Hungary from the Nazis to the Soviets

This is the first book in a Western language to describe in detail the establishment of the Communist regime in Hungary. Hungary was the last ally of Nazi Germany and as such suffered dreadful destruction in the course of fighting during the last year of the war. The war discredited the political and social elite and gave opportunity for a new beginning. Early optimism in democratic circles, however, quickly dissipated. With the help of the Soviet Army, the Communists, who had negligible indigenous support, in a short time managed to destroy any organized opposition to their taking power.

In this concise book, which is based on archival and other primary sources, Peter Kenez describes the methods of Communist conquest of power in one country in Eastern Europe and therefore allows us to better understand the origin of the cold war.

Peter Kenez is professor of History at the University of California, Santa Cruz. He is the author of *A History of the Soviet Union from the Beginning to the End* (1999, second edition 2006); *Varieties of Fear* (1995); *Cinema and Soviet Society* (1992); *The Birth of the Propaganda State* (1985); *Civil War in South Russia, 1918* (1971); and *Civil War in South Russia, 1919–1920* (1976). He is the editor, with Abbott Gleason and Richard Stites, of *Bolshevik Culture: Experiment and Order in the Russian Revolution* (1989).

Hungary from the Nazis to the Soviets

THE ESTABLISHMENT OF THE COMMUNIST REGIME IN HUNGARY, 1944–1948

PETER KENEZ
University of California, Santa Cruz

CAMBRIDGE UNIVERSITY PRESS
Cambridge, New York, Melbourne, Madrid, Cape Town, Singapore,
São Paulo, Delhi, Dubai, Tokyo, Mexico City

Cambridge University Press
32 Avenue of the Americas, New York, NY 10013-2473, USA

www.cambridge.org
Information on this title: www.cambridge.org/9780521747240

First published 2006
First paperback edition 2009

A catalog record for this publication is available from the British Library

Library of Congress Cataloging in Publication data
Kenez, Peter.
Hungary from the Nazis to the Soviets : the establishment of the Communist regime
in Hungary, 1944–1948 / Peter Kenez.
p. cm.
Includes bibliographical references and index.
ISBN-10: 0-521-85766-X (hardback)
ISBN-13: 978-0-521-85766-6 (hardback)
1. Hungary – Politics and government – 1945–1989. 2. Communism – Hungary –
History – 20th century. I. Title.
DB956.K464 2006
943.905'2 – dc22 2005018131

ISBN 978-0-521-85766-6 Hardback
ISBN 978-0-521-74724-0 Paperback

To Penny

Contents

Acknowledgments

Several of my friends read all or part of my manuscript. I thank Jonathan Beecher, John Gams, Paul Hollander, George Springer, and Bruce Thompson for their comments.

Some of my text has been previously published: "The Hungarian Communist Party and the Catholic Church, 1945–1948," *The Journal of Modern History* (Vol. 75, No. 4, 2003, pp. 864–89); "Post Second World War Hungarian Cinema as a Reflection of the Communist Struggle for Power," *Historical Journal of Film, Radio, and Television* (Vol. 23, No. 1, 2003, pp. 11–26); and "Anti-Semitism in Post World War II Hungary," *Judaism* (Vol. 50, Spring, 2001).

I have received friendly help in the Hungarian National Archives and, in particular, in the Political History Institute in Budapest, where most of my source materials are located. It was a pleasure to work there. The head of the archives, Katalin Zalai, gave me access to all the files I needed. I am also very grateful to the Historical Photo-Archive of the Hungarian National Museum, in particular to Dr. Katalin Jalsovszky for her extensive knowledge and kind help, under some time pressure, in finding suitable illustrative photographs.

The Research Committee of the University of California, Santa Cruz, supported my work with three substantial grants.

I received invaluable help from my wife, Penelope, who selected the pictures and spent countless hours editing. This book is dedicated to her with love and gratitude.

Introduction

A great Hungarian liberal political thinker is reported to have said he wanted the following epitaph on his gravestone: "Here lies István Bibó, lived, 1945-1948."[1] He meant to express the great hope and excitement he had experienced in those years, when it seemed possible that his nation had turned away from its feudal past and a better future could be forged on its nascent liberalism. A superficial look at the immediate postwar years makes Bibó's retrospective fondness for this period appear very strange indeed. After all, the war had caused extraordinary devastation: people lived in unheated apartments on the verge of starvation. The soldiers of an occupying army removed much that was movable, raped, and often behaved brutally. The country suffered the worst inflation the world had ever seen. Most important, the ever-growing power of the Communist Party and the lawless behavior of the Communist-dominated political police must have given concern to many for the future of a democratic order in Hungary. In this book, I describe the tumultuous events of the immediate postwar years and explain why Bibó even in retrospect recalled these years fondly. My task is to describe how and why the hopes for a democratic Hungary were gradually extinguished and a Communist regime was installed.

I argue three main points: 1. What happened in Hungary was decided elsewhere, primarily in Moscow. Soviet policy was a series of improvisations, and it developed gradually between the end of the war and the imposition of complete Communist control. 2. The main issue among non-Communist politicians was how best to resist full-scale Sovietization. I argue that those who sought compromise and attempted to get along with the Soviet occupiers were not knaves and fools, but people who had legitimate reasons to

1 This remark was reported by the Nobel Prize–winning author, Imre Kertész, in a speech on December 4, 2002. *Budapest Portál*, April, 2004.

hope that some degree of Hungarian democracy could be saved. 3. As a result of Soviet conquest, a social and political revolution was carried out in Hungary. This revolution could have been accomplished at a lower cost in human suffering; nevertheless, it was a much-needed revolution.

The Hungarian story must be looked at in the context of the origin of the cold war. It was neither the first nor the last time that the fate of the small countries in Eastern Europe was determined elsewhere. The ultimate outcome depended not on what the Hungarians, Romanians, Poles, and so forth would or would not do but on decisions made in world capitals. Postwar international affairs and internal Soviet developments were more responsible than any Hungarian political decisions for the establishment of a Communist regime there. It is easy to answer the question of why in 1948 the Communists came to power. That happened because people in Moscow decided that this was in the best interest of the Soviet Union, and the West was not in a position to prevent it.

The central political issue of the second half of the twentieth century was the confrontation between the West, led by the United States, and the Soviet Union and its satellites. It is understandable that an enormous literature exists on the history of the origins of that great struggle.[2] A major dividing line in that literature concerns the evaluation of Soviet intentions. Did Stalin have a plan? Did he foresee the creation of a Soviet-controlled bloc in a Europe divided into two hostile spheres? Did he just wait for the right moment to carry out his plan? Did he envisage the conquest of Eastern Europe simply as the first stage in the creation of a Communist world? There can be no

2 The literature is so large that it cannot easily be summarized. However, it is worth pointing out that in the immediate postwar period, at a time when the so-called totalitarian paradigm dominated, Anglo-American writers took it for granted that the expansionist politics of the Soviet Union were responsible for the deterioration of East-West relations. Hugh Seton-Watson, for example, believed that he could uncover a blueprint. His argument was that Eastern European countries went through the same stages: 1. genuine coalition, 2. sham coalition, and 3. full Communist domination. Hugh Seton-Watson, *The Pattern of Communist Revolution: A Historical Analysis*, London: Meuthen, 1953. The very similarity implied to him that there had to be a central plan. Others saw the conquest of Eastern Europe as a first step toward world domination, for example, Stefan Possony, *A Century of Conflict: Communist Techniques of World Revolution*, Chicago: Henry Regner, 1953. Such writers as Adam Ulam and Herbert Feis fundamentally agreed that the United States was merely responding to Soviet moves. The great change in Western historiography occurred not because of the availability of Soviet documents but because the war in Vietnam encouraged a generation of young historians to question American motives, and they projected their skepticism onto the past. Some books published in this period, for example Joyce and Gabriel Kolko's *The World and United States Foreign Policy, 1945–1954*, New York: Harper and Row, 1972, put the entire blame for the deterioration of relations on the United States and attributed aggressive motives based on economic interests to Washington, while depicting Moscow as merely responding, which verges on being silly. Ultimately, able historians managed to rise above the simplistic question of who was at fault. Nevertheless, the division between those who saw a well-planned Soviet policy and those who stressed improvisation remained.

absolutely convincing answers to these questions, and we are unlikely ever to find archival documents that would resolve them. Stalin did not confide his innermost thoughts to others or put his plans on paper. All we can do is attribute motives and plans on the basis of his actions.

In this book, I side with those historians who have described Soviet policy in these years as fluid. It appears to me that Stalin in 1944 did not foresee the emergence of two irreconcilably hostile blocs in Europe. I suspect Stalin imagined that powerful countries in the future would compete for influence just as they had before the war; however, he clearly intended that the role of the Red Army in the defeat of Hitler would give the Soviet Union much greater influence and leverage than it had ever possessed before. He apparently hoped at first that the Soviet Union would have a say in Western European politics through the Italian and French Communist Parties. The expectation of a fluid Europe presupposed a situation in which the Soviet Union could prevent the emergence of hostile regimes on its most sensitive Western borders but would refrain, at least for the time being, from openly imposing satellite regimes on the occupied countries. In order to hope to have influence in Western Europe, the Soviet Union would have to make concessions to the Allies in the east of the continent.

Internal developments determined Soviet foreign policy. By the fall of 1946, Stalin and his fellow leaders decided to reimpose the harshest controls on Soviet society after the relative liberalism of the war years. Rightly or wrongly, they feared for the stability of their regime after the dreadful devastation of the war. The war had necessitated the lessening of some forms of repression: the regime had to allow a degree of freedom for peasants on the collective farms; religion was treated more respectfully and even regarded as an ally; artists to a greater extent than before could express genuine sentiments. Perhaps most disturbingly from the point of view of the leaders of the regime, millions of Soviet citizens as soldiers, as prisoners of war, or as slave laborers had come into contact with the more advanced, capitalist West. Soviet leaders saw such contacts with westerners as a form of subversion, and they decided that it had to be stopped. (At the same time, they lost hope for the future of Communism in the immediate future in Western Europe.) The rigid controls and merciless oppression necessitated cutting ties with the outside world, especially the Western allies. For Soviet foreign policy makers that meant that by the middle of 1947 they no longer concerned themselves with Western responses to their actions in Eastern Europe. Imposing uniformity on the bloc of satellites was a corollary of the most deadly conformity at home. The people in the Eastern European satellites, among them Hungarians, came to be victims of

Stalinism as much as the people of the Soviet Union. The immediate postwar period is an important and interesting part of Hungarian history, but it can also be regarded as a case study of Soviet behavior in the early stages of the cold war.

A great deal follows from how we evaluate Soviet intentions. For those historians who believe that the Soviets were already determined at the end of the war to transform this region into a group of satellite states, the postwar years do not form a particular unit. It is characteristic, for example, that in his excellent and well-researched book László Borhi treats the entire period of 1945–1956 as one, moving back and forth in discussing different issues.[3] It is my assumption, by contrast, that these three or four years form a particular and interesting period in the nation's history, years which were very different both from what preceded and from what would follow. I see the 1944–1947 period as a time of imperfect pluralism, a time when different points of view could still be articulated, when newspapers pointed to Communist wrongdoings, and political parties presented genuine alternatives from which voters could choose. It was imperfect pluralism, because from the outset the Communists benefited from the presence of the Red Army and could prevail in matters that seemed decisively important to them.

In retrospect, it is evident that nothing the non-Communist politicians could have done would have prevented the demise of democracy. This is not to say that the future was predetermined and that everything could not have happened differently. A change in the character of Soviet politics or a different turn in East-West relations would have influenced the development of Hungarian politics, but the future was not in the hands of those who had most to lose. To contemporaries, however, this was not immediately

3 Although Hungarian historians have published widely on the postwar era, there is still no single book that attempts to deal with the entire period as a whole. Among historians in the Communist era, of course, there had to be complete unanimity: it was Western, especially U.S., aggression that was responsible for the breakup of the wartime alliance. The most detailed and still useful study of postwar Hungarian foreign policy is Sándor Balogh's, *Magyarország külpolitikája 1945–1950*, Budapest: Kossuth, 1988. In the post-Communist era, by contrast, the dominant paradigm assumes that Stalin and his comrades were simply waiting for an opportune moment to reduce the Eastern European states to the status of satellites. The best and most representative expression of this point of view is to be found in László Borhi, *Hungary in the Cold War, 1945–1956*, Budapest, New York: CEU Press, 2004. The same point of view is expressed implicitly, for example, in Gábor Kiszely's *ÁVH: egy terrorszervezet története*, Budapest: Korona, 2000. See also Róbert Gábor, *Az igazi szociáldemokrácia: küzdelem a fasizmus és a kommunizmus ellen, 1944–1948*, Budapest: Századvég, 2001. They take it for granted that Soviet policy from the outset aimed to reduce Hungary to the status of a satellite. Krisztián Ungváry discusses the historiography of the postwar period. He takes the side of those who believe that the Communist era in Hungary began in 1945. See Krisztián Ungváry, "Magyarország szovjetizálásának kérdései" in Ignác Romsics (ed.), *Mitoszok, legendák, tévhitek a 20: századi Magyar történelemröl*, Budapest: Osiris, 2002, pp. 279–308. See also László Kürti, "Hungary" in Sabrina Ramet (ed.), *Eastern Europe since 1939*, Bloomington: Indiana UP, 1998, pp. 71–93.

apparent. Although many people at the time had serious concerns about the future, it was not at all naive to believe that at the conclusion of the peace treaty Soviet troops would leave Hungary, and then a democratic regime might let roots down and firmly establish itself. The non-Communist parties based their policies on this expectation, and the Communists feared that their opponents might be right, in which case they would have the frightening prospect of being left without Soviet protection. After a great conflagration, people often assume that life cannot simply return to what had existed before. They think that the old way of thinking is discredited by the misfortunes it has caused, and now there is a possibility for something profoundly different and better to be built. In Hungary, too, there was a sense, not shared by everyone to be sure, that a new and better life would begin. The optimism that prevailed at least in some circles does matter in the history of this period because it explains the behavior of many contemporaries.

We will never know what kind of politics would have developed if the Red Army had withdrawn in 1948, as Soviet leaders had repeatedly promised. Although in the immediate postwar years conservatives and nationalists were in retreat, most likely they would have reemerged once again within a few years as a major current in politics. As it was, only József Cardinal Mindszenty and the courageous Catholic nun, Margit Slachta, dared to speak up for an unabashedly conservative and even legitimist position. The liberal consensus that seemed to exist at the end of the war probably would not have lasted. Quite likely, bitter political divisions would have reemerged. It is, however, evident that genuine democrats were in a strong position, and it seems likely that the Hungarians, left to themselves, would have established a far more decent system than the one that was imposed on them by the Soviet-supported Communists. Greece, for example, which had the good fortune to escape Communist rule, experienced repression and civil war in the postwar period and a semifascist military regime for a time; nevertheless, it far outstripped Hungary in the speed of economic development and finally established a democratic regime much earlier than the ex-satellites were able to do.

Among the non-Communist politicians, the recurring issue remained of what attitude to take about the increasing Communist domination. Should the Communists be resisted every step of the way, or, on the contrary, should liberals be looking for a modus vivendi and preserve as much freedom and democracy as they could under the difficult circumstances? Neither side was right, and neither side was wrong, because the ultimate fate of the country was decided elsewhere; nevertheless, those who did everything within their power to find a compromise deserve credit rather than blame. There were some politicians within the leadership of the National Peasant Party (NPP) and the Social Democratic Party (SDP) who at the outset were willing to support Communist policies and, as loyal members of the so-called left-wing bloc, time and again helped the Communist position to prevail within the discussions of the governing coalition. However, many of these people came to be disillusioned by Communist behavior and ultimately ended up within the right wings of their parties. Antal Bán, for example, who took the place of the right-wing Social Democrat Ágoston Valentiny in 1945 as minister of justice, two years later came to be one of those Socialists who were determined to resist the Communists.

The history of the postwar years must be understood not only within the context of the developing cold war but also within the long span of Hungarian history. Hungarians, unlike Croatians, Romanians, and Serbs, for example, belong to a nation with a long history. For more than ten centuries, the country has had an almost continuous existence as a sovereign (or semisovereign) state. The upper classes, although ethnically mixed, proudly regarded themselves as Hungarians, possessed political rights, and exploited a multilingual peasantry. (In 1914, only about half of the population spoke Hungarian as a native language.) In the course of its thousand-year history, the country accumulated a rich and mixed tradition that included dark spots of repression of national minorities but also liberalism and tolerance. Unlike Croatia and Slovakia, which had existed before the 1990s as independent states only as German satellites and were without democratic traditions, Hungary in the twentieth century could have built on a democratic heritage. Between 1867 and 1918, as a part of the Habsburg Monarchy, the country enjoyed spectacular economic growth, although it remained primarily agricultural. Advanced, industrial Budapest, then one of the fastest growing cities in the world with its lively intellectual and artistic life, coexisted with a backward countryside where a multinational peasantry lived in material circumstances not much better than peasants living in the Russian empire. One need not idealize the Austro-Hungarian Empire and remember that the Hungarians terribly mistreated the national minorities, yet still point out that it was a time of optimism.

The period of 1918–1919 was a great dividing line in Hungarian history. The loss in the First World War had more disastrous consequences for Hungary than for any other land. In October 1918, a revolution separated Hungary from the Monarchy and created a republic, headed by Count Michael Károlyi. This liberal government remained in office for less than five months. On March 20, 1919, the Entente made known its decision concerning the line of demarcation between the Hungarian and Romanian troops, implying the future territorial division. The next day, Károlyi was compelled to resign in favor of a Communist-Socialist coalition, in which the Communists played the dominant role. Károlyi's government could neither accept Allied demands nor successfully resist them. Ironically, it was only the nominally internationalist Communists who were willing to fight for the national interest because they expected that Soviet Russia would come to their aid. The Hungarian Soviet Republic remained in existence for only 133 days, in the course of which it carried out a mindlessly radical policy with terror. It failed to gain the allegiance of the peasantry by nationalizing rather than distributing land. All through its existence, the Soviet republic was fighting Czechoslovak and Romanian armies. Ultimately, it failed not because of domestic opposition, though counterrevolution was gathering strength, but because of military defeat by armies supported by the Allies.

The treaty concluded with Hungary at Trianon in 1920 was part of the Versailles settlements. The country lost two-thirds of its territory and more than half of its population, leaving more than 3 million Hungarian speakers just beyond the newly drawn borders. It is indisputable that the terms of the treaty that Hungarians were forced to sign were not only unfair but also unwise. The desire to regain all or at least some of the lost territories came to dominate and therefore poison Hungarian politics. Ironically, Admiral Nicholas Horthy, who became "governor" and regent in 1920 and pursued a nationalist policy, came to power with the aid of foreigners and was compelled to accept peace terms that the internationalist revolutionaries would not accept. Nevertheless, remarkably, he and his supporters succeeded in the completely preposterous pretense that it was the liberals, Socialists, and Communists who were responsible for the defeat in the war and therefore the great territorial losses. The country remained a kingdom, without a king. The surrounding countries, all of them beneficiaries of the collapse of the Monarchy, would not accept a Habsburg restoration, and for the Hungarian political class a republic appeared too revolutionary.

Interwar Hungary was profoundly different from what it had been before 1914. As a part of the Monarchy, the government in Budapest had administered a country of more than 18 million people, and now it was reduced to a population of less than 8 million. The multinational empire was no more, and instead Hungary became the most ethnically homogeneous country in the area. The perceived injustice of the Trianon treaty determined the character of Hungarian politics in the interwar period. Revisionism alienated Hungary from its neighbors and justified a socially repressive policy in the name of national interest. A small landed aristocracy still possessed much of the land and controlled the government. After the war in Eastern Europe, the new countries carried out meaningful land reform, but not Hungary. Only about 8 percent of the land was distributed and that in such small parcels that many of the new owners soon lost their land; consequently, in the 1920s and 1930s about a third of the peasantry was landless. The defeat of the Soviet Republic was followed by a White Terror that claimed at least as many victims as the previous Red Terror. Aside from Communists and left-wing Socialists, Jews suffered in particular. Although prewar Hungary made possible and even encouraged Jewish assimilation, in the changed circumstances a new Hungarian middle class resented Jewish domination in the nation's intellectual and economic life. Before the war, Jews were recognized as Hungarians and the nationalists were glad to count them as such, for they improved the demographic balance. After the Trianon treaty, there was no need for them. The fact that Jews had played a disproportionately large role in the Soviet Republic gave justification for a new wave of anti-Semitism. Hungary was the first country in postwar Europe to introduce anti-Semitic legislation in the form of limits on the percentage of Jews admitted to the universities.

During the interwar period, the left wing played only a small role in the political life of the nation. The SDP was allowed to organize workers but not landless peasants. The Communist Party was outlawed, but in any case it had been compromised by the unhappy memory of the 1919 Soviet Republic and by association with the profoundly unpopular Soviet Union. Whatever opposition there was to the outdated social structure came from the ever-stronger, radical right wing. The realistic choice for a politically minded Hungarian was between a government in the hands of conservatives, serving the interests of a landed aristocracy while retaining some of the restraints imposed by a certain type of liberalism, and a government of the extreme right, socially radical but very much attracted first to the example of Italian fascism and later to German National Socialism.

That Hungary would end up on the German side in the developing international conflict was overdetermined. Nazi war plans promised to overthrow the Versailles settlement, something that Hungarians deeply desired. In addition, Hungary, like other countries in the region, was deeply hurt by the economic crisis and could be helped only by ties to the rapidly reviving German economy. Hungary needed the German market. Allied policies, as represented by the Munich agreement, made it clear to the people of Eastern Europe that they had no choice but to come to terms with a resurgent Germany. The Germans rewarded the Hungarians for their friendship, first by returning a part of Slovakia and in 1940 by giving back to Hungary the northern part of Transylvania.

Prime Minister László Bárdossy declared war on the Soviet Union immediately after German troops crossed the Soviet border. This war also turned out to be a disaster for the country. The 200,000-strong Second Hungarian Army was destroyed on the Don in 1943. After it became clear that the Germans were unlikely to win, ruling circles under a new premier, Miklós Kállay, attempted by various means to contact the Allies in the hope that the country would be liberated by Anglo-American forces rather than by the Soviet army. Given strategic and geographic realities, such plans were utterly unrealistic. On March 19, 1944, the German army occupied Hungary, in spite of the fact that Hungary was an ally. The German High Command feared that Hungary might follow the Italian example and seek a separate peace, and such a development, if successful, would have had disastrous consequences for the German lines of communication. The occupiers forced Horthy to dismiss Kállay and replace him with the pro-Nazi Döme Sztojay. At this point, the Hungarian Jewry, up to this time the largest still intact in the German sphere of interest, became subject to deportations to Auschwitz.

The war, which up to that point had been fought in distant lands, was now brought home with all its horrors.

1

Autumn 1944

At the end of the Second World War, prospects for Hungary in general and for Hungarian democracy in particular did not appear to be good. The country was in ruins, and the social-political system had disintegrated.

The front approached Hungarian territory in the summer of 1944. On August 23, the Romanian government succeeded in switching sides, and this change was a major blow to the German and Hungarian armies. In the apparently solid front, a wide gap had suddenly opened. Within days and almost without resistance, the Red Army moved into northern Transylvania, an area that had come under Hungarian rule in 1940 as a result of German help. In September, the front was already within the 1937 borders of Hungary. Soviet troops entered the country not only from the east but also from the south, through liberated Yugoslavia. On October 20, 1944, after a long tank battle, the Red Army occupied Debrecen, one of the largest cities in the country and the future seat of the provisional government and National Assembly.

The quick advance, however, was then stopped. Unfortunately for the Hungarians, the Germans decided to invest major forces in the defense of Budapest. It was in the interest of the German High Command to keep the fighting away from German territory as long as possible. Determined and skillful defense and the willingness to sacrifice – in particular Hungarian units – did slow down the Russian advance. In western Hungary, the Germans even embarked on an utterly hopeless counteroffensive. Nevertheless, Soviet superiority in men and in armament was overwhelming, and the ultimate victory was only a matter of time. Hungary was a war zone for eight months. As a consequence of the intense fighting, the country, and especially the capital, suffered dreadfully. The task of reconstruction would be long and difficult.

In addition to the damage caused by the fighting, the Germans – and later the Soviet army and its allies, the Romanians – removed much that was moveable. According to postwar estimates, 40 percent of the national wealth was lost. In the course of the war, 340,000–360,000 Hungarian soldiers died, and 600,000 became prisoners of war in the Soviet Union. After Polish, the Soviet, and German losses, Hungarian human losses were proportionally the greatest among all the belligerents in the Second World War.[1]

Perhaps worst from the point of view of the future of Hungarian democracy was the fact that the country, together with the rest of Eastern Europe, fell into the Soviet sphere of interest. Since 1945, there have been many articles and books written concerning how the Western powers had betrayed Eastern Europe at Yalta by allowing it to fall into Soviet hands. Also, considerable significance has been attributed to the so-called percentage agreement that Winston Churchill arranged with Joseph Stalin in an offhand manner, dividing Eastern Europe among the victors. According to this agreement, the Western powers and the Soviet Union would each have 50 percent "interest" in Hungary (later changed to 80 percent versus 20 percent in favor of the Soviet Union). In reality, Yalta, and the famous little piece of paper that Churchill handed over to Stalin, had little consequence. The decisively important fact was that the Red Army, rather than British or American forces, had liberated Hungary from German occupation. No amount of negotiation and pleading could have changed this fundamental matter after the fact. Had the Western powers been willing to sacrifice tens of thousands of their soldiers by invading Western Europe not in 1944 but in 1943, the situation undoubtedly would have been different because the meeting of the Allied armies would have taken place further east. For perfectly understandable and legitimate reasons, the Allies had decided not to make that sacrifice.[2]

To consider it a misfortune that Hungary came into the Soviet rather than the Anglo-American sphere of influence, as did lucky Greece, is not to say that the Soviet Union from the very outset was determined to reduce the country to the status of a satellite. Indeed, on the contrary, from all the available evidence it appears that Stalin and his lieutenants had no blueprint

1 Ignác Romsics, *Magyarország története a XX században*, Budapest: Osiris, 1999, p. 268. Romsics also included in his account soldiers from northern Transylvania, which during the war belonged to Hungary.

2 László Borhi expresses a different point of view. He takes the possibility of Allied landings in the Balkans seriously and therefore believes that there was a possibility of Hungary being liberated by the Anglo-American forces. László Borhi, *Hungary in the Cold War, 1945–1956*, Budapest, New York: CEU Press, 2004, pp. 17–22.

for the future and did not see any more clearly than the Western leaders what shape Europe would take in the postwar world. Stalin's agreement to free elections in Eastern Europe at Yalta was not simply an empty promise meant to be immediately broken. There is no reason to doubt that the Russians assumed that at least in the foreseeable future in Hungary, just as in other Eastern European countries, there would be power sharing between Communist and non-Communist forces. Soviet leaders made their foreign policy thinking not of Eastern Europe in isolation but of Europe as a whole. They were determined not to allow the re-creation of the *cordon sanitaire* that had existed between the wars. A minimum goal of Soviet foreign policy was the prevention of a belt of hostile states at the western Soviet borders, states that could serve as bases for military action at the most sensitive Soviet borders. For understandable reasons, the Soviet leaders wanted friendly states as neighbors. Unfortunately, it turned out that in a country such as Poland and to a somewhat lesser extent in Romania, the only way to prevent the emergence of hostile regimes was direct and brutal intervention in domestic politics. Of the Eastern European countries, it was anti-Russian, anti-Communist Poland whose fate was first sealed.

On the other hand, as long as the war lasted and in its immediate aftermath, the Soviet leaders did not want to alienate the Western powers by establishing Communist regimes in the newly occupied countries. The dissolution of the Comintern in 1943 was obviously aimed at assuring the Allies that the Soviet Union no longer regarded itself as the headquarters of world Communism. Frightening the Western powers while the war still continued would have been a very dangerous policy. The suspicious Soviet leaders constantly feared a separate peace between the Nazis and the Allies. In reality, of course, the Communist parties remained tools of Soviet foreign policy, and the dissolution had little practical consequence.

After the capitulation of Germany, Soviet leaders believed, as it turned out wrongly, that the Italian and the French Communist Parties would have roles to play in their postwar governments. They thought in terms of their past experience, assumed that there would be a competition for influence everywhere in Europe, and did not foresee a clear separation of East and West. Under the circumstances, establishing purely Communist governments in the East would have compromised their larger goals. Initially, Soviet support for coalition governments in Eastern Europe, among them in Hungary, was perfectly genuine.[3]

3 One of the few available pieces of evidence we have concerning Soviet intentions in 1944 is a memorandum written by I. M. Maiskii to V. M. Molotov in January 1944. Maiskii's main concern

Allowing, indeed encouraging, the creation of a multiparty system in Hungary and in the rest of Eastern Europe did not mean, of course, that the Soviet leaders refrained from interfering in the domestic affairs of these countries. From the very first moments, the crucial decisions concerning the establishment of the postwar regime in Hungary were made in Moscow. The Soviet leaders, perhaps for understandable reasons, took a more hostile stance toward Hungary than toward the other ex-satellites of Nazi Germany. Hungary, after all, was the last satellite of Germany. By contrast, Italy, Finland, and Romania had managed to change sides in the last stages of the war; Czechoslovakia and Poland had been victims of Nazi aggression and had a record of resisting the Germans. Russophilia had a long history in Bulgaria, a country that had refused to declare war on the Soviet Union. Tito of Yugoslavia had acquired international prestige and admiration for the organization of the powerful partisan movement that contributed greatly to the liberation of his country. In most Eastern European countries at the conclusion of the war, there were leaders who could come forward untainted by collaboration, possessing independent standing and prestige for having resisted the Nazis. In Hungary, the situation was profoundly different. There was no trusted national leader with an unblemished anti-Nazi past and no Hungarian government in exile. The head of state since 1920 (regent in the absence of a king) was conservative Admiral Nicholas Horthy, who had been brought to power by the counterrevolution that followed the brief Hungarian Soviet regime of 1919.

After Romania's decision to switch sides, it was obvious that the Red Army could not be stopped at the Hungarian borders. This moment offered the best opportunity to get out of an obviously hopeless war. The military situation had deteriorated to such an extent that Horthy decided to accept the inevitable; he turned to the Russians with a request for an armistice and offered to change sides.[4] An agent of Horthy, Count Vladimir Zichy, who had an estate in Slovakia, met a Soviet officer, Colonel Makarov, who was a military agent assigned to work with Slovak partisans. Zichy reported to

was assuring Soviet security for the next two generations. He hoped to bring this about by border adjustments, by having security treaties with Finland and Romania. He envisaged intervention in the domestic lives of the defeated countries by the Soviet Union, but also by the United States and Britain. Maiskii and the entire Soviet foreign policy establishment took a hostile position to Hungary. He recommended that the disputed territorial issues between Romania and Hungary should be resolved in favor of Romania, that Hungary should be obliged to pay reparations, and that at least in the first years after the war Hungary should remain isolated. T. V. Volokitina (ed.), *Sovetskii faktor v Vostochnoi Evrope, 1944–1953: Dokumenty*, vol. 1, Moscow: ROSSPEN, 1999, pp. 23–48.

4 The most detailed description of negotiation attempts by Horthy is in C. A. Macartney, *October Fifteenth, A History of Modern Hungary, 1929–1945*, vol. 2, Edinburgh: The University Press, 1961, pp. 349–355.

1. Admiral Nicholas Horthy, 1868–1951.

Horthy the results of his conversation and was optimistic. The Soviet Union, in exchange for Hungary breaking relations with the Nazis and allowing the entrance of Soviet troops, would permit Horthy to stay in power and would not interfere in the country's domestic order. Hungary would have to give up territories acquired with the help of Germany, but final territorial issues would be resolved later at a peace conference.[5] Horthy, at this late date, still vainly hoped that the Anglo-Saxon powers would somehow participate in the occupation of Hungary. However, Hungarian approaches to the Allies were rejected: they were told that they had to deal directly with the Russians.

It was on the basis of Zichy's report that Horthy sent a high-level delegation to Moscow to negotiate further. This delegation included General Gábor Faragho; Domokos Szent-Iványi, a diplomat; and Géza Teleki, who seemed an appropriate choice because his father as premier had committed suicide in 1941 rather than join the German invasion of Yugoslavia. The Hungarians brought with them a letter written by Horthy himself (in English) and addressed to Marshal Stalin.[6] On October 11, the Hungarians in Moscow were told what the preconditions were: evacuation of all

5 Charles Gati, *Hungary and the Soviet Bloc*, Durham, NC: Duke University Press, 1986, pp. 25–26. According to Gati, Stalin's moderation concerning Hungary was to distract attention from the swift Sovietization of Poland. Poland, of course, was far more important from the Soviet strategic point of view (p. 37).

6 Ibid., pp. 24–25. The tone of the letter is remarkable. Horthy repeatedly complains about the Germans and, in particular, about the Romanians. He refers to Hungary as "poor country" and a second time as "unfortunate country."

territories that the country had acquired after 1937 as a result of the German alliance and declaration of war against Germany.[7] There was no more promise of future discussions on territorial claims. Molotov professed never to have heard of Colonel Makarov. Whether he was telling the truth and Zichy had been misled or whether the Red Army's progress on Hungarian territory made previous concessions unnecessary is difficult to establish. In either case, as the Red Army advanced, Moscow's conditions became less favorable. Horthy, at this point, realized that he had no choice and was ready to make the necessary concessions.

On October 15, he made a proclamation on the radio and announced that his government was asking for an armistice from the enemy. There were about 65,000–70,000 German troops in Hungary as an occupying force and for the purpose of guarding lines of communication.[8] Had the Hungarian leadership been united and decisive, the German forces could have been overcome. But this last moment for saving Hungary from devastation was missed for two reasons. First of all, Admiral Horthy was so fearful of the Russians that he did not act decisively. He still hoped, quite unrealistically, that the Anglo-Saxon powers rather than the Red Army would occupy the country.[9] Second, in order to succeed, the regent would have had to be certain of the loyalty of the senior officer corps. These were the people who could have taken charge of the defense of the capital against the Germans. However, the majority of the senior officers remained pro-Nazi even at this late date.[10] Many of them came from Swab families (the Hungarians referred to the German minority as Swab), and even those who did not had been blinded by their admiration for the German military. The military, just like the rest of society, had been educated in an anti-Soviet and pro-Nazi spirit.[11] How out of touch with reality a large part of the political elite was is illustrated by this rumor: Döme Sztójay, the pro-German premier who had been appointed by Horthy under pressure in March 1944, expressed pleasure on hearing the news that Romania had defected from the German side. He was convinced that, as a consequence of the Romanian

7 T. V. Volokitina, pp. 101–102.

8 Gyula Kádár, *A Ludovikától Sopronkőhidáig: Visszaemlékezések*, Budapest: Magvetö, 1978, p. 718.

9 There had been tentative contacts and desultory negotiations between Hungarian diplomats and the Allies since the summer of 1943. At first, only Hungarian representatives and the Anglo-American powers were involved; later, the Hungarians also negotiated with Soviet representatives. Vojtech Mastny, *Russia's Road to the Cold War*, New York: Columbia University Press, 1979.

10 István Szent-Miklosy, *With the Hungarian Independence Movement, 1943–1947: An Eyewitness Account*, New York: Praeger, 1988, pp. 48–49.

11 On the Hungarian officer corps, see Sándor Szakály, *A magyar katonai elit, 1938–1945*, Budapest: Magvető, 1987.

"betrayal," all of Transylvania would be given to Hungary after German victory.[12]

By this time, however, the Germans were well prepared. Hungary was strategically too important for them to allow the Hungarians to find their own salvation. The advance of the Soviet armies had stopped in the north in Poland, where the Soviet leadership was content to wait until the Germans brutally suppressed the Warsaw uprising. Another route through which the Red Army could reach Germany was via Hungary and Austria. Horthy's clumsy attempts to establish contacts with the Allies for the purpose of a separate peace were all known to German intelligence. His far too belated and ill-prepared attempts to betray his ferocious German allies and to get out of the war on October 15 resulted in a fiasco.

The Germans, forewarned, responded by arresting Horthy and a few anti-Nazi politicians and officers. Whatever secret organization had existed among politicians and soldiers in the course of 1944 disintegrated with these arrests. The last-minute anti-German resistance attempts of General János Kiss and Endre Bajcsi-Zsilinsky were feeble and failed. The Hungarian Nazis executed the resisters, and as a result the Hungarians acquired a few martyrs to the anti-Nazi cause.

The Germans not only compelled Horthy to withdraw his proclamation concerning Hungary's desire to end the war but also to appoint Ferenc Szálasi, the head of the Arrow Cross Party, as national leader. (Stalin was willing to forgive Horthy for his abdication but not for the appointment of Szálasi.)[13] The two houses of the parliament (in which, to be sure, only a small minority of the deputies participated) approved the appointment, and, therefore, the appearance of legal continuity was maintained. Szálasi, in his six-month-long tenure (October 1944–May 1945) created a regime of unparalleled anarchy and terror. By continuing the war on the side of the Germans and helping them to rob his homeland, he did great damage. It was characteristic of the ideological commitment of the regime that when the International Red Cross offered food help in December 1944 to the starving capital, Szálasi refused the offer because it stipulated that some of the supplies must be shared with inhabitants of the ghetto.[14] As the military situation deteriorated, Szálasi's government first escaped to western Hungary and

12 On the other hand, among the population as a whole, getting out of the war was greatly desired. Already in March 1944, according to an admittedly not very reliable public opinion survey, four-fifths of the population would have welcomed a separate peace. Walter D. Connor and Zvi Gitelman (eds.), *Public Opinion in European Socialist Systems*, New York: Praeger, 1977, p. 137.

13 William McCagg, *Stalin Embattled, 1943–1948*, Detroit, MI: Wayne State, 1978, p. 314.

14 Éva Teleki, *Nyilas uralom Magyarországon*, Budapest: Kossuth, 1974, p. 213.

then followed the retreating German army into exile, intent on continuing the war to the bitter end. In May 1945 in Germany, the last group of Hungarian Nazis completely lost touch with reality. In the last meeting of the cabinet, on May 1, 1945, Szálasi discussed his ideas about world politics. He was convinced that Hungary was the most democratic country in the world and that England needed Hungary because it was the only country that could bring order into Central Europe. He expressed his willingness to negotiate with Britain but only if the British declared their intention to join the fight against the "Bolsheviks."[15] The "ministers" spent their last days in freedom planning to change the street names in Budapest, at least those that had been named after prominent Jews. Szálasi, to the very end, followed the example of his idol, the Führer: just before his arrest, he married his sweetheart, Gizella Lutz.[16] He went to his death in 1946 unrepentant and convinced of the justice of his cause.

Because the Szálasi regime could not conceivably be regarded as a partner for armistice negotiations or the basis of a new postwar government, Soviet policy makers in Hungary were confronted with a tabula rasa, quite different from what had existed in any other Eastern European country. In this respect, Hungary was similar to Germany. Historians have referred to the situation in Germany in 1945 as *Stunde Null*, zero hour. The foundations of government had to be laid; everything had to start from the very beginning. The country did not have a written constitution. Hungary was still nominally a kingdom, even though there had been no king since 1918. It was obvious already at this time that a new form of state would have to be introduced and that the future democratic state would be a republic. How public life should be organized and what should be the basis of legitimacy were open questions.

The initiatives to restart public life came from three sources: first and most important, the occupying authorities, that is the Soviet leadership and the Red Army; second, the re-created democratic political parties, among which the Communists were the most important; and third and least important, local initiative.

From the Soviet point of view, Hungary, Hitler's last satellite, deserved no special consideration. In Hungary, there had been no resistance movement. Individual officers and units at the last moment changed sides, but for all practical purposes the Germans did not have to worry about Hungarian

15 On the Szálasi regime, see Béla Vincellér, *Szálasi hat hónapja, 1944 Oktober–1945 Május*, Budapest: Volos, 1996.

16 Ibid., p. 245.

partisans. Consequently, in the near future when the question of reparations would arise, Hungary was treated at least as punitively as Germany. Already then Stalin had decided not to support Hungary's legitimate requests for redrawing the borders in such a way as to take ethnicity into account and to right the obvious wrongs that Hungary had suffered at the end of World War I. Although, from a moral point of view, such a solution was reprehensible and certainly had nothing to do with Marxist ideology, the Soviet leadership acted on the basis of the principle of collective responsibility and collective punishment. In the newly liberated territories in Czechoslovakia, Yugoslavia, and the Soviet Union, the Hungarian minorities were immediately exposed to collective punishment. Innocent people were mistreated just because their native language was Hungarian.

As mentioned before, there is some evidence showing that the Soviet leadership had a special distaste for Hungary. In December 1943, Stalin complained to Edward Benes that the Hungarians behaved even worse than the Romanians in occupied Soviet territories.[17] This observation by Stalin is entirely contrary to fact. In reality, the Romanians had a much larger army fighting against the Red Army. The Romanians, unlike the Hungarians, became responsible for the administration of Soviet territory, "Transnistria," and there they behaved very badly, indeed. After the dreadful defeat of the Second Hungarian Army on the Don in January 1943, the Hungarian army was not engaged in any other major battles, and by the end of that year most of the soldiers were withdrawn from the Soviet front.

As the Soviet troops were fighting on Hungarian territory in the liberated areas, most members of the administrative offices had disappeared. Many followed the retreating German and Hungarian armies. From the point of view of the future, from the point of view of creating a democratic polity, the self-exile of the personnel of the old administration was beneficial. It was essential for the occupying authority to create new organs in such a way as not to alienate but, on the contrary, to win over those Hungarian forces that were still fighting in the rest of the country. The Russians were well aware that as long as the fighting continued it was in their interest to encourage Hungarian soldiers to defect. In order to bring about this result, the Soviet leadership decided to use those Hungarian officers who had been sent to Moscow by the collapsing Horthy regime to negotiate an armistice. They wanted to include these politicians and generals who defected from the enemy in a provisional government that was to be formed. This government

17 Vojtech Mastny, *Russia's Road to the Cold War: Diplomacy, Warfare, and the Politics of Communism, 1941–1945*, New York: Columbia University Press, 1979, p. 154.

was not to have a radical complexion. The Soviets desired to form the broadest possible coalition government including representatives both from the conservative (but now anti-Nazi) officers of the Horthy regime and also, of course, Communists.[18]

Soviet politicians took two important steps to achieve these goals. First, they allowed a group of Hungarian Communists to return from Moscow and begin the work of rebuilding the party. Second, they encouraged the establishment of the Hungarian National Independence Front from those democratic parties that during the last year of the war had operated underground. Indeed, on December 2 in liberated Szeged, five parties formed the Hungarian National Independence Front (HNIF). These parties were (1) the Communist Party (MKP), (2) SDP, (3) NPP, (4) the Smallholders' Party (FKGP), and (5) Civil Democratic Party (PDP). Four of these parties would come to dominate political life in the next few years.

The Communist Party, which in the interwar period had only an ephemeral underground existence, now became decisively important. In 1944, it had perhaps a few thousand members working illegally. Nevertheless, at this time the Communist Party was the major political force in the country because it enjoyed Soviet backing. The Soviet leadership trusted only those Communists who had spent the war years in the Soviet Union and by contrast exhibited great suspicion against those who had operated underground in Hungary. When the Hungarian delegation in Moscow suggested including Communists in the new government, they had in mind those who had worked in Hungary, but these were unacceptable to the Soviet leadership. In fact, the Russians in their internal correspondence referred to these people as "Communists" only in quotation marks.[19]

It was Stalin himself who selected Mátyás Rákosi as the head of the Hungarian Party, and in the next twelve years he would be the Hungarian Stalin. Rákosi was a man of unprepossessing appearance, short, corpulent, bald, and an indifferent speaker but obviously an intelligent man.[20] He

18 "Molotov added that he must say honestly that this arrangement [the setting up of a provisional Hungarian government] was in the interest of the Red Army as it is fighting against the Germans," Vida István (1995). "Orosz levéltári források az 1944 öszi moszkvai kormányalakitási tárgyalásokról, az Ideiglenes Nemzetgyülés összehivásáról és az Ideiglenes Nemzeti Kormány megválasztásáról," in István Feitl (ed.), *Az ideiglenes nemzetgyűlés és az ideiglenes nemzeti kormány 1944–1945*, Budapest: Politikatörténeti Alapítvány, 1995, p. 81.

19 T. V. Volokitina, p. 109.

20 The American representative to Hungary, Arthur Schoenfeld, described him in his report on August 17, 1945, to the secretary of state: "Rákosi with whom this was my first real talk impressed me as

came from a poor Jewish family with many children. In his youth before World War I, he had worked in England for some time. He became a Communist in a Russian prisoner of war camp in World War I. He played a rather significant role in the Communist regime of 1919 but acquired his reputation in the movement in the early 1920s when he traveled widely in Europe as a Comintern agent. He was especially suitable for this role not only because of his remarkable linguistic ability but also because of his willingness to carry out instructions unquestioningly. At this time, he became personally acquainted with the major figures of the international Communist movement, which later turned out to be a great advantage.[21]

Rákosi was instructed to return to Hungary in 1925 with the charge of resurrecting the more or less moribund party. However, he was soon arrested. First, he was sentenced to eight years, and in a second trial in 1933 he received a life sentence. In these trials, Rákosi gave a good account of himself, enabling the international Communist movement to turn the trials into propaganda successes. In recognition of his performance, the Seventh Congress of the Communist International in 1935 elected him as a member of its executive committee. It was, however, rumored that in prison he betrayed some of his comrades. If so, he was forgiven. In 1940 at the time of the Soviet-Nazi alliance, he was exchanged for Hungarian flags that the Russian army had captured at the time of the suppression of the revolution in 1849 and was allowed to return to Moscow.[22] Because some of the prominent Hungarian Communists, most importantly Béla Kun, the leader of the 1919 Communist government, had fallen victim to the purges, Rákosi was undoubtedly the best-known Hungarian Communist leader on the international scene. Fifteen years in a Hungarian prison had conferred added prestige. On his arrival in Moscow, rather incautiously, he inquired about the fate of his comrades who had been arrested and thereby aroused Beria's long-lasting hostility. Rákosi was hardly naïve, but someone who had not spent the worst years of the purges in the Soviet Union could not have understood the prevailing atmosphere of fear. Almost certainly he, who had been an ally of Béla Kun, would also have been killed, along with the entire Kun faction in Moscow, had he been there.

forceful and highly intelligent with advantage of knowing his own mind. His knowledge of English and contact with Anglo-American Communists as well as acquaintance with Anglo-American press certainly make him one of the more enlightened Hungarian public men," *Foreign Relations of the United States* (FRUS), vol. 4, U.S. government publication, Washington, DC, 1945, pp. 849–850.

21 Mátyás Rákosi, *Visszaemlékezések, 1892–1925*, vol. 1 Budapest: Napvilág, 2002.

22 On Rákosi see Árpád Pünkösti, *Rákosi a hatalomért, 1945–1948*, Budapest: Europa, 1991.

At the end of October 1944, five leaders, Ernő Gerő, Mihály Farkas, Imre Nagy, József Révai, and Zoltán Vas, left Moscow for Hungary.[23] Stalin decided that the head of the party should not return for the time being. According to Rákosi, Stalin was concerned about his personal security.[24] However, the more likely reason was that Stalin did not want the heads of the Communist Parties of the newly occupied countries to return too soon because the Allies might think these people were about to take power with Soviet help.[25] Gerő was the second most powerful figure in the Hungarian party and was the leader of the Hungarian Communists in Moscow until Rákosi's arrival. In fact, he expected to be recognized as the leader of the Hungarian faction and was obviously disappointed that Stalin chose Rákosi.[26] He also had extensive experience in Western Europe. He had spent years in France and participated in the Spanish Civil War. It was rumored that he had especially close ties with Lavrentii Beria, the head of the NKVD, and as such was the éminence grise of the regime.

Farkas, who was born in Kosice, had been a member of the Czechoslovak party until 1941 and was transferred to the Hungarian party at Rákosi's request. It was only at this point that he took Hungarian citizenship. Presumably, it was decided in Moscow that the Hungarian party needed to be bolstered. Farkas also had been a veteran of the Spanish Civil War.

Révai was a genuine intellectual with the reputation of being the most hard line among the top leaders. He was to be the Hungarian Zhdanov, the guardian of ideological purity. Révai's standing in Moscow was undermined by the fact that in 1937 he had received an admonition for not having unmasked a comrade, who had been – without reason, of course – arrested.[27] Farkas and Révai were Rákosi's protégées. Vas was the most easygoing among the top Communist leaders, the only one who later achieved a degree of genuine popularity.

It is difficult to envisage and understand the mental world of these major figures of the Communist movement. We would be incorrect to say that

23 The return of the Communist leaders was adventurous. They came via Romania, and, as they approached the border, they were almost shot by suspicious Soviet soldiers. Mátyás Rákosi, *Visszaemlékezések, 1940–1956*, vol. 2, Budapest: Napvilág, 1997, p. 925.

24 Ibid., vol. 1, p. 136.

25 Mihály Korom, "A magyar kommunista emigráció vezetöinek tevékenysége a Szovjetunióban a második világháboru idején," *Múltunk* 2 (1997): 3–51.

26 Korom, p. 10–12. Gerő, as a disciplined Communist, without question accepted Rákosi's leadership, and from his correspondence with Rákosi showed no signs of disloyalty.

27 There were rumors in 1950 that Révai was to be the next victim of a purge trial. Sándor Bándy, "Lakatos Imre arcai," *Beszélő* (December 2003): 92–98.

they were drawn to Communism because power attracted them. (Once they became rulers of Hungary, the situation changed.) At the time when they became Communists, the chances that the Hungarian party would assume power must have seemed remote to these intelligent people. While living in the Soviet Union, they saw around themselves privation and terror. How could they not be repelled? The only explanation for their behavior must be their deeply held Marxist faith. In spite of everything that they saw and experienced, they remained convinced that the future belonged to Soviet-type Communism.

The top leadership, Rákosi, Gerő, Farkas, and Révai, would remain unchanged until 1953, although Révai's influence somewhat receded. These people had a great deal in common, and their background would have considerable significance in the period when the Communist regime was established in Hungary. They were not close personal friends, and during their long years in Moscow they hardly knew one another. In their correspondence they addressed one another with striking formality. Their experiences in the Soviet Union convinced them that close and friendly ties were dangerous, and consequently their contacts with one another were purely official.[28] They were all Jewish. They had no lives or interests outside of the Communist movement. They all spent their entire adult lives in the service of Communism, and, because of their isolation from daily life in Hungary, they could have little appreciation of the particular Hungarian circumstances. With the exception of Farkas, who was a rather crude man, the other three were obviously intelligent and talented people. The leaders of the party proudly regarded themselves as soldiers in the army of the world Communist movement and therefore of the Soviet Union. They were willing without question to carry out policies made in Moscow.

Nagy, who had not been among the top leaders, was evidently selected for early return because of his reputation as an expert on agricultural matters and for the fact that he, unlike the four other men, was not Jewish. Even at this time, the Soviet leadership was conscious of the significance of this fact.[29] Georgii Dimitrov, the ex-leader of the defunct Comintern, and still an important adviser to the Soviet leadership on affairs concerning the international Communist movement, suggested to Rákosi that, in order not to call attention to the unfortunately very large role that Jews played in the Hungarian Communist Party, the "Jewish comrades" should be employed

28 Vladimir Farkas writing in *Élet és Irodalom*, July 14, 2000. Vladimir was the son of Mihály Farkas.
29 Korom, pp. 48–49.

in jobs, such as editorial work, that did not have direct contact with the masses.[30] Molotov was no less aware of the damage that the association with Jews could cause to the Communist movement. In his discussion with the Hungarian delegation on November 13, he attempted to persuade the Hungarians to include in the new government Communists who had spent the war years in exile in Moscow. Molotov "quickly added that he wanted to call attention to the fact that he was not thinking of Hungarian Jews, he was thinking simply of Hungarians."[31] In order to gain popular support, it was essential to make the party more "Hungarian." A manifestation of this effort was the change in the name of the party from the Party of Hungarian Communists to Hungarian Communist Party.

Dimitrov in Moscow selected the first Central Committee of the Hungarian Communist Party with the approval of the top Soviet leaders. The dominant figure until the arrival of Mátyás Rákosi was Ernö Gerő who, with his comrades, knew that because they were representatives of the Soviet leadership their status was superior to those comrades who had worked underground during the war. The natives accepted the Muscovites' superior standing unquestioningly. Those who had just returned from the relative safety of Moscow felt themselves entitled to question and judge the behavior of people who had operated in considerable danger in the underground.

It is difficult to give a balanced description of the role and policies of the Communist Party at the very earliest stages of post-Nazi politics. The record was mixed as regards fairness to non-Communist political programs. On the one hand, the Moscow-trained leaders well understood that at this moment, Soviet policy in Eastern Europe would not allow a program calling for radical transformation of the country. They were also well aware of what seemed to them the "lessons" of the failed revolution of 1919: excessive radicalism, disregard for nationalist feelings, and alienating the peasantry by not satisfying its desire for land had created a powerful backlash. Therefore, some Communists returning from Moscow took it on themselves to help in the organization of other democratic parties. Moscow demanded coalition politics. With automobiles lent by the Soviets, they looked up prominent FKGP, SDP, and NPP politicians and suggested that they start party work. We know the instructions for such behavior came from Moscow because

30 Rákosi, *Visszaemlékezések, 1940–1956*, vol. 2, pp. 924–925.

31 Vida, in I. Feitl (ed.), 1995, p. 82. In Molotov's case, it would be wrong to see traditional anti-Semitism. His wife was Jewish, soon to be sent to camp for this reason. On the other hand, already at the time of the Second World War the Soviet leadership, in particular Stalin, exhibited anti-Semitic tendencies.

the Communists in the other Eastern European countries behaved the same way.[32] However, perhaps understandably, great confusion prevailed. On the one hand, Communists with Soviet aid helped other parties to organize, but, on the other, at the very outset these parties had reasons to complain. Perhaps contrary to what Moscow demanded, the occupying Soviet Army in the localities often allowed only the Communist Party to organize and print leaflets.[33]

The discussions that took place in Moscow concerning the forming of the government took a long time. In the beginning of December, Gerő and Nagy returned from Hungary to consult with their Soviet comrades. First, the Soviet leaders hesitated about whether to set up a committee or a government. V. G. Dekanozov, Molotov's deputy, argued for committee, mentioning that De Gaulle had also set up a National Liberation Committee. The advantage of having a government was that it would possess greater legitimacy and could serve as a counterweight to the Szálasi regime. On the other hand, from the Soviet point of view it would be a disadvantage to have a government formed in Debrecen, because the Anglo-Saxon powers would expect to send representatives there. Having Americans or Britons so close to the Soviet front was a disturbing idea to people in Moscow. Finally, Stalin himself made the decision that it should be a government,[34] and in fact Allied representatives never came to Debrecen.

An agreement was reached about the composition of the future Hungarian government.[35] The Hungarian delegation in Moscow at first suggested Zoltán Tildy, the leader of the FKGP, the largest democratic party, for the role of prime minister. Tildy at the time was in hiding in Budapest. The delegation also wanted to form the government from the representatives of the "Hungarian Front," an underground organization that had been established in May 1944 by the representatives of FKGP, MKP, and SDP.[36] Evidently, the Hungarians were thinking of the inclusion of Communists who had spent the war years at home. For this reason alone, the suggestion was unacceptable

32 Ferenc Nagy, *Küzdelem a vasfüggöny mögött*, vol. 1, Budapest: Europa, 1990, p. 96.

33 Magyar Országos Levéltár (MOL), xix –A–1-j, box 18, collection xx.

34 The documents concerning these discussions are in Vida, in Feitl (ed.), 1995, pp. 65–100.

35 In a conversation that took place in 1982 or 1983 Molotov said to Chuev: "I actively participated in the creation of the first Hungarian government. This was, I think, in 1945. I created that government." Chuev said: "I was in Hungary recently and I was told that there is no one there who believes in communism." Molotov responded: "The Hungarians? They are a petit bourgeois people, profoundly petit bourgeois." F. Chuev and V. I. Molotov, *Sto sorok besed s Molotovym: Iz dnevnika F. Chueva*, Moscow: Terra, 1991, p. 90.

36 Informational letter by G. M. Pushkin and B. Ia. Geiger to V. G. Dekanozov concerning the suggestions of the Hungarian delegation's recommendation for forming the Hungarian government in Volokitina, pp. 109–110.

to the Russians. The Soviet authorities chose Béla Dálnoki Miklós as the new premier. He had been one of the most senior officers in the Hungarian army and had changed sides in time. Dálnoki Miklós, after defecting appealed to the Hungarian soldiers, ordered them to follow his example and change sides. In addition to him, two other generals were chosen to be ministers.

Ultimately, the government was made up of three generals, the son of an ex-Hungarian premier, Géza Teleki;[37] representatives of the Socialist Party and of the FKGP; and three Communists who were chosen chiefly because they were not Jewish. One of them was Imre Nagy; the other an almost completely unknown and insignificant figure, József Gábor; and the third one was Erik Molnár, a historian. General János Vörös became minister of war and General Gábor Faragho minister of supplies.[38] Imre Nagy got the portfolio of agriculture, Erik Molnár portfolio of culture. The Smallholders got the portfolios of foreign ministry (János Gyöngyösi) and the ministry of finance (István Vásáry). This was a very conservative government. The three generals until very recently had passionately served the pro-German cause. Vörös had been chief of staff of the army. Faragho was a particularly odd choice. He had been the commander of the gendarmerie, an organization that had been exceedingly brutal in the extermination of the Jews and in the struggle against political opposition, in particular, Communists. (Indeed, the new government in April 1945 dissolved the gendarmerie.) He was chosen as a delegate sent to Moscow because before the war he had served in the Soviet capital as a military attaché. On the basis of his knowledge of Soviet life, he had published a bitterly anti-Soviet and anti-Communist book that had enjoyed considerable success in right-wing circles.[39] How the generals, who just a few weeks before were loyally serving the Nazis, and a few democratic and Communist politicians, could get along and work together is difficult to imagine. It is hard to believe that the Soviets who were responsible for this list planned a long-term coalition, at least in this configuration.

37 Paul Teleki was a conservative man who became premier in 1939. Under his tenure, extremely restrictive anti-Jewish legislation was passed. However, in 1941, he protested against Hungary joining the anti-Yugoslav coalition by committing suicide. The coalition violated a Hungarian-Yugoslav nonaggression treaty.

38 Remarkably, Faragho had been the head of the gendarmerie after the German occupation of the country in March 1944 and, as such, was responsible for the organization of the deportation of the Jewry. In the interwar period, he had been military attaché in Moscow and learned Russian.

39 Kádár, p. 782.

In retrospect, the Soviet choices seem surprising. Before October 15, the Soviet leadership would even have been willing to retain Nicholas Horthy at the head of the government. Soviet representatives approached István Bethlen, the chief architect of the interwar political system and premier in the 1920s. Bethlen, a descendent of one of the most aristocratic and prominent families, a man who had opposed the Nazis as vulgar upstarts, would have been an acceptable minister in the new government; however, the old politician had no interest in participating in the new political order.[40] Clearly the Russians had in mind short-term considerations: finishing the war as quickly as possible and going as far west as possible were their primary concerns. To accomplish this they aimed at weakening the resistance of the Hungarian army and getting as many defectors as they could. It is unlikely that they had not been informed about the past of a man such as Faragho. The tactic was successful: some Hungarian army officers did draw the conclusion that if people like Vörös and Faragho could become ministers, then officers of the lower ranks who came over to the Soviet side had nothing to fear.

The discussions concerning Hungary's future political system, in which Stalin himself participated, do throw some light on the thinking of the Soviet leader. He made great efforts not to alienate and frighten the Allies. As mentioned before, he resisted the idea that Rákosi or Vas join the new government. Stalin repeated again and again that the Communist program must include references to the defense of private property. He also advised the Hungarians that they should show "flexibility" in purging the administrative apparatus and when talking about land reform should not be explicit about size.[41]

As was to be expected, it was the reestablishment of local government that was the most difficult task. At a time when the front was near and the system of communications had broken down, it is not surprising that anarchy prevailed. Nowhere were these committees actually elected. In some of the towns and villages, the reorganization of local authorities took place spontaneously. Here notables who had not been burdened with a pro-Nazi past took matters into their own hands. In other villages and towns, the Communists took the initiative. At least some Communists who did not know the policy line laid down in Moscow wanted to establish a

40 István Vida, *Koalició és pártharcok, 1944–1948*, Budapest: Magvető, 1984, pp. 37–38.

41 The source for the information is Gerő, *Politikatörténeti Intézet Levéltára* (PIL) 274 7/8. McCagg, referring to an article by Korom, also summarizes the notes. Stalin's "moderation" is extraordinary: he repeatedly advised the Hungarian Communists to be flexible, to stress the role of private initiative in the reconstruction of the economy, and not to scare people. McCagg, pp. 313–316.

Soviet-type regime on the example of the failed 1919 Soviet Republic. In the village of Vésztö, a "Soviet Republic" was formed that intended to send ambassadors to Moscow and ask to be accepted among the constituent republics of the Soviet Union. Soon they were disabused. Representatives came from Debrecen, and the "chairman" of the "Soviet Republic" was chased out of the village.[42] The formation of committees everywhere was haphazard. In some places, the organizers named the committees "soviets," in other places, "executive committees." Ultimately, the name "national committees" came to be generally accepted. Soon after the formation of these committees, representatives of the newly established democratic political parties joined them, hoping to spread their influence. The first significant task of the national committees was the organization of the elections to a Provisional National Assembly.[43]

Before the Provisional National Assembly would be called, the Hungarian National Independence Front was created in Szeged on December 2, 1944. This organization was the successor of the underground Hungarian Front that had been organized after the German invasion in the spring of 1944. Aside from the five anti-Nazi, democratic parties, the trade unions were also represented. On December 3, the Front published its program and its new newspaper, *Délmagyarország* (*Southern Hungary*).

The history of this newspaper is interesting, for it reveals something about the policy of the Communist Party at this early date. The few local Communists in Szeged, a city that had been liberated earlier than Debrecen, established a newspaper (*Szegedi Népakarat, The Popular Will of Szeged*) presumably with the permission of the local Soviet army command. The editors followed a radical line, recalling the policies of the short-lived 1919 regime. However, Révai appeared in Szeged a few days later, and the newspaper was closed down. Révai represented Soviet policies that called for the creation of a broad national front. Révai, with the help of FKGP and

42 Imre Kovács, *Magyarország megszállása*, Toronto: Vörösváry, 1979, p. 213.

43 What these "national committees" were and what would be their proper area of responsibility remained vague for some time. The government discussed the matter on March 19, 1945, in Debrecen. The representatives of the political parties more or less agreed that the committees could not interfere in administration but would have a primarily supervisory role. Interestingly, in this issue there seemed to be a difference of opinion within the Communist Party. Some regarded these institutions as useful allies and expressions of "revolutionary spontaneity," whereas the occupying Soviet authorities regarded the committees as a nuisance. The representatives of the party in the government defended the autonomy of these institutions and opposed the government's attempt to limit that autonomy. A Soviet representative in Budapest, Osokin, on March 6 protested to Foreign Minister Gyöngyösi concerning the behavior of the Budapest national council, which had taken on administrative tasks. *Pártközi értekezletek, 1944–1948*, Budapest: Napvilág, 2003, pp. 23–26.

2. First meeting of the National Chief Council, 1945, with Ferenc Nagy, László Rajk, Béla Varga, Kálmán Kovács, and István Reis. (Source: Hungarian National Museum.)

SDP representatives, revived the old *Délmagyarország* as representative of the National Front.[44]

The program of the Front was that of the Communist Party presented by the leader of the Communists, Gerő, who brought it back with him from Moscow. It was only slightly modified by the Socialist representative on the editorial board, Ágoston Valentiny. The program was impeccably democratic. It advocated armed struggle against Germany, prohibition of extreme right-wing organizations and movements, the punishment of Hungarian war criminals, a new and democratic constitution, radical land reform, election of a constituent assembly, formation of a provisional government, and friendly relations with neighboring countries and with the Allies. In addition, the program also included matters that were of special interest to the trade union representatives, such as improvement of the working conditions by guaranteeing eight-hour workdays, paid vacations, and the right to collective bargaining.[45]

44 Henrik Vass and László Zalai, "Tájékoztatás és hatalmi harc 1944–1948," *Múltunk* 2–3 (1993): 208.
45 Róbert Gábor, *Az igazi szocialdemokrácia: küzdelem a fasizmus és a kommunizmus ellen, 1944–1948*, Budapest: Századvég, 1998, p. 75.

The creation of a Provisional National Assembly for the whole country was more difficult than putting a government together in Debrecen. Given the fact that a large part of the country was still under German occupation, and even in the liberated areas order could hardly be reestablished, it made sense to name the assembly "Provisional National Assembly" rather than a parliament.

Hungarian politicians from all political parties were aware that there was time pressure in bringing together this assembly. It was already too late to become a meaningful participant in the anti-Nazi camp and thereby achieve better terms in the forthcoming peace conference. This assembly had the resposibility to declare war on Germany. By contrast, from the Soviet point of view the creation of anti-Nazi political organizations gradually lost importance as the war was obviously coming to a conclusion. The Hungarian delegation returned from Moscow and arrived in Debrecen on December 12, and within two days it had already established the committee charged with convening the National Assembly.[46]

The politicians chose Debrecen as a temporary capital because of its symbolic significance. It was here in 1849 that the revolutionary assembly declared Hungary's independence from the Habsburgs.[47] The date chosen for the first meeting was also symbolic: December 21, Stalin's birthday. The Soviet army lent trucks to help the work of this committee. These went around the liberated countryside asking people to elect delegates and then immediately took them to Debrecen.[48] Given the circumstances, it is understandable that only a small portion of the population participated in voting. Some observers criticized the elections as undemocratic, but it is hard to see how the organizers could have done better under the circumstances. The nomination for candidates was in the hands of the trade unions and political parties rather than the local assemblies.[49] Altogether 230 people were elected: the Communists had almost 40 percent of the delegates, and the SDP a little less then 30 percent. This way the two Marxist parties possessed a comfortable majority. The Russians were interested in the composition of the assembly, not merely which parties would be represented but also its social composition. In retrospect, it is remarkable that in a little more than a week more than a million and a half people participated in the elections

46 István Feitl, "Az ideiglenes Nemzetgyűlés létrejötte és jogalkotása," in László Hubai and László Tombor (eds.), *A magyar parlament 1944–1949: Tanulmányok*, Budapest: Gulliver, 1991, p. 13.

47 Vida, in Feitl (ed.), 1995, p. 82.

48 Mária Palasik, *A Jogállamiság megteremtésének kisérlete es kudarca Magyarországon, 1944–1949*, Budapest: Napvilág, 2000, p. 30.

49 Ibid.

at a time when hardly more than half of the country was freed and there existed no system of communication and transportation. To be sure, the composition of the assembly did not represent the political commitments of the population; the Communists were overrepresented, as elections carried out a year later would demonstrate. However, because the assembly was not and could not have been a genuine deliberative parliament, Communist overrepresentation had little practical significance.

István Bibó, the most widely respected Hungarian liberal political thinker writing at the time, pointed out that the elections took place under the most difficult circumstances and, therefore, could not possibly be fully democratic. He emphasized, nevertheless, that it was a more democratic election than any other that had ever been conducted in Hungary. In the willingness of the assembly to regard itself as the sole source of legitimacy and in the immediate promise of land reform, he saw the basis of a future democratic Hungary.[50]

The Hungarians and the Russians were both concerned with questions of legitimacy. The politicians considered it important that the legitimacy of the government should arise not from an interparty agreement but from a National Assembly created by free elections. Probably they understood that given the circumstances and the pressure of time, the gathering could hardly become a genuine consultative organ. Since the members of the cabinet had been chosen in Moscow, the election was a formality; nevertheless, this formality gave the government a greater legitimacy than if it had simply been put together by consultation among various political parties. Officially, the Provisional National Assembly elected the government on December 22, 1944.[51]

The plenary session altogether lasted only two days. In these two days, the sessions lasted eight hours. (The next occasion that the entire assembly was called together took place only in September 1945, at which time it was in session for six days.) The Provisional Assembly claimed for itself exclusive state power and authority. It also entrusted the government with concluding an armistice. Given the extraordinarily important matters that the assembly discussed and the brevity of the meetings, one must conclude that there could not have been serious disagreements and debate.

The first task of the assembly was the formation of a political committee (PC) that had the responsibility of carrying out the day-to-day business; this

50 István Bibó, "A demokratikus Magyarország államformája," in *Demokratikus magyarország: Válogatás Bibó István tanulmányaiból*, Budapest: Magvető, 1994, pp. 23–26.

51 Palasik, p. 26.

committee would oversee the work of the government in the name of the Provisional Assembly. Although the PC could not legislate, it could issue regulations, and because it acted in the name of the Provisional National Assembly, its composition was very important. The FKGP had five representatives, the Communists and the Socialists four each, the NPP had three, and the PDP had two. In addition, there were five nonparty representatives. As the liberated part of the country grew, so did the size of the PC. Ultimately, it had thirty-one members. Under the circumstances, it made sense that the PC should reflect the correlation of forces in the larger assembly. The PC, given its relatively small size, could be convened on short notice when it was impossible to convene the entire Provisional National Assembly. In this way, it turned out that the PC in effect played the role of the parliament until the elections in November 1945.

It was the PC that in January 1945 created the National Chief Council (Nemzeti Fötanács) in order to take on itself the role of head of state.[52] Three people made up this council: the premier, the head of the Provisional National Assembly, and a representative of the PC (Béla Zsedényi, Béla Miklós Dálnoki, and Ernö Gerő).[53] Thus the Communists and their allies had a larger percentage of seats in the Provisional Assembly than in the more important PC or in the National Chief Council.

In between the two plenary sessions the country was governed by regulations issued by the government and the PC. As was to be expected, on December 23, the first act of the new government was to ask for an armistice from the Soviet Union and from the Allies. From this point on, matters moved quickly. The Soviet government notified the American and British embassies in Moscow about the request of the new Hungarian government. The preparations for the conditions of the armistice immediately began. On December 28, Hungary declared war on Nazi Germany. On January 1, a Hungarian delegation headed by Gyöngyösi, the minister of foreign affairs, arrived in Moscow to receive the conditions for the armistice.

The Allies debated two issues among themselves: What would be the power of the Allied Control Commission (ACC) in Hungary and within it the power of the British and American representatives? The role of this organization was to be decisively important in the following years. These

52 MOL XVIII–3. The constitutional arrangement was the work of József Bölöny, professor of law.

53 Gizella Föglein, *Államforma és államfői jogkör Magyarországon 1944–1949*, Budapest: Osiris, 2001, pp. 18–24.

commissions were set up in all the ex-Axis countries. The other significant issue was the amount of reparations that Hungary would be obliged to pay not only to the Soviet Union but also to Czechoslovakia and Yugoslavia. The British and the Americans considered the demands too onerous and expressed surprise that it was to be $100 million more than what Romania was required to pay, even though it was demonstrable that Romanian occupation in Bessarabia and in the southern Ukraine had caused more damage to the Soviet population. On both issues, the Soviet position prevailed. These matters concerning reparations and the relative powerlessness of the British and American representatives in the ACC would have far-reaching consequences in the political life of the country in the next few years. Arguably, the conditions accepted by the Allies in Moscow had greater consequences for the future of Hungary than the Yalta conference, which took place at almost the same time, February 4–11, 1945. At Yalta, Hungary was hardly even mentioned in the discussions.

The real source of power after the arrival of the Red Army was the Soviet government. The negotiations in Moscow carried out by the Allied representatives and the Soviet Union legitimized this situation. Nothing significant could happen in Hungary without the permission of the ACC. The ACC very soon developed a large network within the country and was able to intervene everywhere and in everything. The British and the Americans agreed to participate in the ACC in spite of the fact that they had no effective role to play.

On January 18, 1945, the Hungarian delegation received the official text of the armistice conditions, and two days later the delegates signed the document, even though the conditions were exceptionally harsh. In addition to paying heavy reparations, Hungary was required to assume responsibility for supplying the Soviet troops, and the ACC was required to withdraw all personnel from territories occupied after 1937 and to assemble eight divisions to fight against Nazi Germany.

This last provision was never carried out. The idea of creating a Hungarian army to fight on the side of the Allies had arisen even before the conclusion of the armistice. On December 12, János Vörös, the minister of war, had discussed the matter with General Susaikov, a member of Marshal Malinovskii's staff. The Hungarians were anxious to have an army fighting on the side of the victors. General Vörös wanted to recruit his soldiers from among prisoners of war and expected that those who were still fighting on the side of the Germans would be willing to change sides in order to avoid a worse fate. By the time the armistice was signed, however, the Soviet leadership had lost interest in the creation of a Hungarian army. Evidently, the Soviet leadership did not trust the Hungarians to the extent of equipping them with Soviet weapons.[54]

With the signing of the armistice document, Hungary, in fact, left the war[55] and an unhappy chapter in Hungarian history ended.

54 Imre Okváth, "A katonai elit metamorfozusa, 1945–1950," in Imre Okváth (ed.), *Katonai perek 1945–1958*, Budapest: Történelmi Hivatal, 2001, pp. 13–14.

55 For more information about the armistice and its consequences see Sándor Balogh, *Magyarország külpolitikája 1945–1950*, Budapest: Kossuth, 1988, pp. 5–20, and Margit Földesi, *A megszállók szabadsága*, Budapest: Kairosz, 2002, pp. 48–49.

2

Budapest

Budapest has always played a dominant role in the history of modern Hungary. Its population at the end of the war was approximately ten times larger than that of the next largest town. During the war, the size of the population increased to 1.4 million; however, as a result of the murder and deportation of Jews, civilian casualties, and the number of people who followed the retreating German and Hungarian armies, the number fell to 900,000. In 1945, people returned from captivity, and the population of the city once again grew to be 1 million inhabitants.[1] Budapest was not merely the administrative capital but also the center of communications, industry, and cultural life. All railroad lines converged there, and much of the country's industry was concentrated there or in the surrounding districts. Budapest was an outpost of Western Europe surrounded by a poor and backward countryside. In the interwar period, the city supported a lively intellectual life, perhaps not as brilliant as it had been in the last decades of the Habsburg empire but still impressive. As Ferenc Nagy put it in his memoirs, it was possible to govern Debrecen from Budapest, but it was not possible to govern Budapest from Debrecen.[2] As long as Budapest was not liberated, the reconstruction of the country and the revival of political life could hardly begin.

The siege of the capital, from the appearance of the first Soviet tank at the boundary of the city to the final capitulation of German and Hungarian forces, lasted for 102 days and concluded on February 11. This was a far longer siege than that of any German city or indeed any European city

1 László Varga, "Várostörténet, 1945–1956," *Budapesti Negyed* 2–3 (1998). Accessed July 22, 2005 <http://www.bparchiv.hu/magyar/kiadvany/bpn/20_21/varga.htm>

2 F. Nagy, vol. 1, p. 148.

outside of the Soviet Union in the Second World War.[3] (By comparison, the fighting for Berlin lasted two weeks and for Vienna only one week.)

Although the German military authorities had been planning the defense of the city, the Hungarian Nazi (Nyilas) bureaucracy had not prepared for the siege. The population had not been encouraged to leave, nor had sufficient food supplies been amassed. As a consequence of shortages in December and January, hundreds starved to death. The winter of 1944–1945 was especially cold. The weather had the fortunate consequence that epidemics did not spread in spite of the abandoned corpses of people and animals in the streets. On the other hand, during the long siege the inhabitants of the city shivered in the unheated cellars of the apartment houses. Because of the damage to the water supply network, in the last period of the siege people from several districts of the city had to go out in search of water, exposing themselves to the danger of being shot. Gas and water supplies ended altogether at the end of December.[4] In some parts of the city, especially in Buda, where the fighting lasted longest, the water shortage was catastrophic.

Even during the misery of the siege, the anarchy of Nazi rule in which different sections of the party struggled against one another continued. Mindless terror also did not end. The chief of Szálasi's press department, Ferenc Fiala, described the situation: "Order has broken down in the capital. Anyone who possessed a submachine gun could become judge and executioner."[5] No one was safe. Nyilas thugs attempted to murder a Hungarian army officer in order to take his automobile. Others broke into the building of the papal representative, tortured, and ultimately shot Joseph Cavallier, the head of the Hungarian Holy Cross Order, saying that he had given out letters of protection to Jews.[6] Led by a crazed Catholic priest, Father András Kun, a group of men dressed in cassocks with Nazi armbands slaughtered the sick in a Jewish hospital. On another occasion, Father Kun personally shot a police officer.[7] From the end of November until such time as it became too dangerous to approach the Danube because of the nearness of Soviet troops, Jews were regularly taken to the river at night and shot. The German command expressed its disapproval: the nightly shooting upset the public and the Germans wanted to maintain order in the conditions of siege. From the time of the Nazi seizure of power in October until the liberation of the city, the

3 Krisztián Ungváry, *Budapest ostroma*, Budapest: Corvina, 1998. Ungváry's study is the definitive work on this segment of the war.

4 Ungváry, p. 220.

5 Éva Teleki, p. 136.

6 Ibid., p. 140. Also, Béla Vincellér, pp. 102–104.

7 Ungváry, pp. 242–244.

3. Budapest, 1945. (Source: Hungarian National Museum.)

Jewish population of Budapest diminished to a little more than 100,000 people; that is, it was cut in half. (In Budapest, Jews were not systematically deported as they had been in the rest of the country.) As long as it was possible to leave the city, Jews were still forced to march on foot to Austria.[8] In the last hours when resistance was obviously hopeless, Nazis mined the ghetto and were prepared to blow it up. The Jews were saved only by the arrival of Soviet troops.

The defenders destroyed all the bridges over the Danube, and because the fighting had gone from house to house, at the end of the siege the city was in ruins. Eighty percent of the apartment houses were damaged, and 36,000 families were homeless, including 40,000 children.[9]

Budapest was finally liberated in the middle of February, and the difficult job of reconstruction began. How did people in Budapest, who had suffered the most, and also people in the rest of the country at this time, look at the soldiers of the Red Army and, in general, perceive what was happening to them? During the long decades of Communism, the events of 1944–1945 had always been referred to as "Liberation," and the anniversary of April 4, 1945, the removal of the last German troops from Hungarian territory,

8 Ibid., p. 136.
9 Zoltán Vas, *Akkori önmagunkról*, vol. 2, Budapest: Magvető, 1982, p. 30.

was celebrated as a national holiday. No one questioned publicly whether the events of 1945 should be properly described as liberation. Even people who were by no means Communists used the phrase "liberation." Ferenc Nagy, for example, the Smallholder (FKGP) politician and future premier, in his memoirs written in exile described his worries and the concerns of those who were with him at the time of the arrival of the Russians but nevertheless consistently wrote about "liberation."[10] In reality, however, it is highly unlikely that more than a small minority of the population at the time greeted the arrival of the Red Army with unalloyed enthusiasm and felt themselves liberated. For them, the events could be characterized as a conquest by a hostile, foreign army.

It is extremely difficult to reconstruct how Hungarians regarded Soviet occupation at the time. The sources are inadequate. Memoirs and contemporary newspapers are available, but obviously the memoir writers do not form a representative sample. Peasants and simple workers almost by definition do not write memoirs. Neither the accounts of contemporary newspapers, which presented events from a particular political point of view, nor the memoir writers, who turned to these events after the passage often of decades, can be fully trusted. We can, nevertheless, make some safe assumptions. It is likely that aside from a small and committed Nazi minority most people regarded the end of the war with relief. Aside from a few of the German occupiers and their Hungarian allies, most people understood by the middle of 1944 that Germany had lost the war and Hungary was once again on the wrong side. Relief at the end of the senseless destruction, however, did not mean that Hungarians felt a sense of gratitude to the soldiers of the Red Army. A combination of long-standing contempt for Slavs in general and for Russians in particular coupled with years of nationalist, anti-Soviet propaganda, carried out by the functionaries of the Horthy regime, could not have remained without effect. Those Hungarians who had not been personally subjected to Nazi terror had far more friendly feelings for the "civilized" Germans than for Russians. Probably the average Hungarian was ambivalent: glad that the war was over, or would be over very soon, but distrustful of the new occupiers. People were able to hold conflicting views at the same time: one day optimistic about the future of their country and on another deeply concerned about the behavior and intentions of the new conquerors.

The unsettled situation, circumstances in which no one knew or could know what the future would bring, created wild and inevitably conflicting

10 F. Nagy, vol. 1, pp. 78–79.

expectations and fears. István Bibó, writing at the time, saw a danger to Hungarian democracy in the fact that half of the population was afraid of the introduction of "proletarian dictatorship" and the other half was concerned about "reactionary forces."[11] Indeed, a recurring phrase in Communist verbiage in the following years was the struggle against "reaction," fighting against reactionaries. They insisted on depicting all their political opponents – mostly unfairly – as reactionaries. It showed the political skill of the Communists that they managed to depict themselves as "democrats" and their opponents as fascists and reactionaries, that is, antidemocrats. By contrast, the anti-Communist forces propagated rumors – as it turned out, accurately – concerning Hungary's immediate inclusion into the Soviet Union and the introduction of collective farms.

Public opinion concerning Russians and Communists depended not so much on past propaganda but on current realities. People expected Soviet soldiers to behave badly, and in fact they did. One might say that they lived up to expectations. One can find excuses for Soviet behavior. After all, it was German and with them Hungarian armies that invaded the Soviet Union and not vice versa. All occupying armies behave badly: even the U.S. army has been blamed for mistreating Germans in prisoner of war camps in 1945.[12] It is an even more powerful defense that the German, Romanian, and even Hungarian armies in the Soviet Union had created great devastation in the very recent past, introducing bloody terror in occupied territories and mistreating the population that they deemed inferior. Under the circumstances, the soldiers of the Red Army could not have been expected to behave much better. We may disapprove of vengeance, but in human terms, it is understandable. Such mitigating circumstances, however, mattered little to the Hungarians. What they saw was that the occupiers raped and looted, acted arbitrarily, and were the cause of much suffering.

Moscow's policy toward Hungary was reprehensible: it aimed to punish and exploit. Obviously, one of the most reprehensible crimes, the arrest and ultimate murder of the finest hero of the Second World War, Raul Wallenberg, was the responsibility of the Soviet government. Wallenberg had worked selflessly within the Swedish embassy, devoting all his energies and facing danger daily in order to save as many Jewish lives as possible. He was arrested in Budapest on January 17 and disappeared.[13] Presumably, the

11 Bibó, "A demokratikus Magyarország államformája," in *Demokratikus Magyarország*, 1994, pp. 27–28.
12 Günter Bischof and Stephen E. Ambrose (eds.) *Eisenhower and the German POWs: Facts against Falsehood*. Baton Rouge: Louisiana State UP, 1992.
13 There is an enormous literature on the role and fate of Raul Wallenberg. Most authorities assume that he was killed in 1947.

Soviet leaders had assumed that his work on behalf of the Jews was a cover for spying for the Americans. For the Soviets, altruism was unbelievable and, therefore, suspicious.

The Soviet High Command behaved brutally. It usually disregarded complaints, it failed to discipline soldiers, and it acted arbitrarily. It was also responsible for the worst injustice. Because it had overestimated the number of defenders of Budapest in order to justify previous and mistaken reports, now it had to capture a large number of "prisoners of war." Because such prisoners were not available, the Russians made up the shortfall by indiscriminately arresting men in the streets. When Hungarian Communists brought up this matter with the Soviet High Command, the Russians responded by saying that the arrested were really soldiers who had just changed into civilian dress. Sometimes these "prisoners of war" were used for the removal of the rubble and in general for reconstruction. But others were taken to the Soviet Union for work and were not returned, if at all, for years. The phrase *malenkaia rabota* (in a corrupted form *malenkii robot*), a little work, became part of the Hungarian vocabulary at the time. No one was safe. Jews and Communists were arrested in the streets just like anyone else.[14]

It seems that the behavior of the Soviet soldiers in Hungary was worse than in Bulgaria and Romania but not worse than in Germany. This may have had something to do with the difference in High Command. Evidently, Marshall Fedor Tolbukhin was better in disciplining his forces than Marshall Rodion Malinovskii. The fact that in Budapest, unlike in Bulgaria or Romania, the Russians encountered evidence of a higher standard of living and evidence of a Western European style of life also probably contributed to their hostility. The extraordinarily bitter fighting on Hungarian territory, in the course of which tens of thousands of Soviet soldiers died, inflamed the troops.[15] There is evidence that in areas where the fighting was most bitter the victorious Russian soldiers behaved the worst.[16]

Contemporary diaries and memoirs are full of horrors of every kind. Almost every memoir dealing with this period talks about Soviet terror, looting, and in particular rapes. The great writer Sándor Márai began his diary for the year 1945 by telling the story of his neighbor, a rabbi. The rabbi came to him a day after the liberation and said that a Russian

14 András Hegedüs, *A történelem és a hatalom igézetében*, Budapest: Kossuth, 1988, pp. 105–106.

15 Norman Naimark makes this argument in his book, *The Russians in Germany. A History of the Soviet Occupation, 1945–1949*, Cambridge, MA: Belknap Press of Harvard UP, 1995, p. 70.

16 Ungváry, pp. 269–275.

4. Rubble in Budapest. (Source: Hungarian National Museum.)

soldier had come and harassed his wife, searched the house, and finally found the rabbi, who had been hiding in the cellar. "Watch. Watch," the soldier demanded and took the rabbi's watch from his wrist. The rabbi added: "What a disappointment!"[17] Elsewhere, Márai writes that an old Jew, thinking that the Soviet soldier he met was Jewish, went up to him and announced that he too was Jewish. The Russian smiled, kissed the man on his left cheek, then on the right, and confessed that, indeed, he was Jewish. After that, the Russian made the entire family stand at the wall and with his comrades removed everything valuable from the apartment.[18]

At the time, the image of the Soviet soldiers in the Hungarian mind was one of someone dangerous, ill disciplined, primitive, and drunk. It was a well-founded notion that Russians could not resist the lure of alcohol. They looted wine cellars and even confiscated perfume bottles to drink. The sight of drunken Russian soldiers on the streets behaving badly and capriciously was a regular occurrence.

Stories were common about Russians who saw a flushing toilet for the first time and became terrified. The preoccupation of Russian soldiers and even officers with confiscating and stealing watches also contributed to the image of the primitive Russian. Every Hungarian knew the phrase *davaj chasy* (give me your watch). There was something extraordinary, almost comic, about the soldiers' and officers' preoccupation with watches. Béla Király, an officer of the Hungarian army, approached a Soviet officer to give himself up and report that his unit was ready to stop fighting. The Soviet officer "stretched out his hand. I thought, 'well, these Soviet soldiers are not such barbarians as they had been described by propaganda. They know how to receive a parliamentarian.' But the Soviet officer did not accept my hand. With great skill and speed, he removed my watch from my wrist."[19]

There was another aspect of this image also. German behavior in Russia was different from how the Russians acted in the occupied countries. Germans were cold, merciless, and cruel. The average soldier, convinced that he was representing a superior civilization, saw no need to be kind to "a lower form of humanity." There are no stories of German soldiers befriending Russian children. Russians, by contrast, on occasion could be humane. They often responded warmly to children. When the children begged for

17 Sándor Márai, *Napló, 1945–1957*, Washington: Oriental Press, 1958, p. 3.
18 Sándor Márai, *Föld, Föld*, Toronto: Vörösváry, 1972, pp. 24–25.
19 Béla Király, *Honvédségből Néphadsereg*, Paris; New Brunswick; New York: Bessenyei Kör, 1986, p. 40.

bread, they often took pity on them.[20] Together with the words *davaj* and *malenkaia rabota* most Hungarians also learned the word *khleb* or bread. The Russians also respected "culture." Márai wrote in his diary that a Russian soldier he met on the street demanded that he carry his large bag. Then he asked Márai what his profession was. He answered: writer. The Russian immediately took back his heavy bag and gave him a loaf of bread.[21] Béla Király wrote in his memoirs that after his surrender he was taken to meet a Soviet colonel, and the Soviet officer received him graciously and gave him chocolate.[22]

Terror introduced by undisciplined Soviet soldiers was a major problem for the Communist Party. Communist leaders well understood that the people associated them with the occupying army and any misdeed by Soviet soldiers reflected on them. Their internal correspondence was full of complaints. It put the functionaries in a difficult situation. They had to find excuses not only for others but also for themselves for Soviet behavior. For example, a report from Pestszentlörinc on February 10, 1945, included the following: "Comrade Árpád Házi [a major figure in the party who had spent the war years working underground in Hungary] is asking the Center to do something in connection with the behavior of the Russian soldiers. Pregnant mothers are taken to work, the Russians behave rudely, they beat up the members of the police, and the mayor. The comrades are afraid to go out to the street and therefore they do not come to the Party office. The fascists make the Russians drunk in order to frighten the population."[23] It was an amusingly far-fetched idea that the Russians needed persuading to drink. Nevertheless, blaming the "fascists" for the misbehavior of the Soviet soldiers is a recurrent theme in internal correspondence.

The Communists themselves were not exempt from Russian arbitrariness. András Tömpe, one of the organizers of the political police, wrote from Pécs: "It is partially the consequence of the incorrect behavior of the Russian commander that Russian soldiers occupied the police building. Within two hours the police had to move out, but in such a way that everything had to remain in the building. When the Russians arrived they threw the files out of the window.... The behavior of the Russians is very unfortunate. Day

20 I remember standing behind a truck full of Russian soldiers. Together with other children, I begged for bread, and the soldiers took pity on us and gave us loaves. Peter Kenez, *Varieties of Fear, Growing Up Jewish under Nazism and Communism*, Washington, DC: American University Press, 1995, p. 44.

21 Márai, 1958, p. 5.

22 Király, p. 41.

23 Politikai Intézet Levéltár (hereafter PIL) 274/16/1 February 10, Pestszentlörinc.

and night they are in the street drunk." "There is an anti-Russian mood in the city, and that is not helped by the demand of the Russian commander that the citizens are obliged to greet every Russian officer in the streets."[24]

From Obuda, immediately after liberation the local Communist leader reported to the Central Committee: "Communists inform the Soviet soldiers who are the local fascists. Then the Russians arrest the fascists together with the person who made the report. In many instances they let the fascists go, but keep the person who made the report. The Russian command is full of fascist interpreters."[25]

Communist district secretaries in a meeting on March 8, 1945, aired many complaints against the Russians. They said, "People blame the communists for what the Russians do." They also said, "Fascists captured by police are freed by Russians. A major named Visovsky is interested only in drinking, and is completely under fascist influence. This is why it happened that a party member was shot by the Russians, and an old comrade by the name of Klieger was beaten bloody in his own apartment, lost one of his eyes and was called a stinking communist."[26]

Although the Communists among themselves constantly deplored Russian behavior, there was one topic they did not discuss in their official correspondence even though this was the one that occupied the Hungarian public the most. Rape committed by the soldiers of the Red Army remained an absolute taboo as long as the Communist regime existed. Although everyone talked about it, at the time nothing ever appeared in print concerning this issue until the collapse of the Soviet regime. Naturally given the nature of the problem, it is impossible to give exact figures, but the estimates run between 50,000 to 200,000 rapes.[27] These rough estimates are based on reports of abortions, sexually transmitted diseases, and hospital records. There are anecdotal reports concerning Soviet officers who severely punished offending soldiers and also reports about others who took no actions against such soldiers at all. The matter was of such great consequence in the political struggle of the Communist Party for power that Rákosi considered it necessary to report on this issue to Dimitrov and ask for his help. Needless to say, no such help was forthcoming. He wrote on February 19, 1945, shortly after his arrival in Budapest: "Our situation is made more difficult by the occasional bad behavior of soldiers of the Red Army for which we

24 PIL 274/16/1 May 4, 1945, Pécs.

25 PIL 274/16/1 February 13, 1945, Obuda.

26 PIL 274 16/1 March 8, 1945.

27 Andrea Pető, "Átvonuló hadsereg, maradandó trauma . . . " in *Történelmi Szemle* 1-2 (1999). Accessed July 22, 2005 <www.tt.hu/tsz99_1_2_peto_andrea.htm>

5. Ernő Gerő, 1898–1980.

are blamed. Undoubtedly there is some improvement in this matter, but the cases of mass rape and looting are repeated after the liberation of every district, including Budapest. There are still cases when [Soviet soldiers] arrest workers, among them good party members, who are taken to prisoner of war camps where they disappear."[28]

In spite of the embarrassment caused by the Soviet troops' behavior, the growth of the Communist Party was phenomenal. On December 28, 1944, Ernő Gerő wrote to Rákosi, who was still in Moscow, describing the situation he had found on his return. He reported that the party had only 3058 members, although he immediately added that this was an understatement because there were large areas of the country including districts of the capital still under German occupation. He complained about the lack of cadres, organizational weakness, and the inability of the comrades who had lived under German occupation to understand the current policy line. On the other hand, in spite of its small size, Gerő wrote, the Communist Party was the moving force in politics, and its program was widely accepted by the newly formed national councils in different localities.[29] He expected that within a very short time the membership would increase to 10,000–15,000. In reality, the increase of the membership surpassed Gerő's expectations: In February, the party had 30,000 members, in May 150,000, and in October half a million.

28 Henrik Vass, ed., "Dokumentumok Rákositól – Rákosiról." *Múltunk* 2-3 (1991): 247.

29 Gerő to Rákosi December 28, 1944. In *Moszkvának jelentjük: Titkos dokumentumok, 1944–1948*. Budapest: Századvég, 1994. p. 11.

Whether the new members joined the party because of conviction or opportunism is impossible to establish and sometimes self-interest reinforces apparently noble motives. For whatever reason, two strikingly different groups supplied particularly large numbers of new Communists. One of these groups was the Jewry. Jews had been living under a sentence of death; now they suddenly realized they were going to live and this had not happened because of the goodness of the Hungarian people, their neighbors and friends, but because of the valor of the soldiers of the Red Army. This sense of liberation and gratitude to the Soviet Union – however undeserved, given the almost explicit anti-Semitism of the Soviet leadership at this time – explains much about the politics of the postwar years. In Hungary, unlike any other country in Eastern Europe, Jews in the Communist Party and in the political police would come to play a role way out of proportion to their numbers in the population. Many Jews, though, of course, not all, came to feel it was only the Red Army and Soviet power that stood between them and the incorrigibly anti-Semitic people. Whether this was true is another matter. Anti-Communist propaganda had always identified Communism and Jews. Now this identification in the popular mind seemed justified. Anti-Semitism among the Hungarian people continued to be a handicap to the Communist Party in its struggle for power, and therefore it had considerable political significance.

Ironically, the other group supplying many new Communists was the ex-Nazis, those who had not played particularly visible roles in the previous regime. Leaving aside such motives as attempting to cover up an unsavory past, the affinity of ex-Nazis for Communism was not as strange as it might seem. Nazism and Communism had something very significant in common. These were movements that, in an extremely conservative political order, promised social change. Because Communism had been discredited by the unfortunate experiences of the short-lived Communist regime of 1919, and because it was also associated with the unpopular Soviet Union, many, especially the uneducated and politically unsophisticated, gravitated to the Hungarian version of National Socialism. This is not to argue that there was no difference between Communism and Nazism. In Marxism the Communists possessed a sophisticated ideology that could satisfy the craving of many for an all-encompassing worldview, promising to explain the present and the past and even to predict the future. It is, however, necessary to point out that they had attracted their followers from the same social circles. For example, László Rajk, a veteran of the Spanish Civil War, was the most prominent among the underground Communists and as such was arrested by the Nazis. At the same time his brother, Endre, was a high-ranking official of the Nazi party, who had the job of organizing the food supply for the capital.[30] András Hegedüs, a future prime minister and a close associate of Rákosi, confided in an interview, long after he had lost power and become disillusioned, that if he had first come into contact with Nazis instead of Communists, he might have chosen the other radical movement.[31]

The top leaders of the party at this time openly courted low-ranking ex-members of the Hungarian Nazi Party (Nyilaskeresztes Part), "little Nazis," as they were called at the time. The party needed new members in order to penetrate Hungarian society and also to be able to assume a nationalist mantle. Rákosi explicitly stated that, in his opinion, it was easier to make good Communists out of the "little Nazis" than out of Jewish intellectuals.[32] Rákosi, Gerő, Révai, and indeed most members of the top leadership came from precisely those social circles in which the top leader of the party expressed no confidence. One may describe this attitude either as a result of remarkable self-knowledge or, perhaps more likely, self-loathing. Many of the new members of the party were indeed ill educated and came from lower class peasant and worker backgrounds. They had many reasons to join. First of all, by becoming Communists, they could cover up their unsavory past. Indeed, the party in its recruiting work made it explicit: join and your missteps would be forgiven. Given ever-increasing Communist dominance in politics, it was easy to see that membership in the victorious party would lead to material benefits. But in any case, moving from one radical organization into another was intellectually and psychologically not very difficult. These ex-Nazis brought with them their deeply ingrained anti-Semitism. Low-ranking Communist activists often made crude anti-Semitic statements. The anti-Semitism of these new Communists was a different order from the cynicism of the top leaders, who were simply willing to take advantage of the anti-Semitism of others.

The Communists were the first to organize their party. They, of course, had considerable advantages. They had Soviet material support and knowledge of Moscow's policies and clarity of purpose. On the other hand, they had the least to build on; they had to start organization work from practically nothing. A party that grew within a few months from fewer than 4000 members to more than 300,000 needed local organizations and reliable mid-level cadres. The Smallholders and the Socialists had a ready-made

30 Teleki, p. 213.

31 András Hegedüs, *Élet egy eszme árnyékában: Életrajzi interjú*, Vienna: Zsille Zoltán, 1985, p. 52.

32 Losonczy's letter to Révai, July 14, 1949 Published by Éva Standeisky in *Budapesti Negyed* 2 (1995). Accessed July 22, 2005 <http://www.bparchiv.hu/magyar/kiadvany/bpn/08/losonczy.html>

structure that they needed only to revive, but the Communists had to create it. Party cells had to be set up in large factories, counties, cities, and small towns, and all of these had to be staffed with reliable people. In order to overcome the shortage of cadres, the party, in the spring and summer of 1945, organized courses in which working-class people participated, for the most part, but also some peasants. At first, six-week and three-month courses were set up for the preparation of mid-level cadres. In the summer of 1945, 10,000 people participated in these courses. To be invited to study at a party school was a great privilege: people were freed from their regular jobs and could look forward to a fine career.[33] In the following year, the party set up a six-month course as a higher-level school. In these schools, students learned not only Marxism-Leninism but also how to behave and speak like a Communist leader.[34] As long as the course lasted, the participants lived in dormitories and were insulated from the outside world.[35] As in so much else, the Communists learned from and copied Soviet institutions.

An important and much debated question in the historical literature of the postwar period concerns Stalin's intentions in Eastern Europe. Did he already plan to set up satellite states? The extensive correspondence between the Hungarian Communists and Moscow can shed some light not on Soviet plans but on how the Hungarians understood Soviet intentions. The Communist leaders, especially Rákosi, were in constant touch with Moscow. Most of the communication went through Georgii Dimitrov, a Bulgarian Communist, who had been head of the defunct Comintern. He retained his job as the person responsible for relations with the national parties.[36] Between February and September 1945, Rákosi wrote nine rather lengthy reports. Remarkably, although Rákosi and Dimitrov both knew Russian well, the reports were written in German, the language of the Comintern.[37] Rákosi wrote honestly and in great detail about the problems of the party, Hungarian politics and foreign relations. He did not keep silent about the behavior of the Soviet troops and blamed some of the difficulties of the party on the Russians. We can form a fairly clear idea of how the leaders of the party saw their tasks from these reports. They regarded themselves as agents

33 Gerő's report to the international department of the Soviet Communist Party, August 6, 1945, in *Moszkvának jelentjük . . .*, pp. 57–76.

34 Hegedüs, *A történelem . . .*, pp. 123–134.

35 A fine Hungarian film, *Angi Vera*, made in the 1970s, gave a wonderful description of such a school. There is also an excellent description of the training of the young Communist cadres in Tibor Dessewffy, *Iskola a hegyoldalban*, Budapest: Uj Mandátum, 1999.

36 The Comintern was officially dissolved presumably in order to allay the concerns of the Allies. Needless to say, Soviet direction of the international Communist movement continued.

37 For these reports see Henrik Vass (ed.), "Dokumentumok Rákositól – Rákosiról," *Múltunk* 2–3 (1991): 245–288.

6. László Rajk, 1909–1949.

of a higher authority. At no point did they try to assert their independence from Moscow. It never seemed to have occurred to them that Soviet and Hungarian interests might not coincide. There was no question on Rákosi's part of attempting to assert independence. Indeed on the contrary, he complained that he was not receiving enough directions from the "Center." For example, he wrote on June 11: "It would give us great help if we heard your opinions and advice. I have to admit that we are somewhat embarrassed that we have heard absolutely nothing concerning whether our political line is correct or we should change something. We regard this as a sign of confidence, but it would be better if we were acquainted with your views."[38]

It would be a mistake to conclude that the Russians constantly pushed the Hungarians in a radical direction. In fact, the opposite is more likely. G. M. Pushkin, the Soviet ambassador, reported to Moscow:

> The MKP is not following that correct path that is followed in Yugoslavia, Bulgaria, Romania and Finland. In these countries the democratic parties united in a bloc. Here too there was such a bloc that corresponded completely to our policies up to the municipal elections. The communist party could have strengthened its position and its influence on political life only if it remained in the same bloc with the democratic parties.... The difficult tasks can be dealt with only in a peaceful way by a bloc of democratic parties that included not only the SDP and the National Peasant Party, but also the most influential political force in the country, the FKGP.[39]

38 Ibid., p. 275.

39 G. P. Murashko and A. F. Noszkova, "A Szovjet tényezö Kelet Europa országainak háború utáni fejlődésében, 1945–1948," *Múltunk* 2 (1996): 58–59. Pushkin's recommendation of maintaining the National Front for the elections would not have strengthened democracy. In fact, it would

One must conclude that while the main outlines of policy were laid down in Moscow, the local leaders could have had considerable autonomy if they had chosen to use it. It seems that these people lived in constant fear that they might make a mistake and misunderstand what was expected of them. The Soviet leaders did not so much tell their Hungarian inferiors what to do as make them fearful that they might do something that would get them into trouble. People who had lived in Moscow before or during the war must have all been aware of the cost of making mistakes. Stalin was famously inscrutable. As circumstances changed, so did Stalinist policy, but because he usually left his view less than perfectly clear it was rarely necessary for him to admit that Soviet policy in fact had changed. Such a situation put the Communist leaders – not only in Hungary – in a difficult position. Because they could never be certain what was expected of them, they often pushed the current policy line, as they understood it, further than necessary.[40] It was better to appear too eager than to appear insufficiently obedient. Of course, the Communist leaders took for granted that their ultimate task was to establish a Soviet-type regime. Only the issue of timing remained uncertain. It mattered a great deal whether the transition period to a single-party system would occur within a few years or only after decades. From the available evidence, it appears that the Soviet leadership and therefore their Hungarian inferiors expected a far longer transition period than in fact occurred.

Rákosi attempted to monopolize contacts with the Soviet leadership and, in particular, with Stalin. He alone could communicate with Stalin in writing. His direct line of communication was both the foundation of his power and also protection. However, for their knowledge the Russians did not depend entirely on the reports of the Hungarian Communists; they had their own separate channels. Already in 1942 a certain Ernő Szücs had signed a document in which he promised to obey orders of the NKVD. After his return to Hungary, he worked in the ministry of the interior and sent regular reports on the behavior of the Hungarian Communist leaders to Moscow. He had something bad to say about everyone. In particular, he accused Révai and George Lukács of Hungarian nationalism, anti-Sovietism,

have made the elections meaningless. Nevertheless, the Soviet ambassador argued for maintaining a genuine democratic front. The date of his report was presumably the end of 1945.

40 Robert Levy, *Ana Pauker: The Rise and Fall of a Jewish Communist*, Berkeley: University of California Press, 2001, p. 73. Levy describes a remarkable situation. In 1945, Ana Pauker, the leading Romanian Communist, visited Moscow. Before she entered the Central Committee building, she asked her good friend to take care of her child if she did not return. The life of a Communist leader was precarious.

and so forth.[41] Because every Communist leader, including Rákosi, Gerő, and certainly Révai, had some "dark spots" in their career from a Communist point of view, they had reason to fear. In addition, the Russians, of course, had their own observers in Hungary.

In some respects, the Communist Party in these early months of 1945 was like all other parties: it competed for popular support, it had representatives in the Provisional Assembly and in the government, and it published newspapers and pamphlets to present a political program. But, in other ways, it was not just like any political party: it represented the real power in Hungary, the victorious Soviet Union. Consequently, the power and influence of the Communists could not be measured at this early date by the extent of its popular support. Because it represented the Soviet Union, it was able to take possession of two decisively important portfolios in the government: agriculture, enabling it to oversee the coming land reform, and the interior, giving it control of the police, including the political police, a critical component of power. Ferenc Erdei, minister of the interior, nominally belonged to the NPP, but in fact was a Communist and acted in the interests of the party. That Erdei was not a member of the party was actually beneficial to the Communists: they did not have to assume responsibility for the lawlessness, but at the same time they were able to place their people in crucial positions. The secretary within the department of the interior who was directly responsible for the police, Sándor Zöld, was also a Communist, and so was his successor in this position, Mihály Farkas. At the very outset, the Communists took into their hands the instruments of coercion and, consequently, the playing field in the struggle for power was never even. It must be pointed out, however, that the Communists' success in maximizing their position by legal and illegal means does not necessarily imply that they were already preparing to take power within a short time.

On January 21, weeks before the fighting for the city ended, the parties of the National Independence Front established the city's self-government. The parties' representatives elected János Csorba, a Smallholder politician, as mayor. The work of reconstruction began even before the siege ended. On February 7 in Pest, the first streetcar line started to operate, and two days later the first train arrived at the North railroad station. Within a few months the correlation of political forces changed to the advantage

41 Magdolna Baráth, "Valaki figyel," *Beszélő* 11 (1999). Accessed July 22, 2005 <http://www.beszelo.c3.hu/99/11/08 barat.html>. Szücs's Soviet contacts did not ultimately protect him from the fate that befell so many of his comrades. Szücs was arrested, presumably with Soviet permission, in 1950. The Hungarians found copies of his reports to Moscow in his safe.

of the Communist Party, and on May 5 the representatives elected Zoltán Vas as mayor, who held his office until the municipal elections in October.[42]

Our best source for the situation in Budapest in January and February 1945 is a letter that János Kádár, the senior Communist leader in Budapest at the time, sent to Erdei. In it, he painted a depressing picture. He wrote:

> The part of the city that had been liberated by January 18th is full of demolished houses and barricades. There are demolished cars everywhere, and thousands of human and animal corpses. Bombs or fire demolished a large proportion of the houses; the rest is unlivable because of broken windows. The population has been living in cellars and 80% of it is still there. There is a shortage of food. Order has broken down. The Germans and the Nyilas removed everything that could be removed from the factories, stores and from a large part of the private apartments. But the robbery has not stopped after liberation. A large part of the population has participated and is participating in the robbery. Because of the inability of the police and the lack of action on the part of the Soviet army, the robbers can act with impunity and public safety has completely disappeared.[43]

As Kádár wrote, it was not only the Soviet soldiers who looted but also Hungarians who took advantage of the general confusion, abandoned apartments, broken shop windows, and so forth. The occupation army had neither the ability nor the commitment that was necessary in order to impose order. Under the circumstances, the district national committees in the city and the political parties took it upon themselves to organize police detachments. This effort resulted in confusion plus the coexistence and competition of more or less independent organizations. Some of these were self-appointed groups, made up of shady characters. They gave themselves names such as "Hungarian GPU" and "Interior Safety Brigade." Members of the professional police, Jews, and people with German names, who hoped for protection by becoming policemen, joined. The primary obstacle in the work of organizing a functioning and much-needed police was the Soviet army. The Soviet command had no understanding of Hungarian politics, so at times they released prominent Nazis arrested by the Hungarians. On the other hand, they arrested half of the newly recruited police. According to Kádár, 2000–3000 of them were in a prisoner camp in the nearby town of Gödöllö. Because the Russians refused to give weapons to Hungarians, the functioning of the police was strictly circumscribed in any case. They could

42 Varga, 1998, passim.

43 Kádár to Erdei February 9, 1945, MOL XIX-B-1-r. The document is reprinted in *Társadalmi Szemle* 1 (1997): 82.

7. First meeting of the Provisional Assembly in Budapest, September 4, 1945. Members of the government include Sándor Rónai, Imre Nagy, Erik Molnár, and Ernő Gerő. (Source: Hungarian National Museum.)

not operate after sunset because it was too dangerous. After a few weeks of complete chaos, the Russians finally relented. Soviet soldiers and Hungarian policemen organized combined units that patrolled the streets of the capital.

Meanwhile, in Debrecen on January 12, the cabinet discussed the reorganization of the police. The gendarmerie, which had been the repressive arm of the old regime, was officially dissolved only in the spring, although it had played no role since liberation. Erdei suggested and the cabinet agreed that the police had two major tasks, the preservation of public order and the defense of the democratic system, so they should have two separate departments, a criminal and a political one.[44] The political department later became the AVO (Állam védelmi osztály) and later still AVH (Állam védelmi hatóság) and became responsible for repression and terror. It also became a decisively important weapon in the hands of the Communists in their struggle for power. We should remember, however, that at the time of its creation the major task of the political department

44 Palasik, p. 58.

was the struggle against the Nazis. Erdei instructed the department to make every attempt to capture the party headquarters of the Hungarian Nazis in order to take possession of documents that in the future would be needed to establish criminal responsibility. He also instructed the department as to how the captured Nazis should be treated, how they should be fed, and so forth.[45]

The political department had a confused origin. Erdei entrusted András Tömpe, who enjoyed the confidence of the Moscow Communists, with the organization of the department. Tömpe arrived in Budapest at the end of January to begin his work. However, with fighting still going on in the capital, the decision of the cabinet, meeting in Debrecen, had little impact on what was happening in Budapest. Here the Communists took matters into their own hands. Zoltán Vas, soon to be mayor of the city, suggested that János Kádár, one of the most prominent Communists in the city, should take the chief of police job. Kádár demurred and insisted that a Communist army officer, László Sólyom, should assume the responsibility, and in that case he would be willing to become his deputy.[46] Sólyom had been among the few high-ranking officers who chose to go into retirement in 1941 rather than fight in the war against the Soviet Union. During the last year of the war, he had participated in the small resistance movement.[47] Kádár was correct in saying that in the unsettled conditions a military officer was more prepared to deal with the problems of reestablishing order than he would have been.

On January 17, the Budapest National Council, dominated by Communists, entrusted Gábor Péter with the organization of the political department, and he began his work on February 2, even before Budapest was entirely liberated. The Political Committee of the Communist Party approved the choice of Péter, and he, unlike Tömpe, was an entirely Communist appointee and a particularly unsavory character. He had already joined the party in 1931 and survived the war in Hungary. Soon he came to be the most dreaded figure in the country. He became the chief instrument of terror in the hands of Rákosi's leadership and possessed considerable

45 MOL XIX-B-1-r. It is not clear who composed these instructions. Probably, it was the minister of the interior himself.

46 The description of the organization of the Budapest police is largely taken from Zoltán Vas, *Akkori önmagunkról*, vol. 2, pp. 37–40.

47 On Sólyom, see, Antal Oroszi, "*A Sólyom – per.*" In Imre Okváth (ed.), *Katonai Perek*, pp. 141–162. Sólyom was a remarkable person. He would not fight in a war that he disapproved of. In March 1946, he resigned his job as the head of the police because he believed that the deportation of the Swabs – a task that was entrusted to the police – was wrong. Then he served as a general in the army until his arrest. He became a victim of the purge trials, and in 1950 he was executed.

autonomy. Péter enjoyed close personal relations with Rákosi and recognized him as the only individual entitled to give him commands.[48]

For some time, Tömpe and Péter competed, having more or less the same number of people working under them and each writing letters to the minister of the interior or the Central Committee criticizing the other.[49] For a while, both groups worked in the same building. It is not clear why it was Péter who ultimately emerged victorious.[50] Reading reports of the two men, one gets the impression that Tömpe was a more intelligent person.[51] Tömpe soon left the capital and assumed responsibility for political police work in the rest of the country.

Péter reported to Gerő that his intention was to have only Communists serve in the department, but that turned out to be impossible because of the lack of reliable cadres. The desire to have only Communists in the political police was not surprising. Trying to persuade Kádár to work for the police, Vas argued: "let us be sure that communists will not once again be arrested in Hungary and in the capital. From now . . . let us, communists, decide whom we consider to be enemies of the people."[52] What kind of people came to work at this early date for the political police? Among the first 113 people, 83 were members of the Communist Party, and 23 were social democrats. None belonged to the largest party, the Smallholder party. (The proportion of Communists in the countryside in the organization headed by Tömpe was similar.) Péter in his report described 21 as "intellectual," 23 as "petit bourgeois," and 70 as "worker." Jews were overrepresented. There were 28 of them, making up a little less than a quarter of the personnel.[53] For understandable reasons, Jews were regarded as reliable workers at a time when the main task of the political police was the capture of Nazi war criminals. As far as educational qualifications were concerned, it was a very heterogeneous group. Some had diplomas, but others were scarcely

48 Rákosi in his memoirs denied that he had close relations with Péter. This is what he wrote about him: "When I got to know him better I saw that he was a pathologically vain man, uneducated and in vain did I direct him to educate himself, he did not change." Rákosi, *M. Visszaemlékezések, 1940–1956*, 1997, vol. 2, p. 748.

49 PIL 274 11/11 Tömpe to Central Committee, March 27, 1945. Tömpe complained that Péter was naïve, petty, and overly self-confident and did not tolerate criticism

50 Péter and Tömpe quarreled with one another publicly. Péter declared that he did not recognize the provisional government in Debrecen. Tibor Zinner and Róna Péter, *Szálasiék bilincsben*, vol 1, Budapest: Lapkiadó Vállalat, 1986, p. 85.

51 Tömpe fought in Spain, returned to Hungary, and had served in the Hungarian army. He defected to the Russians and joined a partisan unit. Consequently, he was well known to the Moscow Communists. He retired as a lieutenant general in 1963. In 1967, he was named ambassador to East Germany. In 1968, he protested against the Soviet intervention in Czechoslovakia. He committed suicide in 1971. One would like to know how he saw his life and career during his last days.

52 Ibid., p. 38.

53 PIL 274 11/10 April 30.

literate.[54] Péter himself was barely educated: he had completed only four years of elementary school.

The first offices of the department were in the party headquarters on Tisza Kálmán Square, which itself demonstrated that the political police was a party organization. Soon, however, the department was moved: first into Eotvös Street and finally into the infamous building, Andrássy Boulevard 60, the ex-headquarters of the Nazis. The Nazis had named the building "house of loyalty"; it was here that they tortured their victims.[55] The first task of the new tenants was to clean up after the previous ones in order to begin their work, not very different from that of the previous occupants.[56] The choice of headquarters betrayed extraordinary insensitivity. It symbolized the fact that Nazis and Communists may be different, but as far their use of terror was concerned, they had much in common.

In a report to Gerő, Péter described his meeting with the Smallholder mayor of Budapest, János Csorba, who wanted to know who had given him his job. Péter was conscious of the fact that he was more powerful than the mayor, who indeed, lost his job within weeks. Péter rather jocularly wrote to his Communist superior that he had not told Csorba that he had his position before the mayor had his.[57] What is remarkable in this situation is that this crucial office had come into being entirely outside of the government's control. The next month, Péter reported that the premier, Dálnoki Miklós, had visited and expressed his dissatisfaction that the political police was entirely in the hands of the Communists. He declared that his government would not allow the police to be reduced to the level of a party agency; however, in this matter the premier was powerless.[58]

The size and power of the department constantly grew. Péter at first established six sections, each with ten people. By April, as he reported to Rákosi, the political police already had eight sections, employing 410 people. The sections included supervision of the press and reporting on public opinion, record keeping, detective work, special assignment, and economic

54 Zinner and Róna, vol. 1., p. 86. Timár recollected that he taught his colleagues how to write correctly.

55 PIL 274 11/10 February 1945.

56 Zinner and Róna, vol. 1, p. 85.

57 PIL 274 11/10 March 17, 1945.

58 PIL 274 11/10 March 30, 1945. Of course, the Smallholder politicians were well aware of the significance of the Communist control over the political police. Zoltán Tildy, in an interparty meeting devoted to the discussion of the work of the police, complained about the lack of Smallholder party members within that organization. He also would have liked to remove Jews from the political police, arguing that their presence greatly contributed to the rise of anti-Semitism. *Pártközi értekezletek*, May 15, 1945, p. 71.

crimes. At this time, the primary responsibility of the political police was the apprehending of Nazis. In this work, the department was successful: on April 12, 5722 men were under arrest, on April 30 11,922, and at the end of July 22,021. There was no room for all these people in prisons, and consequently the authorities set up internment camps in Budapest or in the suburbs. Péter wrote that 60 percent of the information came from denunciations and only 40 percent was the result of detective work. He complained that many of the denunciations were unfouded.[59]

It stands to reason that from the very beginning there was a close connection between Soviet intelligence organs and the Hungarian political police. Erdei's representative in Budapest, a Social Democrat, András Andreánszky, reported from Budapest to Debrecen that a certain Orlov, a Soviet officer in civilian dress, acted as an adviser in the political police department and that Orlov also had the role of maintaining contacts between the Hungarian and Soviet intelligence organs.[60] In March, Fedor Bielkin, a general in the Soviet intelligence service, had conversations with the Hungarian authorities. He also acted as an adviser to the ACC and later had the responsible job of supervising the Soviet intelligence network in Eastern Europe. In the following years, he continued to maintain close ties with the Hungarian organs. But even aside from the participation of Soviet agents in the work of the political police, many of the Moscow-trained Hungarian Communists regarded themselves as fighters for a cause whose headquarters were in the Soviet Union. The deputy of Péter was János Kovács, who had been born in Hungary but was a Soviet citizen and a lieutenant colonel in the NKVD.

According to Vladimir Farkas, who was a high-ranking official in the AVO and AVH, and therefore was in a position to know ex-Nazi officials in the organization of the political police, played even more important roles than Soviet advisers. He remembers András Diener Dénes, an ex-gendarmerie officer who acted as an adviser to Péter.[61] Evidently, Diener Dénes was something of an intellectual, a scholar of the works of the great Hungarian poet, Sándor Petöfi. He made an impressive career in the AVO, but ultimately, like so many others, became a victim of the purges. The case of Tibor Wayand was even more curious. Wayand had been a high-ranking gendarmerie officer, a man who had tortured Communists and, therefore, was sentenced to death and executed. Nevertheless, before his

59 PIL 274, 11/10 April 12, 1945.

60 Palasik, p. 62.

61 Vladimir Farkas, in *Élet és Irodalom*, July 14, 2000.

death, presumably hoping to save his life by demonstrating his usefulness, he advised Péter about police methods.[62]

In addition, yet another political police was formed in April 1945, Katpol (military-political police). This functioned within the Army to screen ex-Nazi officers and attract reliable people – from the Communist point of view – into the army that was to be formed. György Pálffy, who had been a staff officer in Horthy's army and a secret Communist, headed the organization. The situation within the army reproduced what was happening in the country at large. A right-wing ex-Horthyist officer headed the army, but the political police was safely in the hands of the Communists.[63]

The other political parties were well aware of the danger of having the political police entirely under Communist control. In the course of the early months of 1945, the representatives of political parties repeatedly expressed their dismay at the actions of the police. On one occasion, the minister of justice, Ágoston Valentiny, a right-wing Social Democrat, encouraged the cabinet to vote, against the Communists and left-wing Social Democrats, to establish yet another police organization which would supervise all the others.* The Communists, presumably with Soviet help, succeeded in preventing the realization of this plan.[64] The Communist response to the attacks on the police time and again was that those who criticized the work of the police were helping the fascists to escape punishment and, therefore, were reactionaries. The consequence of Valentiny's plan was a sharp struggle within the SDP, ultimately leading to Valentiny's resignation. István Ries, a left-wing Social Democrat, took his place. The Socialists and the Smallholders succeeded in placing their representatives as deputy directors under Péter, but this was a hollow victory. Péter isolated these men, their rooms were bugged, and they had absolutely no influence on the course of affairs.[65] The Communists jealously guarded their monopoly over the instrument of coercion.

From the very beginning, the Communists used the political police for their own political advantage, including the creation of a homogeneous, Soviet-style party. Those who had just returned from Moscow considered themselves superior to their Hungarian comrades. They knew that they alone had the Soviet leaders' confidence and an understanding of the new policy line. They assumed that they had the right to judge the behavior of

* This affair is discussed in greater detail in Chapter Four.

62 PIL 274, 11/23.

63 Pál Kornis, *Tanuként jelentkezem*, Budapest: Zrinyi, 1988, pp. 64–66.

64 Palasik, pp. 68–69, and Rákosi, vol. 1., p. 175.

65 Zinner and Róna, vol. 1, p. 90.

people who had had to work in illegality. They acted harshly. The most outrageous example of the heavy-handed behavior of the recent exiles was the Demény affair. The political police in February 1945 arrested Pál Demény and Aladár Weisshaus immediately after the liberation of Budapest. They accused these two men of all sorts of crimes, such as being police agents, embezzling money, and, above all, factionalism. Demény, an extraordinary and colorful character, had organized the largest Communist movement in Hungary after the failed revolution of 1919. From 1924, however, he acted outside of official (i.e., Moscow-directed) control. He was convinced that people in Moscow had no understanding of the circumstances at home and that following their directions would be suicidal. For underground activities, he had spent six and a half years in prison during the Horthy regime.

In 1944, during German occupation, he and his followers participated in the resistance, helping to prevent the Germans from removing the equipment of the factories of Csepel. In this industrial district, the followers of Demény were particularly numerous. Demény's cells in 1944 united with the official Communist Underground Party. This unity, however, did not save him.[66] Demény now had no intention of acting outside of regular Communist channels and, in January 1945, wrote to Rákosi expressing his desire to work together with him. But there was no forgiveness.

László Rajk wrote a secret report to the Central Committee saying that the Demény affair could not be discussed openly because there was not enough proof against him.[67] The political police, in fact, attempted to create "proofs" by compelling ex-officials of Horthy's police to say that Demény had cooperated with them.[68] But evidently, the confessions were not convincing enough to hold a public trial at the time. Demény was handed over to the Russians, but the occupiers did not know what to do with him. After some months, he was returned to the care of Gábor Péter. Finally in the spring of 1946, a trial was held, but it was not publicized, and his followers were excluded from the hall. He was sentenced to four and a half years as an informer, but was not freed until 1956. Until the end of the Communist regime, he remained a nonperson. In vain he continued to protest his Communist convictions to the end of his days.[69]

The Demény affair could serve as an illustration of the political situation that existed in Hungary immediately after liberation. The political police was

66 Pál Demény, *A párt foglya voltam*, Budapest: Medvetánc, 1988, p. 25.

67 PIL 274/11/18 December 19, 1945, Rajk's report.

68 PIL 274/11/23 Confession of Tibor Wayand. After his confession he was executed.

69 László Varga, "Forradalmi törvényesség," *Beszélő* 11 (1999). Accessed July 22, 2005 <http:www//beszelo.c3.hu/99/11/09varga.htm>

in Communist hands, and it could arrest and hold in prison anyone it desired without any legal niceties. Even when the country had few Communists with underground experience, at a time of considerable anarchy and confusion there could be no toleration of deviation from hierarchical organization of the party. The simple fact that a comrade had once operated outside of the regular organization was unforgivable. A man who had spent his entire adult life in the Communist movement was arrested whereas the head of the gendarmerie of the previous regime, one who had been responsible for arresting Communists, was a member of the government. The Communists and the Russians evidently considered Demény more dangerous than Faragho.

3

The Armistice and Its Consequences

THE ALLIED CONTROL COMMISSION

In 1945, Hungary was under foreign occupation, and its sovereignty was strictly circumscribed. On January 20, 1945, delegates of the newly formed provisional government signed an armistice agreement in Moscow with the representatives of the victorious powers. According to this agreement, the ACC had the right and obligation to assure that the Hungarians lived up to the terms of the armistice. Because the British and the Americans had merely observer status within the ACC, in reality the ACC was an instrument of Soviet policy. The signing of the armistice document became the legal justification for Soviet intervention in every aspect of Hungarian life.

Before the Second World War, there had been no precedents for these commissions. The first of these was set up in 1943 after the successful Allied invasion of Italy. For all practical purposes, the Soviet Union was excluded from formulating the terms of the Italian armistice and also from supervision of the restructuring of political life in that country. At the time, the Red Army was still fighting deep in Soviet territory, and although the Russians greatly resented their exclusion from Italian affairs, there was not much they could do about it. The Americans and, even more, the British wanted to prevent the expansion of Soviet influence into the strategically important Mediterranean region.[1]

From the point of view of the defeated countries of Eastern Europe, the Italian example was unfortunate because it supported the Soviet diplomatic claim that they were simply following the example set by the Western powers

1 This description is based on *Documents of the Meetings of the Allied Control Commission for Hungary, 1945–1947*, Bendeguz Gergő Cseh (ed.), Budapest: MTA Jelenkor-kutató Bizottság, 2000, and Margit Földesi, *A megszállók szabadsága*, Budapest: Kairosz, 2002.

in setting the terms of the armistice without substantive participation of the other Allies. In countries that had been liberated by the Red Army, such as Finland, Bulgaria, Romania, and Hungary, the Soviet position was dominant. At the outset, the British and Americans envisioned that there would be two periods in the administration of the defeated countries: the first of these would be from the signing of the armistice to the final defeat of Germany and the second from the end of the war to the signing of a formal peace treaty. In the first period, the country that provided the occupying army would necessarily predominate, but in the second period all the Allies would play more or less equal roles. Reality proved to be different: there was, of course, no distinction between the two periods. By 1947, when the formal peace treaty was signed and the ACC ceased to exist, relations between the victorious powers had changed drastically. Soviet influence in the countries of Eastern Europe had not decreased; on the contrary, it had become so entrenched it would go unchallenged for years to come.

On May 14, 1945, George Kennan, always a sober and level-headed observer, wrote, less than a week after the conclusion of the European war, to Ambassador Averill Harriman in Moscow:

> I believe that our only hope of getting anywhere would be to make up our minds that if we do not get full tripartite treatment we will withdraw not only our participation in the Control commissions but our political representatives as well. (Consular representatives might be left). If this threat works and causes the Russians to grant us equal participation, so much the better. If it does not, then I think it preferable that our people get out anyway. Their presence in those countries thus far has not had any appreciable influence on the course of events there, nor has it been effective in protecting American interests. On the other hand, it has been effective in misleading public opinion both in the United States and in the countries concerned and in saddling our government with a share of responsibility for policies which has nothing to do with American ideals or American interests.[2]

In the functioning of the ACCs in Eastern Europe, the British and American representatives were indeed reduced to the role of observers. Kennan was absolutely right: it would have been better if the Allies had excluded themselves altogether, because their presence on the commissions conferred a degree of legitimacy on an institution that was simply an instrument of Soviet domination.[3]

2 FRUS, 1945, vol. 4, p. 814.

3 Alexander Kirk, political adviser to the supreme Allied commander, reported to the secretary of state on March 27, 1945: "It seems clear that despite these efforts (condemning anti-Soviet comments by Hungarians), the Russian attitude remains one of surface moderation combined with essential negation. . . . In effect the Russians have not seen fit to permit the real work of ACC to begin and

At the outset, the British and the Americans did play some role beneficial to Hungary in setting the terms of the armistice. The Soviet representatives wanted to impose the heaviest possible reparation terms on Hungary. They demanded $400 million, of which the Soviet Union would have received $320 million and Czechoslovakia and Yugoslavia would have received the rest. At the insistence of the Anglo-American powers, that amount was reduced to $300 million, of which the Soviet Union was to receive $200 million. The British and the Americans remembered that the heavy reparations imposed on Germany after World War I were the source of later instability. Also, the British, and especially the Americans, had economic interests in Hungary and were concerned that the great burden placed on Hungary would harm these interests.

The ACC officially came into existence with the signing of the Hungarian armistice on January 20, 1945, and its first meeting took place on February 27 at the Russian headquarters. The chairman of the ACC was Marshal Kliment E. Voroshilov, who as a consequence of this position became in reality the ruler of Hungary.[4] Voroshilov had an enormous staff of approximately eight hundred people. The Soviet delegation was almost a second government with a complex organization that included personnel, economic, and political departments. The ACC, that is, the Soviet representatives, appeared not only in every government department office but also in the counties, in every major factory, and even in railroad stations. The Americans, by contrast, had only sixty-seven people and the British ninety. The rules governing the ACC established that the Anglo-American representatives could establish contacts with Hungarian authorities only through the intercession of the Soviet chairman or his deputy.[5]

The Hungarian government was already responsible for the feeding and clothing of the Red Army on Hungarian territory.[6] In addition, that they had to provision the ACC's almost thousand members imposed a considerable burden.[7] The large Russian contingent was the most expensive, but

have handicapped even its administrative functions by policies that give the effect of negation and delay." FRUS, 1945, vol. 4, pp. 811–812.

4 Vida, 1986, pp. 11–12.

5 Földesi, 2002, pp. 55–56.

6 MOL NXIX-J-1-j 24 box, IV, 482.1. Although the armistice agreement did not mention Hungary's responsibility for supplying the Red Army on Hungarian territory, the Russians imposed this obligation also.

7 The eleventh point of the armistice agreement said: "The government of Hungary will make regular payments in Hungarian currency and provide commodities (fuel, foodstuff, etc.) facilities and services as may be required by the Allied (Soviet) High Command for the fulfillment of its functions as well as for the needs of missions and representatives of the Allied states connected with the Allied Control Commission." *Documents of the Meetings of the Allied Control Commission for Hungary*, p. 427.

the Allies were also demanding. Imre Kovács, an anti-Communist politician many years later in exile in the United States, wrote in his memoirs:

> The Western members of the ACC also did not hesitate to place the burden of their expenses on destitute Hungary, just like the Russians. There was, however, a difference. The Russians did not send a bill to the government: they took what they wanted. The British and the Americans without hesitation, without pangs of conscience added even the bills from the flower shops to their long list, for flowers that they had sent to their girlfriends. The communists knew how to take advantage of such matters and used the opportunity to create hostility against the British, but especially against the Americans."[8]

According to the armistice agreement, the Soviet Army through the ACC was supposed to submit to the government every quarter their supply requirement. In reality, the Russians simply took want they wanted without formalities.[9] Whenever they needed housing, they simply removed inhabitants from their houses, even in the middle of the winter. Hotel managers in vain complained to the government that Soviet officers simply took over rooms in their hotels and did so, of course, without payment.[10]

Marshal Voroshilov was viceroy of Hungary. He was not as much disliked by the Hungarians as some of his subordinates or his successor. He gave a relatively good account of himself as Soviet representative. He was sixty-four years old when he came to Hungary and had an illustrious career behind him, as a commander in the Russian Civil War and as a soldier who in the 1920s and 1930s had much to do with the reorganization of the Red Army. He had considerable standing within the Soviet hierarchy and personal ties to Stalin that allowed him a degree of independence. Of course, he had no special knowledge of Hungary and spoke no foreign languages.Thus, whether negotiating with the representatives of the Anglo-Saxon powers or the Hungarians, he always depended on interpreters. On occasion at least, he could charm Hungarian politicians, even those who were not sympathetic to the Communist cause. He gave the impression that he was enjoying himself in Hungary and was fond of the country. However, he was not the person who formulated policy. The policy was made in Moscow, and he faithfully executed instructions.

8 Kovács, p. 267. When an article appeared in the Communist paper, *Szabad Nép*, the Allied representatives protested. The affair was even discussed at ACC on January 7, 1946. Instead of being embarrassed that they charged the Hungarian government for a personal gift of flowers, the British and the Americans attached to the ACC protested the article and suggested that the paper ought to be suppressed at least temporarily. The Soviet representative promised to consider the suggestion. *Documents of the Meetings of the Allied Control Commission for Hungary*, p. 115.

9 MOL XIX-J-1-j 24 box IV, 482.1, Soviet soldiers.

10 Ibid.

8. Kliment Voroshilov, 1881–1969.

Voroshilov stayed in Hungary until February 1946. Although nominally he remained the head of the ACC, his role was taken over by his deputy, General V. P. Sviridov. After Voroshilov's departure, it was Sviridov who was the chief Soviet representative in Hungary until the dissolution of the ACC in September 1947. Because he did not possess the same degree of prestige as his predecessor, he had to turn to Moscow even for minor decisions. The Hungarians, even the Communists, found him to be a much more difficult person to deal with than Marshal Voroshilov.

The highest civilian Soviet representative in Hungary was Georgii Maksimovich Pushkin, who in spite of his youth (he was thirty-six in 1945) had already had considerable diplomatic experience. When the Soviet Union recognized the Hungarian government in November 1945, Pushkin became the first Soviet ambassador. The American representative, Arthur Schoenfeld, described him in his note to the secretary of state: "Pushkin has not been in the U.S. He seems younger than his probable age, about 45. His eyes and expression are remarkably hard. He is completely successful in preventing an indication of emotion or reaction appearing while he is listening. While talking he can, at will, produce an almost spectacular smile but his eyes do not lose their coldness. His speech is low and quiet yet distinct. He appears to have a determined ruthlessness verging on the fanatical yet controlled and less blunt than that of a Soviet military man like Starhusky [his name in fact was M. M. Stakhurskii, chief of staff to Voroshilov] for instance."[11] Obviously, Pushkin was a product of the great purges of the diplomatic

11 FRUS, 1945, vol. 4, p. 818. Schoenfeld to secretary of state, May 19, 1945.

corps in the 1930s. In other words, he was a typical Soviet diplomat of his time.

Moscow firmly controlled its diplomats. Soviet representatives in Budapest did not even have the authority to issue visas to Allied journalists and businessmen. An American traveler to Hungary had to turn to Moscow for permission and only then did the Soviet Union notify its representatives in Budapest to issue the necessary permit.[12] Soviet authorities closely supervised every aspect of Hungarian life and politics. Voroshilov, for example, played an active role in the development and timing of the land reform legislation. He put pressure on the Hungarians to hold early elections, which he believed would favor the Communists. He decided whether to allow the formation of new political parties. The armistice agreement explicitly allowed the Soviet representatives to censor newspapers, film, and radio.[13] Indeed, in April 1945, Gyula Ortutay, the minister of education, turned to Voroshilov, asking him to assign a censor so that radio broadcasting might recommence.[14] The Russians censored all newspapers, but, because they had very few reliable Hungarian-speaking officers, the censorship was haphazard. It often happened that a censor permitted the very same material on one day that another censor had forbidden the next day.[15] In the armistice treaty, the Hungarians obligated themselves to remove the residues of fascism. This meant, among other things, holding people responsible for their past actions, cleansing the government and civil service from people "not committed to democracy," closing down fascist organizations, censorship of newspapers and movies, and removal of fascist books from the libraries.

CENSORSHIP

From the very beginning of Soviet occupation, the authorities took a great interest in purging libraries of anti-Soviet and "anti-progressive" books. Already on February 26, 1945, following Soviet instructions, the government issued a regulation, ordering the destruction of "fascist and antidemocratic books." The regulation threatened those who did not obey with six-month imprisonment.[16] The government also organized a campaign to

12 Ibid., p. 841.

13 The sixteenth point of the agreement specified "the publication, introduction and distribution in Hungary of periodical and non-periodical literature, the presentation of theatrical performances or films, the operation of wireless stations, post, telegraph and telephone services will take place in agreement with the Allied (Soviet) High Command." *Documents of the Meetings of the Allied Control Commission for Hungary*, p. 428.

14 MOL XIX-J-1-j 24 box IV, 482.1, April 16, 1945.

15 Kovács, p. 268.

16 Földesi, 2002, p. 162.

collect books that were considered hostile to the new regime. In April 1945, Béla Zsedényi, the president of the Provisional National Assembly, following Soviet instructions, ordered libraries that fascist, anti-Soviet books had to be destroyed although some of those could be retained with special permission if they could be safely kept in closed places away from the reading public. At the same time, the government set up a special commission to draw up an index of books that were to be destroyed. This commission, headed by Imre Faust, had twenty members, representing social organizations and political parties. It labored for many months, first meeting three times a week and later once a week.[17] Even as late as December 1946, the commission still continued to add titles to the index.

What were the principles on the basis of which books could be put on the index? Books that were critical of the Soviet Union, Communism, or the 1919 Hungarian Soviet Republic, of course, had to be eliminated. Anti-Semitic and profascist books also, naturally, got on the list. Nevertheless, as was to be expected, the list was haphazard. It included a well-known history of Hungary that Gyula Szekfű had written with Bálint Hóman. Szekfű was the first Hungarian ambassador to Moscow, but Homan, a minister of education during the Horthy regime, was in prison.[18] It also included, not surprisingly, the anti-Soviet book that a current member of the government, Faragho, had written just four years earlier about his stay in the Soviet Union as Hungarian military attaché.[19] Prominent Hungarian writers, such as Krudy and Féja, also were put on the list of forbidden books. The insightful study of Rene Fülöp Miller, *The Mind and Face of Bolshevism*, also had to be destroyed. Other entries on the list were curious. For example Heinrich Rückert's German-language book *Lehrbuch der Weltgeschichte in organischer Darstellung*, published in 1857, also had to be destroyed. One suspects that Rückert must have expressed anti-Russian views, which in 1945 at a time of intense Russian nationalism could not be tolerated. The same fate awaited a collection of pictures of the Austro-Hungarian navy. This book got on the list, presumably, because Miklós Horthy, decades earlier, had been an admiral in that navy.

17 Faust had fought in 1919 in the Red Army and after the defeat of the Béla Kun regime went into exile. On his return, he spent some years in a Hungarian prison. Although not a member of the MKP, he was considered to be a reliable person by the Communists. Like many others, he was arrested in 1949 and spent some more years in prison.

18 According to Kovács, the first three volumes of the seven-volume work were written by Homan and these had to be destroyed, but the later volumes by Szekfű could be retained. Kovács, p. 268.

19 *Szabad Nép* did not hesitate to point out the anomaly. It called for the removal of Faragho from the cabinet, which indeed happened shortly. *Szabad Nép*, June 7, 1945.

The Russians, and therefore the Hungarians, took the task of destroying books extremely seriously. Soviet soldiers accompanied the trains that took the confiscated books from the provinces to the capital. Regulations required that the Soviet representative sign the list of books for which he had taken responsibility.[20] The urge to destroy sometimes had ludicrous consequences. The organization of lawyers in Debrecen, for example, turned to the police for permission to retain a list of anti-Jewish laws that had been abrogated because knowledge of these laws was necessary to protect the interests of those who had been persecuted under the laws of the recent past. University libraries had to ask for special permission to retain some of the forbidden books in closed collections for research purposes. In some instances, the collectors were overzealous: the statistical bureau complained to the prime minister that all journals and magazines going back to 1920 had been removed from their offices.[21] It is estimated that, in the course of this campaign in 1945–1946, approximately 3 million books were destroyed.[22]

The Communist-dominated youth organization, Madisz, played a major role in the book-collecting campaign by turning book collection into a mass movement. It asked and received the cooperation of the youth organizations of the SDP and also of the FKGP. Young people, armed with a list of forbidden titles, offered their services to people, promising to check their libraries in order to save the owners of the libraries from serious unpleasantness.[23] They made it known that searches would soon be carried out by representatives of the ministry of the interior, and if those people were to find forbidden books, bad consequences would follow. If people behaved suspiciously, the zealous youth were to report this to the relevant authorities. Madisz obviously drew on Soviet experience, because this book-collecting campaign functioned very much like a Soviet-type "voluntary" mass movement.

In August 1945, István Balogh, a prominent FKGP politician and state secretary in the office of the prime minister, could report to a meeting including a Soviet representative that an index of 2000 titles had been prepared, and 400,000 books had already been destroyed. He promised that those who gave up their books voluntarily would not be punished, implying that those who had retained or hidden proscribed books would be. Balogh

20 MOL XIX – 1 – j 18 box XXI unit, April 20, 1946. Prime minister's office to ministry of industry.

21 Ibid. Statistics office to Nagy Ferenc, February 17, 1947.

22 Földesi, 2002, p. 172.

23 Sándor Rákosi, Lajosné Ikladi, and Lajos Gál (eds.), A *Madisz, 1944–1948: Dokumentumok az ifjusági mozgalom felszabadulás utáni történetéből*, Budapest: Kossuth, 1984, pp. 135–137.

insisted that his people would find all "fascist" books even if they had to look for them under the rubble.[24] On February 20, 1946, Prime Minister Ferenc Nagy reported to Voroshilov that books collected by youth activists could not be burned for lack of fuel. He mentioned that there had been 9809 searches, and the agents had found 13,201 books. He also mentioned that there had been 235 denunciations, resulting in ninety-nine court sentences with forty-six cases still pending. In order to demonstrate how seriously his government took this matter, he wrote that 20,463 posters had been printed about the campaign.[25] Nevertheless, the Russians were not satisfied. Major General A. M. Belianov, the head of the administrative department of ACC told the Hungarian representative, Dr. János Wolff, that the ACC was concerned that the speed of book collection was too slow. In reality, this was exclusively a Soviet concern; the matter of book collection was never discussed with the Allies. Belianov also wanted other parties aside from the Communists and their mass organizations to be involved.

In discussions with the Hungarian-speaking Russian officer, Grigoriev, the special problem of textbooks came up. It was obviously impossible to equip in a short time grade schools and high schools with properly "progressive" history textbooks. The Russian allowed that old textbooks could be used after offending passages were blacked out.[26] Dealing with textbooks was a particularly difficult task because there was much in the discussion of Hungarian history that could be regarded as creating anti-Soviet, or at least anti-Russian, feelings among the young. For example, the discussion of the Revolution of 1848–1849 was a particularly delicate matter. March 15, the anniversary of the outbreak of the revolution, was a national holiday. It was difficult not to remember that the revolution was defeated not by the Habsburgs but by the invasion of the army of Tsar Nicholas I.

Because Hungary at the time suffered from a shortage of paper, the idea emerged that the books should not be burnt but instead used for producing paper. The prime minister's office wrote to the ministry of industry that this could be done, but not for the time being for security reasons. First, control over the collected books would have to be firmly established.

The committee dealt with films, theater, and fine arts as well as books and other printed material. In the case of cinema censorship, films that were anti-Soviet or "anti-democratic" in substance of course were put on the index; also proscribed were films in which actors appeared who had discredited themselves by collaborating with the Nazis. Because some of the best-known

24 MOL XIX – 1 – j 18 box XXI unit.
25 Ibid.
26 Ibid.

actors fell into this category, this regulation greatly reduced the available films. This was a particular blow at a time when there was a shortage of entertainment, and the industry was hard put to meet the demand for films.

In April 1945, the Budapest city council also began to deal with the question of statues that were considered to be politically undesirable.[27] Statues erected for statesmen of the interwar period and, indeed, in some cases for some of the politically unacceptable figures from Hungarian history had to come down. Such was the fate of the statue of the sixteenth-century jurist, István Werböczy. (Werböczy was responsible for the laws regulating serfdom.) In some instances, the destruction was turned into a public event: Madisz organized the removal of the statue of the pre–World War I prime minister, István Tisza. Pictures of the event appeared in the newspapers and were supposed to demonstrate the political commitment of Hungarian youth.

REPARATIONS

For the future of the nation a far more important matter than the introduction of censorship or the purging of libraries was the economic burden imposed on the defeated country by the Soviet Union. It is difficult to exaggerate the suffering of the Hungarian people and the damage done to the economy by merciless Soviet exploitation. Both the short- and long-term consequences were far reaching: in the immediate postwar years, people suffered hunger and privation; in 1946, Hungary had the greatest inflation the world had ever seen; the prewar standard of living was slow to recover; the structure of the economy that came into being was different from what had existed before; and, arguably, the foundations of a centralized, command economy were established at least partially in order to satisfy the heavy reparation demands.[28]

Recently a Hungarian historian, László Borhi, argued that Soviet economic policy in Eastern Europe was a conscious first step toward reducing these countries to satellites. It is unquestionably true that deliveries to the

27 János Pótó, *Emlékművek, Politika, Közgondolkodás*, Budapest: MTA, 1989, p. 25.

28 A. B. Göllner, "Foundations of Soviet Domination in Post-War Hungary," in N. F. Dreisziger (ed.), *Hungary in the Age of Total War*, New York: Columbia University Press, 1998, pp. 196–198. In this article, Göllner argues that the Russians removed Hungarian factories not only because they needed the product for their own economic benefit but also because they consciously wanted to destroy private enterprise. He points out that machines and products often were left lying scattered in the fields rusting, or these machines were left in sealed boxcars. In my view, Göllner seriously overestimates Soviet efficiency.

Soviet Union and Soviet penetration into every sphere of the economy tied these countries to the Soviet Union and thereby prepared the soil for the establishment of Soviet-style "people's democracies."[29] However, one might make the opposite argument. Soviet determination to squeeze as much out of Hungary and the other occupied countries as possible, regardless of the long-term economic consequences, might suggest that the Soviet leaders were not consciously planning the creation of a satellite. Had they planned to create a satellite they should have paid more attention to the problems of reconstructing the economy. Instead, they had a single aim: to squeeze as much as possible out of the population and to remove to the Soviet Union everything that might be beneficial for reconstruction at home. Indeed, in 1947 and 1948, when Hungary and the other countries of the region were being reduced to the status of satellites, Russian demands lessened.

Soviet behavior also had political consequences. The Hungarian people saw casual looting by Red Army soldiers and organized reparation activities as two parts of the same well-conceived policy made in Moscow. The public perception of the misbehavior of Soviet soldiers and the reparation demands blended together. Whether it was individual soldiers taking away watches from citizens or organized Red Army detachments dismantling factories, it meant the same thing to the Hungarian observer: Russians were despoiling the country. The Communists well understood that the people blamed them also for the actions of the Soviet government and Red Army soldiers, but they were powerless against their Soviet superiors.

Admittedly, the sources of economic misery did not start with Soviet exploitation. Although in the first years of the war damage to the Hungarian economy suffered minimally, in 1944 the situation drastically changed. First, the Germans occupied the country and compelled the Hungarians to produce for the war effort. As a consequence, Hungary acquired a huge debt from Germany, which, of course, became uncollectible. Then the desperate resistance that the Nazis put up to the advancing Red Army caused enormous damage, primarily to industry but also to agriculture. Finally, the Germans and their Hungarian allies carried away everything that could be moved in order to prevent these from falling into Soviet hands. They dismantled and removed approximately five hundred factories. They blew up the bridges over the Danube and took ships, trucks, and railroad rolling stock to Germany. They also took the country's gold and silver reserves. What they could not carry away they destroyed.[30] It was heavy industry, in particular machine building, that suffered the most. A substantial portion

29 This is also argued by Borhi, 2000, pp. 7–9.

30 Göllner, in Dreisziger (ed.), p. 186.

of the national wealth was squandered in this way. Later, the Allies were not quick to return Hungarian property from territories that came under Anglo-American occupation, partly because they wanted assurances that Hungary would pay its rather large prewar debts to British and American interests and partly, perhaps, because they correctly assumed that anything of value would end up in Russian hands. Much of the property was never returned by the Allies but was confiscated and used to satisfy prewar Hungarian debt to the citizens of Western countries.

As German despoliation of the Hungarian economy ended, Soviet exploitation immediately started. Of course, Hungary was not the only country in Eastern Europe to suffer this way. Nevertheless, it appears that aside from Germany, in particular the eastern zone of Germany, no country suffered as much. In Germany, the pickings were greater than in economically less developed and mostly agricultural Hungary. The Soviet justification for the merciless exploitation then and later was not altogether unreasonable. No matter how much was taken from the defeated countries, those goods could not possibly compensate for the consequences of German aggression against the Soviet Union, an aggression in which Hungary was a willing partner. In the immediate postwar years, reconstruction in Germany and Hungary was difficult, but not as difficult as it was in the Soviet Union. Poverty and starvation were dreadful in the defeated countries, but still not as bad as the famine in the Soviet Union was; in 1946, people were reduced to cannibalism.[31] Needless to say, the Hungarians neither knew nor cared how people in the Soviet Union lived at the time.

The twelfth point of the armistice agreement obligated Hungary for the payment of $300 million. In addition, the next point of the armistice specified that citizens of member states of the United Nations could claim reparations for the damages they had suffered on Hungarian territory as a consequence of war.[32] To satisfy these various claims, the Hungarian government paid out another approximately $160 to $170 million in the following three years.[33] An additional and particularly onerous obligation was that the Soviet Union claimed all German property on Hungarian territory. This was a rather large category because the Germans had been deeply involved in the Hungarian economy before and during the war. Hungarian factories produced for the German war machinery.

31 On the Soviet exploitation in Germany, see the excellent book by Norman Naimark, cited earlier, *The Russians in Germany*, pp. 141–205.

32 The armistice treaty is reprinted in Sándor Balogh and Éva Földesi (eds.), *A Magyar jóvátétel és ami mögötte van, 1945–1949: Válogatott dokumentumok*, Budapest: Napvilág, 1998, pp. 19–23.

33 Ibid., p. 9.

9. Allied Control Commission, 1945, in front of Andrássy Avenue 42. General Edgecumbe is fourth from the right; to his right is General Sviridov and to his right, cap in hand, is General Weems. (Source: Hungarian National Museum.)

Furthermore, in 1944 the Germans compelled prosperous Jews to sign over their wealth to the German state in hope of saving their lives. Given the fact that a considerable portion of large enterprises had been in Jewish hands, this demand included a sizeable portion of the national wealth. The ironic consequence of German economic penetration into Eastern Europe, especially Hungary, was that the Soviet Union ultimately benefited. The Soviet Union also became the beneficiary of the German persecution of the Jews. Under these terms, the Soviet Union claimed four hundred industrial enterprises on Hungarian territory, which included some of the largest Hungarian factories. The Russians shamelessly manipulated the agreement to their own benefit: any property in which the Germans had a financial interest, no matter how small, the Russians now claimed as their own.

The most egregious Soviet demand was taking care of the financial obligations between German and Hungarian companies. The Hungarians argued that the amount owed by Germany to Hungary was much larger than vice versa. This was understandable because, until the very end of the war, Hungarian industry had produced for the German army, and the Hungarians had received little or no compensation. Germany owed Hungary

\$280 million.[34] The Soviets, however, insisted that Hungary give up all demands on Germany, whereas whatever Hungary owed to German companies operating in Hungary now had to be paid to the Soviet Union. Hungarian negotiators believed that this was not a very significant matter, perhaps costing an additional couple million dollars, and therefore they were willing to settle without objections. However, they were soon bitterly surprised. The Russians demanded an additional \$200 million, which exactly doubled Hungary's reparation obligation to the Soviet Union. The Russians came up with this enormous figure because of their evaluation of the German mark. They insisted on counting the value of the German mark as 3.8 for a dollar, which it had been in 1938. However, during the war when the transactions between Hungary and Germany had been concluded, the value of the mark was 100 for a dollar.[35] Hungarian negotiators offered 10 million dollars to take care of this matter, but the Russians would not concede.* In vain did the Hungarians ask the Russians to look into the account books available in Germany to demonstrate the true financial relations between Hungary and Germany.

In addition, the Hungarian government had to accept responsibility for the damage done to these properties after the signing of the treaty on January 20, 1945. Because some of the most bitter battles took place after that date around Budapest and in Transdanubia, where almost all the industry was located, obviously considerable damage was done to these properties by both sides after the treaty signing.

The \$300 to \$400 million price tag for reparations was not as important in itself as the appraisal for the goods delivered primarily to the Soviet Union. The timing of reparation deliveries was also a critical issue. Obviously, the moment when the country had been destroyed and reconstruction could hardly begin was the most disadvantageous from the Hungarian point of view, but Soviets wanted the largest amount in the shortest possible time. Furthermore, the Russians insisted that the evaluation of material delivered should be done on the 1938 (i.e., prewar) price level, although the armistice agreement said nothing about price levels. Although Western ambassadors in Moscow tried to alleviate the burden by using current price levels, Soviet negotiators would not budge. This was a matter of utmost significance: the manipulation of price levels allowed the Russians to increase wildly

* At this time, the entire Hungarian industry was valued at \$500 million, and that was less than Hungary owed to the victors.

34 Iván Pető and Sándor Szakács, *A hazai gazdaság négy évtizedének története*, Budapest: Közgazdasági és jogi kiadó, 1985. p. 23.

35 MOL XIX-J-1-j – box 28, Reparation problems, Note, April 10, 1947.

Hungarian obligations. The Russians would not even accept 1938 Hungarian prices in setting values for goods; they would consider only world prices. Because Hungarian industry was less developed and therefore less efficient, Hungarian prices even in 1938 were higher than world prices. Further, there were items that had not been produced in 1938 in Hungary at all, in which case the Russians set prices arbitrarily. Naturally, in peacetime the prices were significantly lower than at the present moment, which meant that the burden of deliveries was bound to be much greater. The Russians gave a small concession: the value of industrial equipment to be delivered was raised 15 percent and that of other goods 10 percent.[36] They also allowed that the deliveries of goods could be carried out in six years rather than five as originally demanded. In addition, the Hungarians had to pay for the transportation of goods to the Soviet Union.

The Soviet authorities wanted to begin reparation deliveries immediately. On February 9, even as the struggle for the capital continued, Béla Miklós, the premier, notified his cabinet that Voroshilov had demanded that the Hungarians should submit a concrete proposal concerning the reparation deliveries within five days. This was the beginning of a long bargaining process between the two sides. In each and every instance, the Soviet position prevailed. The Hungarians pointed out in vain that the burden placed on the economy would impede reconstruction and result in a great inflation. The Russians responded to the Hungarian document by presenting a list of demands for goods to be delivered in the course of 1945 and also in the course of the next five years.[37] From the quick Russian response, it would appear that they had drawn up their own plans considerably before the end of the war. The large Soviet ACC contingent included a department that dealt with reparation matters. The Hungarians also created an office within the ministry of foreign affairs for reparation issues. General Hermann Pokorny, who from this time on was responsible for negotiating with the victorious powers, headed the department that was set up on March 22.[38] While these negotiations continued, the Soviet army on its own was removing entire factories or parts of them and reassembling them in the Soviet Union. The Hungarians were not even in a position to inspect the factories being removed because the government did not possess the logistical means to

36 This agreement was included as an annex to the twelfth point of the armistice agreement. See Balogh and Földesi (eds.), p. 23.

37 Földesi, 2002, pp. 109–110.

38 Pokorny, a professional army officer, was born in Moravia. His first language was Czech, but he learned Russian and achieved distinction in the First World War. His memoirs were published after his death. *Emlékeim: A láthatatlan hirszerő*, Budapest: Petit Real, 2000.

travel to the countryside. In vain did the Hungarians ask help from the Russians in this matter.[39] We now know that at least some of the machinery taken from Hungary was left rusting at Soviet railroad junctions. The Russians were not very efficient in using their confiscated goods.[40]

In an appendix, the document specified Hungary's obligations in great detail: how much machinery, how much railroad-rolling stock, how many ships, how much and which agricultural goods, how many animals, and so forth.[41] The product mix was disadvantageous to Hungary, inasmuch as it emphasized heavy industry, especially machine production. The Hungarians would have preferred to send agricultural products to the Soviet Union. Although the Hungarian negotiators were not aware at the time, there was a dreadful shortage of food in the war-devastated Soviet Union. The Russian negotiators, however, insisted on industrial products.[42] The agreement concerning reparations was finally concluded on June 15, 1945. Prime Minister Miklós signed it in the name of the Hungarian government and Voroshilov in the name of the Soviet government.

Hungary also had to pay restitution to Czechoslovakia and Yugoslavia. The Czechs and the Yugoslavs had no occupation army in Hungary, so they were not in a position to get whatever they wanted. Hungary owed 70 million dollars worth of goods to Yugoslavia and 30 million to Czechoslovakia. Here also the price level was the same as with the Soviet Union, that is, 1938 world prices. As in the case of the agreement with the Soviet Union, only agents of the recipient countries could establish that the quality was satisfactory. Also, as in the case with the Soviet agreement in the case of late delivery, 5-percent interest was to be paid by the Hungarian side.[43] The Czechoslovak demands on Hungary were particularly disagreeable to the Hungarians. After all, Slovakia, a German satellite, had collaborated very enthusiastically with Germany, and as a proof of its commitment to the German cause, had deported its Jewish population under its own volition. In 1945, the Slovaks were expelling their Hungarian-speaking minority and taking possession of their property. For these reasons, it made little sense to the Hungarians that they had to pay reparations to the Czechoslovaks.

Satisfying Soviet demands was nearly impossible. How could Hungarian factories produce high-quality goods, on which the Russians insisted, at

39 MOL XIX-J-1-j Hungarian-Russian reparation agreement, p. 3.

40 Zoltán Bay, *Az Élet erösebb*, Budapest: Csokonai, 1990, pp. 109–132. Bay, a chief engineer, described in his memoirs how carelessly the Russians removed everything from the Tungsram factory, including desks and chairs, and how much they destroyed in the process.

41 Balogh and Földesi (eds.), pp. 28–35.

42 MOL XIX-J-1-j Hungarian-Russian reparation agreement. The treaty is reprinted on pp. 5–6.

43 Balogh and Földesi (eds.), pp. 42–44.

a time when factories were in ruins, when the soldiers of the Red Army occupied those factories that were still capable of producing, and when hundreds of thousands of workers were either in Germany or in Soviet prison camps? How could one realistically talk about Hungarian economic policy at a time when factories and mines were under Soviet military control? In any case, Soviet demands on Hungary were open ended. Soviet soldiers from the very outset of the occupation took charge of mines and still-functioning factories, and compelled workers to produce, often without payment, to satisfy the needs of the occupation army. (Most of the coal mines were flooded because the pumps had no electricity to operate.) Yet goods and services taken by the Russians in this way were not officially counted against Hungarian reparation obligations.

On May 18, 1945, Minister of Finances Vásáry sent a note to the ACC piteously complaining that Hungarian authorities could not deliver the tobacco and alcohol demanded by the Russians, because the factories producing these goods were already under Soviet control.[44] Gyöngyösi, the foreign minister, requested that in order to make rational planning for the deliveries possible, Soviet demands should be submitted to the relevant Hungarian ministries rather than to local organs. Voroshilov turned down this reasonable request. The Russians tolerated no limitation on their operations in Hungary.[45]

To reconstruct and to begin deliveries at the same time was nearly impossible. In 1945, the output of heavy industry was reduced to 35 percent of prewar levels; 15–22 percent of the national income went into reparation payments. Aside from the difficulties caused by the occupation authorities, another serious problem was that the country was cut off from the world economy. Its diplomatic and economic isolation meant that the economy needed iron and coal, but it could not buy them abroad because it did not have the currency to pay for imports.

Deliveries to the Soviet Union placed such a heavy burden on industry that the factories could not produce for domestic consumption. Under the circumstances, the peasants had no incentive to part from their products because there was nothing for them to buy. In order to begin production, the government was forced to issue loans to companies, which could be done only by printing money. The inflation that would do enormous damage to the economy in the following year began immediately after the end of hostilities. In December 1945, 95 percent of the budget was financed by printing money.[46] Between 1945 and 1948, approximately a third of the

44 MOL XIX-J-1-j 24 box IV, 482.1.
45 Ibid., finance minister to Voroshilov, October 5, 1945.
46 FRUS, 1945, vol 4, p. 919.

national income went to satisfying demands arising out of the armistice agreement.[47] Only after Hungary became a full-fledged satellite did the obligation to pay reparations to the Soviet Union come to be a relatively small percentage of the national income.

A note written on November 15, 1945, by an anonymous author at the time of the negotiations with the Soviet Union concerning an economic agreement included the following:

> The food supply is catastrophic. Animals have died and are dying. The introduction of land reform has created confusion. Agricultural machinery has been destroyed. There is no fertilizer. There is no public transport. People cannot work when there is nothing to eat. Our obligation to provide everything for the Red Army places on us a great burden. Heavy industry now is producing at 35% of the prewar output. If we cannot provide the peasants with goods, the peasants will not produce for the market.[48]

A very heavy burden was the Soviet requirement that Hungary supply the Red Army with food and lodging. In fact, the consumption of the occupying army was greater than the total amount of food that was left for the feeding of the approximately 9 million Hungarians. On occasion the food supplies sent to keep miners at work was confiscated by the Red Army for its own use.[49] The feeding of the Red Army was not included in the armistice agreement, which spoke only of the obligation of supplying the ACC and providing logistical means for the movement of the Soviet army for the purposes of fighting the common enemy, the Wehrmacht.

The Soviet Union not only removed as much from the country as quickly as it could but it also attempted to take advantage of its dominant position for long-term gain. Because Hungary was cut off from the rest of the world in 1945, it was only the Soviet Union that was in the position to deliver much-needed raw materials in exchange for Hungarian goods. As much as the non-Communist politicians hoped for Western help, it was not forthcoming. In order to conclude the rather modest agreement concerning the exchange of goods, Ernö Gerő, as minister of trade, and Antal Bán, a left-wing Socialist, as minister of industry, traveled to Moscow in August. The Russians wanted to combine a short-term treaty concerning immediate exchanges with long-term agreements. Even at the time, it was clear to foreign and domestic observers that this agreement aimed at tying

47 Pető and Szakács, p. 23.

48 MOL XIX-J-1-j 28, box IV, –526.2, Reparation problems.

49 MOL XIX-J-1-j Discussions between Hungarian government and Soviet delegation, Sept. 15, 1945.

Hungary economically to the Soviet Union in the future. In Hungary, as elsewhere in Soviet-controlled Eastern Europe, the Soviet Union proposed creating joint stock companies. The Soviet contribution was to be their ownership of ex-German assets; thus they did not have to make any direct investment. Owning of 50 percent of the stock and having de facto leadership of the companies ultimately enabled the Russians to control the most important segments of the economy. In the near future, such joint companies would control shipping on the Danube, the Hungarian airline, and bauxite and oil exploration, among other things. Although the chairmen of these companies were usually Hungarian, the general managers were almost always Soviet citizens. The companies were exempt from Hungarian taxes and import and export duties. They enabled the Soviet Union to penetrate the economic lives of the countries that had them. These joint stock companies in Hungary, as elsewhere in the region, came to be critical components of Soviet exploitation.

Gerő initialed the agreement for which he had permission from the prime minister.[50] However, at this point just before the national elections, the government was hesitant to sign, at least for the time being. The FKGP ministers hoped to use the Anglo-Saxon powers as a counterweight to Soviet penetration. Indeed, the British and the Americans saw the envisaged treaty as something that would negatively affect their economic interests. The Americans, for instance, had had considerable investment in the Hungarian petroleum industry before the war. Both the British and the Americans protested against the economic agreements drawn up by Gerő and the Russians. They protested both in Moscow and also to the Hungarian government in Budapest.[51]

Interestingly, as concerned Hungary, the Allies had few reasons to complain about the course of politics in 1945, limiting their protests to Soviet economic treatment of Hungary.[52] They were concerned partly because Soviet policy harmed their economic interests, but also because they saw the impoverishment of the country as something that would make the economic revival of Europe more difficult and because they saw Soviet economic

50 F. Nagy, vol. 1, pp. 178–183. The naive Premier Miklós, indeed, gave permission to Gerő at least to initial such agreement.

51 MOL XVII- 3 IV 548, box 34, Joint companies.

52 For example, in May the Americans protested to Voroshilov the removal of the Tungsram factory in which American citizens had a financial interest. A month later, the Russians responded that the factory during the war passed into German hands. The Hungarian government should reimburse American shareholders for their losses. FRUS, 1945, vol. 4, p. 813. On May 30 General Key protested to Voroshilov against the removal of MAORT (Hungarian American Oil company) properties, p. 815.

penetration in Eastern Europe as a base for further Soviet political encroachment in this area. The vast majority of reports sent to Washington by American representatives in Budapest concerned economic issues, namely Soviet penetration of the Hungarian economy that was detrimental to American economic interests.

The Hungarians were in no position to resist for long. On the one hand, the Soviet Union was able to put political pressure on the hesitant ministers, and on the other, the economy desperately needed Soviet trade. The Russians, Voroshilov, and Pushkin put great pressure on the provisional government to sign the economic agreement before the elections and the formation of a legitimate government. The FKGP ministers and politicians feared that the agreement would tie Hungary permanently to the Soviet Union; nevertheless, on October 12 the cabinet approved the agreement with the stipulation that it did not preclude economic cooperation with other countries.[53]

Unlike contemporaries, we know the outcome of the political and economic struggle. Within a few years, a Soviet-style economy was introduced in the countries of Eastern Europe, including Hungary. In retrospect, some historians, such as Göllner and Borhi, saw in Soviet behavior a purposeful undermining of free economic enterprise. Even at the time some politicians, for example FKGP Minister of Finances Ferenc Gordon, expressed his suspicion to the American representative in December 1945 that the Russians desired an economic collapse in order to create a revolutionary situation.[54] This was almost certainly not the case. A social revolution in Eastern Europe would not have served Soviet interests. At the time, all parties' economic programs, including the Communists', envisaged the inclusion of private enterprise in the difficult task of reconstruction. It was the extremely difficult economic circumstances that necessitated centralization at the expense of private firms. Policies, which led to the kind of command economy in the near future, were probably not consciously introduced.

53 FRUS, 1945, vol 4. Schoenfeld to secretary of state, October 6, 1945, pp. 881–883.
54 Ibid., Schoenfeld to secretary of state, December 5, p. 918.

4

Politics in a New Era

PARTIES

The Communist Party was the first to organize, but the building of the other three parties of the National Front also progressed quickly. They were, however, internally divided from the very beginning, and these divisions greatly weakened their resistance to the ever more aggressive Communists. The issue was always the same: should one recognize that there was no alternative to cooperation with the Communists and seek the least damaging compromise, or should one resist them every step of the way on every matter of significance?

The SDP established in 1890, was the oldest party still in existence. After the defeat of the Hungarian Soviet Republic in 1919, in which the Communists dominated but the Socialists also participated, the moderate leaders of the SDP and the counterrevolutionary government of Admiral Nicholas Horthy arrived at a compromise. According to the December 1921 agreement, the party was allowed to function legally and participate in elections but had to refrain from organizing state employees and, more significantly, the village poor. In the interwar period, suffrage in Hungary was based on property and educational qualifications, and only people in the cities voted in secret elections. Under these restrictions, the SDP was able to operate reasonably freely. However, its support gradually declined in the economically difficult times of the 1930s. Those who wanted to struggle against the conservative social and political structure of society increasingly turned to the extreme right, which offered radical change. The Hungarian Nazis gained strength at the expense of the Socialists even among the working classes.[1]

1 László Hubai, "A politikai irányzatok választási eredményeinek kontinuitása, 1920–1947," *Múltunk* 1 (1999): 44–69.

The attitude of the Socialists toward the Communists had always been ambivalent. The programs of the two Marxist parties profoundly differed. The SDP envisaged a gradual movement toward Socialism, and it was committed to observing democratic norms. The Comintern until 1935 regarded the Socialists as dangerous enemies and constantly attacked them, and the Socialists responded in kind. In Hungary, the Soviet Union and the Communist Party were both extremely unpopular, even among the working classes. With the rise of Nazi danger, the Comintern at its last congress adopted a policy of "popular front," which implied temporary cooperation with "democratic forces" including the Socialists, but this policy change had little consequence in Hungary, where the Communist Party remained an insignificant political entity. The SDP leaders explicitly rejected the idea of a "popular front": they well understood that associating with Communists would compromise them among their supporters, and it would also endanger their agreement with the government.[2] In these circumstances, infiltration into the SDP was the only way the Communists could become relevant in the political struggle. After 1941, during the war, Communists took advantage of the fact that the Socialist Party was still legal and participated in its work. In this sense, it is fair to say that Communists had already secretly penetrated the SDP.

On March 19, 1944, the Germans occupied the country, and the situation changed. The Socialists also had to go underground, and their best-known leaders were arrested. Under these circumstances, the Socialists were compelled to cooperate not only with the Smallholder Party but also with the Peace Party, as the Communists had renamed themselves. The newly created and, of course, illegal Hungarian Front called on Horthy to change sides in the war. A new generation of Socialist leaders, more radical, less disturbed by the experiences of 1919 when cooperation between the two Marxist parties turned out to be very difficult, looked more favorably than their elders on their "brother party," the MKP.

In October 1944, when the end of the war was obviously near, representatives of the two parties, László Rajk and Árpád Szakasits, signed an agreement promising that the two parties would work for the unity of the working classes and the realization of Socialism.[3] However, within the SDP even at this time, there was no agreement over the issue of relations with the Communists. Disagreements among the leaders became ever stronger and more visible. Szakasits, the head of the party, György Marosán, and Pál

2 István Simon, "A szocialdemokrácia uj arca," *Múltunk* 1 (2001): 213. Simon quotes from an article by the chief theorist of the party, Illés Mónus, in *Népszava* September 27, 1936.

3 R. Gábor, 1998, pp. 66–67.

10. Combined election meeting of the Communist and the Socialist, Árpád Szakasits and Mátyás Rákosi, Rákoscsaba, September, 1945. (Source: Hungarian National Museum.)

Justus belonged to the left wing and supported the idea of close cooperation. Anna Kéthly, Ferenc Szeder, and other leaders, on the other hand, would have liked to keep the Communists at arms length.

After the demise of the Horthy regime, and after the experience of the last year of the war in which Socialists and Communists had managed to find common cause in resisting the Germans, it was perhaps understandable that from the point of view of many, though by no means all, Socialist leaders, the Communists had become close allies. Although many surely entertained doubts about Communist tactics and disliked unquestioned Communist allegiance to the Soviet Union, they still shared the Communist belief that at the moment the real danger was presented by the "reactionaries," a notoriously slippery term. Although during the Horthy regime it was in the interest of the SDP to keep aloof from the Communists, after the appearance of the Red Army on Hungarian territory the situation changed completely. In January 1945, Szakasits, who in 1943 wanted to draw close to the Smallholders in order to hold back Communist influence in case of the victory of the Red Army, decided to follow an entirely different political line.[4] He surrounded himself with people who supported his policy of close cooperation

4 F. Nagy, vol. 1, p. 111. Nagy describes a conversation with Szakasits that took place in 1943.

with the Communists.[5] The representatives of the "right wing," that is, moderate Socialists who had doubts concerning the wisdom of this policy, were gradually pushed out of the leadership.

There was a general understanding, even among the right-wing leaders of the SDP, that the new circumstances demanded new politics. The old leadership was blamed for the fact that in the interwar period the SDP had been regarded by many as an accomplice of the Horthy regime. A change in leadership was inevitable. A thorough repudiation of the old policy made it possible for the left wing of the party to emerge victorious and remove the old leadership.

The two workers' parties set up a committee with the task of resolving disputes and encouraging cooperation. Cooperation, however, was never easy. Even left-wing Socialists constantly complained about Communist tactics. Especially in the countryside, aggressive Communist functionaries continued to regard the Socialists as enemies. The Socialists had to compete with the "brother party" for working-class support, and against their better judgment, they had to assume a more radical policy line in order to compete. Pál Justus, head of the propaganda department, considered this competition as one of the main reasons for the decline of support for the Socialist Party. Because the Communists did not disdain demagogy, the Socialists felt that they too had to use radical slogans at a time when the population was tired of such radicalism.[6] Both parties had their popular base in Budapest and both wanted to increase its influence among the industrial workers and within the trade unions. In the past, the SDP and the trade unions had been closely connected, and it was here that the Communists intended to make the greatest inroads. The Communists were not loyal allies; among working-class audiences, they attacked the earlier policies of their Socialist allies and led the workers to believe that the SDP had no future in the new Hungary. No wonder Szakasits often felt betrayed and realized that he had to struggle on two fronts.

The SDP was no longer a fully independent party as early as 1945. That summer Károly Peyer, the leader of the party in the interwar period, a man whose name symbolized compromise and cooperation with the Horthy regime, returned from the infamous German concentration camp, Mauthausen. He found it necessary to visit Rákosi and find out whether the

5 Ibid. See also Klára Schifferné Szakasits, *Fent és Lent, 1945–1950*, Budapest: Magvető, 1985, pp. 90–91. In her book the daughter of Szakasits describes how her father struggled against those who opposed his line within the party, primarily Valentiny, Szeder, and Kéthly, and at the same time were against the Communists who wanted to incorporate the SDP within the MKP.

6 PIL 283/34/4. Report of propaganda department to secretariat for September and October, 1945.

Communists would have any objection to his resuming his office as head of the SDP.[7] Indeed, Rákosi and the Communists did have objections: they supported the left wing of the SDP, and Peyer, in post-1945 Hungary, had no major role to play in the party that he had long led.

The organization of the SDP started later than that of the Communist Party, and it did not have Soviet support. Indeed, the Russians on occasion prevented the Socialists from printing their posters.[8] Nevertheless, in the beginning the SDP had many more members than the MKP: at the end of 1945, the SDP had between 350,000 and 400,000 members. At least half of the membership was in Budapest.[9] Well entrenched in the trade union movement, the SDP was particularly strong among the better-educated workers, for example, among the printers. It also attracted a large number of small merchants and tradesmen.[10] Only in 1946 did the SDP membership begin to lag in comparison with the Communist Party.[11]

The gap between the left wing and right wing of the party widened. The left with few hesitations followed the Communists. The Socialist ministers in the cabinet did not always vote together. One may speak confidently about the Communist economic program. It is more difficult to clarify the economic ideas of the other parties because they were not unified. Under the circumstances, one can only talk about dominant or prevailing views. Interestingly, the Socialists, perhaps less afraid of being associated with the Soviet Union and not having to follow Moscow's instructions, put out a slogan in 1945 and used it in the following years of transition that seemed more radical than what the Communists were saying. The Socialist slogan was: "Today we work for democracy, and tomorrow for socialism."[12] Unlike the Communists, they were not afraid to say at this earliest time that their goal was the creation of the preconditions for building Socialism. They did say explicitly that they aimed at increasing the role of the state in the economy, establishing a governmental monopoly in foreign trade, and the introduction of a steeply progressive taxation system.[13] The majority in the Socialist leadership looked to the British Labour Party, which had just come to power and was carrying out an ambitious nationalization program. Their hope for effective support from the British, however, did not materialize.

7 M. Rákosi, *Visszaemlékezések, 1940–1956*, vol. 1, pp. 188–189.
8 PIL 283/34/4 April 20, 1945.
9 Gábor, pp. 84–85.
10 PIL 283/32/65 June 8, 1945.
11 PIL 283/34/5 propaganda department report to secretariat, December 1946.
12 PIL 283 32/31 February 6, 1946.
13 Pető and Szakács, p. 28.

The Communists were able to influence the policies of the SDP, and the left wing of that party was willing to follow policies inspired by the Communists, but the NPP was even more under Communist influence than the SDP. The NPP was organized in 1939, but it had only an ephemeral existence; it was more of a group of intellectuals than an organized political force. The great debate that lasted through the twentieth century among Hungarian intellectuals was between the "urbanists" and "populists." The urbanists were mostly Jewish, Western oriented, and sympathetic to Socialism. The populists, by contrast, devoted themselves to describing and improving the deplorable lot of the peasants. From the outset, populist intellectuals, so called village explorers, played a major role in the NPP. They agreed with the Socialists that the country desperately needed a social revolution, but unlike the members of the working-class party, they were particularly concerned about the fate of the peasantry, the poorest segment of the population. Compared to the Marxists, they were nationalists; they professed to believe in the particular virtues of the Hungarian peasant. They were emphatically not Western-style liberals; their commitment to a democratic form of government was questionable.

In 1944, the NPP had to be recreated anew. It wanted to represent the interests of the agricultural workers, the hitherto landless and therefore poorest segment of the peasantry, and also those who had so little land that they could barely survive. The party also received support from a segment of the village intelligentsia, such as teachers and agronomists, that was attracted to radical, propeasant policies. From the outset, this party was to be an ally of the Communists, and Communists actually played a role in the leadership of the party. The NPP helped the Communists to extend their influence in the countryside. It is possible the party was created to increase Communist influence in the villages, where the Communists had little indigenous strength. The purpose of the NPP from the Communist point of view was to attract support from peasants who otherwise would have voted for the more established and better-known Smallholder Party. Writers and sociologists, who in the interwar period devoted their energies to the description of the lives of the poor peasantry, now became political actors. The leaders of the party, Péter Veres, a writer of some consequence, and village explorers, József Darvas, Ferenc Erdei, and Imre Kovács, all acquired their reputation by taking the side of the poor peasants during the Horthy era. Darvas and Erdei stood close to the Communists in their radicalism and in their passionate desire to destroy old, feudal Hungary. In fact, Ferenc Erdei actually petitioned to join the Communists but was told that he was more useful to the Communist cause as a leader in the

11. Zoltán Tildy, 1889–1961.

peasant party.[14] Aside from Erdei, Darvas and Veres also considered joining the Communist Party.[15] Although his request was not publicized, it was an open secret that Erdei worked for the Communists. (After the Communists acquired a monopoly of power in 1948, Erdei, Darvas, and Veres, unlike left-wing Social Democrats, continued to play political roles.)

The party's strength in the cities remained, not surprisingly, minimal; however, it did succeed in gaining some support in the countryside. In its propaganda, the NPP stressed Hungarian nationalism, and in this respect it differed from the two other left-wing parties. The NPP did not develop a comprehensive economic program; it was satisfied with representing the interests of the poor peasantry. NPP leaders envisaged an economic system that would be based on small peasant lots. They explicitly opposed the introduction of collective farms.

At the end of 1945, the NPP had 170,000 members.[16] The leadership of the party from the outset was bitterly divided between Erdei and Darvas on the one side and Kovács, who distrusted the Communists, on the other. Veres, who cultivated the look and speech of a peasant, attempted to moderate, but being politically naïve, was an ineffectual leader. Nevertheless, he came to be the symbol of the party. Kovács in his memoirs rather cruelly

14 Gerő's letter to Rákosi, December 28, 1944, in *Moszkvának jelentjük*, p. 13. Gerő reported to Rákosi, who remained in Moscow, that for the time being Erdei's admission to the MKP would be kept a secret.

15 Péter Benkő, "A Nemzeti Parasztpárt az Ideiglenes Nemzetgyűlésben és a kormányban," in Feitl (ed.), 1995, p. 172.

16 Sándor Balogh, *Parlamenti és Pártharcok Magyarországon, 1945–1947*, Budapest: Kossuth, 1975, p. 24.

described Veres as a "talking dog": "It was simply unbelievable that a man whose appearance was no different from that of a poor peasant could have his speaking and writing talent."[17] Veres's Hungarian populism was not free of anti-Semitism.[18] In an election campaign speech in 1945, he made clear his attitude: he did not want Jews in his party.[19] (He need not have been concerned: few Jews were attracted to the ideology of the NPP.) Every meeting of the leadership deteriorated into a struggle between the pro-Communist wing and those who were suspicious of the Communists.

Erdei, who had the crucially important position as minister of the interior, in each and every instance explicitly sided with the Communists. When on July 3, 1945, he was criticized within his own party leadership for his performance, he responded: "No one is capable of defending democracy the way the communists can. Today in Hungary democratic transformation means two things: land reform and possession of the police power. The tempo is set by the communists in both of these, and perhaps there have been mistakes made, but without the communists nothing would happen."[20]

In terms of electoral base, the FKGP was the strongest. A party with a similar name had existed even before the First World War; however, the organization that maintained its continuity was really founded only in 1930 by Zoltán Tildy and Ferenc Nagy. Tildy, a future premier and later president of the republic, had been a protestant minister, and Nagy came from a peasant family. Tildy's father-in-law, Antal Gyenis, a judge, was a victim of the White Terror in 1919. From the Communist point of view, this family connection was a recommendation.[21] As the party's name indicates, it was organized to defend the interests of the landed but still rather poor peasantry. The first party program called for land reform, secret and universal suffrage, and improvement of the conditions of the peasantry by increasing agricultural prices in relation to industrial products.[22] During the Horthy era, when the left was more or less missing from the political landscape, the FKGP, fundamentally a moderately conservative organization, nevertheless represented a democratic alternative. Had the peasantry been able to vote in a secret ballot, the FKGP probably would have emerged as the largest

17 Kovács, 1979, p. 241. Kovács mentioned that the phrase "talking dog" came from the famous Hungarian poet Gyula Illyés.

18 His views on the Jewish question are analyzed in János Gyurgyák, *A Zsidókérdés Magyarországon*, Budapest: Osiris, 2001, pp. 574–578. Veres regarded the Jews as alien. He identified them with capitalism and exploitation of the Hungarian peasantry.

19 Gati, p. 103.

20 Benkő, in I. Feitl (ed.), 1995, p. 177.

21 György Haas, *Diktaturák Árnyékában: Tildy Zoltán Élete*, Budapest: Magyar Napló, 2000, p. 22.

22 F. Nagy, vol. 1, pp. 31–32.

party. The conservative government, however, was determined to defend the interests of the landlord class and by electoral trickery prevented the emergence of a powerful peasant party.

The leaders of the Smallholders' Party had opposed the German-oriented foreign policy, and as a consequence the party had to go underground after the Germans occupied the country in March 1944.[23] The FKGP leaders had cordial relations with major figures of the other moderate opposition party, the SDP; indeed, the right wing of the SDP found a natural ally in the FKGP. Working underground, the two parties easily cooperated.

In the government of Debrecen and in the Provisional Assembly, the FKGP did not receive the representation that it deserved on the basis of predictable popular support. It had fewer representatives in the assembly than the Communist Party (fifty-five versus seventy-one), and only two portfolios in the government. János Gyöngyösi became foreign minister and István Vásáry minister of finances. The best-known leaders of the party, Zoltán Tildy and Ferenc Nagy, were hiding in the capital still surrounded by the Red Army. Also, the party did not have the logistical means possessed by the Communists and to a much lesser extent the Socialists and NPP.

Nevertheless, the growth of the FKGP was phenomenal. After the liberation of Budapest in February, the organization of the party began with great enthusiasm. By the middle of 1945 it was the largest party, having local organizations everywhere. Its newspaper, *Kis Ujság,* was the most popular in the country, selling more copies than *Szabad Nép*, the Communist paper, or *Népszava,* the Socialist newspaper.[24] Of all the parties it had the most heterogeneous base. The FKGP benefited from the unwillingness of the Communists and the Soviet authorities to allow right-wing parties to organize. It was able to count on the support of the great majority of the peasantry, its traditional base, but beyond that it found support among those who had felt more or less comfortable in the old regime, or who feared a Soviet-imposed Communist regime. The Communists' criticism that the FKGP included "reactionary" elements was not altogether unfounded, if by "reactionary" they meant partisans of the old order. Those who wanted to prevent the advance of the Communists were likely to find their political home in the Smallholders' Party. Under the circumstances it is not surprising that the FKGP came to be a coalition of forces, with some leaders representing the more or less leftist old party, and other, new elements, who came to

23 Ibid., pp. 67–78. On East Germany, see also Wolfgang Leonhard, *Child of the Revolution*, trans. C. M. Woodhouse, Chicago: Regnery, 1958.
24 PIL 274, 23/29.

this party because it already appeared to be the most likely counterbalance to the Communists. Thus it came about that a party that was explicitly founded and dedicated to representing the interests of the peasantry developed nationally into a major force in the cities of the country, including Budapest. In the countryside it was necessary only to rebuild already existing cells, but in the capital the organization had to start from next to nothing.

In the optimistic period immediately after liberation, the left wing of the party, led by Tildy himself, was dominant. At this time it still seemed likely that collaboration with the Communists and with the Soviet Union would be possible. In that spirit the party was willing to accept a radical reorganization of the prewar political and social system.

Of course, the Smallholder leaders saw perfectly well the danger posed to the future of Hungarian democracy by the Communists' ability to place their people in responsible positions, particularly in the police. They put their hopes in the first free elections, assuming that a strong demonstration for the party by a majority of Hungarians would end the political injustices. If it was not to be the elections, then the turning point would come when the peace treaty was signed, for it was widely believed that once the treaty was signed the Soviet army would leave the country.

The economic program of the largest party, the FKPG, did not fundamentally differ from that of the Marxist parties. It also called for progressive taxation. It took for granted the survival of a free economy but did not oppose an increased role for the state. As the party's name indicated, it paid particular attention to the interests of the peasantry, and its primary goal was to create an agricultural system on the pattern of the Scandinavian states.[25] The FKGP program envisaged raising the level of Hungarian agriculture to the Western European level. Under the circumstances it was not difficult to construct an economic program for the coalition, the National Independence Front. This program reaffirmed the commitment of the political parties to free enterprise, although the representatives of all parties well understood that in reality, given the dire economic situation, the government must be involved in every significant economic issue.

Aside from the four most important parties, MKP, SDP, NPP, and FKGP, there was another party that was a founding member of the Hungarian Independence Front, the Civic Democratic Party. The most important person in this party was Count Géza Teleki, who had the portfolio of education in the provisional government. Of the five parties that were members of

25 In the description of the economic programs of the different parties, I largely base my discussion on Iván Pető and Sándor Szakács, pp. 27–31.

12. János Kádár speaks to voters in Budapest, August 1945. (Source: Hungarian National Museum.)

the Independence Front, this was by far the weakest. It claimed to represent the middle classes and as such it had its base of support in Budapest. At the initiative of the Communists, this party was excluded from the Hungarian Independence Front in May 1945.

The Catholic Church desired to participate in political life, and its supporters established the Christian Democratic People's Party.[26] Although Premier Dálnoki Miklós permitted the functioning of this party, the Budapest National Committee, dominated by Communists, simply disregarded the decision of the premier and the Christian Democratic Party was not allowed to function.[27] In the following years the Catholic Church became a significant factor indeed in the political life of the nation, but its influence was a direct result of its moral authority and not through a political party. The other parties, in particular the Communist Party, objected to the official recognition of this organization, and it was not a participant in the Hungarian Independence Front.

26 Lajos Izsák, *A Keresztény Demokrata Néppárt és a Demokrata Néppárt, 1944–1949*, Budapest: Kossuth, 1985.

27 S. Balogh, 1975, p. 37.

ISSUES

The provisional government moved to Budapest on April 12, 1945, and remained in office until the first elections in November. The tasks facing the new government were immense. First it had to establish some degree of autonomy from the occupying Soviet army, which, according to the armistice agreement, was only temporarily exercising sovereign powers in the country. The Russians, who were extremely demanding, did not make this task easy. The major task was simply to begin the rebuilding of the infrastructure under extremely difficult circumstances. Restructuring of the local administration had begun in January when the government named thirteen chief executive officers for the counties. These were distributed according to estimated party strength: MKP and the FKGP received four, the SDP three and NPP two positions. There was some dispute about the title for these men. Ágoston Valentiny, the minister of justice, was concerned that the old title *föispán* had unpleasant connotations and therefore "government agents" should be used instead, but the Communist Gerő suggested that it was necessary to retain the old title because everyone knew what it meant.[28] (In the previous regime the *föispán* was the representative of the government in the county, as opposed to the *alispán*, who was elected locally.) These county chiefs had the task of reorganizing and democratizing local government. Their authority at a time of poor communications was considerable. The difficult task of reestablishing law and order in the countryside fell on their shoulders.

In the makeup of the Provisional National Assembly, the left was dominant. After the liberation of Budapest, more delegates were added to the Assembly, but the left retained it dominance. In the government, however, the correlation of political forces was different. That this coalition government had a great deal of difficulty in working together was to be anticipated. Given the extremely heterogeneous makeup of the cabinet and the circumstances of its creation, it was unlikely that it would become a well-functioning, cooperative leadership. This government encompassed representatives of the Horthy regime, such as Faragho, Vörös, and Dálnoki Miklós, people who had been personally close to Horthy, along with ministers who hoped to establish a Western-type democratic and liberal political order, such as Valentiny, Vásáry, and later Ferenc Nagy. Finally, to add a third ideological corner, there were Communists and a crypto-Communist. The Communists were in no position to dominate. József Gábor and Molnár

28 MOL XVIII – 3 – 1 Notes, January 3, 1945.

Erik were not among the top leaders of the party, nor were they particularly able politicians. The two important portfolios the Communists had were agriculture under Imre Nagy and the ministry of the interior under Ferenc Erdei. (Erdei, of course, nominally belonged to the NPP.) The Communists desperately wanted this ministry for themselves, but because the other parties objected, a compromise was reached that was acceptable to the Communists. On the other hand, Erdei, however devoted he was to the Communist program, could not be brought under strict party discipline.

The most significant issue the government faced was land reform, but it was not the most divisive.* The matter that caused the most passionate disagreements was control of the political police. The moderate and right-wing members of the government were increasingly and rightly concerned that the political police was becoming an instrument of Communist power. The non-Communist ministers wanted to examine some of the outrageous and illegal acts of Communist authorities. Furthermore, Ágoston Valentiny, a moderate Socialist and minister of justice, planned to set up within his ministry an investigating organ that would have been in a position to reveal Communist manipulations. This organ in effect would have been a competitor of the Communist-led political police that existed within the ministry of the interior. The government accepted Valentiny's proposal in a six to four vote. Erdei, the Communist ministers Gerő and Molnár, and the left-wing Social Democrat, Bán, voted against Valentiny. The Communists immediately saw the danger. One may assume that they consulted with the Soviet authorities, which at this point intervened. Ambassador Pushkin summoned Foreign Minister Gyöngyösi on July 2 and protested that the ACC had not been consulted. He maintained that acting on Valentiny's proposal would hinder the punishing of war criminals.[29]

Ultimately, not only was the proposal defeated, but the issue also led to a reorganization of the cabinet. The Communists and the SDP leadership had been dissatisfied with the composition and policies of the government. It had been in the Soviets' interest to put conservative figures in the government while the war continued, but after the armistice circumstances changed, and there was no need to retain compromised people such as ex-gendarme General Faragho. After the government moved to Budapest in

* Land reform is discussed in the next chapter.

29 István Vida, "Az Ideiglenes Nemzeti Kormányátalakitása 1945 juliusában és a szovjet diplomacia," in Lajos Iszák (ed.), *Vissza a történelemhez*, Budapest: Napvilág, 1996, p. 390. Vida in his article reprinted the documents composed by Pushkin on his conversations with Hungarian leaders.

April, it was subject to the influence of a press that expressed much more radical opinions than were popular in the provincial city of Debrecen. The Communist and Socialist newspapers more and more strongly criticized the right-wing members of the cabinet.

In the middle of July the cabinet was reformed: those who had been most troublesome for the Communists were removed. Valentiny, István Vásáry, an able and determined FKGP politician, and also Faragho had to go. SDP and FKGP politicians who belonged to the left wing of their respective parties took their places. On the other hand the Smallholder leader, Ferenc Nagy, joined the cabinet in the newly created post of minister of reconstruction, which, at the time, was a very important position because it enabled the party to claim credit for successes in enabling the country to start life anew. The left-wing SDP, István Ries, took Valentiny's place, and he immediately withdrew his predecessor's proposal. (Five years later Ries was tortured to death in an AVH prison.)[30] These changes in the composition of the government brought it closer to the makeup of the Provisional National Assembly; that is, it moved the cabinet further to the left. To be sure, Dálnoki Miklós remained premier, but being neither a commanding personality nor an able politician, his role was circumscribed.

The struggle over the control of the political police in 1945 was the first time that the Communists were defeated in a serious matter. It was also the first time that they turned defeat into victory by carrying out a minor coup d'etat, removing troublesome political opponents from positions of power.

ELECTIONS

The politicians of the FKGP, counting on the anti-Communist views of the great majority of the Hungarians, assumed that they would do well in the first free elections. Therefore, István Vásáry, the minister of finances, urged the cabinet as early as March 18 to hold elections as soon as possible. He referred to the decisions of the Yalta conference that had just taken place and promised free elections. However, at a time when the entire country had not yet been freed, holding national elections was obviously impossible.[31] When the conditions for holding elections had been created and the laws for the elections were being discussed, naturally, each party hoped the laws and the timing would be favorable to their own political interests. After some disputes, the parties agreed that the right to vote would be extended

30 Gábor, p. 193.

31 S. Balogh, 1975, p. 53.

13. Election posters, September 24, 1945. (Source: Hungarian National Museum.)

to every citizen over the age of twenty. For the first time in Hungarian history no distinctions were made between the sexes, and no educational qualifications were required for the right to vote. The Communists were aware that the women tended to vote more conservatively than men, but for ideological reasons it was impossible for them to oppose the extension of suffrage. The voting was to be on the basis of party lists. That is, the citizens would be choosing from among party programs and not voting for individual candidates. Only war criminals and members of twenty-five right-wing organizations that had been outlawed were deprived of the right to vote.

These were to be the first genuinely free elections in Hungarian history. That the elections took place as early as they did had something to do with the international agreements among the Allies promising free elections in the countries of Eastern Europe. Voroshilov, the head of the ACC, informed the Hungarian premier on August 16 that the elections should be held as soon as possible.[32] The FKGP, concerned about

32 Vida, 1986, p. 122.

the fairness of the coming elections, would have welcomed international observers (i.e., Anglo-American representatives), but that did not happen because of the opposition of the Soviet Union and of the MKP.[33] The parties did agree on setting up committees, including representatives of all parties, in order to decide disputed issues. The elections were not limited to the four participating members of the National Front. Aside from them the Citizens' Democratic Party, formed by Géza Teleki, and the Hungarian Radical Party also fielded candidates.

The Communists won two major concessions at this stage. First, the other parties agreed that before the national elections municipal elections would be held in the capital and in the surrounding districts. The rationale behind this demand was that the Communists assumed they would do better in Budapest, and especially in the industrial belt surrounding the city, than in the rest of the country and consequently hoped to build on their success in the capital. The municipal elections were to be held on October 7 and the national elections four weeks later on November 4. Second, the Communists persuaded the Socialist leaders to allow the two workers' parties to present a common electoral list. Within the SDP, predictably, the left wing approved the idea, but the right-wing Socialists opposed it. Once again, the left, led by Szakasits, prevailed.

The Communists understood that because national elections had to take place, from their point of view the earlier the date the better. In a speech to the Central Committee on July 7, Rákosi explained[34]:

> In the understanding of the public, the party is responsible for every trouble, every confusion . . . therefore it would be an error to postpone the elections, because it is going to be a hard winter, and that would be used against us. . . . It is not possible to exclude all fascists from the electoral roles because their number is in the hundreds of thousands. . . . Considerable portions of these are industrial workers or landless peasants. Think of the ex-members of the Böszörményi type "kaszáskeresztes" movement [a radical right-wing rural organization of the 1930s]. Many of these are now members of our party. I believe the views of the ex-fascists are no different from those of the population as a whole.

He expressed extraordinary optimism:

> Our thinking is that if we proceed with the Socialists then we will have a very substantial majority in Budapest. Maybe 70 percent or maybe even more or a little less, but in any case convincing, better than what we can achieve by ourselves.

33 FRUS, 1945, vol 4. Arthur Schoenfeld repeatedly reported to Washington that the non-Communist politicians were concerned about the fairness of the coming elections. They expressed fear of Soviet intervention and hope that the Allies would send representatives who would supervise the elections.

34 PIL 274 1/28 KV July 7, 1945, "Központi Vezetöség" Central Committee.

Clearly, Rákosi understood that it would be an advantage to win in Budapest before the national elections. He also made practical suggestions:

> We should not put women on our list in village constituencies. This can only be done in the cities and perhaps in industrial centers. The peasant, even a democratic peasant, does not like political women. With such nominations we would only help the reactionaries.

This speech by Rákosi, delivered to the top leadership of the party, shows how the Communists at this time overestimated their support. They apparently believed that it would be possible to acquire power legitimately, although, not being democrats or liberals, they did not hesitate to use all available means including the political police and the aid of the Red Army. Two years later, after the next elections, Rákosi's attitude toward the Hungarian people would be different. In a speech to the Political Committee of the leadership in September 1947 evaluating the results of the 1947 elections, he called Hungary "a reactionary country."[35]

The Communists, who had never participated in elections before 1945 and therefore had no experience in such matters, started to work hard. People who had spent years in Moscow, of course, were aware of the significance of propaganda and took this matter seriously. They soon found, however, that methods that worked in a totalitarian state were not always useful in the context of meaningful political pluralism where it was possible to contradict Communist propositions and pose alternatives. Rákosi addressed party activists in September 1945 before the elections. The major political issue of the day was the decision of the two workers' parties to run in the Budapest district elections on a common list. The slogan that Rákosi recommended to his listeners was "Workers' unity and workers' plurality." He pointed out, however, that such a slogan might be effective among worker constituencies but would not work elsewhere. It was important to win over small traders, merchants, and clerks. He therefore recommended other slogans such as "Let us rebuild Budapest!" This time, as all through the period of the struggle for power, the Communists tried to depict their political role as a fight against reactionary forces. Consequently Rákosi wanted his listeners to look at the election as a phase in this struggle and wanted Communist agitators to point out that the reactionaries feared only the Communists. He also hoped that the electorate would believe that a victory of the Communist and Socialist slate would it make it more likely that the Soviets would return the Hungarian prisoners of war. The question of bringing home prisoners

35 PIL 274 2/42 September 11, 1947.

of war from the Soviet Union was a politically very significant one and remained on the agenda for years. The Communists continued to argue that they were in the best position to satisfy this demand. Further, Rákosi wanted the agitators to take advantage of the popularity of some Communist leaders, and the people he mentioned were Imre Nagy, whose name was associated with land reform, and Zoltán Vas and Ernő Gerő, who both had made significant contributions to the process of reconstruction.[36]

An activist at this meeting named Ferenc Bercznai made his own recommendations[37]:

> It is important not only to convince but also to produce an emotional impact. In our posters let us completely avoid any modernist drawings or paintings, for these are not liked either by peasants or by workers or even by the intelligentsia. In our marches the masses should not see any hesitation or weakness, because people are drawn to strength. . . . A person with a Jewish face or Jewish behavior *should not participate under any circumstances* in house-to-house agitation [italics in the original]. That is the explanation of the lack of success of Madisz and MNDSZ [mass organizations for youth and women].

One wonders what he had in mind when speaking of "Jewish behavior."

Aside from the MKP, the competing parties did not present formal and elaborate electoral programs. The party slogans of the four main parties did not explicitly contradict one another: each promised democracy, building a new Hungary, and reconstruction; each professed to be a defender of land reform. After the admonition of Stalin himself scarcely a year before, that the Communists should stand for the defense of private property, the Communists were not in a position to advocate explicitly the establishment of Socialism through large-scale nationalization. On the other hand, the Smallholders did not object to the nationalization of some segments of the economy. Each party professed to be in favor of Hungarian independence while making veiled references to influences threatening this independence. For Communist agitators this threat came from the Western Allies, who were just then criticizing a recently signed Hungarian-Soviet economic agreement and who repeatedly expressed skepticism concerning the freedom of the coming elections. The FKGP, by contrast, clearly saw the threat to independence from the occupying Soviet army. Each party wanted to be regarded as defender of the nation and national traditions, though the FKGP stressed this point more than the Socialists and the Communists. The Smallholders talked more about the freedom of religion, but of course the two Marxist parties did not openly attack the churches at this time. Each party talked about the sad plight of the Hungarian minority in the neighboring countries, in particular

36 PIL 274 21/5.

37 PIL 274 21/5 September 5, 1945.

the newly reestablished Czechoslovakia. (At this time tens of thousands of Hungarians were ruthlessly expelled by the Slovaks.) The NPP talked about the importance of peasant unity and the Socialists and Communists about "workers' unity." The Smallholders, by contrast, aimed to present themselves as a party that stood above class interests. Indeed, among all the parties it alone succeeded in getting support from all segments of the population.

In spite of the many common themes the differences among the parties were clear to the public. The voters well understood that when they voted for the Socialist-Communist list they were voting for a program of radical social change. The FKGP dominated the other side. It advertised its ideology as a *polgári* program. *Polgár* in Hungarian means simply citizen, and consequently the word could not have had much content, because, of course, every voter was a citizen. The word became meaningful only in contradistinction to "Socialist." *Polgár* has a connotation in Hungarian that includes bourgeois but without a pejorative sense. Hence it was somewhat ironic that a nominally peasant party claimed to be bourgeois. The "civic" program implied to the voters that these politicians were not Socialists. Politicians at the time contrasted *polgári demokrácia*, "civic democracy," and *népi demokrácia* (i.e., "people's democracy"). At this time the phrase was not yet further defined though it would receive much attention later from Communist theorists. The FKGP became the most popular party in the country for the simple reason that it was not Socialist. Those who voted for the Smallholders voted against Soviet occupation and against following the Soviet example. On the other hand not everyone who voted for the Socialists or for the NPP was an admirer of the Soviet model. (Interestingly, the words *polgár* and *polgári* have remained part of the Hungarian political vocabulary. Today one of the two main political forces defines itself as Socialist and the other as *polgári*, i.e., civic.)

The tension between the left and the right was considerable; their visions of a future Hungary were irreconcilable. Their past and values were profoundly different. Communists who came out of the Moscow school of political education could not fit easily into an altogether different political environment. Their commitment to observing democratic niceties was limited. For example in a meeting of the Central Committee in September, Rákosi encouraged his followers to break up meetings of the opposition. He said[38]:

> The FKGP provokes us in their newspapers. In the future such provocation will get worse. We have to respond sharply to their fascist-like statements. We must take up

38 PIL 274 16/8.

the struggle in the press as well as in other areas. We will not allow them to hold a successful mass meeting. Of course we will not make our plans open.

At the same time both sides in the struggle had reason to prevent the further deterioration of relations. The right wing was concerned about the intervention of Soviet troops, and the Communists did not want the elections to be tainted to such an extent as to embarrass the Soviet Union. The Allies correctly had held the Soviet Union responsible for crude violations of democratic norms in the recently held elections in Bulgaria. The Communists, at least before the October Budapest municipal elections, believed that they had no need for the use of force.

When the results came in on October 7, they were bitterly disappointing for the Communists. The FKGP achieved an absolute majority in Budapest, (50.5 percent), and the two combined Marxist parties received only 42.7 percent. The Communists were devastated.[39] From these results, it followed that the FKGP would win the national elections and that the combination of the two workers' parties was a tactical error. People who would have voted for the Socialists did not do so because of this combined list. The elections demonstrated the correctness of the views of the right-wing Socialists who had protested against the common list. Because men and women received different colored voting envelopes, it was easy to establish that it was the majority of women who voted for the Smallholders, and women, because of the great wartime losses of men, made up more than 60 percent of the electorate. Rákosi, blamed the unfavorable results at least partially on the votes of conservative women. According to Rákosi, even proletarian women, influenced by the churches, voted for the Smallholders.[40]

In the course of the four weeks between the Budapest municipal elections and the national elections, the political struggle became ever more bitter. Pro- and anti-Communist demonstrators came to the streets. Contrary to original expectations, the results in Budapest made it more rather than less likely that the FKGP would be the great victor in the national elections. Voroshilov was greatly concerned. He suggested that the four parties of the National Front should present a common list.[41] Such an act, of course, would

39 Vas remembered that Rákosi personally promised Voroshilov victory of the workers' parties. When the results came in, the Communist leaders were devastated: "Rákosi, pale as a corpse sank into the chair without saying a word." László Varga, "New Yorki beszélgetés Vas Zoltánnal," *Magyar Nemzet*, October 31, 1992. Quoted in Béla Zselitski, "Postwar Hungary, 1944–1946," in Norman Naimark and Leonid Gibianskii (eds.), *The Establishment of Communist Regimes in Eastern Europe, 1944–1949*, Boulder, CO: Westview, 1997, p. 78.

40 Rákosi, M. *Visszaemlékezések, 1940–1956*, vol. 1, p. 216.

41 FRUS, 1945, vol. 4, p. 895.

14. Elections, November 4, 1945. (Source: Hungarian National Museum.)

have made elections meaningless. The representatives of the four parties ultimately decided that the national elections should proceed as originally scheduled. Nevertheless, they were concerned that the electoral struggle, the sharpening of political differences, in the given situation would be against the national interest. Although the idea of the common list was rejected, largely because of the understandable opposition of the FKGP, the politicians did agree before the elections that the coalition government would continue regardless of the results. This agreement was based on the correct assumption that the Soviet Union would not allow the exclusion of the Communists from the government. Because the Communists could not be excluded, the Socialists and the NPP also had to be included.[42] Furthermore, the FKGP recognized that in the circumstances assuming the responsibility of governing alone and allowing the left to be in opposition would not have been in its interest.

Following the victory of the Smallholders in the Budapest municipal elections, the results of the national elections held on November 4 were not surprising. An astounding 92 percent of those who had the right to vote actually participated in the elections. Fifty-seven percent voted for

42 S. Balogh, 1975, pp. 91–98.

the Smallholders, 16.9 percent for the Communists, 17.4 percent for the Socialists, and only 6.8 percent for the NPP. The two other parties, the Radical Party and the Democratic Party, together had less than 2 percent. The victory of the FKGP was convincing: it won in every county, including the capital. It is remarkable that the committee set up to discuss controversies arising out of violations of the election laws had no work at all. Not a single complaint was made. There could be no question concerning the cleanness and fairness of the elections.

Because the parties had agreed before the election that the coalition government would remain in existence, the only issue to be decided was the distribution of the portfolios among the parties. That Tildy, as leader of the FKGP, would become premier was accepted without discussion in view of the election results. The FKGP without protest conceded half of the ministries to the three other parties of the National Front. Predictably the most contentious issue was which party would receive the portfolio of the ministry of the interior. Not only the FKGP and the MKP, but the Socialists and the leaders of the NPP also wanted to see the minister of the interior come from their own party. It was Stalin himself who gave directions to the Hungarians via Voroshilov, the head of the ACC. Stalin directed them to insist on controlling that most important ministry.[43] Tildy offered a compromise: the division of the ministry into a ministry of the interior and a newly created ministry of state security. In one of these, there would be a Communist minister and an FKGP state secretary, and in the other, it would be the other way around. The Communists, however, having behind them explicit Soviet support, would not compromise and once again prevailed. The other debated issue was less significant. The Communists wanted to make Rákosi and Szakasits deputy premiers, and Tildy offered them only seats in the cabinet without portfolios. Once again, the Communist position prevailed.

The Communists argued that, although they had received only 17 percent of the votes, behind them stood the working class, which was the best-organized force in the country. Therefore the political significance of the working class was greater than its numerical strength; in other words,

43 Voroshilov's report to Stalin and Molotov in Volokitina, pp. 243–245. Voroshilov wrote: "Today Tildy and Nagy Ferenc gave their answer to Rákosi's proposition in connection to your directions." These directions were that the Communists must insist on having the ministry of the interior. In fact, the Hungarian Communists were willing to concede the ministry to the FKGP in exchange for control of the political police. The Central Committee agreed to this arrangement in its meeting on November 8. The Communist position became more intransigent because of directions from Moscow. Balogh, who writes about the change in position, does not mention the directions from Moscow on November 10.

one vote was more valuable than another. This was exactly the same rationalization that Lenin made in 1918 when he disregarded the result of the elections held in November 1917 and dispersed the Constituent Assembly. The Communists further argued that a substantial Communist presence in the government would in itself guarantee to the Soviet Union the good intentions of the Hungarians.[44] It is unlikely that Tildy backed down because of the force of Rákosi's arguments.

Paradoxically, although the left-wing parties were in a majority in the Provisional National Assembly, they were underrepresented in the government; now after elections had created a parliament less favorable to the left, the Communists and their allies actually had much more power where it mattered. The three Socialists belonged to the left wing of the party (Antal Bán, industry; István Ries, justice; Sándor Rónai, trade and cooperatives). Among the FKGP ministers, Gyöngyösi, who was regarded as belonging to the left wing of the party, remained in his post as minister of foreign affairs. István Dobi, a left-wing FKGP leader, joined the cabinet without a portfolio. The Soviets and the Communists most disliked Béla Kovács, who became minister of agriculture. A Soviet agent in Hungary reported to Moscow that Kovács was a determined enemy. The others he described either as politically untried (Károly Bárányos, supplies; József Antall, reconstruction; and Antal Balla, information) or, a worse category, anglophile (Ferenc Gordon, finances; and Jenő Tombor, defense). The NPP got the portfolio of education (Dezsö Keresztury). Of the three Communist ministers, only Gerő, who became minister of transportation, had the full confidence of the Russians. Erik Molnár, who became minister of social welfare, was not among the top leaders. The choice for the much-coveted post of minister of interior fell on Imre Nagy. The Soviet agent reporting to Moscow described him as "weak."[45] Presumably, the Communist leaders chose him because they believed that he possessed a degree of popularity as a result of being associated with land reform. Also, because Nagy was not regarded as a hard-line Communist, his choice was less threatening. He was something of a compromise candidate and satisfactory from the Communist point of view. All that they needed was that the minister should not interfere with the work of the Communist-led political police. The new government had eighteen ministers, of whom nine belonged to the FKGP, four to the MKP, four to the SDP, and one to the NPP. Both the Soviet Union and the United States immediately recognized this

44 Ibid.
45 Tugarev to Paniushkin, December 14, 1945, *Moszkvának Jelentjük*, pp. 87–90.

government.[46] One of the reasons for the quick U.S. recognition was that Washington wanted to stress the distinction it drew between Hungary, where genuine elections had taken place, and the two Balkan countries, Romania and Bulgaria, where they had not.[47]

Now that Hungary had a democratically elected parliament and a coalition government, it was possible to resolve one of the anomalies of the country's constitutional system. Since the Austro-Hungarian monarchy had been dissolved in 1918, Hungary had been without a king. The conservative leaders who came to power in 1919 after the defeat of the short-lived Soviet republic, wanted to preserve the 900-year-old form of state. In any case, the idea of a republic seemed too left wing and "democratic" to them. However, for reasons of international politics, it was impossible to restore the Habsburgs. The surrounding countries that had received large chunks of Hungarian territory vociferously objected to Habsburg restoration. Because all Hungarian rulers from the sixteenth century on came from the Habsburg family, there were no other legitimate claimants to the throne. Under the circumstances, the country remained a kingdom without a king. The "governor," that is, Admiral Nicholas Horthy, was regent. It was obvious that in the vastly changed circumstances this situation could not continue, and the country should become a republic.

On December 1, 1945, it was a Socialist representative in Parliament, Ferenc Szeder, speaking in the name of his party, who raised the question of the declaration of a republic. Immediately, the Communists and the NPP joined in support of the idea. Although the majority of the FKGP was republican, there was a small legitimist wing. But even some of the republicans argued that it was inappropriate to do away with the form of state that had existed for such a long time at a moment when the country was still occupied by foreign troops. Others maintained that in such a significant matter the parliament was not entitled to make a decision, all the more so because the topic had never been mentioned during the electoral campaign.[48] The leaders of the party, Tildy and Ferenc Nagy, argued for the declaration of

46 Although it was the United States that first expressed willingness to establish diplomatic relations with Hungary if free elections would take place, the Soviet representatives requested that the press would say that it was the Soviet Union that recognized the new government first. F. Nagy, vol. 1, p. 217.

47 FRUS, 1945, vol. 4. Leslie Squires, secretary of mission in Hungary, to Schoenfeld, U.S. representative in Hungary, October 11, 1945. Squires wrote: "It was felt, I believe rightly, that the restoration of normal diplomatic relations between Hungary and the United States would emphasize and give added validity to our refusal to do business with the present governments of Rumania and Bulgaria," p. 886.

48 The SDP in its Thirty-Fourth Congress in August did mention that the establishment of the republic was one of its goals. Föglein, pp. 56–57.

15. Hungary becomes a republic, February 1, 1946. (Source: Hungarian National Museum.)

a republic, and the FKGP parliamentary caucus after long debates accepted the arguments of the leaders.[49] There were only two holdouts. The only significant opposition came from the Catholic Church, more precisely from the head of the Church, Cardinal Mindszenty. On January 31, after several days of discussion, the parliament voted for the republic against one negative vote: Margit Slachta, a nun, who in her speech defended not only the idea of monarchy but also the Habsburgs.[50] On February 1, 1946, Hungary became a republic.

Who should become the president of the new republic was discussed even before the vote was taken in parliament over the republican form

49 Ibid., pp. 56–74. The British and the Americans let the Smallholder politicians know that they had no objection to constitutional change. The fact that Hungary was a kingdom in the interwar period had caused concern in the neighboring countries, which regarded the form of state as a manifestation of revanchism. It seemed a good idea to get rid of this irritant before the peace conference.

50 Slachta was a remarkable woman. She was a nun and became the first female representative in the Hungarian parliament in 1920. Her political views were anti-Socialist, antiliberal, and antimodern. In the parliament, her most famous vote was to impose corporal punishment on speculators. She was a legitimist, and after the end of the Second World War she entirely agreed with the politics of Cardinal Mindszenty. Time and again, she showed great political courage. Among the prominent members of the Catholic Church, she spoke up against the persecution of the Jews most courageously.

of state. One possibility was Mihály Károlyi, a scion of one of the most prominent aristocratic families and the leader of the democratic revolution of 1918; he had spent the interwar years in exile. He was supported by the majority of the SDP and also by the two small liberal parties. Had he returned immediately after the war from exile, he might have improved his chances. As it was, he received no support from the Communists, and the leaders of the FKGP insisted that they should be able to name the president. Under the circumstances the real choice came down to two leaders of the FKGP, Tildy and Ferenc Nagy. Because Nagy was regarded as a centrist and Tildy a left-wing leader of his party, the Communists preferred Tildy.[51] On February 1 with a voice vote, the parliament unanimously elected Zoltán Tildy as first president of the republic.

The elections in the fall of 1945 were a turning point in the politics of the Communist party and to a lesser extent in the attitude of the Soviet leadership toward Hungary. It is clear that the Communists had expected far greater support than they in fact received. Such an outcome did not moderate their ambition; on the contrary, they came to believe that their enemies – and they made no distinction among conservatives, reactionaries, and fascists – were out to get them. They insisted on having control over the machinery of repression (i.e., the political police) not only because they were determined to take the offensive, but also because they were afraid that their opponents, if given a chance, would use the police against them. In the Communists' perception of politics, the defeated deserved no mercy, and they were genuinely concerned that their enemies would treat them the same way as they would deal with the defeated. Similarly, the Soviet leaders came to appreciate that if the Hungarians were allowed to select their leaders freely, an anti-Soviet government would arise.

51 Tildy's father-in-law, a teacher, who in 1919 was a member of a local Communist-led directorate, was murdered by the White guardists. This fact made him more acceptable to the Communists. Haas, p. 22.

5

Land Reform

In the self-perception of the Hungarian people, Hungary was a peasant country, and the peasantry was the possessor of particular national virtues and characteristics. A large and intellectually impressive segment of the pre-war intelligentsia had devoted their talents to the study and, they hoped, the betterment of the impoverished, often landless peasantry. Their writings, objectively descriptive but at the same time passionate, prepared the soil for the social transformation that was to take place in 1945.

Land reform was by far the most significant social issue the country faced at the end of the war. Hungary needed a social revolution, and that meant, above all, the destruction of the great estates together with the social and political system resting on them. The conquest of the country by the Red Army was the source of a great deal of suffering and misery, but at the same time that army made it possible, indeed, inevitable, that this much-needed revolution would be carried out immediately and rapidly. The Soviet Army brought with itself the land reform that solved an age-old problem. Therefore, according to István Bibo, the great liberal political theorist, 1945 could be regarded as a "liberation" because the land reform finally destroyed the antiquated feudal system. As he put it, "for the first time since 1514 [the date of the codification of serfdom] the rigid social system started to move, and move in the direction of greater freedom."[1]

At the end of the war, two-thirds of the population lived in villages, and aside from Budapest the country had only three cities with a population larger than 100,000.[2] Although economic development in the inter-war years had been substantial and Budapest had become an industrial enclave, Hungary remained primarily an agricultural country. Half of the

1 Bibó, 1994, p. 325.

2 Tibor Valuch, *Magyarország társadalom története a XX század második felében*, Budapest: Osiris, 2002, p. 62.

population continued to be engaged in agriculture, producing 40 percent of the national income.[3] A handful of aristocratic families possessed a disproportionate amount of cultivated land, and 40 percent of the village population were landless or possessed such small plots that they could not support themselves. Politics and economics were interrelated. The prewar Horthy regime, in which the old feudal aristocracy continued to play a dominant role, had been determined to protect the large estates.[4] As a consequence, Hungary had the most unfair land distribution anywhere in Eastern and Central Europe. After World War I when all countries in this region carried out land reform, the Hungarian version was the stingiest and least meaningful. Not only was an extremely small portion of the agricultural land distributed (about 8 percent), but that land was then divided among too many landless peasants, with each receiving such small, economically unviable parcels that the new owners soon fell back into poverty. Mechanization and the use of fertilizers hardly increased in the interwar period, and therefore agricultural productivity remained static. Per-acre productivity fell ever more behind that of Western Europe. The great depression was a particularly hard blow to Hungary. The fall of agricultural prices on the international market reduced a large segment of the peasantry to destitution and further delayed the introduction of mechanization. Contemporary observers often spoke of 3 million beggars in a country of 9 million.

The Communists had been preoccupied for years with the question of land reform. They had spent a great deal of time and effort evaluating the reasons for the failure of the Hungarian Soviet Republic of 1919. They attributed their failure in 1919 in part to their unwillingness to distribute land among the peasants, thereby winning them over. What made such a conclusion all the easier to reach was that in the Soviet revolution of 1917, on the first day after victory, Lenin proclaimed his famous "decree on land," allowing the peasants to cultivate the land as if it were their private property. The critics never failed to point out that the fault of the Hungarian leadership had been that it chose not to follow the Russian example.[5]

In the fall of 1944, the Hungarian Communists, enjoying the relative comfort of Moscow, were the only party able to prepare a political program

3 Romsics, 1999, p. 160.

4 How committed the Horthy regime was to the maintenance of the system of large estates, and how out of touch Horthy himself was with reality, is demonstrated by an exchange between Horthy and Tildy. On October 11, 1944, Horthy met Tildy and Szakasits. Even at that late a moment, Horthy attempted to persuade Tildy to drop the demand for land reform from the party program. István Vida, *A Független Kisgazda Párt Politikája, 1944–1947*, Budapest: Akadémia, 1976, p. 29.

5 Péter Gunst, "A Magyar agrártársadalom 1919–1945 között," in Péter Gunst (ed.), *A magyar agrártársadalom a jobbágy felszabadulástól napjainkig*, Budapest: Napvilág, 1998, p. 239.

16. Imre Nagy, 1896–1958.

appropriate for postliberation Hungary, and their program would give land reform a central place. In September 1944, Imre Nagy, an agricultural economist, was entrusted with the task of working out a reform plan. The importance attributed to land reform by the Communists was signaled by their insistence on claiming the portfolio of agriculture in the provisional government. Imre Nagy was the obvious candidate for this post, which he, in fact, assumed at the end of December 1944, and, with very few modifications, his plan became the basis of what was introduced by the provisional government a few months later.[6]

That land reform must be introduced after the war was not a debated issue; the need for it had been widely discussed even before the war. By the beginning of 1945, there was no longer any organized opposition to the idea, but the practical details of what kind of land reform and how radical it would be soon led to an intense struggle among the political parties. The first debate concerned the Council of Ministers' right to resolve such an important matter by issuing regulations rather than waiting for a legislative resolution. The problem in March 1945 was that the war was still unfinished, making it very difficult to reconvene the Provisional National Assembly, which had been suspended after only two days of meetings in December 1944.[7] The Smallholder Party politicians, not without justification, accused the Communist Party of pushing through the land reform without proper preparations.

6 János Rainer, *Nagy Imre: Politikai Életrajz, 1896–1953*, Budapest: 1956–os Intézet, 1996, pp. 236–237.

7 MOL XVIII – March 3, 1945, Kecskemét. Indeed the representative of the Civic Democratic Party wrote to the head of the Provisional Assembly, Zsedényi, asking why the law concerning land reform was not issued by the Provisional Assembly.

The Communist Party did not oppose convening the Provisional National Assembly; it was not convened, however, because K. E. Voroshilov, the head of the ACC, intervened. In fact, the Soviet authorities took a great interest in the Hungarian land reform from the very beginning. From their point of view, it was essential that the land be divided as soon as possible in order to encourage defections from the still-combatant Hungarian army. The Russians believed that land reform would favorably influence peasant soldiers, making the Red Army's task easier.[8] Voroshilov wanted land to be promised to those who defected from the Hungarian army and wanted the full text of the reform project to be distributed in those parts of the country not yet liberated.[9] Although a few months earlier Stalin himself had instructed the Hungarian Communists to avoid appearing as enemies of private property, now both military and foreign policy considerations impelled the Russians to support an immediate land reform project expected to find wide support among the Hungarian peasantry.

The Communists presented their plan in the form of a government regulation at a meeting of party representatives on March 15. In earlier proposals the Smallholders and the Socialists had planned the division of estates larger than 500 holds (710 acres). The Communist plan of 100- and 200-hold limits was therefore more radical. Some participants in this meeting, for example, Imre Kovács representing the NPP, expressed concern that a radical division of the land would create problems providing food for the cities in the short run and therefore proposed a two-tier program, starting first with a division of estates larger than 500 holds and only later taking away smaller estates.[10] The Communist plan of making a distinction between the holdings of large landowners and peasants was difficult to carry out in reality. In fact, the Communists introduced a third category as well: those who had resisted the Nazis were allowed to retain 300 holds. The distinction between "landlord" and peasant categories enabled the Communists to declare some peasants who seemed to be anti-Communists as "landlords."

The interparty meeting of March 15 was something of a formality. The plans had been prepared, the posters had been printed, and Soviet support assured. Voroshilov once again intervened in support of the Communist position, and on March 18 the government issued a regulation concerning the implementation of the land reform.[11] It is noteworthy that this most important piece of legislation was issued as a government regulation,

8 Rainer, p. 272, and Rákosi, vol. 1, p. 226.
9 Eric Roman, *Hungary and the Victor Powers, 1945–1950*, New York: St. Martin's Press, 1996, p. 41.
10 Kovács, p. 235.
11 *Pártközi értekezletek*, p. 21.

and the Provisional Assembly gave its imprimatur ex post facto only on September 16.

The regulations started out with a preamble, which pointed out that ending the system of large landowning was essential for building a democratic polity in Hungary. The land reform project envisaged the creation of a national land fund created from the confiscated estates. The state confiscated all lands from "traitors," that is, those who had collaborated with the Nazis, and also from the German minority, the so-called Swabs, who had identified themselves with Nazi Germany. Landowners lost their property greater than 100 holds, but peasants who worked their own lands could retain 200 holds. The government also confiscated forests, vineyards, and agricultural implements that had belonged to the great estates. The regulations promised compensation for land that was to be taken over, but estates larger than 1000 holds were to be confiscated without compensation. Of course, traitors did not receive compensation. The overseeing of the land reform was entrusted to the ministry of agriculture. The charge, made by FKGP leader, Ferenc Nagy, that this project served political rather than economic goals was difficult to dispute. Ferenc Nagy would have preferred the reform to be carried out gradually and the task of supervising it to be entrusted to agronomists rather than committees made up of poor peasants.[12] He would have allowed all landowners, regardless of the size of their estates, to retain at least 100 holds. However, his idea that the land reform should be carried out gradually did not even have the support of his own party. The left wing of the FKGP agreed with the Communists that the reform had to be carried out immediately.

Under Communist direction and with the aid of the Soviet army, the peasants who claimed land from the newly created land fund set up committees in the villages.[13] Setting up these committees was a crucial aspect of Communist propaganda work. The Communists attempted to convince the peasants that the Communist Party was now in a position to help them, and it was doing so. The organization of the committees began immediately after the arrival of the Red Army. They came into being in February, that is, before the actual publication of the land reform project and before the entire country had been liberated. The Communists on occasion encouraged spontaneous land grabs by the peasants. The party regarded these acts as a mobilizing device. It was to be expected that under the circumstances there would be a great deal of confusion and lawlessness in the process of

12 Nagy, vol. 1, pp. 144–147.

13 There is a good description of the process of the land reform by Sándor Szakács, "A földosztástól a kollektivizálásig," in Gunst (ed.), *A magyar társadalom . . .*, pp. 285–314.

occupying land. This was a revolutionary process, often carried out within a few days and at times with the aid of Red Army soldiers. The haphazard, spontaneous taking of land well suited the Communists' conception of social revolution. On the other hand, the land reform project was seen by the country, and in particular by politicians from the other parties, as an entirely Communist project, and they resented it.[14]

The most radical acts took place in the early months after liberation. It was the most confused period, at a time when people paid the least attention to legal niceties. Furthermore, Eastern Hungary, which was liberated first, was also the poorest and most radical part of the country. Here the demand for land was the greatest, because it had the largest number of landless peasants and the least land available for distribution. There was no force to prevent the peasants from taking more property than the land reform plan had called for.

From late spring, the process became more orderly. From this point on, it was possible to complain about lawlessness, and, indeed, there were more and more complaints that lands had been seized contrary to the provisions of the regulations. Also, petitions started to come to the Political Committee of the Provisional National Assembly asking that the petitioners be allowed to retain certain lands because of their left-wing past, or because they had saved Jews or otherwise publicly opposed the previous regime.[15]

The result of the reform was that altogether 75,000 estates, 5.6 million holds, were expropriated or confiscated, which represented 35 percent of the country's territory.[16] Even this large-scale expropriation did not provide adequate land for the claimants: the average amount of land that was given to a family was only five holds (7.1 acres). Who should get land was difficult to establish, at least in part because a considerable number of landless peasants were still prisoners of war. The land committees made an attempt to help families with several children. On the other hand, there were peasants who were afraid to claim their share because of concerns that the Germans might return and punish those who had taken landlord land. Between 1945 and 1949, the onset of collectivization, the percentage of landless peasants dropped from 46.8 percent to 17 percent. At the end of 1945, every third peasant was a beneficiary of the reform, because not only the landless received property but also those who had cultivated uneconomically small plots. A special problem was what to do with Church property. Before the

14 PIL 274 7/25 Rákosi's letter to Gerő, March 27, 1945.

15 MOL XVIII – 3 – 1.

16 Ivan T. Berend and György Ránki, *The Hungarian Economy in the Twentieth Century*, London: Croom Helm, 1985, p. 183.

17. Land reform, 1945. (Source: Hungarian National Museum.)

war, the Catholic Church had been the largest landowner in the country, possessing 16 percent of the cultivated land. The land reform plan took away most of the property belonging to the bishoprics, but allowed 100 holds for the support of village priests. The Communists hoped to insert a wedge between the village priests and the Church hierarchy.

Those who received land did not get it without paying compensation. There was general agreement that the new owners should pay. Interestingly, not only did all the political parties and those who lost land believe in the necessity of paying compensation, but the new owners also took it for granted. They assumed that they could own something only if they had paid for it. On average, peasants paid approximately one quarter of the assessed value of the land. They were obliged to pay the state in installments over the next ten or twenty years. Those who had the smallest estates were allowed longer terms for repayment.[17] The peasants' debt to the state had political significance. In the immediate postwar period, the state made no serious attempt to make the peasants pay, but at the time of collectivization this became one additional source of pressure on peasants who were reluctant to

17 Ibid., p. 85.

join the collective farms. In reality, the ex-landowners did not receive any compensation. At this time of inflation and extraordinary economic hardship, the state could not have repaid the landowners even if it had intended to. After the Communist monopoly of power was established in 1948, compensation of landlords was taken off the agenda. The Hungarian land reform was the most radical carried out anywhere in the postwar period.[18] It was here that radical change was most needed.

What kind of agriculture would be created after the land reform? The Communist party's program in the immiediate postwar years called for the defense of agricultural private property. At a time when it was still fighting for public support, any other policy would have been harmful. Among the peasantry there was already constant talk that the Communists would force them into joining collective farms, an institution that was deeply unpopular. In this matter, the Communist agitators were constantly on the defensive. The Communist position at this time was that the period of transition into a Socialist society would be a long one. Communist leaders in their speeches emphasized that peasant property was not exploitative, so there was no need to destroy it.

The government's economic policies, however, did not favor the peasantry. When it succeeded in overcoming a dreadful and destructive inflation, it still was not ready to free agricultural prices. The authorities set prices not on the basis of the world market or by supply and demand, but to satisfy political and economic goals. In order to stimulate industrial recovery, the government set the relation of agricultural versus industrial prices so as to favor industry. As compared to prewar prices, the increase in industrial prices was much higher than that of agricultural prices.[19] If we add to the artificially low prices the compulsory delivery system, then it becomes evident that in spite of the recent land reform, the lot of the peasantry remained desperate. As a consequence, it could be said that it was the peasantry that paid most dearly for the successes of the reconstruction, even though the peasantry remained the most disadvantaged class in the emerging social structure. The peasants did not have capital for improvements or for buying agricultural machinery. The machinery of the large estates had been distributed, but what was appropriate for the large estates was not what was needed on the small strips of land.

The situation in the countryside remained desperate. In spite of the radical land reform, not every landless peasant was able to acquire land. Also, there

18 Berend and Ránki, p. 184.

19 Iván Pető and Sándor Szakács, p. 68.

18. New landowners receive their documents, July 5, 1947. (Source: Hungarian National Museum.)

remained many whose property was so small as to be incapable of supporting a family. The small strips of land that most peasants cultivated were not likely to produce even as much as the antiquated but large feudal estates had before the war. The countryside suffered both from urban and especially rural unemployment. The disappearance of large estates meant that agricultural laborers had no job opportunities. Public works, such as road building, which in the past gave employment to many, now were suspended for lack of funds. Meanwhile, the size of the village population was growing as the collapse of industry and the shortage of food in the cities encouraged many who still had relatives in the villages to return to the countryside. In the fall of 1947, there were at least 100,000 unemployed in the villages.[20] Those who had recently acquired land remained insecure and feared the return of the old order and the loss of their newly acquired land. In order to reassure the new landowners that they were legal owners, the government continued to employ land surveyors and issue ownership documents.

Under Communist auspices, the National Organization of New Landowners (UFOSZ) was created in March 1946 to defend the interests of

20 Sándor Orbán, *Két agrárforradalom Magyarországon: Demokratikus és szocialista agrárátalakulás, 1945–1961*, Budapest: Akadémia, 1972, p. 46.

the new landowners. Within a year, out of the 3280 villages, 2100 had local UFOSZ organizations.[21] In September of that year, UFOSZ held its first national conference. The Communists used UFOSZ as a counterweight to the Peasant Union, set up by the FKGP, that hoped to unify the peasantry under its own influence. In UFOSZ meetings, the peasants expressed repeatedly the same concerns: the determination not to return land (even if at the time of the reform it was taken in contravention of the paragraphs of the land reform law) or to return animals (even if these had been taken from Jews who had been deported). The peasants also wanted a reduction of government obligations, loans, seeds, and so forth.[22] The demands for reduction of obligations and loans were not satisfied. The government, even before the Communist conquest of power, was primarily interested in the revival of industry, which then received most of the investment and loans. The production of artificial fertilizers did not begin in the postwar years.

It is evident from the reports of the village agitators that the influence of the Communist Party remained weak in the villages. Communist ideology had little appeal to the peasants, the economic program of the party did not favor them, and the party had no reliable cadres in the countryside. Talking about a "proletarian revolution," as some of the Communists were wont to do, obviously made a bad impression in the countryside. Imre Nagy in his report to Moscow admitted that the Catholic Church was a stronger presence in the countryside than the Communist Party. He also mentioned as an example of weakness that the local committees often included no peasant members but only people sent from the cities.[23] The fundamental dilemma of Communist agricultural politics was that, on the one hand, the party aimed to modernize and improve efficiency, while on the other, it claimed to defend the interests of the peasants who had just received mostly small parcels that could not be efficiently cultivated.

In the fall of 1946, the peasant policies of the party were still strikingly moderate. Imre Nagy was the man responsible for agricultural policies within the Communist leadership. In his speeches and articles in these years, he usually took a more moderate tone than the other leaders of the party, in particular, Rákosi. He saw the improvement of agriculture in increased mechanization, better agricultural education, and developing cooperatives. In his speech to the Third Party Congress, Nagy stressed

21 RTsKhIDNI fond 17, opis 128, delo 315, p. 44. Report by Imre Nagy.
22 PIL 274 17/12 March 16–17, 1946.
23 RTsKhIDNI fond 17, opis 128, delo 315, p. 44. Report by Imre Nagy.

that the Communists were not aiming at the creation of a Socialist society. He said:

> Already before the war our party had developed its theoretical position and made clear its views concerning the agrarian question. Already then we stated the fundamental principle of our agrarian policy: in Hungary the time has not come for moving from capitalism to socialism. The time has not yet come for the struggle between two social systems. The task is to get rid of the still powerful remnants of feudalism. What we are dealing with is a struggle within the capitalist system: a struggle between democracy and reaction.[24]

He repeatedly emphasized that the goal of the party was the protection of the small estates.

The radical land reform of 1945 introduced a new social and economic system in the Hungarian villages. The landowning aristocracy disappeared, and the number and percentage of landless agricultural laborers greatly diminished. The new agricultural system, based on small estates, functioned for a very short time, only four years. During that period, a number of factors made the economic environment unfavorable: the destruction of the war, the confusion caused by the reform itself, industry's inability to provide the peasantry with the necessary implements, and even bad weather conditions. In view of the unfavorable circumstances and the brief period of this new system, it is impossible to know whether it could eventually have overcome age-old backwardness and approached Western European standards of production.

24 Rainer, p. 329.

6

Salami Tactics

HUNGER

The bitter political struggles of 1945 and 1946 took place against a background of wretched poverty and privation. Ironically, even though the sponsor of the Communist Party, the Soviet Union, was responsible to a considerable extent, the dreadful economic conditions helped the Communists' struggle for power. Their radical policies seemed more reasonable at a time when normal economic policies did not promise quick relief. They could use demagogic slogans blaming the troubles of the nation on "reactionaries," black marketeers, and other ill-defined enemies, though it was obvious that the black market was not the cause but the consequence of the economic problems. Help could come only from the Soviet Union, and the Communists could argue that they were in the best position to ask for such help. Indeed, the party to a considerable extent succeeded in claiming credit for successes in reconstruction and for the introduction of a stable currency that took place on August 1, 1946.

It is hard to describe the extent of the misery of the first postwar year. The entire country suffered, but the capital was in a particularly bad position. Because fuel was unavailable, people were shivering in their cold, windowless apartments. In the middle of the winter, schools had to be closed down temporarily because the schoolrooms could not be heated. People worked in unheated offices. A new word was coined, *szénszünet*, meaning "coal vacation."

In Budapest, the food supply situation in late winter and early spring of 1945 was indeed catastrophic. When the siege had just ended, a deputy mayor of the city, accompanied by representatives of political parties, traveled to Debrecen to report to the provisional government on the supply situation and said among other things: "There are families whose members have not seen bread for weeks. A segment of the population during the siege received its sustenance from animal cadavers on the streets. Budapest would need 100 supply wagons daily. Only once did we receive 40 wagons, but since then nothing."[1]

Because the authorities could not help, people took matters into their own hands. Many traveled to the countryside on trains, which operated unpredictably, and were so overcrowded that people were sitting on top of the wagons, hanging on to one another. They traveled in order to exchange with the peasants their clothes or other valuables for food. From the villages, they brought back potatoes, flour, lard, or whatever they could get to alleviate hunger. On the edge of famine, Budapest reverted to bazaar-like barter on the main avenues and squares of the city.[2] The government could not assure even a minimal food supply. It experimented with soup kitchens in order to feed the neediest, but it could not even supply these. Some of the workers in the factories, once these factories started to work once again, managed to receive food in their workplace. Zoltán Vas, who was appointed commissar responsible for the capital's food supply on February 15, 1945, ordered that all available land in the city be cultivated. Most people had to resort to a flourishing black market. Black marketeers, not surprisingly, created great hostility among those who could not afford the exorbitant prices. The Communists did not refrain from using the opportunity for political benefit by agitating against private traders.

Although a system of rationing had been introduced at the end of the war, the authorities could not deliver even what was promised on the ration cards. In Budapest, the daily bread ration at the end of 1945 was reduced from twenty to fifteen decagrams.[3] The situation in the spring of 1945 was the most difficult, but matters did not improve a great deal during the first year. The wheat harvest in 1945 was only one-third of the prewar average. The disastrous harvest was the consequence of three factors: 1. under wartime conditions normal agricultural work could not be performed,[4] 2. in 1945 and in 1946 the country suffered from a drought, and 3. the recent land reform created confusion and uncertainties.

Aside from an absolute shortage of food, the government had great difficulty in organizing a network of distribution. Because of the lack of coal and

1 *Népszava*, February 16, 1945. Reprinted in *Pártközi értekezletek,* pp. 18–19.

2 Vas, vol. 2, p. 98. According to Vas, who was responsible for supplying the capitoal with food, in March the Soviet Union organized a delivery of food to the capital that included potatoes, wheat, and sugar. Of course the food products were Hungarian while the Russians provided trucks and railroad carriages. The Russians gave the food for which the Hungarians paid.

3 Varga.

4 Pető and Szakács, p. 43.

the destruction of train engines and rolling stock, the rail network could not function. The government also lacked trucks. As a result, at the end of 1945 the rationing system in Budapest provided only 550 calories per day, less than that in any major European city. Even in Berlin, the rations were twice as large.[5] (By contrast, during the interwar period the daily average calorie consumption in Hungary had been 2700.[6]) Perhaps with the exception of Romania, the situation of food supply in Hungary was the worst among the surrounding countries.[7]

Because of the lack of fodder, the peasants slaughtered their horses and other draft animals. Before the war, only about 10 percent of the arable land had been cultivated with the use of tractors, but now even the undamaged tractors could not be used because of the lack of fuel. The diminished number of horses and oxen very much delayed recovery.[8] The consequence of the slaughter was that animal husbandry was very slow to recover. The country did not have enough grain to cover the seed requirements for next year's harvest.

During the war, the Horthy regime created a new government department for food supply. In 1943, Béla Jurcsek, the minister responsible for the new department, had imposed compulsory deliveries of grain on landed properties, the amount depending on the size of the estate.[9] Gábor Faragho, the ex-gendarmerie general, headed this department in the provisional government. The ministry continued the system of requiring compulsory deliveries and extended it to an ever-larger list of products. The fundamental problem was that the free market could not function because the peasants' incentive to sell was undercut both by the hyperinflation and the fact that industry was unable to provide goods for the peasants to buy in any case. The government had no other means available but coercion. It issued more and more regulations concerning peasant obligations and organized committees to see that the regulations were carried out.

Obviously, the problems of agriculture and industry could not be separated. As long as the factories could not produce consumer goods, the revival of normal free market exchange could not be expected. In the first months after the conclusion of hostilities, the majority of industrial enterprises were under Soviet supervision and produced to satisfy the needs of the occupiers. The government, in order to make sure that the demands for reparations would be satisfied and the peasants would be provided with

5 FRUS, 1945, vol. 4, p. 919. Information from Károly Bárányos, minister of supplies, to Schoenfeld.
6 Pető and Szakács, p. 42.
7 Ibid., pp. 45–51.
8 Ibid., p. 42.
9 *Pártközi értkezletek*, p. 7.

the necessities, had to interfere in every aspect of industrial production. It was these circumstances rather than ideological commitment that prevented the revival of the free market. The rights of owners of industrial enterprises came to be further diminished by the increased role of trade unions, which were steadily coming under Communist, rather than Socialist, domination.

The Western contribution to recovery was minimal. Aladár Szegedy-Maszák, the Hungarian ambassador designate in Washington, begged for assistance on his arrival in early 1946. The United Nations Relief and Rehabilitation Administration (UNRRA) approved an aid package of $4 million in January 1946. Aside from UNRRA, the American Jewish charity organization, JOINT, provided help. Although any help was welcome, clearly this was only a drop in the bucket. In February, Ambassador Schoenfeld reported to the state department that the economic situation in the country was desperate. Money had become worthless, rioting was to be expected in Budapest, and the Hungarian authorities seemed incapable of dealing with the crisis. American diplomats, of course, were well aware of successful Soviet efforts to tie Romania and Bulgaria into the Soviet economic sphere and saw that the Hungarian situation would not be different. The particular points of the Soviet-Hungarian economic treaty, negotiated in Moscow in August and finally ratified by the newly elected parliament in December, plus the establishment of Soviet-Hungarian joint stock companies, indicated that, in spite of the democratically elected government, Hungary would be part of the Soviet sphere of influence at least economically. The ambassador saw a consistent and conscious Soviet policy aimed at reducing Hungary to the status of an economic satellite. In his view, Moscow would be interested in rehabilitation of the economy only after that goal had been achieved. Then the United States would be faced with a dilemma: to help the country, even though it would be obvious that such help would primarily benefit the Soviet masters, or to allow the creation of an economic basket case in the middle of Europe.[10] Such a situation would have a negative impact on the reconstruction of Europe and therefore would be contrary to American interests.

Nevertheless, by the spring of 1946 the United States gave up on Hungary, at least to the extent that it did not consider it worthwhile to extend material support. The ambassador, who in the winter of 1945–1946 still supported the idea of giving some help to the country and engaging it in commercial relations, by May changed his opinion and advised against assistance.[11]

10 Ibid., pp. 258–260.

11 Ibid., pp. 293–294.

The United States was not only unwilling to extend significant help but also was uninterested in entering normal commercial exchange with Budapest. The Americans refused to buy Hungarian meat (at a time when there were considerable supplies, because the peasants had to slaughter their animals for the lack of fodder) or even the famous Hungarian export article, paprika.[12] Whether the Americans were correct in deciding that there was no point in giving any support to Hungary is difficult to say. But unquestionably, they contributed to the misery of the population and discouraged and demoralized their Hungarian friends. In general, American representatives showed little understanding and sympathy for the centrist politicians in the government who were forced to give one concession after another to the Russians. American intervention and appeals came only in defense of American economic interests, and even in that area they were rarely successful. The Hungarian government had no alternative but to open up the country to Soviet economic penetration.

In the winter and early spring of 1946, the government had three basic tasks: 1. providing enough food for the population to avoid starvation; 2. getting enough coal to make the trains run, heat apartments in the cities, and restart the factories; 3. stopping the inflation that had acquired a dynamic of its own and was reaching levels that had never been seen in world history. In order to deal with the seemingly overwhelming problems, the government established the Chief Economic Council, headed by the premier, Tildy, and including the left-wing FKGP István Dobi, a minister without portfolio; the two deputy premiers, Rákosi and Szakasits; Ernö Gerő, minister of transport; and Antal Bán, minister of industry. However, the real force in this powerful organization was not the members of the government, but the secretary of the Council, the Communist Zoltán Vas. Vas was an energetic and able man, who, although not a trained economist, had acquired experience in this field first as a man responsible for the supply of Budapest in the immediate postliberation period, and then as mayor of the capital.[13] One of the few Communist leaders possessing at least a degree of genuine popularity, Vas nonetheless lost the job of mayor as a result of the FKGP victory in the Budapest municipal elections.

The establishment of the Chief Economic Council meant that the Communist party in fact took possession of the direction of the economy. There

12 FRUS, 1945, vol. 4, November 26, secretary of state to Schoenfeld, pp. 912–913. The Americans refused a proposed agreement according to which the Hungarians would deliver textiles for American cotton. They were, however, willing to sell cotton, assuming that the Hungarians were able to pay. Ultimately, the cotton came from the Soviet Union. See also Borhi, p. 33.

13 Vas, vol. 2, p. 164.

were several factors that assured Communist domination. The most important of these was Soviet support. Hungary was prostrate before a victorious Soviet Union that continued to demand deliveries of goods as reparation, and Communists were best placed to moderate Soviet requirements. The non-Socialist politicians' position was weakened by the lack of Western aid. In any case, the economic situation – not only in Hungary but also in other countries that faced similar problems – required government intervention in the economic life of the nation.

The bottleneck for the recovery of industry was the lack of coal. Vas, aside from his role on the Economic Council, was also named government commissioner for coal production. In this crisis situation, the government decided to nationalize the mines, which was the first step leading ultimately to the complete destruction of private enterprise. This step was popular among the workers. According to a survey carried out by the socialist public opinion research organization, 66 percent of the workers supported the idea and only 21 percent opposed it. Even among the intelligentsia, a plurality supported it (45 percent versus 33 percent), arguing that only the state possessed the capital to modernize the mines.[14]

Of course, nationalization in itself could not solve the problem. It was a vicious circle: the government could not feed the miners, therefore there was not enough coal, and in the absence of fuel the factories could not produce. A Soviet representative in Hungary, M. Burtsev, reported to Mikhail Suslov that 5000 miners decided to go on strike to protest the lack of food in the coal mines of the Mecsek region in the beginning of May. He added approvingly that sixty-five ringleaders had been arrested. He also reported on disturbances in Hodmezövásárhely, where the crowd, mostly women, had attacked small merchants in the market and proceeded to break into the building where the city's food supply was kept. The cause of the disturbance was the poor quality of bread that had been distributed on the basis of rations cards.[15]

Whether the critical situation should be used for imposing further limits on private enterprise was a debated issue within the Communist leadership. That government intervention in the economy was a necessity at the moment was not open to question. The issue was how far these controls should go. On the one hand, Gerő wanted to go as far as possible, whereas, on the other, Vas wanted the revival of small private industry and trade at

14 PIL 283 32/31 February 6, 1946.

15 RTsHIDNI fond 17, opis 128, delo 124, p. 56.

19. Mátyás Rákosi, 1892–1971.

least temporarily as a necessary condition for economic revival.[16] For the time being, Vas prevailed.

An aspect of the economic collapse was the inflation that reached its height in the first half of 1946. The problem had not started in 1945, but during the war as the government financed war expenditures by printing money. With the collapse of the economy, the government's intake was reduced to close to zero while the demands of reparations and the necessities of reconstruction could be accomplished only by printing more and more money. In addition to the government, the Soviet occupation authorities also printed money. The government was compelled to issue loans to industrial enterprises that lacked capital. From June to December 1945, the value of the pengö declined two-hundred-fold.[17] Wages could never keep up with the rise of prices, and the condition of the working classes accordingly deteriorated. The inflation became so extreme that the normal banking system of lending money to enterprises came to a halt. The inflation also made the normal taxation system impossible because, in the time between the establishment of a tax obligation and its payment, the value of the pengö declined to such an extent as to make taxation useless as a source of government revenue. The finance ministry introduced the so-called "tax pengő," whose value changed from day to day. At the height of the inflation, at the end of July 1946, the daily inflation rate was 158,486 percent and the value of a dollar was 4,600,000 quadrillion.[18] Given the extent of the inflation, the population was compelled to turn to barter. Under the circumstances,

16 Vas, vol. 2, p. 167.

17 In fact, the intake of the government in the second half of 1945 covered only 7 percent of the expenses. Pető and Szakács, p. 58.

18 Ibid., p. 61.

it was inevitable that there would develop a large-scale black market in dollars, gold, and other valuables. Those who made their living on the basis of wages and salaries bore the brunt of the financial collapse.

The decisively important step in revitalizing the economy was the ending of inflation by the introduction of new currency, the forint, on August 1, 1946. The date was chosen to correspond to the new harvest and the availability of food. The government decided to take drastic steps in order to assure the success of stabilization. On this issue, the representatives of all parties agreed that they would not use prostabilization propaganda for political gain against one another. There was agreement also on the necessity of reducing the number of government employees. The harsh measures included fixed prices, depressed wages, and the requirement that the population hand over to the state gold and foreign currencies, mostly dollars. The Smallholder representatives did not dispute the need for capital punishment of economic crimes.[19]

Of course, it was not possible to put the new currency on the gold standard, nor was it possible to get a foreign loan large enough to protect the forint. Nevertheless, it helped that the United States returned the country's gold reserves, which it had recovered from the Germans, and that the Soviet Union rescheduled reparation deliveries.[20] Financial policy was based on the state setting prices both for agricultural products and for the most important industrial goods. These prices were set in such a way as to favor the industrial working class; that is, agricultural prices were set artificially low. But even industrial wages did not keep up with the recovery of industry. At a time when industry was already able to produce 75 percent of prewar output, real wages were only 50 percent of the 1938 level.[21]

The artificially low agricultural prices meant that the burden of stabilization was disproportionately borne by the peasantry. It also meant that there was a very great incentive for the peasants to take advantage of the continued flourishing of the black market. The government fought back by extending control over more and more aspects of the economy. It was inclined to use force increasingly often. Already in June 1945, the Communist-led police established an economic department, which punished severely those who did not observe regulations.[22] In the course of 1946 and 1947, thousands of people were jailed. The Communist Party also saw the opportunity for

19 *Pártközi értekezletek*, pp. 248–254.

20 FRUS, 1946, vol. 6, p. 329.

21 Pető and Szakács, p. 71.

22 PIL 274 11/8. The reports of the police repeatedly mention hatred against those who live well and a demand to take action against the black marketeers. The police occupied factories and confiscated goods.

demagogic agitation against black marketeers, an agitation that often had anti-Semitic overtones.

It would be a mistake to lose sight of the genuine achievements in reconstruction while depicting the evident and difficult problems of the economy. The peasants, in spite of the unfavorable market conditions and without any outside help, did begin to work and produce. The workers in the cities removed the rubble remarkably quickly, demolished buildings that could not be saved, and attempted to restart work in the factories. Public transport in Budapest did resume practically within weeks after the end of the siege. At least some of the bridges in the capital were rebuilt with Soviet help. Ernő Gerő, the Communist minister of transportation, claimed credit for this success. Most important, in spite of the hardships, many people were optimistic. They believed that it was worthwhile to rebuild and to start businesses, and enterprising people ventured to open restaurants or shops. In spite of the problems and pain, a striking degree of optimism remained among segments of the population. Most people believed in a better future.

COMMUNIST GAINS, SPRING 1946

The establishment of a democratically elected parliament and the creation of a coalition government encouraged various political forces to formulate or reformulate their ideas about the future of the country. The peculiarity of the political situation was that while a majority of the Hungarian people obviously supported the political ideas of the FKGP, and consequently that party now possessed the offices of president and prime minister, the party was not in a position to govern on the basis of its announced principles, and, indeed, on occasion it had to act like an opposition party rather than the leader of a coalition. The reason for this situation was obvious: the presence of the Soviet Army. The Soviet authorities never made it clear, and probably did not know themselves, how much autonomy the Hungarians would be allowed. Indeed, the limits were not something constant, but as the international situation changed so did Soviet policy. In other words, ever more explicitly and ever more strongly, the Russians backed the Communists in their attempts to increase their power.

Communist advances were made a great deal easier by the fact that the other parties were not unified, and in both the Socialist Party and the NPP there were crypto-Communists always willing to cooperate. But even those leaders who were not secret Communists to a certain degree shared the radical ideas of Rákosi and his comrades, at least to the extent that they were also afraid of the reconstruction of the Horthy regime. To them the fight against "reaction," however absurd it seems in retrospect, was not merely verbiage. Consequently, in the spring of 1946 under Communist leadership at first informally, but later in an organized form, a left-wing bloc was created in which the MKP, the SDP, the NPP, and the trade unions participated. This bloc time and again successfully opposed the moderate leaders of the FKGP.

All political forces appreciated that the democratic order was fragile. In view of what would happen in the near future, it is easy to forget that the Communists, returning from the Soviet Union or emerging from the underground and seeing the results of the elections, genuinely feared what they called the forces of the "reactionaries." Educated in the Leninist school of politics, and well remembering Lenin's phrase, *kto kogo* (loosely translated, "who will eliminate the other"), they assumed that in a genuinely democratic Hungary they would have no political role to play. They increasingly came to regard the Hungarian people as reactionary and therefore believed that organizing elections on the basis of wide suffrage was a mistake.[23] After all, the far-from-democratic Horthy regime was not something in the distant past. Rákosi and his comrades frequently asserted that large landowners, capitalists, and the Catholic Church would not easily accept their loss of wealth and power.

The FKGP politicians, with more justification, saw the threat to the democratic order in the presence of the Soviet army and in the Communists' total control over the means of coercion. Ironically, in view of how the law was later used, it was FKGP politicians who advanced the idea of passing laws aimed at the defense of the democratic, republican order. Perhaps naively, they believed that such laws could protect the country from the danger of a Communist coup.[24] Very quickly, it became evident that different groups had different ideas concerning exactly which aspect of the political order needed defense. Rather than debating abstractions, concrete issues dominated the discussions. Non-Socialist politicians wanted the law to be used against civil servants who violated the constitution. In other words, they wanted to remove police officials who abused their power. They saw the danger of "proletarian dictatorship" and hoped that they could construct a legal defense against it. The Communists, of course, would not agree to the inclusion of that issue. Instead, they insisted, the law should punish legitimist, antirepublican agitation and rumor mongering. The Communists also deemed it necessary to try cases under this law not in the regular

23 *Pártközi ertekezletek*, p. 299, October 30, 1946. 24 Palasik, p. 110.

courts but in "people's courts," the same institutions that handled war crimes and in which, not coincidentally, they enjoyed majorities.[25] In each and every instance, the FKGP was compelled to compromise. Ultimately, the law that the parliament accepted in March 1946 became an instrument of political leverage in Communist hands.

It was precisely the impressive victory of the FKGP in an obviously free election and the disappointing performance of the Communists and their allies that impelled the Communists and the Soviet authorities that stood behind them to sharpen the political struggle, using demagoguery and ever more brazen antidemocratic and brutal methods. Probably a pluralist political order survived longer in Czechoslovakia because there the Communists possessed greater popular support. It was as if the Communists said to themselves: if the Hungarian people will not listen to reason, then we have to show them that we have other means at our disposal to assert our power and influence.

The Communists greatly benefited from the fact that achieving a parliamentary majority had not unified the FKGP. Some politicians in the left wing of the party, such as István Dobi, Lajos Dinnyés, and Gyula Ortutay, were crypto-Communists who would later make careers in the Stalinist regime. By contrast, people in the right wing had joined the party because it was the most conservative, legitimate, anti-Communist political force. The decisively important issue for non-Communist politicians was how to preserve the independence of the country, given the presence of an occupation force that subtly and not so subtly interfered in the domestic political struggle. The FKGP, unlike the other three parties of the new government, was itself a coalition. This, indeed, was the source of its success in the elections, but it was also a cause of serious weakness. The political differences between the right, the center, and the left wings were profound; at times of crisis, the two wings each would have liked to exclude the other from the party. When Tildy became president of the republic, he vacated the post of premier. The leaders of the victorious party wanted the post to go to Dezsö Sulyok, a representative of the right wing. However on January 30, 1946, Sulyok gave a speech in the parliament in which he provocatively attacked the Hungarian Soviet Republic of 1919 and thereby aroused the hostility of the Communists.[26] He asserted, quite unnecessarily and incorrectly, that the Communist regime in 1919 had fought the newly established Czechoslovakia for irredentist purposes. After this incident the Communists

25 Pártközi értekezletek, pp. 193–195.
26 Dezső Sulyok, *A Magyar Tragédia*, New Brunswick, NJ: Sulyok, 1954, p. 562.

opposed his appointment and instead supported the centrist Ferenc Nagy. They reasoned that it was to their advantage to have a centrist as opposed to a left-wing FKGP leader as premier because they feared that the rest of the party would move into opposition, which at this point they did not desire. It indicates the degree of limitation on Hungarian democracy at this time that a party that had received only 17 percent of the vote was nevertheless in a position to determine who the next premier would be.[27] In his memoirs written in exile in the United States, Sulyok exhibited more bitterness toward his colleagues in the FKGP than toward the Communists. He described the leading figures of his party, such as Tildy, Nagy, Varga, and Balogh, as scoundrels and traitors who were responsible for the fate of the country. Sulyok asserted that these people gave concessions to the Communists not because they believed this was the best policy under the circumstances, but because they had given in to blackmail. According to him, Tildy, Nagy, and Varga were blackmailed by the Soviets because they had earlier supported Hungarian participation in the war, and Dobi, Dinyés, and Oltványi were blackmailed because of their allegedly brutal behavior as soldiers on the Eastern Front.[28]

Sulyok in his speeches in the parliament continued to express a point of view that was probably shared by many of his comrades in the party, who, however, recognized that it was politically unwise to articulate a position that was bound to provoke the Communists and the Russians. He blamed the extremely difficult economic situation of the country on the necessity of paying reparations, a view that was considered to be anti-Soviet. He also opposed the treaty that was to be signed with Czechoslovakia and blamed the Hungarian negotiators for making too many concessions. In addition, he expressed concern that the Chief Economic Council, under the direction of Vas, allowed the Communists to take over the management of the economy, opening it to Soviet exploitation. He argued bitterly and voted against the law aimed at the "defense of the republic," calling it an "executioner's law." Most of Sulyok's criticisms were well taken, even if the wisdom of making such views explicit in the given political situation could be questioned. Ferenc Nagy, a cautious politician, repeatedly found it necessary to dissociate the party from the views expressed by Sulyok.

One of the first tasks of the new government under Ferenc Nagy was to lessen its financial burden by greatly reducing the number of employees.

27 F. Nagy, pp. 233–237. Nagy describes in his memoirs that the Socialists and the Communists were willing to accept Sulyok before this speech, but not afterward.

28 Sulyok, p. 559. Sulyok produces no proof whatsoever for his accusations.

During the war, the civil service had vastly expanded. The perfectly reasonable desire to economize gave an opportunity to the Communists to advocate the firing of people they described as "reactionaries." It was to be expected that reduction in the number of government employees would be concentrated on those in the bureaucracy who had actively and enthusiastically supported the old regime. Indeed, already in December 1944 the program of the National Independence Front promised the removal from the civil service of those who had compromised themselves by their service in the old regime.[29]

The purging of the civil service started immediately after the end of the war. At first civil servants and later people who worked in private firms were required to fill out questionnaires that contained a large number of queries concerning their past political behavior. Special commissions set up by representatives of political parties and trade unions evaluated the questionnaires. In some instances, the commissions not only fired individuals from their jobs but also forwarded their dossiers to the people's courts.[30]

In spite of these earlier firings, the Communists considered the work unfinished: precisely who should be fired and what agency should decide became one of the first bitterly debated issues within the new coalition government. Not surprisingly, the FKGP wanted to create a decision-making organ in which its representatives had the majority, while the Socialists and Communists wanted to involve the trade unions they controlled. Cleansing government service of people they considered hostile was a significant step in the Communists' struggle for complete dominance. The parties of the newly formed coalition government agreed that it was necessary to draw up so-called "B lists," that is, a list of people who would be fired. For the FKGP, this was only a necessary antibureaucratic measure, whereas the Communists and Socialists from the very beginning saw a political opportunity. The discussions concerning the composition of the committees lasted until May 1946 when the FKGP conceded. Altogether some 60,000 people lost their jobs, the majority for political reasons.[31] The Communists and to a lesser extent the Socialists succeeded in placing their people in the vacated posts.

The Communists soon realized that they could force concessions from their opponents, and after each round of concessions their attacks on the

29 Pártközi értekezletek, p. 4.

30 Gábor Kiszely, *AVH: Egy terrorszervezet története*, Budapest: Korona, 2000, pp. 21–22.

31 Balogh, p. 216. Rákosi wrote to Nagy on March 1, 1946, demanding the inclusion of the trade unions in drawing up "B-lists." PIL 274 3/27 March 1. According to other sources, the number of people fired was close to 100,000. Kiszely, p. 62.

FKGP became stronger and sharper. The Communist, Socialist, and NPP newspapers attacked the government and called for struggle against the "reactionaries."[32] The tactic of the Communist leadership was to avoid attacking the entire FKGP, which might have created resistance and also might have led to the dissolution of the coalition and the formation of a purely Smallholder government. Instead, the goal of the party was to break up the unity of the FKGP by attacking the right wing in the hope of isolating it. The Communists used mass demonstrations against individuals they disliked and government policies that they opposed.[33] In this respect, they had a considerable advantage over the FKGP. What made this kind of mass politics possible, aside from the organizational abilities of the Communists, was the growing desperation over inadequate food supplies and the ever-increasing inflation. This was a good time for demagogy. Workers and the unemployed were ready to look for scapegoats for their obvious misery. Although demonstrations taking place all over the country were centrally organized, it was not possible to control these in every instance, and the crowds on occasion turned their anger against Socialist and Communist leaders as well.[34] The mass demonstrations also were often infected by manifestations of anti-Semitism. Because the police were in Communist hands and Laszló Rajk, minister of the interior, favored the demonstrators, the police refused to take steps against them even when they behaved unlawfully.*

From the spring of 1946 on, the FKGP gave one concession after another. It agreed to the nationalization of the mines, an important piece of the Communist program from the time of Germany's defeat. It accepted the inclusion of the trade unions into the committees that drew up the "B-lists" and thereby enabled the Communists to get rid of their opponents among the civil servants. As a result of demonstrations, it agreed to remove Béla Kovács from the politically important post of minister of agriculture and

* On March 20, 1946, Rajk took the place of Imre Nagy. The Communists probably regarded Imre Nagy's appointment as temporary. The Smallholders disliked Rajk more than the other Communist leaders. Whether this was because of his personality or because of the position he held is difficult to say.

32 It was at this time that the personal relations between the Communists and the FKGP leaders deteriorated. In spite of their political differences, in early 1945 they on occasion played cards together and went to hunt together. By 1946, such manifestations of friendly activities no longer took place. M. Rákosi, *Visszaemlékezések, 1940–1956*, vol. 1, p. 200.

33 RTsHIDNI fond 17, opis 128 delo 124, p. 54. Lieutenant A. Chigirev reporting from Budapest to M. Suslov in June 5, 1946. Remarkably, he described the waves of demonstrations as a sign of increased activity on the part of the reactionaries.

34 No demonstrations took place in Fejér County. The leadership there protested: they had not received instructions from the center. PIL 274 16/89. Rákosi in his memoirs made it perfectly clear that the demonstrations were centrally planned and organized. M. Rákosi, *Visszaemlékezések, 1940–1956*, vol. 1, pp. 242–246.

gave this portfolio to István Dobi, who belonged to the left wing of the FKGP and who willingly cooperated with the Communists. Kovács had been determined to resist illegal land seizures taking place in the name of land reform and to remove those who had no legal right to the land. Dobi, by contrast, explicitly refused to take such steps.

The most important concession forced on the FKGP was the expulsion from the party of twenty-two parliamentary deputies that the Communists and their allies characterized as "reactionary." This group included Sulyok, who had opposed the Communists most strongly and explicitly, and also István Vásáry, the minister of finances in the provisional government. Ousting these deputies from the FKGP delegation, the Communists were supported by the leaders of the Socialist Party and the NPP. Once again, the left-wing bloc proved to be a useful Communist instrument in the struggle against the FKGP.[35] This left bloc continued to exist until the complete destruction of the pluralist political system and greatly facilitated Communist efforts to destroy the political organizations of the "reactionaries."

The removal of twenty-two deputies from the FKGP delegation meant that the party lost its majority in the parliament. However, those who had been expelled from the party did not lose their mandates and in all important matters voted with the FKGP. Sulyok and his supporters were planning to establish the Hungarian Freedom Party already in April 1946, but the ACC did not give the new party permission to operate until June. The formation of this party actually served the interests of the Communists, inasmuch as it divided the opposition.

Destroying the unity of the FKGP had considerable political significance. It was the first and the most visible manifestation of the policy that came to be called "salami tactics," that is, removal from the political scene one by one of those who resisted the Communist takeover. Those who were compelled to leave the FKGP were by no means reactionaries in any accepted sense of the word. They differed from the majority of their party primarily because they vigorously resisted the ever-increasing Communist demands and pressure. They did not hesitate to call attention to every illegal act of the Communists and loudly warn of the growing danger of dictatorship. The most prominent representative of this group was Dezső Sulyok, who continued to irritate the Communists with speeches in which most of his criticisms were justified.

35 *Szabad Nép*, March 6, 1946. Reprinted in *Pártközi értekezletek*, pp. 199–200. The left bloc was formally created on March 5 with the participation of the MKP, SDP, NPP, and the trade unions. Földesi, *A Megszállók . . .*, p. 261.

The question remains as to why Ferenc Nagy as premier, and the centrist politicians who surrounded him, decided to give in. One answer is that the Smallholder politicians were frightened by the powerful wave of demonstrations organized by the Communists. Some FKGP leaders wanted to respond in kind and organize demonstrations by their supporters.[36] FKGP deputies in the parliament denounced Communist wrongdoings more and more bitterly. The political atmosphere in the country became extremely tense. Nagy and Tildy feared that it would be impossible under the circumstances to retain a coalition government, yet they believed that such a government was essential. The FKGP leaders feared that if the Communists left the government, they would mobilize workers and trigger a civil war in which Soviet troops would inevitably become involved. As mentioned before, Nagy and Tildy assumed, incorrectly but not necessarily naively, that once the international peace conference took place and a formal peace treaty was signed, Soviet troops would leave the country, and then the political situation would change to their advantage.

Ferenc Nagy, in a conversation with the American ambassador, Schoenfeld, made it clear that the breakup of the coalition would lead either to a new FKGP government that would soon be paralyzed by Communist strikes and demonstrations or to the formation of a left-wing government, that, in Nagy's view, would bring a repetition of the disaster of 1919. Nagy understood that developments in Hungary were dependent on Soviet-Western relations, and he expected a lessening of tensions among the allies.[37] The policy of the FKGP leadership was basically to hold on to office until such a time as the will of the Hungarian people as expressed by the recent elections could be realized.[38] The expectation that the signing of the peace treaty would mean the removal of Soviet troops, thereby saving Hungarian democracy, was widely shared in the country.

But the main reason for the series of compromises was Russian pressure. The Soviets were, of course, in a position to put pressure on the government. The Soviet ambassador, Pushkin, criticized the parliamentary speeches of FKGP deputies, calling them "reactionary" and "anti-Soviet," and, of course, some of the speeches in fact were implicitly anti-Soviet. Soviet representatives were able to apply pressure by demanding the satisfaction of reparation requirements. They could insist that the government

36 Ferenc Nagy consulted with the British and the American representatives in Hungary. The British counseled caution, the Americans confrontation. Földesi, 2002, p. 263.

37 FRUS, 1946, vol. 6, March 6, 1946. Schoenfeld's report to secretary of state.

38 F. Nagy, pp. 261–263.

pay back the food loan that the country had received in the previous year. They could warn that the government was not supplying the Red Army satisfactorily and the army would have to begin requisitioning to solve the problem. They announced that because the government was not carrying out its obligations, the Soviet Union would not continue to supply raw materials. These threats and warnings brought the necessary concessions. When Nagy went to see the Soviet ambassador to discuss the political crisis, Pushkin responded by saying that the recent demands of the Communist Party leadership merely aimed at defending democracy.[39] Obviously, the Communists and the Soviet authorities had coordinated their moves against the FKGP.

It would be unfair to blame the FKGP leaders for the ultimate outcome. There was nothing that they could have done that would have saved the country from dictatorship. By being accommodating, they proved that they did everything in their power to work with the Soviet Union and that the Russians could not be appeased. The leaders assumed that their resistance to Communist demands would result in the breakup of the coalition. Given the difficult economic problems and the dependence of the country on Soviet goodwill, or at least tolerance, the FKGP leadership rightly feared assuming the responsibility of running the government alone.

COMMUNIST GAINS, SUMMER AND FALL 1946

After the concessions and defeats in the spring of 1946, the leaders of the FKGP decided to take a stand and present their own demands. They were following the example of the Communists. Their minimum demand was a call for new local elections and a redistribution of government offices. Unquestionably, the FKGP had a strong case. The most popular party in the country had an insignificant share of major government posts. Traditionally, the deputy heads of counties (*alispán*) were important figures. They were the highest elected officials in the counties. In the spring of 1946, there were only two FKGP *alispáns* among twenty-three. Not a single major city had an FKGP mayor, and in the leadership of the police the party was almost completely excluded. Among police officers only 7 percent belonged to the FKGP.[40]

The memorandum of the FKGP was phrased diplomatically. It spoke of "ex-Nazis penetrating some political parties" and stated "these people abuse peaceful and honest citizens on the basis of their party commitments." In

39 Ibid., p. 260.

40 *Pártközi értekezletek*, pp. 231–241.

other words, ex-Nazis now working in the Communist-led police persecute those who work for the FKGP.[41]

In an interparty meeting called to discuss FKGP demands, Socialist and Communist representatives explicitly connected new elections to the "strengthening of reactionaries." The protocol of the meeting of June 3 said:

> Imre Szélig, expressed those concerns which we (sic) had concerning the right wing of the FKGP, or more precisely concerning those fascists who hide in the FKGP, and emphasized that elections or the redistribution of political posts would facilitate the strengthening of rightist forces which we could not explain to the great masses of the two workers' parties."[42]

Remarkably, Szélig belonged to the right wing of the Socialist party, which demonstrates that by this time even moderate Socialists supported the Communist position. What he was saying in effect was that Socialists and Communists could not trust the people because they would elect "reactionaries," and he implicitly threatened to call the "masses" into the streets to demonstrate.

Reading the press and party protocols of the time, one sees that the so-called civic (i.e., non-Socialist) parties were at a disadvantage. They were maneuvered into accepting the terms of their opponents, and in their memoranda they also talked about the dangers of fascism and reaction. They conceded that the police had performed a useful and necessary task in fighting against fascists and protested only against "errors" in their work. The leaders of the party could not afford to call a spade a spade and to talk about the danger of Communist terror and Soviet exploitation. The Communists first talked about their opponents as "fascists," and it could not be denied that at the end of the war there were people who could fairly be described as fascists. Indeed, it would have been a miracle if within a few months all the enthusiastic partisans of the old regime had disappeared. But the Communists also talked about "reactionaries," a much more vague term that could be applied to anyone who opposed the establishment of "people's democracy," yet another vague term. Ultimately, everyone who opposed the Communist program was a "reactionary." The distinction between "fascist" and "reactionary" gradually disappeared.

The left bloc's response to the memorandum of the FKGP was phrased moderately. Communist, Socialist, and NPP leaders accepted the need for local elections but maintained that these should be held only after the

41 Ibid., p. 233.

42 Ibid., p. 231.

accomplishment of financial stabilization that was planned for August 1. They accepted that corruption existed within the civil service and needed to be addressed. They recognized the difficulties faced by the FKGP leadership and promised further discussions to try and save the coalition.[43] They agreed that the representatives of parties participating in the coalition government ought to have a common program for the next few years. However, in spite of the tone of compromise, in the most important matter, namely allowing the Smallholders to have a say in the leadership of the police, the left bloc was unwilling to concede. In this instance, however, Ferenc Nagy appeared unmovable. He prepared to resign and made it known that if the president once again entrusted him with the job, he might form a government without the Communists. Government crisis seemed inevitable. This was the first instance when the moderate leaders of the FKGP were taking matters to a breaking point. There were several factors, however, that made the collapse of the coalition unlikely. The Paris peace conference and the attempt to stabilize the currency were imminent. Nagy once again in another conversation confided in Ambassador Schoenfeld that he feared the collapse of the coalition would lead to civil war.[44] It was the wrong time to provoke a government crisis.

But most important, the coalition survived because of Soviet intervention. On June 4, the Soviet ambassador, Pushkin, warned Nagy not to break up the coalition: in case of a government crisis, he threatened unspecified Soviet action. According to the information of the American ambassador, Pushkin also had a conversation with Rákosi and advised him to make concessions.[45] Indeed, at an interparty meeting the left bloc representatives promised to hold local elections "very soon," but at an unspecified date, and to give positions in the police and in administration to FKGP.

The crisis in the summer of 1946 demonstrated that however weak the democratic system was, pluralism still survived. The Communist police and the Soviet army continued to commit illegal acts, but it was still possible to criticize them, and the criticisms did act as a restraint on the

43 Ibid., pp. 236–238.

44 FRUS, 1946, vol. 6, Schoenfeld to secretary of state, June 28, 1946, pp. 316–317.

45 Földesi, 2002, pp. 278–279, incorrectly quotes István Vida, *A Független Kisgazda Párt Politikája, 1944–1947*, p. 191. The information about this meeting is to be found in Schoenfeld's report to secretary of state, June 11, 1946, FRUS, 1946, vol. 6, pp. 304–305. One wonders how the American ambassador received such precise information. There is no reason to doubt the correctness of the information because only Soviet intervention can explain why Nagy changed his mind. It is interesting that although Pushkin's intervention must have been decisively important in resolving the crisis, Nagy does not mention his conversation with the Soviet envoy in his memoirs.

Communist forces of coercion. Furthermore, at this point the Soviet representatives, undoubtedly on the basis of instructions from Moscow, still did not want the collapse of the coalition form of government in Hungary. The peace conference was about to take place in Paris, and Soviet leaders obviously wanted to maintain the appearance of a democratic government in Budapest.

The agreement permitting the survival of the coalition, not surprisingly, failed to bring peace into political life, and the country lurched from one crisis to another. On July 17, 1946, a young man by the name of István Pénzes killed two Soviet soldiers (and a Hungarian girl). The attack occurred on a busy street in the middle of the day. The true motives for his act have never been established. At the time, people speculated that the cause of the murder was sexual jealousy, but it is conceivable that Pénzes killed out of hatred of the occupiers. It is out of the question, however, that Pénzes acted as a part of a large conspiracy, as the Russians charged. One gets the impression that the political police decided immediately to use the occasion for political gain. An hour after the incident, the charred body of the young assassin was found in a nearby attic in which was found a strangely intact membership card of a Catholic youth organization. General Sviridov, in the name of the ACC, demanded the dissolution of several Catholic youth organizations, arguing that Pénzes was a member of KALOT, an organization for village youth.[46] Although Pénzes indeed had been a member of KALOT in 1943, it appears he had long since moved to Budapest and had had nothing to do with KALOT for several years. The accusation that KALOT had organized a conspiracy to kill Soviet soldiers was obviously and self-evidently false.

At the same time, Sviridov launched a fresh attack on anti-Communist forces within the FKGP. In addition to the dissolution of Catholic organizations, he demanded the confiscation of weapons from the population; he also demanded the removal from political life of several FKGP politicians and, in addition, their prosecution for anti-Soviet and pro-fascist propaganda.[47] The FKGP had to part with more of its members and the number of its deputies

46 *Documents of the Meetings of the Allied Control Commission for Hungary*, pp. 168–169. General Sviridov in the meeting of July 24, 1946, certainly used hyperbole when he said: "The basic principle of these organizations is to educate their members in a fascist spirit. Besides these groups, Catholic schools and High Schools all have proto-fascist ideas. All these organizations have as their main purpose to fight the Red Army." Although the British and American representatives expressed some mild disapproval that General Sviridov acted in the name of the ACC without consultations, they took no position on the substance of the matter.

47 *Pártközi értekezletek*, pp. 258–263. The matter was also discussed at the July 24 meeting of the ACC. The British and American representatives protested that they had not been notified before Sviridov sent his letter and expressed skepticism concerning the existence of fascist organizations. *Documents of the Meetings of the Allied Control Commission for Hungary*, pp. 166–173.

in the parliament was further reduced. What the Communists could not achieve on their own, they achieved with Soviet help. The Russians could not be resisted.

The leaders of the FKGP would have liked to get the support of moderates within the NPP to create a unified peasant movement that would have counterbalanced the left bloc to a certain extent. However, they failed in this effort because of the strength of the NPP's pro-Communist left wing and the reluctance of the moderates, led by Imre Kovacs, to split their party.[48] In another attempt to seize the initiative and again borrowing from the tactics of the Communists, the Smallholders decided to organize a national peasant demonstration in Budapest on August 20. That day, the Feast of St. Stephen (the first king of Hungary) is a great national holiday with religious overtones. The FKGP leaders expected the largest number of peasants would be able and willing to travel to the capital on August 20 and the mass event would demonstrate the extent and strength of their support among the people in spite of recent setbacks.

The Russians and the Communists perfectly understood the political danger in having a visible exhibition of the appeal of their opponents. Nagy had to request the permission of the ACC for a national gathering. Sviridov attempted to dissuade him by expressing concern that such a demonstration might lead to a hostile confrontation between "workers" and "peasants." When Nagy threatened to resign over the issue, Sviridov proposed that it might take place at a slightly later date together with an exhibition of agricultural machinery. Because the Soviet Union would want to participate and they needed time to send their material, the date was set for September 8.[49]

When the day came, Communists were well prepared. They did everything in their power to lessen the political damage to themselves. Rákosi wrote in his memoirs that the Communist-led ministry of transportation sent half as many trains from the countryside to Budapest as the Smallholders had requested, maintaining "there was not enough coal." Furthermore, the Communists sent agitators to the trains, hoping to win over the peasants.[50] They distributed newspapers expressing Communist views, but published by the NPP. As is usual in such instances, the organizers and the opposition gave widely different estimates of the number of participants. Rákosi wrote about 50,000 people, while Ferenc Nagy about a half a million. The mass

48 Kovács, p. 305. Kovács, on a previous occasion, told the NPP leadership meeting that he believed he was under police surveillance. PIL 284 8/13 September 17, 1946.

49 Nagy, vol. 1, pp. 351–364.

50 M. Rákosi, *Visszaemlékezések, 1940–1956*, vol. 1, pp. 310–311.

meeting took place without incident. Ferenc Nagy gave the major speech, but Rákosi also appeared on the tribune. Nagy proudly reports in his memoirs that the peasants marched under Hungarian tricolors rather than under the red flag as the workers did at their demonstrations. Indeed, it was far easier for the Smallholders to take advantage of the nationalism of the Hungarian people than for the Communists, no matter how hard they tried. Nationalism was intrinsic to the Smallholders' appeal, yet they were never able to compete with the Communists in terms of mass mobilization. It is easier to organize workers than to organize peasants, and the Communists, having Soviet experience and practical help behind them, were also more able propagandists.

As a result of Soviet pressure and constant concessions, by the end of 1946 the position of the FKGP was much weaker than it had been a year before at the time of the elections. Nevertheless, at interparty gatherings the representatives of political parties could still talk to one another politely and honestly, each making an effort to understand the other. The two sides made efforts to resolve problems. For contemporaries, the ultimate outcome of the political struggle was not yet evident.

7

Postwar Retribution and Pogroms

THE PEOPLE'S COURTS

At the end of the war, life seemed cheap. Millions had died in battle and as a result of senseless violence. In Hungary, the last few months of the war were particularly destructive. During the anarchy of the Szálasi regime, blood was flowing in the streets of the capital. In the Budapest suburb of Zugló, one group of Nyilas alone was reputed to have "executed" (i.e., murdered) 1200 people.[1] Not all the victims were Jewish. Military tribunals on both sides passed down death sentences without scruple.

At this time in most of the defeated countries people took justice into their own hands and punished those who had chosen the wrong side in the great conflict. According to estimates in France, 10,000 people became victims of spontaneous vengeance. In addition, 126,000 people were interned between September 1944 and April 1945; 7037 people were sentenced to death, and 767 were actually executed.[2] In Poland and Yugoslavia, the situation was similar. It was to be expected that people would demand justice, and in the course of assigning punishment some of the legal niceties would be disregarded. In Hungary, lawless punishments were no more widespread than elsewhere. Unlike in France, for example, lynching – taking revenge outside of the law – with a very few exceptions, did not take place. Given the circumstances, one is impressed by the attempts to maintain legality or at least the appearance of it.

The National Independence Front had published a program in December 1944, almost a month and a half before the armistice, stating clearly its

1 Krisztián Ungváry, "Második Sztálingrád," *Budapesti Negyed* 3–4 (2000): 29–30.
2 Ferenc Gazdag, *Franciaország története, 1945–1995*, Budapest: Zrinyi, 1996, p. 17.

position on the treatment of war criminals. Signed by representatives of all political parties that would form the government, it stated:

> The traitors, the war criminals, must be arrested and they must be handed over to people's courts created for this purpose. Their wealth must be confiscated. All fascist, anti-people, pro-Nazi organizations must be dissolved. Their property must be confiscated. Their press must be closed down. Their re-creation must be prevented by issuing strict regulations.[3]

Membership in these organizations was regarded as a crime. By signing the armistice agreement, the provisional Hungarian government assumed an implicit obligation to hold war criminals responsible for their actions.[4] Indeed, already in November 1943 the Allies had indicated their determination to punish people responsible for war crimes.

Only five days after signing the armistice, on January 25, 1945, the provisional government published a regulation concerning the creation of people's courts in order to start the process of holding people accountable for their wartime activity. The purpose of setting up a new system of courts was to take political cases out of the purview of regular courts. In the regular court system, of course, all the judges had been appointed by the previous regime and consequently their personnel could not be used for the prosecution of political and war crimes. (Similar courts were established in other defeated countries after the conclusion of hostilities.) Ultimately, twenty-four people's courts were created in Hungary. Although most of their work took place in the first three years, they continued to exist until 1950.

The regulation explicitly stated that crimes could be punished even if at the time of the act such behavior was not considered criminal.[5] Some protested the notion that people should be punished on the basis of ex post facto laws. They appealed to the principle *nullum crimen sine lege*. For example, on July 2, 1945, Endre Hamvas, bishop of Csanád, wrote to Géza Teleki, minister of religion and education, that Mihály Csernus, an abbot in Endröd, had been sentenced to ten years of forced labor because he had written anti-Communist articles. According to Hamvas, this had not been a crime at the time, and therefore he could not be sentenced. Teleki responded that he could not interfere, and the abbot was punished for his anti-Communist articles.[6]

3 *Pártközi értekezletek*, p. 4.

4 Article 14 of the armistice agreement said: "Hungary will cooperate in the apprehension and trial, as well as the surrender to the governments concerned, of persons accused of war crimes." *Documents of the Meetings of the Allied Control Commission for Hungary*, p. 428.

5 Palasik, p. 42.

6 MOL XIX – A – 1 – j box 31, XXIII b, Criminal cases.

Parties of the National Front and trade unions nominated people, and from these nominations the heads of counties selected judges. Five laypeople under the guidance of a trained jurist made their decisions. In effect, the lay judges functioned like a jury. The intention behind the selection of laypeople was to give the appearance that it was the "people" who were holding war criminals responsible. The prosecutor, who dominated the proceedings, was always a professional jurist. The law limited the right to appeal. Appeals were addressed to the National Council of the People's Courts, whose members were also named by the political parties; however, these people did have to have legal experience. The National Council often made the sentences lighter and thereby aroused the hostility of the Communist and Socialist parties. Socialist and Communist politicians and newspapers blamed the members of the National Council for taking the side of fascists. The gap between the people's courts, made up of laypeople, and the professional jurists on the National Council was great. In the people's courts, because of the participation of the representatives of the trade unions, the left was usually dominant. However, in the National Council, where the trade unions were not represented, this was not the case. During their life, these courts handled 58,629 cases and sentenced to death 477 people, of whom only 189 were executed.[7]

At the same time as these courts were being set up, teams working within the ministry of justice started to assemble a list of people who would be charged with war crimes. The list included everyone who could be held responsible for the country's entering the war, as well as all the Nyilas parliamentary deputies and those military men who had prevented Horthy's attempt at concluding a separate peace. The list also included actors, writers, and judges – civilians who had actively collaborated with the Hungarian Nazi regime.[8]

Who could be judges and prosecutors in a defeated country? In such confusing times, it was to be expected that people's careers would be checkered. People who had legal training almost by definition had served the old regime, most of them as late as 1944. For example, one of the judges, Károly Kis, had pronounced in 1944 that "the Red hordes will be repelled." Another

7 Palasik, p. 44. Palasik took her figures from Tibor Zinner, "Adalékok az antifasiszta számonkéréshez és a népi demokracia védelméhez különös tekintettel a Budapesti Népbiróságra," in *Budapest fővárosi levéltár közleményei,* 1984–1985, pp. 150–151. Zinner and Róna, vol. 1., p. 70, give slightly different figures. They also mention that 26,997 people were punished, but 80 percent of these served less than a year in prison. Only 2,003 people were sentenced to terms longer than five years. According to Zinner and Róna, in Hungary relatively fewer people were executed for war crimes than in the other defeated countries (pp. 71–73).

8 Zinner and Róna, vol. 1, p. 65.

difficulty was that an individual who had committed unsavory acts on one occasion might be found to have resisted the Nazis on another. For example, in 1944 Zoltán Szabó wrote a study justifying the discriminatory laws against the Jews; yet in December 1944 the Nazis removed him from his post, and he had to escape, presumably because of his oppositional views. In February 1946, someone filed a complaint against Ernő Késmárky, a people's judge. Késmárky's brother-in-law, László Ferenczy, had been a major war criminal, who in his capacity as a colonel in the gendarmerie had been responsible for the deportation of Jews. Késmárky, using his connections, illegally provided Ferenczy's attorney with legal documents. In this instance the judge was not removed from his post but merely received an admonition.[9]

The process at the outset was inevitably haphazard. Ákos Major, the first head of the people's court, described in his memoirs how he got his job.[10] He had been a military judge in the Hungarian army during the Horthy regime but refused to serve after October 15. Because of his brother, Tamás, a famous actor and, what was more relevant, a prominent Communist, in January 1945 Major was summoned by the Budapest National Committee and appointed head of a people's court with the responsibility of trying war criminals.

Major started his work at a time when the battle for the city was far from over. The first case that he tried was that of two noncommissioned officers, József Rotyis and Sándor Szivós, who had been responsible for the torture and murder of 124 men who had served in a workers' battalion. The victims had been Jews and political prisoners. The two men argued in vain that their superior had told them that none of the men in the battalion should be allowed to return from the Eastern Front. Major later wrote proudly that he was the first judge in 1945, before the Nuremberg trials, who explicitly repudiated the defense argument that the accused had just been carrying out orders. The court quickly found the two men guilty and sentenced them to death. (The court also sentenced the commanding officer, Alajos Haynal, in absentia to death.) Zoltán Vas, perhaps the most powerful leader in the Budapest National Committee at the time, insisted that the hanging should be carried out in public in one of the main squares of the city. Vas wanted to turn the execution into a political demonstration. He also wanted to give satisfaction to those who had just days before suffered under Nazi terror. Major had misgivings but acquiesced.

9 Information about these cases is to be found in MOL XX – 4 – a, Complaints against NOT.

10 Ákos Major, *Népbiráskodás, forradalmi törvényesség*, Tibor Zinner (ed.), Budapest: Minerva, 1988.

It turned out to be no easy matter to arrange the hanging. Not only were the authorities unable to find a hangman – one of the guards had to kick a chair out from under each of the men sentenced to death – but they could not even find rope. They had to weave together twine that they found at the ex-headquarters of the Hungarian Nazis. However, this rope broke, and one of the unfortunate men had to be hanged again. Furthermore, on February 4, the day of this gruesome event, the Germans and their Hungarian allies in Buda began bombarding this particular square, so the crowd quickly dispersed.[11] Although not many people actually saw the public hanging, the news of the event quickly spread through the entire city in spite of the continued fighting.[12]

The AVO (*Államvédelmi osztály,* state defense department) under Gábor Péter arrested a large number of people and interned them. However, the trials of the important figures of the old regime could begin only after the conclusion of hostilities, when the Allies were able and willing to return their captured enemies to Hungary. The Americans were actually anxious to get rid of the large number of Hungarians who were found in territories under their occupation at the end of the war. General Key through Marshall Voroshilov, head of the ACC, approached the Hungarian government concerning the repatriation of approximately 400,000 people. Prime Minister Miklós responded in September 1945 that the country was ready to receive them. The ministry of the interior drew up plans according to which the returnees would be put in camps where committees would examine each and every one of them. Military officers along with members of the gendarmerie and SS would be separated from the soldiers and housed in different cities. The ministry was so concerned about security that it considered emptying sections of towns where these camps would be set up.[13]

The run of the mill fascists did not receive public trials. It was different with the major war criminals. The most important figures of the old regime had escaped and left the country with the retreating German armies. Through the ACC, the Hungarians presented to the Allies a list of people whose repatriation they requested. In the confusion of the postwar situation in Germany, it was not easy to find some of the accused. The first group of important figures arrived in Hungary only in October 1945. By

11 Ibid., pp. 125–127. According to Major, and probably he is correct, the public executions were perceived as Jewish-inspired vengeance and increased anti-Semitism. The Soviet command directed the Hungarians not to carry out public executions as long as fighting in the city continued.

12 I did not see the execution itself, but as an eight-year-old boy I saw the bodies hanging.

13 XIX – A – 1 – j box 31, XXIII b, Voroshilov to Miklós and Miklos' response.

August 1946, the Allies had returned to their native land 312 people whose names appeared on the list.[14]

During the first postwar months, the people's courts and the National Council could try only relatively unknown figures, such as journalists, soldiers responsible for killing Jewish men in the workers' battalions, and some other figures who had cooperated closely with the Germans. The leaders of all political parties were concerned that a large number of the judges and prosecutors in these trials were Jewish. They very much wanted to avoid the impression that holding people responsible was an expression of a Jewish desire for revenge.[15] In this, they did not succeed.

In October 1945, the Allies returned to Hungary Ferenc Szálasi and two ex-prime ministers, Béla Imrédy and László Bárdossy, among others. In the following months, one public trial after another took place. In a comparative context, these trials were as fair and as competently carried out as anywhere else in Europe. As was to be expected, the behavior of the accused varied. They had, however, two things in common. Not a single one of them considered himself guilty, and every one of them would have preferred to stand trial in Nuremberg rather than in Hungary.[16]

The first major trial began on October 29, 1945. The accused was László Bárdossy. The most important charge against him was that as prime minister he had declared war on the Soviet Union in June 1941. Bárdossy did this without the legal formality of asking the approval of parliament, an approval that without doubt he would have received. He was also responsible for violating a nonaggression pact with Yugoslavia under German pressure. His predecessor had committed suicide rather than violate his word. Also, it was during Bárdossy's tenure that about 18,000 Jews from the newly occupied territories had been transported to Kamenetz-Podolsk in the Ukraine to be killed. Presumably, he was the first tried because from the Soviet point of view he had committed the worst crime: initiating war against the fatherland of Communism. However, from a political point of view it was an unfortunate choice. That he deserved his punishment was not in question. It is possible and indeed likely that in the long run the country could not have avoided being involved in the world war. Nevertheless, Bárdossy's pro-German policies speeded up the process. However, among all the accused he was the most able to present a coherent and sympathetic defense. He conducted himself with dignity. He was a well-educated man who spoke several languages. He assumed responsibility for his actions

14 Zinner and Róna, p. 111.
15 Major, p. 187.
16 Zinner and Róna, pp. 112–119.

20. Execution of Ferenc Szálasi, March 12, 1946. (Source: Hungarian National Museum.)

without considering himself guilty. He sparred with the prosecutors with intelligence and a better knowledge of recent history than his prosecutors. He defended his actions based on the need to repair the damage done to Hungary by the Trianon treaty. Of course, he knew that he would be sentenced to death, and, unlike all but one other accused, he did not request clemency. The court sentenced him to hanging, but the National Council of Judges changed the sentence to death by firing squad.[17]

There were disagreements among the political parties concerning who should be punished and how. But as far as the major figures were concerned, no such disagreements arose. In the trial of the other former prime minister, Béla Imrédy, which took place in the next month, the prosecutor was Dezső Sulyok, the leader of the right wing of the FKGP.[18] Imrédy was also an intelligent man, but his guilt was much more obvious than Bárdossy's: as premier, Imrédy had been responsible for the anti-Jewish laws of the late 1930s. He was the closest confidante of the Germans among the major politicians of the Horthy regime. In fact, the Germans wanted Horthy to name him premier in 1944, but the governor refused. Imrédy had also served in the government that was established under German occupation. He too was executed by firing squad.

Following the Imrédy trial came the trial of the three men who had been responsible for the deportation of the Jews, Andor Jaross, the minister of the interior in the Sztojay government, and his two undersecretaries, László Endre and László Baky. Jaross was shot, and Endre and Baky hanged. Members of the Sztojay and Szálasi governments were all sentenced to death. Szálasi's case was the last of the major trials. He was so much out of touch with reality that he could fairly be described as mad. In a meeting of his cabinet on April 17, 1945, he mulled over an isolated sentence from a speech of the newly installed President Truman and found in it secret Freemason messages. He told his comrades that the death of President Roosevelt would enable the Germans to achieve alliance with Britain, and ultimately it would be the Germans who would eradicate the British.[19] When the Allies apprehended him, he threatened them with an appeal to the International Court of Justice in the Hague.[20] On every occasion when he was asked, What is your profession?, he always answered, "Nemzetvezető," which is the Hungarian equivalent of Führer. He was allowed to keep a diary in prison,

17 I base my description of the trial on Major, who was the chief judge at the trial. Major, pp. 195–241.
18 Sulyok, pp. 545–554.
19 The sentence according to Szálasi was the following: "The moon, the sun and all the stars fell on us." Zinner and Róna, pp. 200–201.
20 Zinner and Róna, p. 118.

which gives a good account of his worldview. He spoke about his desire to establish an order based on the word of Christ and a world order of nationalism and Socialism.[21] Unlike most of the other accused, he did not deny any of the charges and steadfastly refused to acknowledge the competence of the court.

The major war criminals whose trials were open to the public were remarkably well treated: they were decently fed at a time when the capital was starving. The thousands of lesser-known prisoners in camps, however, were not so fortunate. Here there was not enough food or medicine and not even enough beds, so prisoners slept on the floor.[22] Between 1945 and 1948, the police arrested thousands of people for political reasons other than war crimes. These arrests were somewhat random. Often, they occurred because of denunciations and even personal vendettas. Sometimes people were freed and then quickly rearrested.[23]

Ultimately, in the Communist era the line between people imprisoned for war crimes and those charged with other antiregime activities disappeared.

POGROMS

We tend to assume that the revelation of the horrors of the Holocaust, which immediately after the war had made the dreadful consequences of prejudice clear for everyone to see, diminished anti-Semitism in European and American societies. However, this was not the case at all. On the contrary, at least in Eastern Europe, the opposite occurred. To be sure, the situation of the Jews and the nature and strength of anti-Semitism varied from country to country, and everywhere there were special circumstances. In the Soviet Union during the years between the end of the war and the death of Stalin, anti-Semitism was almost explicit, and it was a government-inspired policy: Jews were singled out for special persecution. This was the time of the "anticosmopolitan campaign" ("cosmopolitan" being a transparent allusion to Jew) and of the infamous "doctors' plot" in which almost all the accused – doctors who were alleged to have planned to murder their highly placed patients – just happened to have obviously Jewish-sounding names. In the Czechoslovak purge trials, Jewish Communists were the most likely victims. The worst anti-Jewish attacks, however, took place in the country where Jews had suffered the most: Poland. With tragic irony, popular anti-Semitism

21 Ibid., p. 268.
22 XIX – A – 1 – j box 31, XXIII b, Report to the minister of the interior, August 24, 1945.
23 PIL 274, 11/10 April 1945.

was strongest where there had been the largest number of victims. Some Poles asked this obscene question from their returning fellow Jewish citizens: how come you have survived? The mention of Kielce, the town where the largest postwar pogrom took place, terrified many Eastern European Jews at the time. It is estimated that 2000 Jews were killed in postwar Poland between 1945 and 1947.[24]

In Hungary, the anti-Semitic outbursts were not as bloody as in Poland, but here also there were tragic incidents. The character of postwar Hungarian anti-Semitism differed from previous versions. In the interwar period, it had been the government that had been primarily responsible: immediately after World War I, it passed anti-Jewish laws, most significantly a *numerus clausus* limiting the number of Jews in institutions of higher education. (After the passage of a few years, the government quietly allowed this law to lapse.) However, beginning in 1938, under the influence of Hitler's Germany, the government once again passed a series of ever more stringent laws restricting Jewish economic activity. This government also tolerated, indeed, inspired, anti-Semitic propaganda. There is no way to measure the strength of popular anti-Semitism, but there is little doubt that simple people, especially the lower classes in the cities, were anti-Semitic and accepted the demagogic accusations against Jews at face value. The vast majority of them certainly showed little sympathy to Jews at the time of their greatest tragedy. On the other hand, in the interwar period there had been no spontaneous outbursts of violence against Jews.

The situation changed after 1945. Immediately after the defeat of the Nazis, of course, the new provisional government abrogated all anti-Jewish legislation, although it said nothing about the necessity of returning to the Jews their lost property.[25] At the same time, archival records show a great increase of anti-Semitic sentiment among the common folk, especially among the peasantry. Not only the common folk but also journalists and politicians expressed, if not open anti-Semitism, then what seems to us remarkable insensitivity. In this respect, there was no difference among the political parties. Hungarians, including the intellectuals, took it for granted that the destruction of the Jewry had been entirely the work of the Germans and a handful of native helpers, who now were punished. They explicitly rejected the claim of special Jewish suffering. On March 25, 1945, even before all the camps were liberated and the surviving inmates could return,

24 Antony Polonsky (ed.), *Studies in Polish Jewish Jewry*, London: Littman, 2000, p. 39.

25 MOL XVIII – 3 Provisional National Assembly (INGY) Constitutional Committee, February 5, 1945.

József Darvas, a crypto-Communist leader of the NPP, wrote in the Communist daily, *Szabad Nép*:

There is today a part of the Jewry, fortunately a smaller part, especially those bourgeois figures, who have done nothing against fascism and for democracy, who expect, indeed, demand recognition for special suffering. The workers and peasants also suffered and yet now they work. Those who do not want to work will be expelled from society together with the other saboteurs, and reactionaries.[26]

His fellow leader in the NPP, Péter Veres, said in a mass gathering: "In the Peasant Party there are only Hungarians, we do not need foreigners, neither Swabs, nor Jews."[27] Dezső Sulyok, a liberal, who had voted against the anti-Jewish laws of the late 1930s, nevertheless regarded the Jewish leaders of the Communist Party as non-Hungarians and explained the pogroms as a response to the behavior of the Jews in the police.[28] Leaders of all political parties agreed that there were too many Jews in positions of power, especially in the police.

In 1946, a series of small-scale pogroms occurred, something that had not happened in the interwar period. How are we to explain this phenomenon? Several factors contributed to this unfortunate development. First of all, one should not underestimate the lasting power of Nazi propaganda: it would have been surprising if all those Nazi stereotypes about Jews, in which people had come to believe, had disappeared overnight. Perhaps a more powerful explanation is a psychological one. By and large, people in Eastern Europe, certainly including Hungary, did not acquit themselves well during the years of Nazi rule. Too many became accomplices, but even those who did not could not have had a clear conscience, knowing that they had done nothing to save their innocent fellow citizens. Under the circumstances, it was comforting to believe that Jews had deserved their fate, that they were in fact an alien, subversive, and exploitative people. It is a well-known psychological phenomenon that the worse we behave toward an individual the more we dislike him. It lessens our sense of guilt if we can believe that the person we have mistreated was, in fact, a wicked human being. Undoubtedly, the same mechanism also works on the level of social groups.

Furthermore, it was true that non-Jewish Hungarians also suffered greatly during the war. The Second Hungarian Army fighting on the Don in January 1943 was for all practical purposes eliminated. Tens of thousands of

26 Szabad Nép, March 25, 1945.
27 Gyurgyák, p. 585.
28 Sulyok, p. 525.

soldiers died and an even larger number fell into Soviet captivity. In 1944, Hungarian territory was bitterly fought over, causing enormous destruction, and Budapest became one of the most heavily damaged European cities. Under the circumstances, the Hungarians liked to regard themselves as victims and were not impressed by the obvious fact that their Jewish countrymen suffered incomparably more. They were unwilling to accept responsibility for the destruction of the Hungarian Jewry and liked to believe, incorrectly, that the entire guilt fell on the Germans. The very notion that they also might be responsible added to their hostility.

Another explanation for the wave of anti-Semitic outbursts might be that although prewar Jewry had played extraordinarily significant roles in the economy and cultural life of the nation, it had been completely excluded from political power. Now, Jews were in leadership positions not only in the powerful Communist and Socialist Parties but also in the political police. Peasants in particular found it hard to accept Jews in positions of authority and were willing to listen to demagogic voices deploring Jewish power. In anti-Semitic discourse, it was a recurring theme that Jews now control everything and they are determined to take revenge. In the mind of the Hungarians, justifiably or not, Jews and Communists came to be identified with one another. The Communist Party did everything in its power to counteract this identification but ultimately failed. This identification had considerable significance in postwar Hungarian political developments, and it did great damage both to Communists and to Jews.

Hungarian Jewry, and especially the Jews of Budapest, was like no other Jewry in the world: it was a Western type of Jewry, living in an Eastern European economic and political environment.[29] For our purposes, Western European Jewry is defined by the following: a high degree of assimilation, large number of converts, low birth rate, substantial Christian-Jewish intermarriage, speaking the local language instead of Yiddish, and contributing not to the minority Jewish culture but to the native, in this instance, Hungarian, culture. Hungarian Jewry was every bit as well assimilated as the German Jewry, and it regarded itself as Hungarian just as enthusiastically as the German Jews regarded themselves as German. The difference was that Hungary, unlike Germany, was an Eastern European country: before 1945, the last genuine European feudal ruling class governed it. The country was largely agricultural and the landed gentry owned most of the land. As a consequence of the particular Hungarian social structure, in the late nineteenth

29 The distinction between eastern and western types is taken from the work of Ezra Mendelsohn, *The Jews of East Central Europe between the World Wars*, Bloomington: Indiana UP, 1983.

century a tacit compromise was reached between the aristocracy and the Jewry: middle-class occupations, trade and industry, and the liberal professions were conceded to Jews. The aristocracy had no interest in such affairs, but at the same time it was keen to advance economic modernization and needed an urban middle class with its entrepreneurs and cultural leaders.

After the collapse of the Austro-Hungarian monarchy, a new Hungarian middle class gradually developed, which competed for jobs with Jews, and with it suddenly a modern type of anti-Semitism appeared. A convenient justification for this newfound anti-Semitism was the extraordinarily large role that Jews had played in the short-lived Hungarian Soviet Republic of 1919. Although only a small proportion of the Jews were attracted to Communism at that time, nevertheless the small Communist Party's leadership was largely in Jewish hands: after all, Jews made up a dominant part of the intelligentsia, and these were the people traditionally attracted to radical, Socialist politics. So it was that Hungary, which had been an excellent place for Jews, suddenly became much less than excellent. In spite of the anti-Semitic laws that were introduced in interwar Hungary, however, the extraordinary role of Jews in economic and intellectual life did not altogether vanish. Very few Jews became manual workers, and there were practically no Jewish peasants. The Jews who had been deported by the Nazis to death camps in 1944 were still a relatively prosperous group, in spite of the previous Hungarian government's attempts to reduce their role in the economy and impoverish them. Most of them had been merchants, clerks, and professional people. There was much to be taken away from them when they were deported and much to be reclaimed on their return, which, as we shall see, came to be a major source of conflict.

The demagogic accusation that Jews were exploiters and at the same time subversives has been used by anti-Semites often and in many societies. It was obviously a part of Nazi propaganda and appeal. In Hungary, however, these charges were especially powerful for the simple reason that Jews were, in fact, both the captains of industry and at the same time the leaders of the Communist Party. This duality had much to do with the character of postwar anti-Semitism and also with the behavior of the Jews at this time.

Because Hungary had been an ally (or a satellite) of Germany in the war and was occupied by the Nazis only on March 19, 1944, the destruction of the Jewry began only on that date. (There had been some exceptions: from the Carpatho-Ukraine thousands of Jews had been sent to their deaths earlier.) The fact that Hungary was an ally, rather than an occupied land, had another consequence: military-age Jewish males, subject to deportation elsewhere and barred from the Hungarian army by the anti-Jewish laws, were conscripted instead into labor battalions. This particular institution existed nowhere else in Nazi-dominated Europe. In the labor battalions, the chances of survival depended on the decency of the Hungarian officers, but by and large survival rates were much better than in concentration camps. When these men returned after the war and could not find their murdered families, they were likely to join the Communists. Many of them felt an understandable bitterness toward their Hungarian compatriots, a feeling that influenced their actions and behavior.

Calculating the losses of the Jewry during the Holocaust is a difficult task. First of all, there is a difference between who was Jewish according to the census data and according to the Nazis. In the territory of wartime Hungary, according to census figures, there were 725,000 Jews, the largest Jewry in Europe after Poland and the Soviet Union. These figures do not include converted Jews, whose number, especially in Budapest, was sizeable. So, if we look at the number from the point of view of those who were victimized by the Nazis, we must add another 100,000.[30]

This was not a homogeneous Jewry. About half of the Jews lived in territories that Hungary had acquired just before the war, as rewards for its alliance with Nazi Germany. These newly occupied territories contained a very large number of Jews, whose social and economic situation was quite different from the "original" Hungarian Jewry, especially from the Jewry in Budapest. When we look at the postwar situation, it is more relevant to look at the number of victims and survivors from only the territory of so called "Trianon" Hungary. (That is, Hungary as it was geographically constituted by the Trianon Peace and before significant territories were added or "returned" because of the alliance with Germany in the late 1930s). According to the Nazi definition of "Jew," approximately 490,000 Jews lived in "Trianon" Hungary at the outbreak of the war. At the end of 1945 – that is, by the time those who had survived returned from camps and from labor battalions – there were fewer than 100,000 Jews in Budapest and fewer than 50,000 in the rest of the country. Hungary lost more than two-thirds of its Jewry, and in absolute numbers only Poland and the Soviet Union lost more Jewish citizens to Nazi slaughter.

The behavior of the Hungarian people in 1944, and let us immediately add that it was not very different from that of other Eastern European peoples, convinced many Jews that their assimilation had been a sham, that they had not been accepted, and that their lives and livelihood would never be secure in the country of their birth, and many decided to emigrate. We

30 Ferenc Szabó, *Egy Millióval Kevesebben*, Pécs: Pannonia, 1998, pp. 44–62.

do not have precise data, but estimates put the number between 20,000 and 50,000 people. Most of them went to the United States and to Palestine. The Zionists for the first time achieved considerable influence, especially among the youth. The possibility of leaving the country, however, ended by 1949, at which time the borders were tightly sealed.

For our purposes, however, the relevant part of Hungarian Jewry is the part that decided to stay either because of inertia or because of conviction. A disproportionate number of these Jews were attracted to leftist, radical policies and came to support either the Socialist or the Communist Party. Even though the economic policies of the Communist Party threatened the economic interests, indeed, livelihood, of the Jews, the Communists appeared to many as the only force capable of protecting them against the anti-Semitic Hungarian people. After all, the Communist and Socialist Parties possessed a nearly perfect record in opposing the fascists (not counting the years of 1939–1941). This was particularly true about the Communist Party that had been illegal before 1945. The Soviet Union and the Red Army stood behind the Communists. That fact was a great handicap in the eyes of many Hungarians, but for the Jews it was the other way around. The majority of Hungarians did not greet the Soviet occupation with pleasure. Russians had never been popular in Hungary, and the behavior of Soviet troops in 1945 turned this unpopularity into hatred among many Hungarians. But for Jews, it was an obvious and indisputable fact that the Red Army had saved their lives. Jews and perhaps only Jews could regard the Soviet occupation of 1945 as an unambiguous liberation. Jews naïvely understood Soviet ideology as an ideology of internationalism, the exact opposite of German and Hungarian nationalism, which, in their view, had culminated in Nazism.

The promise of Socialism was the promise of transcending nationalist and racist prejudice. For these reasons a pro-Soviet bias became a prominent feature of Jewish thinking, leading thousands of Jews into the Communist Party, the Communist bureaucracy, and the organs of state repression. Even when the party pursued policies that were almost explicitly anti-Semitic, most Jews could not forget the experience of 1945, when their lives had been saved from one day to the next by the arrival of the Red Army. For many Jews, joining the Communist Party was itself an act of assimilation.

Let us admit that some Jews who joined the Communist Party, especially the Communist political police, the infamous AVO, joined not simply because they wanted to fight for Communism but also because that organization offered the opportunity to take revenge on those who had abused them in the past. (Indeed, there was one instance of an organized retaliation by Jews on their enemies. In 1945, Jewish men returning from worker battalions to the village of Gyömrő and finding that all their relatives had been killed, joined the Communist political police; then with weapons received from the Red Army they killed some sixteen people whom they considered responsible for Nazi atrocities.)[31] The Communists employed Jews in these capacities because Jews were reliable, and association with the previous regime had not compromised them. Nowhere else could the party have found so many educated and reliable cadres as among the Jews. No precise numbers exist, and anti-Semites and anti-Communists, for their own reasons, overestimated the number and percentage of Jews in the Communist Party and especially in the AVO. Still, there can be no question that Jews were overrepresented in this organization and also in the party. According to the best estimates, about one-seventh of the party membership was Jewish in 1945 at a time when Jews made up between 1 and 2 percent of the population. At the same time, it is also evident that the great majority of Jews did not become Communist Party members.

According to contemporary figures, no doubt imprecise, approximately a quarter of the Jewish population voted for the Communists in the 1945 elections. (Nationally, the Communist Party received 17 percent of the vote.)[32] For the 1947 elections, we have no comparable figures, but it is estimated that the Communists received an even larger share of the Jewish vote than in 1945. The party not only did nothing to gain the allegiance of the Jews, but on the contrary, it took steps to emphasize that it was not beholden to Jews. Jewish voting behavior becomes comprehensible only when we remember that in 1946 there was a wave of anti-Semitic outbursts. The party did nothing to prevent these; indeed, its antibourgeois rhetoric contributed to the anti-Semitic atmosphere, but from the point of view of the Jews, the Communist Party remained their only protection.

The unusual aspect of the Hungarian situation was that the government was largely in Jewish hands. Jews played prominent roles in the other Eastern European countries also, but nowhere was their domination as complete as in Hungary. All four of the most prominent and powerful leaders of the Communist Party were Jewish.

It is true that these Communists were not in full control of the government until 1948, but, from the very outset, they had behind them the power of the Red Army, and therefore the Communist Party unquestionably was

31 PIL 274/16/1. Workers' battalions were a particular Hungarian institution. Jewish men were not allowed to serve in the army but were drafted into these units to perform particularly dangerous and unpleasant tasks. Of course, they were not given weapons.

32 Róbert Györi Szabó and György Borsányi, *A Kommunista Párt és a Zsidóság Magyarországon: (1945–1956)*, Budapest: Windsor, 1997, pp. 86–87.

the decisive force in Hungarian politics. How Jewish Communists made possible and in some ways even encouraged native anti-Semitism is an interesting psychological and political phenomenon, which deserves further exploration. The Communist leaders, of course, did not think of themselves as Jewish. They naively believed that, by becoming Communists, they had ceased to be Jewish. They all survived the Nazi era, not in German-occupied Hungary, but in the Soviet Union. Perhaps if they had experienced the Holocaust directly, their sense of community with their fellow Jews would have grown stronger, and they would have understood that no one is entirely free to choose his or her identity.

Nowhere else do we find such a clear example of anti-Semitic policies carried out by Jews as in postwar Hungary. The behavior of the top Communist leaders was entirely cynical. Of course, a Rákosi or a Gerő was not an anti-Semite in the narrow sense of the word. They nevertheless carried out policies that harmed their fellow Jews and on several occasions led to pogroms. They well understood that the association of the party with Jews was harmful to the Communist cause. (It was harmful not only within Hungary but also in their relationship with an increasingly anti-Semitic Stalin. It is true that he tolerated Jews in the top leadership positions in Hungary, but that was perhaps because these were the people who had lived through the war years in Moscow, and therefore Stalin knew them or knew of them and consequently believed that they could be trusted to carry out obediently policies that were favorable to Soviet interests.) The Communist leaders did everything within their power to deny their Jewish origins. They went to ridiculous lengths to cover up their background. Rákosi, for example, went so far as to imitate a peasant accent and peppered his speeches with what seemed to him to be village expressions.[33] Needless to say, such attempts were in vain.

The archives of the Communist Party from these years are full of news about anti-Semitic sentiments and outbursts. Reports flooded in demonstrating not only simple, ignorant anti-Semitism, but also the people's association of unpopular Communist initiatives with Jewish self-interest. In 1947, for example, a silly rumor spread in the countryside that because the war in Palestine was not going well for the Jews, the government was going to import thousands to Hungary. (This was at a time when thousands of Hungarian Jews were, in fact, going from Hungary to Palestine.) The peasants professed to believe that Jews did not have to pay taxes. When the government decided to nationalize church-run schools in 1948, women

33 Árpád Pünkösti, *Rákosi a hatalomért: 1945–1948*, Budapest: Európa Könyvkiadó, 1992.

demonstrated against nationalization saying that the government was going to hire Jewish teachers.[34]

Anti-Semitism had a particularly long tradition in Szabolcs County, the district in which the last Hungarian blood libel trial had taken place in the nineteenth century. A Communist functionary reported from this county that in the village of Kisvárad a worker being interrogated said: "Everyone knows that it is the Jews who are in power here." He also wrote: "In the village of Nyirbátor, when someone is arrested by the police, people simply say: 'the Jews took him.' "[35]

Anti-Semitism was also strong among workers. A functionary reported in 1947: "There is a strong anti-Semitic wave in the factories. There were no Jews among the workers before deportations and there are none now. Among Communist leaders there are many Jews who defend the special privileges of Jews." And elsewhere: "Minority rules and majority starves." In a trade union meeting of the bookbinding trade, a Communist speaker by the name of József Sárközi said: "Only Jews benefited. We have achieved nothing." Ferenc Katona, a trade union official, went further: "In the past also Jewish capitalists ruled over us, and they still do. This cannot continue."[36]

Beyond the usual sources of anti-Semitism, there were several new and specific ones in the postwar period that the party had to deal with. One of these was the issue of property taken from Jews in the previous years and the understandable desire of the Jews to reclaim what had been theirs. For many Christians, it was an insult that someone wanted to take away what they had come to regard as their own. A sad joke that Jews were telling one another at the time is revealing: A Jew who survived the camps runs into a Christian friend. "How are you?" the friend asks. "Don't even ask," the Jew replies. "I have returned from the camp, and now I have nothing, except the clothes you are wearing."[37] It was explicit Communist policy not to support Jewish efforts to take back what was legally theirs. In the case of Jewish-owned apartments and houses that Christians had taken over, the police were instructed not to allow the removal of the Christian tenants.

In the dire economic situation, black markets flourished. The Communists, given their hostility to free markets, naturally blamed problems on speculators. On this volatile issue, their demagogy, based on their visceral dislike of private enterprise, easily slipped into anti-Semitism, at times with tragic consequences.

34 PIL 274/21/7. Report from Nograd county. 35 PIL 274/16/1.
36 PIL 277/16/246. This is the source for both quotations.
37 R. Róbert Györi Szabo, p. 126.

For the series of pogroms that took place in 1946, the responsibility of the Communist Party is undeniable. For demagogic reasons, the party decided to use the dreadful economic situation and the misery that followed for "sharpening the class struggle," which in reality meant that it made small traders scapegoats for the genuine problems. In this struggle, the Communists explicitly approved, indeed advocated, mass movements, spontaneous demonstrations, and even lynching. The party had organized a retaliation against "speculators" by promising to hang black marketeers. The leaders knew or certainly should have known that many of these traders were Jewish, and even if they were not, in the eyes of the common folk they were. It published posters in which the "enemy," the capitalist, the speculator, often had Semitic features. The Communists did not create anti-Semitism, but consciously or unconsciously they contributed to it. In effect, the party attempted to turn the powerful anti-Semitic currents, which were present in Hungarian society at the time, to its own advantage in its struggle for power, and in the process they sacrificed the interests and, in a handful of cases, the lives of Jewish citizens.

In February 1946, the disturbances in Ozd, a mining town, showed the complexity of the situation and the dilemmas faced by the Communist leadership. A Communist leader, who was a well-known anti-Semite, was murdered under mysterious circumstances. The following day a large crowd of miners and workers came to demonstrate. The Communist Party welcomed the demonstration at first, regarding it as a move against "reactionaries" and "fascists." However, the mood quickly turned into something different: the masses demonstrated against Communists and Jews and looted Jewish-owned stores and apartments. When the police arrested some of the looters, the masses were increasingly incensed and maintained that there could be no solution to the social and political problems until they got rid of the Jews. Révai, the man responsible for ideology, reported to the Central Committee: "The demonstration which was undoubtedly justified and correct as a move against a fascist assassination, soon turned into looting, provoked by fascists."[38]

Although there were anti-Jewish demonstrations and attacks on individual Jews in at least a dozen places in 1946, the bloodiest and worst manifestation took place in Kunmadaras in May and in Miskolc in July.[39] The Kunmadaras affair even included the ancient anti-Jewish calumny of blood libel, which,

38 R. Róbert Györi Szabo, p. 149.

39 The most detailed description of the pogroms of 1946 is in János Pelle, *Az utolsó vérvádak*, Budapest: Pelikan, 1995, pp. 149–246.

especially among the peasantry, was still widespread all around the country. The rumor spread in Kunmadaras that Jews made sausage out of Christian children, and it was said that in the nearby town of Karcag several Christian children had mysteriously disappeared. The pogrom, however, against the tiny local Jewry (out of a Jewish population of 250 before the war, only 73 had survived) began only when the police arrested and attempted to transfer to Karcag a popular person who had collaborated with the Nazis. A crowd prevented taking the man to court, and the aroused people beat up the local Socialist Party secretary. The Socialist functionary later reported: "When the crowd kicked out my teeth I suddenly realized that I was beaten not because I was a socialist, but because I was a Jew." The next day, the crowd attacked local Jews, killing 2 and wounding 15. Here, just as in Ozd, violence against Jews quickly turned into looting. Although in this instance the Communist Party could not be held directly responsible for the events, the Communists attempted to make political capital out of the pogrom by unjustly blaming the Smallholder Party for it.

The situation was different in Miskolc. Here the Communist Party was directly responsible. Miskolc was an industrial town, where the working class was in particularly dire straits. The Communists crudely used this disaffection for their own political purposes. They attempted to mobilize the people by making speculators and black marketeers scapegoats for the genuine problems. In the summer of 1946, the misery was the greatest, and inflation reached unheard of proportions. Plans called for the introduction of a new and stable currency, the forint, on August 1: to its credit, the Communist Party was playing a major role in the work of financial stabilization. In June and July, prominent Communist leaders came to Miskolc and harangued the workers. Gerő said: "Why have you not hanged a single black marketeer?" Rákosi himself came to Miskolc and in his speech demanded death to those who speculated and were therefore the enemies of the new, stable currency. The complexity of the situation and the inherent dangers for the Communist Party in its own policies are shown by the fact that before Rákosi's arrival in the town, anti-Jewish graffiti had appeared on the wall calling Rákosi a rotten Jew. Instead of attempting to calm the crowds, the Communists' policy was to demonstrate that it was not a "Jewish party." The local Communist organization was aware of the anti-Semitic mood of the workers, and, instead of attempting to combat this anti-Semitism, it decided to remove party functionaries who came from the Jewish bourgeoisie.

Violence broke out on July 30 during worker demonstrations against the economic hardships. News spread that three "speculators" had been arrested and that they were being moved to an internment camp outside of the city. It seems likely that the demonstrators had been notified ahead of time where and when the prisoners would be marched. The crowds attacked the unfortunate men, killed one, wounded another, and let the third one escape. It could not have been an accident that of the three he alone was not Jewish. The police stood by without attempting to stop the lynching. After the tragic events, the police did arrest some of the participants. However, on August 1 the crowds attacked the police station where the men were kept and there lynched the Jewish-Communist police lieutenant.

Later, it transpired that the "speculators" had been victims of a provocation. The Communist head of the county, István Oszip, had persuaded three mill owners to sell flour at several times the fixed price. He did this in order to show the crowds that the authorities were fighting against the black market.[40] Clearly, he did not foresee the consequences. It is remarkable that Rákosi, writing his memoirs in Soviet exile in the late 1960s or early 1970s, would say only a few words about the Miskolc pogrom:

> In the days preceding August 1st at two places there were serious disturbances. In Diosgyör the Political Police arrested a few troublemakers, and consequently the enemy managed to persuade some of the workers to march to Miskolc, and in the confusion two workers of the Political Police were killed. It was possible to reestablish order quickly.

After an interval of several decades, that is all that Rákosi found necessary to say about this sorry event.[41]

After 1946, the wave of attacks on Jewish life and property subsided. The political and economic situation stabilized, and the regime, increasingly under Communist domination, was able to maintain order. While the party was struggling for power, mass movements and demonstrations served their purposes. Once the Communists were in power, disorder not only did not serve their interests, but on the contrary, it became dangerous. The lack of spontaneous violence against Jews, of course, did not mean that anti-Semitism had disappeared. At the time of the Hungarian Revolution of 1956, anti-Semitic incidents occurred once again, although, in view of the brevity of the revolutionary period, it is difficult to say how important and widespread they were.

The Communist Party in the immediate postwar period pursued a contradictory and confused policy regarding overt anti-Semitism. This confusion followed from the facts that the leadership of the party was largely in

40 Róbert Györi Szabo, p. 162.

41 M. Rákosi, *Visszaemlékezések, 1940–1956*, p. 298.

Jewish hands and that popular anti-Semitism was strong especially in these years. As far as the Communist leadership was concerned, the interests of the Communist cause were far more important than the defense of a persecuted minority. The leaders believed that by dissociating themselves from Jewish claims for restitution and by encouraging demagogic agitation against speculators they could divert anti-Semitic sentiment from themselves and the party. Such a policy was bound to be unsuccessful and only imposed more misery on the Jews without making the public any less anti-Communist.

8

The Catholic Church

Already in 1945, it was obvious that the Communist Party, with the support of the Soviet army, presented the greatest danger to the survival of pluralism. It was not clear, however, which was the best way to parry the danger: should non-Communist groups give concessions and thereby prove their good will, hoping to moderate the Communists, or, on the contrary, should the Communists be resisted by all available means? The non-Communist segment of the political spectrum was divided on this issue: were the leaders of the Smallholders Party correct in giving in to the demands of the Communists? Or was the Catholic Church, led by Joseph Cardinal Mindszenty, pursuing a more intelligent policy by fiercely resisting?

The discussion of the relations between the leaders of the Catholic Church and the Communists show that there were debates within the Church, within the anti-Communist coalition, and to a lesser extent even among the Communists themselves. It was inevitable, of course, that the Church and the Communists would end up on the opposite sides of the struggle, given their mutually exclusive worldviews. Nevertheless, what was the best tactic for each side to pursue in this conflict was not self-evident. Intelligent Communist leaders in 1945 understood that a frontal attack on the Church would backfire, and therefore the Communists attempted at first to avoid open conflict as much as possible. The decision to take the offensive came only when they felt themselves strong enough to do so.

According to a public opinion survey carried out in 1948, more than 90 percent of the population considered themselves believers (95 percent in the countryside); half of the population attended church regularly and another 25 percent occasionally.[1] These were larger percentages than before the war.

1 Magyar Távirati Iroda, Public opinion survey, Confidential report, PIL 274 23/26, pp. 23–25.

Some contemporary observers attributed this phenomenon to the people's craving for consolation in religious faith at a time of great poverty, misery, and uncertainty.[2] It is also possible that some were attracted to religious worship, especially in the Catholic churches, because it was one way to express opposition to the new order in which the Communists played an ever-greater role.

Two-thirds of the population was Roman Catholic. Although in Hungary the Catholic Church did not possess the same degree of influence and certainly did not enjoy the same degree of identification with the nationalist cause as it did in Poland, nevertheless, before 1945 it had possessed considerable power. (Because of the Catholic Church's close identification with the Habsburgs, Protestants, who made up only a quarter of the population, had played a greater role in the nationalist movements all through Hungarian history.[3])

Unlike Tsarist Russia or, indeed, democratic England, pre–Second World War Hungary had no official church, and, in theory, Protestants, Catholics, Greek Orthodox, and even Jews enjoyed the same rights. In practice, however, no attempt had been made to separate church and state.[4] The representatives of the churches sat ex officio in the upper house and the head of the Church, the cardinal of Esztergom, was a prince of the realm, his title being "prince-cardinal." The Catholic Church played a major role in education, had an extensive charity network, and maintained hospitals and orphanages. Most significantly, the Catholic Church was enormously wealthy: it owned a considerable portion of the arable land of the country. The churches, in particular the Catholic Church, had become very much a part of that anachronistic, almost feudal, system that existed in prewar Hungary. With the collapse of that system, it was inevitable that the churches would lose some of their privilege, even if the country were not Sovietized.

In the interwar period, the Church's hierarchy was thoroughly enmeshed in the existing political-social system and was intensely conservative. When a young Jesuit priest, Jenö Kerkai, had the opportunity to address a gathering of bishops on the question of land reform, one of the bishops interrupted him: "Do not dare to mention that word!"[5] Representatives of Christian churches, including Justinian Cardinal Serédi, voted in the upper house of the parliament in 1939 for the "Second Jewish Laws." These laws drastically

2 József Mindszenty, *Emlékirataim*, Toronto: Vörösváry, 1974, pp. 70–71.

3 Jenő Gergely, *A Katolikus Egyház Magyarországon, 1944–1971*, Budapest: Kossuth, 1985, p. 11.

4 Before 1947 there were three types of church in Hungary: 1. national, 2. recognized, and 3. nonrecognized (i.e., sects). In 1947, these distinctions were abolished.

5 Margit Balogh, *A KALOT és a Katolikus társadalompolitika, 1935–1946*, Budapest: MTA, 1998, p. 45.

21. Joseph Cardinal Mindszenty, 1892–1975.

limited the role of Jews in national life in the name of defending Hungarian culture, Christian values, and the economic well-being of the nation.[6]

There were some priests who believed that unless the Church took a position on the critical social issues of the time it was in danger of losing the faithful. These churchmen, many of them Jesuits, were influenced by the ideology of European Christian Socialism. They felt that it was essential to offer an alternative to Communism, to left-wing radicalism. In the middle of the 1930s, young Jesuit priests established a movement known as KALOT (an abbreviation of Christian Agrarian Youth Organization); it was nationalist, anti-Socialist, and anti-Semitic. Its leaders, Kerkai and Töhötöm Nagy, advanced some of the same demands and subscribed more or less to the same worldview as the Hungarian Nazis, the Arrow Cross Party of Ferenc Szálasi. In Hungary at that time, only the radicalism of the right found public support.[7] Because they were most concerned with social justice, perhaps it is not surprising that those young priests who had been most willing to cooperate with right-wing radicals of the Nazi variety were also the most likely to accept the inevitable and compromise with the Communists after the war.

In Hungary, as elsewhere in Eastern Europe, it was obvious that the Communist regime, which was in the process of being created, would sooner or later collide with the churches, because Communist ideology and Christian faith were not reconcilable. But what form the conflict would take and how

6 Gyurgyák, pp. 149–150.

7 M. Balogh, p. 64.

bitter it would be was not immediately apparent. In 1945, even those who made foreign policy in the Kremlin had no clear idea of the future of Eastern Europe, and the religious policies of the Communists were a function of the general political struggle. As bitterly as the Vatican had opposed Communism heretofore, when the war ended with Soviet armies occupying a large part of Europe, the Church recognized that some sort of modus vivendi with the Russians might be inevitable in order to preserve at least some influence in Eastern Europe. How the relations between church and state would develop in each newly occupied country and how strongly and with what means the Catholic church would resist the new authorities very much depended on personalities. That the Church in Hungary in this critical period was led by Cardinal Mindszenty turned out to be decisively important. Mindszenty was the most rigid among the senior churchmen, but the archbishops and bishops were almost as conservative. Lajos Shvoy, the bishop of Székesfehérvár, was as determined an opponent of cooperation with the new authorities as Mindszenty. In his pastoral letter written in 1948, the leader of the moderates, the archbishop of Eger, Gyula Czapik, implicitly argued that accepting the changes introduced by the government, such as laws concerning secular marriage and easier divorce, were irreconcilable with Catholic faith. In the same pastoral letter, rather tactlessly in view of the very recent past, he repeatedly denounced the Jews as murderers of Christ.[8] In his description, Pilate was only a hypocrite, for he gave into the Jews when he knew that Jesus was innocent, but the Jews were responsible for "terror." It must be added, however, that the Church of Rome at this time continued to view the Jews as Christ killers, so Czapik's views were not considered extreme.

In March 1945, Justinian Cardinal Serédi died, leaving the Church without a titular head at a time of revolutionary transformation. In the absence of a cardinal, it was the Conference of Bishops that had to deal with the day-to-day questions. During the months following the end of the war, land reform was by far the most important issue in Church-state relations. The Catholic Church, the largest landowner in Hungary, lost seven-eighths of its land, 1,087,271 acres out of 1,225,039 English acres.[9] The state, in exchange, promised financial support for the maintenance of religious institutions. The secularization of church lands was long overdue, and from the point of view of the Church it could have been regarded as a benefit. In the modern world, it was incongruous that the Church stood together with the most conservative landed aristocracy in Europe. Indeed, at least a

8 PIL 274 7/262, pp. 1–3.

9 Gergely, p. 24.

minority among the churchmen regarded land reform favorably or at least as inevitable under the circumstances. The Conference of Bishops, however, was of a different opinion. In their protest, the bishops made two arguments: they disputed the right of the provisional government to make a decision of such major importance, and they maintained that church lands should belong to a different category than privately held estates, because the wealth of the Church was to be used for charitable purposes. József Grosz, the archbishop of Kalocsa and the most senior churchman in the absence of a cardinal, wrote to the prime minister of the provisional government, Béla Miklós, protesting the land reform.[10]

Not only was the Church without a prince-cardinal but the official contacts with Rome had also been interrupted. The ACC directed all diplomats who had maintained ties with the Szálasi regime to leave the country. Although the papal nuncio, Angelo Cardinal Rotta, had behaved courageously in 1944 and was among the very few senior Catholic churchmen who publicly protested the deportation of the Jews, he too fell into the category of diplomats to be expelled. The provisional government was not permitted to have independent diplomatic relations; it had no diplomats anywhere, and consequently no diplomat could be accredited to Hungary. It was, however, expected that the papal representative would soon be allowed to return.[11]

Nevertheless, some direct contact with the Holy See continued through the efforts of the remarkably intelligent, restless, and adventurous Jesuit priest Töhötöm Nagy, a close friend of Kerkai, and with him a cofounder of KALOT. By 1944, it was clear that the Germans would lose the war and that the Red Army would occupy Hungary. Under the circumstances, the leaders of KALOT understood that it would be necessary to come to terms with the victorious powers. In November 1944, Nagy succeeded in crossing the front line and was received by Marshal Voroshilov. Nagy's political goal was the establishment of a Christian Socialist Party in Hungary and finding some sort of agreement between the victorious Soviet Union and the Hungarian Catholic Church. In 1945 by illegal and circuitous means he went to Rome twice and was on each occasion received by Pope Pius XII.

Töhötöm Nagy had the opportunity at the time to comment on various Catholic figures that might have been considered to lead the Hungarian

10 PIL 274 7/247 April 4, 1945, Grosz to Miklós. The government was willing to leave more lands for Bishops Mindszenty and Shvoy in recognition of their anti-Nazi stand in 1944, but Mindszenty refused this concession.

11 Gergely, pp. 35–38.

Church. Mindszenty was his number one candidate because, he argued, the bishop of Veszprém was an excellent organizer and a man of blameless personal life and enormous willpower. He did mention, however, that Mindszenty was excessively strict, inflexible, and a legitimist. Very soon he was sorry that he had made this recommendation.[12]

Indeed, in August 1945, Pope Pius XII named József Mindszenty the head of the Hungarian Church. This was a surprising choice for several reasons. Not only did the pope disregard the recommendations of the Hungarian provisional government but also the bishop of Veszprém was the most junior among the bishops and was not well known even within the Church. The bishopric of Veszprém had a relatively low standing in the hierarchy of church offices. (Historically, Kalocsa and Eger, both archbishoprics, were the most important Church seats after Esztergom.) Furthermore, Mindszenty had been bishop of Veszprém for only one year.[13] There were two considerations, however, that may have influenced the pope. During Nazi rule in 1944, Mindszenty had organized some of the senior churchmen of Western Hungary and delivered a letter in their name to the Nazi authorities advising them not to make western Hungary a battlefield. (In this letter, there was no mention of Nazi terror or the fate of the Jews, whose extermination at this time proceeded with renewed force.[14]) For his efforts, Mindszenty was promptly arrested; consequently, he could not be accused of collaboration with the Nazis. At a time when the Croatian and Slovak hierarchies had been deeply compromised by their cooperation with the Nazis, this was a significant consideration. Furthermore, in the course of the first few months following the end of the war, Mindszenty had shown no interest in cooperating with the new authorities. His conservatism and his distaste for Socialism and Communism were well known to Angelo Rotta, who must have been the adviser of the pope in this matter. Presumably, it was Rotta's, rather than Nagy's, recommendation that was decisive. In the past, Rotta had been a patron of Mindszenty. It was he who had recommended Mindszenty to the pope as bishop of Veszprém a year before, even though this decision

12 Töhötöm Nagy, *Jesuiták és Szabadkőművesek*, Szeged: Universum, 1990, pp. 182–183.

13 Gergely, pp. 35–38.

14 In 1991, the pope visited Hungary and prayed at the grave of the cardinal, whose body had been returned to Esztergom in that year. At that time, some Jews protested, saying that Mindszenty had been an anti-Semite and did not raise his voice against mass murder in 1944. He had allowed priests in Veszprém to hold a mass on June 25, 1944, at which they prayed to God to free their town of Jews. On the basis of the available evidence, it seems that he was no more anti-Semitic than most churchmen. When he courageously chose to protest turning western Hungary into a battlefield, he found no reason to mention that Jews were being killed. In 1944, there were some senior churchmen, who, however cautiously and belatedly, raised their voices in defense of Jews. Mindszenty was not among them. The *New York Times*, August 19, 1991.

did not please Cardinal Serédi.[15] It was characteristic of the foreign policy of Pope Pius XII that in 1945 he chose a man to be the head of the Hungarian Church who was known to be an opponent of accommodation with the victorious Soviet Union.

Although Mindszenty was by no means the first choice of the provisional government, the politicians, including the Communists, did not foresee the difficulties they would have with the new cardinal. They saw in him a man who came from a humble family, and one who had been arrested by the murderous Szálasi regime. At his inauguration, the government was represented by Minister of Defense János Vörös, and even Lieutenant Colonel General Sviridov, the Hungarian-speaking Soviet officer who later became the head of the ACC, was also present.[16]

Mindszenty's background, worldview, and character came to be extremely important in the history of this transition period from pluralist to totalitarian state. He turned out to be the most influential and powerful opponent of the Communist takeover; no single individual was such a thorn in the side of the Communist leaders as the cardinal. He had been born to a poor peasant family in the little village of Csehimindszent, in western Hungary. His family name was Pehm, which allowed his Communist opponents later to stress that he came from the Swab minority and to imply that somehow he was not a "real Hungarian."[17] In 1941, at a time when others for opportunistic reasons wanted to call attention to their German ancestry, he, on the contrary, changed his name to Mindszenty to stress his identification with the Hungarian nation.[18] In his autobiography, he went to great lengths to show that his family had lived in Hungary for centuries and that he was a pure Hungarian.[19]

The future cardinal did not have the education that one might have expected from such a senior church official. After secondary education, he attended a seminary but refused the offer of a scholarship at a Catholic University in Vienna to study theology.[20] Aside from Latin, he spoke no foreign languages. He was by no means an intellectual; he was strict, ascetic, and courageous but also narrow-minded, conservative, and

15 Gergely, p. 37.

16 Ibid., p. 39.

17 The NPP was particularly anxious to get rid of the German minority in order to have more land to distribute among the peasants. A hostile report on Mindszenty described him as "Swabian." PIL 284, volume 13, June 14, 1948.

18 Friedrich Wilhelm Bautz, Biographisch-Bibliographisches Kirchenlexikon, vol. 5, Hamm (Westf.) 1993, p. 1552

19 Mindszenty, pp. 13–14.

20 Ibid., p. 16.

extremely inflexible.[21] The bitterness of his opposition to the modern world was extreme even among senior churchmen, not only in Hungary but also in Europe. He was a man who never changed his ideas and beliefs. As a young priest after the collapse of the monarchy in 1918, he had written articles opposing the democratic revolution, because Mihály Károlyi, the leader of that revolution, wanted to abolish the Habsburg Monarchy and introduce land reform. Mindszenty was arrested in February 1919. (Much later his conservative admirers incorrectly depicted him as a victim of the Béla Kun Communist regime, although his arrest had taken place at a time when Kun himself was in prison.) He opposed the abolition of the monarchy because he was a legitimist and remained so to the end of his days. Even in the 1970s, he had not given up hope that the Habsburgs would be restored. In his room in Viennese exile, he had a picture of Otto hanging on the wall, and he even sent money to him for the Hungarian education of his daughter.[22] (It is something of a mystery why he thought that a Habsburg needed the financial support of an exiled churchman.) His conservatism also made him oppose the Hungarian extreme right, the Arrow-Cross Party: radical change was the goal of the Hungarian Nazis as well. Even his Hungarian nationalism was in the style of the prewar ruling class. In fact, there was no aspect of the policies of the defunct Horthy regime that Mindszenty found necessary to repudiate. His admiring last secretary reported that shortly before his death in 1975 the cardinal encountered a Slovak priest and found it necessary to point out that Slovakia was part of Hungary.[23] His conservatism, his unwillingness to accept the inevitable, and his inability to understand the spirit of the times occasionally reached ludicrous proportions.

Not for a moment did he show any willingness to cooperate with the victors. Immediately after his liberation from Nazi captivity, two priests who played major roles in the newly reestablished center right Smallholders' Party, István Balogh and Béla Varga, approached him. They suggested to him that as bishop of Veszprém he should establish contact with Marshal Voroshilov, head of the ACC, and thank him for his liberation and for the presumed good

21 In the 1970s Pope Paul IV asked Mindszenty, then living in exile in Rome, to resign his seat in order to enable him to name a new cardinal in Esztergom and come to terms with the Hungarian government, which had become the most liberal in the Soviet bloc. Mindszenty rejected the argument that cooperation with a Communist government would improve the life of the faithful and refused to resign. He left Rome and chose to live in exile in Vienna.

22 Tibor Mészáros, *Akit övei be nem fogadtak: Mindszenty Biboros titkárának Visszaemlékezései*, Pécs: Pro Domo, 1997, pp. 226–228. In 1991, when Mindszenty's body was being returned to Esztergom, Mészáros protested. He chained himself to the grave. He maintained that the cardinal's body should not be returned until the last Russian solider left Hungary. This was in the spring, and the recall of Russian soldiers was scheduled only for the summer. May 3, 1991, the *Daily Telegraph*.

23 Ibid.

will toward the Church. Mindszenty rejected the idea: to him the Russians were enemies and the new coalition government, established under the auspices of the Red Army, possessed no legitimacy.[24] He had only contempt for politicians who were willing to compromise with the Communists and the representatives of the Soviet Union.[25] As long as he remained in his office in Esztergom, he could find no allies among the major politicians and supported the Smallholders' Party only because it seemed to him the lesser evil.

The first conflict between the Church and the new regime was over land reform, but the second came shortly after Mindszenty's assumption of his seat as head of the Hungarian Church. As head of the Catholic Church, he jealously guarded his prerogatives, or, one might say, he suffered from delusions of grandeur. Because he considered the coalition government illegitimate, in his opinion the chain of legitimacy was broken, and therefore he alone could represent the state. He regarded himself in the absence of the king as the regent[26] and as such the highest legitimate secular authority. From his belief, it followed that he was responsible to take a position on every political issue. In his inaugural speech, phrased in quaint, anachronistic language, he made it clear that his conception of his role went far beyond taking care of the spiritual needs of the faithful. Legitimacy was broken, but he promised that he, as prince-cardinal, was ready to take charge.[27] He never hesitated either in turning to the faithful in the form of sermons or writing letters to ministers and prime ministers on every controversial political issue, including matters in which the Church had no obvious concern.

He wanted to make the Church's influence felt as the country was preparing for the first postwar elections. Mindszenty found it necessary to protest the decision by the Communists and the Socialists to run on the same list. He wrote to the premier of the provisional government, Béla Miklos, on October 17, 1945:

> I have learned that the communists are forcing a common list on the socialists. This is violating the freedom of elections. This is contrary to the most basic human rights, to the self government promised by the Crimean conference and to the much touted democracy.[28]

It is not obvious why the decision of two parties to collaborate was anti-democratic. The sneering reference to "much touted democracy" made it

24 Mindszenty, pp. 67–68.
25 Ibid., p. 104.
26 Gergely, p. 41.
27 Mindszenty, p. 83.
28 PIL 274 7/247.

abundantly clear what Mindszenty thought of the democratic reforms that were taking place.

Mindszenty, concerned that the Communists might win, decided to appeal to the Hungarian nation. At the first Conference of Bishops under his chairmanship, he showed the participants a draft of his letter and received their approval. It increased the weight of the letter that it was written in the name of the bishops and therefore represented more than Mindszenty's private views: he spoke in the name of the Catholic Church. His pastoral letter was read in every church in the country on November 1, one week before the elections.

He pretended to give no instructions to his followers on how to vote, and, indeed, he mentioned no parties by name, but it was the most transparent of pretenses. In his letter, he enumerated the various acts of the provisional government that he perceived as directed against the Church: most significantly, the law that made divorce easier. He protested against the spirit in which the land reform was conceived. In his opinion, it was motivated by a desire for revenge against the landowning class. He described the lawless behavior of the political police, which, as every Hungarian knew, was in the hands of the Communists. From his description, it appeared that the country was once again living in a situation of tyranny. And he continued:

> We turn to you, dear faithful, to take our words to heart, and at the time of the election give your votes to that candidate who is going to fight for moral purity, for legality and truth against the sad current situation. Do not be frightened by the threats of the sons of evil. It is easier to resist threats once and suffer than to start on a road to which men without conscience want to seduce the Hungarian people. Terror and tyranny will be all the greater depending how little resistance it encounters. . . . A Hungarian father, a Hungarian Catholic mother who has a sense of responsibility for their children's spiritual purity, earthly and heavenly happiness, cannot hesitate. He can vote only for that candidate who guarantees that the contemporary errors can never reoccur in Hungary. Amen.[29]

It did not require much imagination to guess who "the sons of evil" were. It is, of course, impossible to establish how much difference the pastoral letter made. Later, in fact, Mindszenty in his memoirs claimed credit for the electoral victory of the Smallholders' Party, the most conservative of the competing political forces.[30] There were reports of people going directly from church services to the polls on the Sunday morning of the election.[31] We can take it for granted that the influence of the Church, especially in

29 PIL 274 7/246, pp. 8–9.

30 Mindszenty, p. 98.

31 PIL 274 16/133.

the countryside and especially among women, who after the war made up more than half of the electorate, was very great. Mindszenty deplored that no explicitly Catholic party participated in the elections. Under the circumstances, the party that Mindszenty considered the least undesirable, the Smallholder Party, achieved a great victory.

The four parties of the so-called Popular Front, the Communists, the Socialists, the NPP, and the Smallholders' Party, protested the pastoral letter as an intervention in secular politics. The initiative for the protest, understandably, came from the Communists, but the representatives of all parties considered it necessary to give their signature.[32] It is interesting that the Smallholders, the party that had greatly benefited from Mindszenty's intervention in the political struggle, also found it necessary to distance itself from the head of the Church. The leaders of the party genuinely disagreed with Mindszenty's politics, and from a practical point of view they considered it dangerous to be associated with Mindszenty's conservatism and uncompromising stance. Mindszenty was disgusted that the Smallholder politicians joined the protest, and he made his feelings abundantly clear.

The new premier, Zoltán Tildy, and his colleague Béla Varga, the speaker of the parliament, almost immediately paid an official visit to the head of the Catholic Church. Mindszenty according to his own description received the politicians coolly and let them know that he was not satisfied with what seemed to him their pusillanimous behavior.[33]

The next conflict between Mindszenty and the governing political circles came almost immediately. The issue was the abolition of the monarchy. A corollary of the abolition of the kingdom was the abolition of the upper chamber of the parliament. Obviously, in the new Hungary there could be no special chamber reserved for the landed aristocracy. It was this reform that the senior churchmen, especially Mindszenty, opposed most vigorously, for it meant the loss of princely title and the loss of a secular role for the head of the Church. Mindszenty's legitimism was a central feature of his worldview. In the fall of 1945 on two occasions with two different messengers, he sent letters to Otto Habsburg, assuring him of his undying loyalty.[34] When he was in Rome to receive the cardinal's hat, it was made clear to him that Rome considered the re-creation of the monarchy in Hungary as unrealistic. Even that information did not shake the new cardinal's hope for the restoration of the Habsburgs.[35] He thought that a war between the Soviet Union and

32 PIL 274, 7/247.

33 Mindszenty, pp. 104–105.

34 Nagy, pp. 190–192.

35 Ibid., p. 190.

the Western powers was not only inevitable, but that it might break out in the nearest future.[36] It must be said that rumors concerning a renewal of the war were widespread in Hungary, especially in the countryside.[37] While in Rome, Mindszenty was preparing for a future in which the Russians would be expelled from the country. He approached the moderately conservative ex-premier, Miklós Kállay, who had served under Horthy during the Second World War, and suggested the formation of a government in exile, ready to take office when circumstances allowed. Kállay, a realist, rejected the idea and privately expressed his amazement at the cardinal's lack of political realism.[38]

It did not show great political acumen on the part of this senior churchman that he chose to challenge the new regime on an issue in which he had little popular support and could not possibly win. In this matter, even the majority of bishops failed to support their superior, for it was obvious that the struggle in the given circumstances was fruitless. Mindszenty was not the sort of person who easily accepted defeat. On December 31, 1945, he wrote to the premier:

I have learned that the Parliament in the near future is planning to raise the issue of constitutional reform, including the introduction of a republic, and the ending of the 1000 year old kingdom. If this report proves to be correct, even if I have not received an official notification, in the name of the 900 year old right of the Hungarian Prince Cardinal, I protest.[39]

Even after the election of Tildy as president of the new republic, the cardinal continued to send protesting letters. Of all his struggles, the fight to retain the monarchy was the most quixotic. He continued to bombard the premier, whoever he was, with letters on issues related to the Church as well as on completely secular matters.[40] On October 10, 1945, he wrote

36 Ibid., p. 208.

37 These rumors persisted for years. PIL 274 21/7, Report on the public mood to the Central Committee of the Communist Party, October 1947.

38 Nagy, p. 209.

39 Mindszenty, p. 106.

40 Mindszenty exasperated even the right wing of the political spectrum. István Balogh, undersecretary of state in the premier's office and a priest himself, had a conversation with the American ambassador, Schoenfeld. Schoenfeld reported to the secretary of state: "Balogh told us today he spent vain hour attempting to convince Primate he should take more cooperative line with the Hungarian democracy. Specifically he asked Primate to make statement to press regarding his trip to Rome, suggesting he might also take note of difficulties Hungarian democracy faced while pledging help of Catholic Church. Primate was obdurate and refused to consider any conciliatory measures. Balogh says Primate is doing Catholic Church immense harm since all priests are prima facie now being branded reactionaries. He says Primate is stubborn, has small intellect, basically uncultured and surrounds himself with narrow, provincial priests and a few former aristocrat landowners who are offering him bad advice. For example he says Primate is convinced Americans will soon use atom bomb to drive Soviets out of Hungary. FRUS, March 29, 1946.

to Premier Miklós protesting the deportation of Germans. He was the only person in a position of authority who spoke out in defense of this newly persecuted minority. He complained that it was unfair that committees made up of two presumably ignorant and envious peasants and a Communist functionary should decide who had to leave and who could stay. These committees were empowered to make their decisions on the basis of the census of 1941: whoever had declared German as their language was to be expelled. Mindszenty pointed out that the committees were especially likely to deport the rich because they wanted to seize their property. He complained that the committees also deported nuns and priests, and there was no appeal against their decisions. He went on to point out that now the Germans were taken, as the Jews had been a year before. Perhaps the comparison with the Jews was not in good taste, because he had not protested their deportation. Also, Jews had been sent to their deaths, and the Germans were sent merely to West Germany. Nevertheless, he was undoubtedly correct in protesting these deportations, even though they were endorsed and encouraged by the great powers including the United States and Britain.[41]

Mindszenty also protested against the treatment of the Hungarian minority in Yugoslavia and especially in Czechoslovakia. He was quite justified in doing so, for the large Hungarian minority in Slovakia was badly mistreated, and many Hungarians were expelled. In this matter, however, Mindszenty was not alone. The entire political spectrum, certainly including the Hungarian Communists, agreed with him. The government, however, was powerless to protect its compatriots in neighboring countries, and the great powers on no occasion took the side of the Hungarians.

A week later he wrote again. This time he protested the Soviet-Hungarian economic agreement. He did not seem to realize that the government at this point was in no position to resist. By the terms of the armistice, Hungary was burdened with extremely heavy reparation obligations, and the government was trying to make the best of a bad situation. The Soviet army occupied the country, and the Russians could and did impose whatever terms they wanted.

On November 23, 1945, in his letter to Tildy, Mindszenty protested against the rulings of the people's courts. He argued that people had been sentenced either on the basis of ex post facto laws or for crimes they had committed during the era of the so-called White Terror in 1919–1920, and

41 PIL 274 7/247.

therefore the statute of limitations had run out. That a number of unjust sentences were handed down in these confused and emotionally charged times is undeniable. However, the postwar trials of war criminals in Hungary were not more unfair than elsewhere. Mindszenty lent the Church's prestige to the defense of some very unsavory characters.[42]

THE COMMUNISTS AND THE CATHOLIC CHURCH

During the time of struggle for power, the Communists formulated their policy toward religion in general and toward the Catholic Church in particular. They remembered their political errors of 1919, when they had made no concession to public opinion and were determined not to repeat the mistakes of the past. During the next three years, they again and again emphasized that they were not against religion and even attempted to win the allegiance of at least some believers.

The fundamental principle was simple: on the one hand, the Catholic Church was a powerful enemy, but on the other, the faithful ought not to be alienated. Mátyás Rákosi went to Moscow in June 1945 in order to report to the Soviet Central Committee on the Hungarian situation. In his report, he devoted some attention to the party's policies toward the Church.[43] He credited the Church with great power and stated that the Communists were struggling against it. He said that one of the goals of the land reform legislation was to divide the Church. Although the vast bulk of the church lands had been nationalized at Communist insistence, the village priests were given some land in the hope that this concession would turn them against the hierarchy, which was resisting reform. In addition, the priests were given salaries. Rákosi concluded: "Of course they know that we dislike them as much as they dislike us." József Révai, the person responsible for ideology within the Politburo, addressed village agitators in August 1945. On the one hand, he warned them not to attack religion, but on the other hand he told them that it was essential to respond to every attack by "reactionary" priests.[44] Rákosi in a meeting of party activists at the time of the election campaign of 1947 said: "We have to win over women. The majority of the working people are religious, and the Hungarian Communist Party (MKP) is the guardian of all types of freedom, including freedom of conscience. As long as the MKP has a role in the government, we can assure people that

42 Ibid.
43 RTsKhIDNI 17f, 128 opus, 750 delo, pp. 230–231.
44 PIL 274 21/3 August 14, 1945.

they can safely attend church and we will assure that no sacrilegious hand will disturb them."[45]

Rather hypocritically, the Communists offered help time and again in the reconstruction of churches.[46] Indeed, the party received letters of thanks from priests from various parts of the country. The hierarchy was clearly annoyed; the bishop of Györ wrote to a local priest that the Communists should not be allowed to get a new bell for his church. Or, if that had already happened, he was forbidden to thank them.[47] Remarkably, two years later in 1948, the Soviet Party's Central Committee also criticized the Hungarian Communists for the same reason as the bishop of Györ. In an evaluation of the work of the Hungarians in connection with the break with Tito, the Communists were scolded for a number of errors. One of these was that they had accommodated the priests too much by helping them to reconstruct churches, by inviting priests to the opening of houses of culture, and so forth. The Soviet report mentions the extraordinary fact that a Communist Party office in one village had pictures of Stalin and Rákosi hanging on the wall along with a cross.[48] By 1948, times had changed: as pluralism disappeared, there was less need to accommodate believers.

45 PIL 274 21/8 August 1947.
46 PIL 274 16/17 reports from village agitators, October 1946.
47 PIL 274 7/245 October 1946.
48 "Uroki iz oshibok kompartii Iugoslavii dlia Vengerskoi partii trudiashchikhsia," June 12, 1948, in T. V. Volokitina, pp. 596–597.

9

Methods of Mass Mobilization

AGITATION

The Communists were extraordinarily ambitious. They did not simply want to take power; they also wanted to create a different kind of society and even a new kind of human being. Just like their Russian comrades at the time of their civil war, they believed that they were bringing "culture" to the countryside as they attempted to win the peasants over to their type of politics. The people who had been trained in the school of Leninism were well aware of the importance of propaganda. They paid more attention to winning over the population to their worldview than leaders of the other political parties and used more imaginative methods for winning converts. Their most powerful opponents, the FKGP politicians, tended to assume that the majority of the population would see through Communist demagogy and would therefore support their political position. Consequently, they saw less of a need to build an elaborate propaganda machine. Although it is impossible to measure precisely the influence of propaganda, it would certainly be a mistake to explain the success of the Communist Party in the political struggle entirely by its monopoly over the means of coercion and the support of the Red Army.

The Communists succeeded in winning the allegiance of at least a minority of the population. After the dreadful suffering of the war there were people who believed that an entirely new way of social organization was not only possible but desirable, people who were susceptible to utopian promises. None of the new Communists had the slightest idea of the great bloodletting that had taken place in the Soviet Union in the 1930s and was again about to commence. And, of course, they could not have known what kind of system Rákosi and his comrades would soon introduce. Those who voted for the Communists in 1945 did not vote for mass terror, concentration camps, and forcing peasants into collective farms.

It is evident that the Hungarian Communists were imitating their Soviet masters and teachers. They used all the same instruments that the Soviet Communists had developed since the time of taking power in 1917. This was a system that included mass meetings, party schools, "voluntary" organizations, street demonstrations, wall newspapers, organized individual agitation, sending groups of activists into the villages to provide help and services in order to gain followers, and a skillful use of the press and cinema. There was nothing that was particularly new in their work; their Soviet comrades had tried everything before.[1]

At the outset, the Communist Party created a propaganda department.[2] In 1947, the department had three subsections: party education, mass agitation, and cultural work. The Central Committee also maintained a six-month party school in order to train district secretaries. At any given time, the school had forty to fifty students. This school trained the future top leadership, and in the course of their education they listened to lectures from the most powerful figures of the party, including Rákosi, Gerő, Imre Nagy, Lukács, and so forth. In addition, there were twenty-three lower level, three-week training courses for party activists.[3] The propaganda department also published brochures for agitators, which appeared at short intervals. From these, the agitators learned the current issues that the leadership considered necessary for discussion.

In 1945, the propaganda department was already preparing monthly reports on its agitation work. László Orbán, a leader in this department, argued in his report that, contrary to the common understanding of the word, Communist propaganda was nothing more than spreading the truth. Like most propagandists before and since, he was dissatisfied with the results of his work. He bemoaned the fact that many "comrades" still did not understand the significance of this work, and consequently the first task was to make them understand. As a good Marxist, he said: "It is the knowledge of theory that makes it possible for us to predict the future." First of all, party cadres needed to be trained. Because the vast majority of the new members of the party did not know Marxism-Leninism, he found it essential to organize seminars, party schools, and a central party school that was to train the highest level of the leadership of the party. The party had enormous difficulty in finding reliable and capable people.

1 Peter Kenez, *The Birth of the Propaganda State: Soviet Methods of Mass Mobilization*, Cambridge and New York: Cambridge UP, 1985.

2 PIL 274 21/1.

3 RTsKhIDNI fond 17, opis 128, delo 315, p. 31. Report by Nográdi.

Second, Orbán continued, more attention had to be paid to agitation among the masses. The task was, of course, the popularization of the policies of the party. He considered the organization of mass meetings an excellent method. He mentioned as a positive example that when the newspapers reported on the Soviet food loan, the Communists organized meetings in several factories in order to express their appreciation for the help. Other methods of propaganda he recommended were organizing street demonstrations to show the strength of the party and printing posters and pamphlets. He mentioned other Soviet propaganda instruments, such as wall newspapers that aimed chiefly at "unmasking the enemy."[4]

As if to demonstrate Orbán's argument about the difficulty of finding appropriate cadres, on June 4, 1945, István Sebes, the deputy head of the department of mass organizations, complained to the Central Committee in a pitiful letter: "I would like to add that I have no talent whatever for journalism; I write with extreme difficulty, and preparing an article takes me days. Furthermore, my sentences do not move smoothly, but haltingly. In the past nine years writing materials have hardly entered my hands."[5]

Among the top leaders, it was József Révai who was ultimately responsible for propaganda work. Supervising propaganda and watching for the purity of ideology went hand in hand. Révai, therefore, could fairly be regarded as the equivalent of Andrei Zhdanov in the Soviet leadership. He was obviously an intelligent and well-educated man who had a well-developed aesthetic sensibility. It was said about him, perhaps as a joke, that when he really liked a novel or a short story, he knew he had found something too dangerous for wide distribution, and he had to ban it. On August 14, 1945, he gave a speech to the party activists. The speech was revealing of the mentality of the leadership at the time. As with most propagandists, he was concerned that his party was not doing enough. He described propaganda work as "a matter of life and death" and saw the enemy as strong and threatening. The party needed to train cadres who could resist enemy propaganda and find a way to hit back. The greatest danger was in the countryside, especially in Transdanubia, which was a conservative region. He said they needed to train agitators who knew the countryside, people who could talk to the peasants in their own language. In his view, people in the countryside, by and large, did not like people in the city. He admitted that the peasants were hostile to the Red Army and therefore to the Communists, and they rightly associated the two. The peasants had to

4 PIL 274 21/2 report of the propaganda department, June, 1945.
5 PIL 274 17/2 report to Central Committee, June 4, 1945.

be convinced that although compulsory delivery of food was not in the interests of the peasantry, nevertheless, it was essential. He put it this way:

> We must be careful about agitation, comrades, we must tell the truth. There is no other method, but we must wrap the bitter truth in such a way, as to make it possible for the people to swallow.

He added the party must always be on the attack and not be defensive, except concerning religion. He understood that a frontal attack on religion at this time would backfire. On the one hand, activists in the countryside ought not expect everything from Budapest: they had to show initiative and organize their propaganda work so as to correspond to local problems. On the other hand local organs needed to be strictly supervised: he complained for example, that a newspaper in Pécs had written about British politics, resulting in a protest from the British embassy. The newspaper had to be closed down for a few days. "Let the local organs deal with local issues and leave world politics to us."[6]

The immediate political task of propagandists in the fall of 1945 was to win over voters for the crucial fall elections. The Communist Party exerted greater efforts, organized more meetings, and published more pamphlets than activists in other parties. Their propagandists attracted people to meetings by presenting amusing programs, by choral singing, and by organizing torchlight parades.[7] They could do this not only because they paid more attention to propaganda but also because they had Soviet practical support, enabling them, for example, to borrow trucks from the Red Army. The Communists also developed a more detailed political program than the other parties. The results of the elections demonstrated, however, that propaganda could achieve only so much.

The organization of agitation work in the factories was much easier and apparently more successful than in the countryside. At least some workers accepted the argument that the Communist Party was a party by and for the workers. It was also easier to organize workers: they could be called together for a meeting at a moment's notice. They could be persuaded to go to the streets and demonstrate for some Communist goal. The methods of agitation, aside from mass meetings and demonstrations, were wall newspapers and also sending individual agitators to visit people in their apartments. These visits were usually awkward affairs, where the agitators were anxious

6 Report sent to Moscow by Soviet army command in the spring of 1946: "[I]n the villages the majority of the peasants are hostile to the Red Army and to the Soviet Union." Murashko and Noszkova (eds.), p. 52.

7 PIL 274 21/5.

to finish their prepared speeches and leave, and the hosts were just as anxious to accompany them to the door. The subjects of the "discussions" were some contemporary foreign or domestic affair. The agitators did not expect to be contradicted or to be asked hostile questions, and, indeed, such "unpleasantness" very rarely happened.

László Orbán spoke to agitators on February 7, 1947, about the themes that agitators in the factories were to emphasize. He stressed the need to develop propaganda encouraging production and argued that the workers should compete with one another. The standard of living would increase if they produced more, he said. In the past, producing more was not in the interest of the workers. Some people protested, Orbán continued, that if the workers produced too much it would result in unemployment. People were afraid of work competition because they thought that hard work would only result in higher norms:

> They say that we cannot have competition because there is not enough raw material. Let us explain to them that this is not the case. Let us take advantage of local pride. We should celebrate the best workers by putting their pictures on the wall. Let us put these workers on a pedestal.[8]

Production propaganda, of course, was also a weapon taken from the Soviet arsenal.

The question of nationalization, which began in 1946 with the nationalization of the mines and followed with the nationalization of the banks and large enterprises, was an important issue for worker audiences. Workers were understandably concerned, afraid that nationalization would lead to lower salaries. The agitators reported that the technical intelligentsia was by and large hostile to nationalization, and the workers were divided.[9] Although peasants did not pay as much attention to the issue as workers, they were more likely to be hostile to it, fearing rightly that it would be followed by the nationalization of land and the introduction of collective farms.

The elections of 1945 once again demonstrated what the Communist leaders well understood: the party was weak in the countryside. In order to overcome this weakness, the party organized a network of "village educators" (the Hungarian word *népnevelő* is more precisely translated as "educators of the people"). The task of these people was twofold: win over the peasants to the Communist point of view by providing some help and at the same time to report on the mood of the village. Speakers at party meetings frequently made the point that the "comrades underestimated the

8 PIL 274 21/11.

9 PIL 274 21/53 March–May 1948.

importance of agitation work." The work was not popular. A report from the town of Sopron, for example, said: "Among the comrades agitation is not the most popular work. It happened that in our factory there was a woman comrade who was often late. The party court sentenced her to be sent out to the countryside as an agitator."[10] Understandably, being sent to an often-hostile audience was not desirable. Presumably, agitation work was also not the most helpful in advancing in the party hierarchy.

Who were these agitators? The majority came from a poor peasant background, but there were not enough Communists in the villages. Under the circumstances, the party needed the services of workers who volunteered for the assignment. Few of the agitators were women. This was not only because men greatly outnumbered women in the party, but also because of a conscious decision by the leadership. The organizers of the campaign believed that the peasants more than city people would find women "politicians" distasteful, so women agitators would make a negative impression. Jews were also consciously kept out of the ranks of "village educators." However difficult it might be to send reliable, intelligent people to agitate, it was repeatedly stipulated that Jews were not appropriate for this task.

The party even gave specific instruction on the agitators' personal appearance and behavior. Károly Nándor told the village agitators:

> We have to be careful that the agitator should visit not only the well-to-do. People will say that he came only to eat and drink. Dress is important. Let us not appear in dress that we received from the army, especially from the Russian army. Such a situation occurred in Tolna county, Völgység district, where the district secretary, comrade Toth, appeared in such attire. He even put a military map kit around his neck. So they said in the district that he works for the Russians. Under the circumstances it is difficult to show the patriotic nature of the party in the district.[11]

Women were discouraged from wearing lipstick or rouge and from smoking.[12] (Smoking, of course, was all right for men.)

The agitators were instructed to stress nationalism. Nándor made sensible suggestions:

> Instead of singing the International in the villages, peasant songs should be sung. In mass meetings we are talking in vain about nationalist politics if afterwards we sing: "and the world will be internationalist." A peasant who has some land does not want to be regarded as a "proletarian." In the village issues of *Szabad Nép* let us remove: "Proletarians of the world unite" and put instead: "flourishing agriculture and a well to do peasantry." In the village we should not use the greeting: "Szabadság" but

10 PIL 274 21/7 June 4, 1948, p. 96.
11 PIL 274 16/23 May 17, 1947.
12 PIL 274 16/50 report on the work of village agitators, May 1947, p. 79.

instead: "good evening, good day." Let us hungarianize words such as sympathizers, functionaries, activists, etc.[13]

In the archives, there are hundreds of reports sent by the village agitators to the propaganda section of the party. From these, one can construct a picture of the Hungarian village in these years. First of all, the backwardness and poverty are striking. In most villages, there was no electricity or even a telephone. People were called to meetings by the ancient method of a drummer walking through the streets of the village. Mail service hardly functioned. Newspapers were delivered in many places only twice a month.[14] Although the land reform was a genuine social revolution, it was not accompanied by agrarian reform. There was no credit available for improvements or reconstruction. The mere redistribution of land could not alleviate the dreadful poverty of the village at once. Complaints about lack of food and the high prices for industrial products were constant. Industrial products and clothing were often simply unavailable. There were villages where the peasants had to walk three kilometers for water.[15] In winter time, the agitation work had to stop because roads became impassable. (Agitators from the cities usually traveled on trucks.) Even maintaining contact with the central organs was difficult. In a generally optimistic, typewritten report, sent on December 23, the county party secretary added in his handwriting: "I need an answer quickly, before the coming of spring!"[16]

Second, the reports demonstrate how weak the party was in the countryside. Two-thirds of the villages had no party organization at all.[17] The party did not have educated and reliable agitators. The great majority of the reports were obviously written by people who were barely literate. Many of the reports are illegible and full of grammatical errors; one may assume that the propagandists and the people they were trying to influence were of a similar background. On occasion, there are complaints that the group of agitators spent their entire visit in the bar, some of them getting roaring drunk.[18] There were also complaints that they did not pay for their drinks. People who lacked education and had the most rudimentary understanding of Marxism-Leninism made up not only the agitators but also the entire village network. This fact was hardly surprising, and it is difficult to see how it could have been otherwise. Reports speak about habitually

13 PIL 274 16/34 January 1947.
14 PIL 274 21/21 meeting of agitators, December 12, 1947, Kis Ferenc from Györ.
15 PIL 274 16/51 September 4, 1947, p. 156.
16 PIL 274 16/51 December 23, 1946, p. 35.
17 Rákosi speaking to village agitators, PIL 274 21/21 March 10, 1947.
18 PIL 274 16/51 October 18, 1947, report from Székesfehérvár, p. 189.

drunk party secretaries and party functionaries who were regular gamblers or rude to the peasants. Others were denounced for not going out to the village at all but simply summoning peasants and rudely giving them instructions.[19] Two-thirds of the villages had no party buildings or even a room for meetings.[20]

A report from Fejér County in December 1946 indicts the village agitators there, mentioning some accused of stealing and others of buying large quantities of wine. This report concludes: "Taking into consideration what I have already enumerated, I can speak only of negatives. I do not know of a single instance when we could report on this activity's political benefit resulting from well-planned work."[21]

Perhaps that report was excessively pessimistic. A report from Somogy County written in the same month speaks of a success achieved by different methods.[22] Here a sheet metal worker, shoemakers, a doctor, and a typist, presumably carrying his typewriter with him, accompanied the group of agitators. According to the report, the shoemakers were always the most popular and the peasants would bring twenty to thirty shoes to them for repair. What they could not fix, they took with them with the promise of returning to them within a couple of weeks. We may assume that when the peasants saw help coming from the Communists, at least some of them were won over.

A national summary for 1947 spoke of 203 agitators (only 6 of them were women) visiting 1657 villages. The summary mentions recurring complaints, chiefly about compulsory deliveries and high taxes. The delivery quotas were so high that peasants were often left not only without bread for their families but also without seed for next year's planting. The peasants had to pay three times as much for their grain on the open market as they got for compulsory deliveries. The new owners, peasants who had just recently received land as a consequence of the radical land reform, were in an especially desperate economic position. Everything was in short supply, including salt and kerosene. Articles of clothing, in particular shoes, were often unavailable.

A Mihály Schmidt, an activist who had been sent from the capital, reported on December 1, 1947: "When we advertised that a communist speaker was coming, no one came to the meeting. We changed tactics and said that some representatives were coming from the central bureaucracy and then the peasants were much more likely to attend." Evidently, the agitators

19 PIL 274 21/22 reports from Vas county, for example.
20 PIL 274 21/21 Rákosi's report, March 10, 1947.
21 PIL 274 16/51 December 14, 1946, p. 29.
22 PIL 274 16/51 pp. 34–35.

had other tasks beyond spreading the Communist message. The same person, a certain Mihály Schmidt, a Budapest factory worker, continued in his report: "As I traveled on the train at Dombovár, István Pusztai, a teacher boarded. He openly described comrade Rajk as a scoundrel and described democracy as a system created by a bunch of thieves. I arrested the man and handed him over to the political police in Pécs."[23]

Rumors spread in different parts of the country, and the same ones emerged time and again. One of these was that war between the West and the Soviet Union was only a matter of time. On occasion people even gave the exact date for the outbreak of the war: October 28–29, 1947. The peasants predicted that the British would win, occupy the country, and hang the Communists.[24] (This was undoubtedly an expression of wishful thinking.) A few months later, an agitator reported that people believed that diplomatic ties between the Soviet Union and the United States had already been broken.[25] People explained the lack of consumer goods as a result of preparation for the war.

In the summer of 1948, a rumor spread that the Russians would take two children from a family of four children and three out of six. Also, those children who signed up to join the Pioneers (a Communist organization for children) would be taken to the Soviet Union. Everywhere there was constant fear that people would be taken by the Russians to the Soviet Union for work, a fear which, on the basis of the experiences of 1945, was not altogether unfounded. It was said that after the nationalization of factories, free love would be introduced. Another amusing rumor was that the Soviet Union had become greatly indebted to the United States and therefore was planning to sell Hungary to the Americans.[26]

Clearly there was at least a kernel of truth in many of the rumors, however far fetched, and in some cases popular scepticism of the Communists' intentions was perfectly accurate. It was rumored, for example, that in the Soviet Union the people were starving. Indeed, they were. There was constant talk about the introduction of collective farms in Hungary and the Communist agitators spent a great deal of time and effort trying to convince people that word of a future introduction of collective farms was merely a fairy tale, spread by the enemy. The Communists were well aware of the almost universal and deep hostility of the peasantry toward collective farms, which, of course, did not prevent their introduction a short time later.

23 PIL 274 21/25 November 1947.
24 PIL 274 21/7 September 1947.
25 Ibid., May 11, 1948, by Edit Varga from Székesfehérvár.
26 PIL 274 21/15 June 9, 1948, summary report.

The agitators maintained, and it may have been true, that information about the outside world came from Western radio broadcasts, which were then spread by the village intelligentsia. It was particularly disturbing to the agitators that the population was well informed about the much higher standard of living in the West, particularly in the United States. The reports complained that even party members were on the fence, not knowing whether to believe information spread by the party or information coming from Western broadcasts. It is striking how much concern the peasants expressed about foreign affairs. At the time of the Yugoslav-Soviet break, the peasants said that now that Yugoslavia had left, Romania and Bulgaria would follow the Yugoslav example, and once again Hungary would remain the last ally of the loser, just as in the previous war.[27] As time went on, and as international relations changed, Communist agitators spent more time trying to convince their audiences that life in the West was getting worse. This was a hard sell, because many of the peasants had relatives in the United States who not only wrote letters but also sent packages of food and clothing.[28] The agitators had a somewhat easier task showing that America suffered from racial prejudice against blacks and that Jews and Catholics were also subject to discrimination.

In April 1948, the propaganda committee discussed the themes that were to be emphasized in "the struggle against imperialism." The agitators were to say that the Soviet Union was getting stronger every day and that life in the United States was getting worse and worse: "While here we use terror against a few, in the United States terror is exercised against many progressives."[29]

A great concern for the peasantry was the large number of prisoners of war (POWs) that the Soviet Union refused to return to their homeland. In fact, the peasants were so concerned about their POW relatives in Russian captivity that they became prey to various confidence schemes. There are several reports of scoundrels' collecting money for "train fare" from the poor victims by promising it would enable their loved ones in the USSR to return home.[30] Obviously, this issue contributed to the unpopularity of the Soviet Union and reflected badly on the Communists, although the Communist Party propaganda continued to argue that the party was in the best position to bring home these POWs. Before the 1947 elections the

27 Ibid., June 3–4, 1948, Edit Varga's report, p. 85.
28 PIL 274 21/47 report from Abauj, April 1948.
29 PIL 274 21/12 Miklos Vásárhelyi, April 9, 1948.
30 PIL 274 16/51 p. 35.

Communist agitators took the line that a vote for their party was a vote to return the POWs from Russia.

A propaganda device in the countryside was the organization of "Free Land" Sundays and "Free Land" winter evenings. The idea was to combine agrarian learning, literature, and music with "political education." There were some reports of interest, but by and large the results were not encouraging. István Gyertván, a party secretary from Nográd County, wrote on April 10, 1948:

> We did not hold "Free Land" Sundays, because we had had experience with winter evenings, which did not take place because of lack of interest. There are no factories here, only peasants, who are very poor, and apathetic. They are convinced that the authorities always want to squeeze the people, as if the people were an inexhaustible.[31]

Another report in the same month from Zala County included: "It is impossible to have "Free Land" Sundays here because I am the only communist here. The people are full of hatred for democracy. The education of people is in the hands of a reactionary teacher. The children of Satan should be entrusted to him, not the children of the Hungarian people."[32]

Yet another method of agitation, also copied from the Soviet experience, was factories and army units adopting villages and providing help to them. The Soviets called this method of agitation *shefstvo*. Workers or soldiers traveled to the countryside to provide free service. This was regarded as social work, expected from party members. In some instances, the workers to be sent to the countryside first had to participate in a three-week course of political education.[33] A specially favored task, ironically, was the repair of churches. They fixed windows in church schools; they repaired water mains that had been damaged during the war; they fixed agricultural instruments. In most places, people responded favorably to this help but not everywhere. In some instances, the group complained that the peasants received them coldly.[34] On one occasion in a village in 1945, the priest rang the church bell at the appearance of the propagandists, wanting to indicate that the end of the world had arrived.[35]

It is difficult to evaluate the success of propaganda campaigns. Nevertheless, it is impressive how much effort the Communists devoted to this work and how imaginative they were. The ultimate conclusion must be,

31 PIL 274 21/48.

32 PIL 274 21/48.

33 PIL 274 16/51 report from Belapátfalva, September 6, 1947, p. 158.

34 PIL 274 16/51 report from Zalaegerszeg, September 5, 1947, p. 157.

35 PIL 274 16/50 p. 46. This event occurred in a village of the district of Aszod.

however, that the vast majority of the peasantry was hostile to Communism and to the Soviet Union from the outset, and this hostility actually increased over time. Once again the simple and obvious conclusion is inevitable: the power of propaganda is limited when it is aimed at bringing people over to a worldview that is alien to them.

MASS ORGANIZATIONS

After the success of their revolution, Russian Communists established a number of organizations that pretended to be voluntary and autonomous but in reality were neither. The aim of these organizations was not to represent particular social interests but to penetrate society and tailor the Communist message to different groups. In a contemporary metaphor, the party was thought of as the engine of society, providing energy and force, whereas mass organizations were the transmission belts, mobilizing society to move forward toward the goals announced by the party. Hungarian Communists, as was to be expected, attempted to copy Soviet institutions, and for this purpose they created a section of mass organizations within the department of propaganda of the Central Committee.

However, the political context in Russia at the time of the civil war and that in Hungary in 1945 differed. Whereas in Soviet Russia even during the civil war no political parties could legally function, in postwar Hungary there existed an imperfect pluralism. Although the Communists were hostile to these, for some time genuine mass organizations could still exist. For example, not only the Boy Scouts but also Christian youth movements for a time at least were allowed to operate.[36] There was also an organization of war orphans, widows, and invalids that, in the Communist view, was in "reactionary hands."[37] The Communists considered the trade unions as the main "transmission belts" for societal organization and made great and ultimately successful efforts to wrest these organizations from the Socialists. As long as there was private enterprise, the unions could provide actually function to represent workers' interests. However, once industry and trade were nationalized, the unions lost their original role and became yet another instrument of Communist control and ideological indoctrination.

There were, however, mass organizations that were from the outset under Communist leadership. The two most important ones were MNDSZ

36 In June 1945, Rákosi described the founder of the Boy Scout movement, Baden Powell, as "an English spy" and expressed concern that the movement was under clerical influence. PIL 274 18/2 June 18, 1945, speech to party activists.

37 PIL 274 17/2 June 4, 1945.

(acronym for Hungarian Women's Democratic Association) and MADISZ (acronym for Hungarian Democratic Youth Association). MNDSZ helped the party to gain strength among the women. It was a typical Communist front organization. In vain did the Communists try to persuade the Socialists to abandon their own organization for women.[38] The results of the 1945 elections showed that women were less likely to support radical policies than men. In particular, the influence of the Church among women was strong, and the party faced a difficult task in gaining followers. Communists made half-hearted attempts to pretend that they did not dominate the association, but everyone saw through the pretense. In some villages, the MNDSZ office was in the same building as the party headquarters.[39]

The Communists attributed particular significance to the youth organization. All political systems, but especially those that aim for total control, consider the education of the youth a most important task. It is a truism that the youth represents the future. Therefore, agitation among the young was a priority for the Communists. In addition to the basic idea that propaganda among the young and politically unformed was beneficial, the Communist agitation among young Hungarians was driven by the recognition that only a few years earlier Hungarian youth had responded fervently to nationalist and militarist appeals by fascist leaders. The so-called *levente* movement, a quasi-military organization, attracted thousands. Nazi propaganda had to be counteracted. On the other hand, in the tiny underground Communist party, there had been very few young activists, and these cadres needed to be amplified.

After the appearance of the Red Army, the party immediately began seeking contacts among young people. Already on October 15, 1944, four days after the liberation of the provincial town of Szeged, twenty young people established the Communist Youth Organization (KISZ).[40] New, young Communists soon established similar cells in the rest of the country. However, at the very outset it was clear to the senior Communist leadership that the best strategy would be to have a unified, nonparty movement under Communist influence. Almost immediately after returning from the Soviet Union, Ernő Gerő argued against a separate Communist youth organization.[41] Clearly, this policy decision had been made earlier in Moscow, but it was not uniformly welcomed. What the Communists called "sectarianism"

38 RTsKhIDNI fond 17, opis 128, delo 315, p. 29.

39 PIL 274 16/50 Szamor village, November 6, 1946.

40 Report on the establishment of the Szeged KISZ organization. In the collection of documents already cited: S. Rákosi, et al., pp. 39–40.

41 Ibid., November 9, 1944, pp. 41–42.

was especially strong among the young. Some of the young Communists were impatient and wanted to take advantage of the victory of the Red Army and move immediately to a Communist system. The leaders patiently explained that the "masses" at this point did not support "proletarian dictatorship" and that the experience of the 1919 Communist regime counseled caution. They pointed out that even the Soviets decided to collectivize agriculture only twelve years after coming to power.[42] It was in this context that MADISZ was organized in Debrecen on December 7, 1944.[43]

The Communist policy of preferring a unified, nonparty youth movement, as an extension of the National Front, created a curious situation. The Communists failed to dissuade the representatives of other parties from forming their own youth movements and were prevented by their own policy from forming an openly Communist youth movement. Meanwhile the Social Democrats, Smallholders, and religious organizations created their own youth movements in order to train the next generation of leaders. It was not too difficult to see through the pretence that MADISZ was a Communist organization, but the consequence of this ambivalent situation was that MADISZ could not openly participate in the electoral struggle in the fall of 1945. Its members campaigned for the Communists as individuals.

It was the Communists alone who had no separate organization. Usually the KISZ organizations simply renamed themselves MADISZ and requested the other youth organizations to join. The plan was to include non-Communists in the leadership, yet to assure that behind the scenes Communist dominance would remain secure.[44] Communist MADISZ leaders came under party discipline and were punished for not following instructions from above.[45] Creating a unified youth movement was difficult not only because of the resistance of the other political parties but also because the youth was heterogeneous. The interests, education, and backgrounds of peasant young people and high school and university students in cities were very different. Under the circumstances, it was hard to develop a program appealing to all.

The differences in outlook among the various political parties were reflected also in their youth movements. Indeed, they appeared in an exaggerated form among the youth. The young Communist sympathizers were contemptuous of competing ideologies and impatient with the policies of their elders who were unwilling to build a Soviet-type political system

42 PIL 274 18/1.
43 S. Rákosi, et al., p. 42.
44 PIL 274 17/2 report to Central Committee, June 4, 1945.
45 PIL 274 18/1 April 7, 1945, István Kende.

immediately. At a national leadership meeting of MADISZ, several speakers spoke of the FKGP youth organization members as fascist thugs.[46] By contrast, the leaders of the youth organization of the FKGP, "Independent Youth," denounced Communist shenanigans so strongly and stressed nationalism in their appeal so explicitly as to embarrass their elders.[47] They signed their letters and reports "with Hungarian greetings" and with "patriotic respects." They described the leaders of MADISZ as anti-Hungarian and anti-Christian. One speaker defended Bárdossy, an ex-premier, who had just been sentenced to death for war crimes.[48]

On several occasions, the disagreements among the youth organizations came to physical violence. The Communists invariably initiated these. In the archives, there are numerous reports of Communists breaking up meetings of the FKGP's Independent Youth organizations and arresting their leaders. In November 1945 in the little town of Jászberény, for example, Communist youth accompanied by Russian soldiers broke into a meeting of the Independent Youth and threatened the participants with weapons.[49] In September 1945 in Hajdúböszörmény, the Communist police dispersed the meeting of the Independent Youth, in spite of the fact that the organization had permission for the gathering from the local Soviet authorities.[50] The Communist-dominated political police was even more willing to use force against young activists than against the better known elder leaders of the Smallholders' Party. Some young people responded to the pressure by changing party affiliation and joining the Communists.[51]

As long as MADISZ faced competition, it had to make efforts to attract people by offering amusements and sports and participation in various sorts of social work. The organization also consciously imitated Nazi mobilization techniques such as organizing marches and giving out uniforms.[52] Above all, MADISZ offered its members a sense of belonging and a sense of participating in building a new and better society. One ought not underestimate the force of an idealistic appeal to the youth to participate in reconstruction.

46 PIL 286/5 November 28, 1945.

47 PIL 286/5 December 19, 1945. Here is a report on a meeting: "After singing the national anthem, B. Rácz István opened the meeting. After that followed Racz's opening speech about youth, humanity, Hungarianness. We must be an example to the other organizations of youth. Youth, Humanity, Hungarianness. This is what we wrote on our flag. It is great to be young, it is a holy obligation to be human, and it is a great obligation to be Hungarian."

48 PIL 286/5 January 19, 1946.

49 PIL 286/5 November 6, 1945, p. 43.

50 PIL 286/5 pp. 50–52.

51 PIL 286/5 p. 371.

52 Meeting of MADISZ leaders. Bárdi: "However strange it sounds we must take some methods from the fascists. They knew how to organize the broad masses. . . . Appearances, uniforms, marches." PIL 274 18/1 April 7, 1945.

Many later well-known functionaries of the Communist regime started their political activities in the youth organization.

Communist leaders, however, were dissatisfied with the achievements of MADISZ. They were dismayed at the relatively small size of the organization and by the general disorder within it. In the summer of 1945, MADISZ had 70,000 members.[53] (In the following years, however, hundreds of thousands participated in MADISZ activities.) Rákosi later complained that it was difficult to find "good comrades to work in mass organization, because good communists did not appreciate the significance of the work."[54]

As long as the pluralist system existed, the Communists could not achieve their goal of having a unified youth movement entirely under their control. Pluralism ended among the youth movements as it also ended among the political parties. In 1948, the independent youth organizations finally buckled under pressure, and the Communist goal of a unified youth movement under their control was finally achieved.

The trade union movement experienced a major transformation. Immediately at the end of the war, it was under exclusive Socialist influence. Very quickly, however, the Communists managed to achieve a major success in bringing the unions under their control and marginalizing the Socialist leaders. Unionization progressed rapidly, and by the spring of 1947 the unions had a million and a half members.[55] The Communists formed factory committees, which explicitly aimed at limiting the power of the owners. The management could make no major decisions without the agreement of the workers' representatives. The committees had the right to supervise the use of scarce raw material and also had a say in how much white-collar workers could earn. The trade unions were also used to organize politically inspired strikes against "reactionaries." On one occasion, for example, the union carried out a strike that made it impossible to print an anti-Communist newspaper.[56] Once private enterprise was eliminated, the trade unions retained their role in "Communist education," that is, channeling the party's current policy to working-class audiences.

There was another mass organization, which, though not as large or as significant as MNDSZ or MADISZ, nevertheless deserves particular attention. This was the Hungarian Soviet Cultural Society (MSZMT). The Communist leadership well understood that in the understanding of the Hungarian people, Communism and the Soviet Union were inextricably tied together.

53 PIL 274 17/2 István Kende, February 18, 1945.

54 PIL 274 2/38 Rákosi speaking to a Central Committee meeting in January 1947.

55 RTsKhIDNI fond 17, opis 128, delo 315, p. 37. Report by István Kossa.

56 Ibid.

In order to come to power, it was therefore essential to increase not only the popularity of the party but also that of the Soviet Union. This was a difficult task at a time when the Soviet army was occupying the country, its soldiers were behaving badly, and Soviet policy was egregiously exploitative.

For the purpose of popularizing Soviet culture and the Soviet Union in general, the MSZMT had already been organized under Communist inspiration in June 1945.[57] Similar societies were created in all the countries that came under Soviet influence after the war. The Hungarian Communist leadership was keenly aware that they were competing with the neighboring countries for Soviet favor. They were pleased when a Major Gurkin, a Soviet official in the office responsible for contact with newly occupied countries, regarded Hungary as the second most successful in spreading Soviet culture after Romania.[58] However, the Hungarian Communists wished to be first in this competition and to become model disciples.

Gyula Hay, a Communist writer who had just returned from Moscow, took the lead in creating this society. He reported to Rákosi in September 1945 that the organization had been established three months earlier. The honorary chairman of the society was a great Nobel Prize–winning scientist, Albert Szent-Györgyi, and the chairman was a well-known, non-Communist writer of popular novels, Lajos Zilahy. Szent-Györgyi enjoyed enormous respect at the time, not only for his scientific accomplishments but also because of his courageous stand against the Nazis and for his efforts to arrange a separate peace between Hungary and the Allies. In December 1944, he was elected to the Provisional National Assembly. He belonged to that group of prominent intellectuals who in the past had shown little sympathy for the Soviet Union or Communism but who understood that in the prevailing international situation there was no choice for Hungarians but to develop as friendly relations as possible with the powerful neighbor to the east. The Communists, of course, did not trust these people; nevertheless, they possessed the political wisdom to take advantage of their prestige and use their services in the struggle for power. Once they were firmly established, most of the intellectuals were either pushed aside or themselves decided that they could no longer cooperate with the Communists. In 1947, Szent-Györgyi, for example, disillusioned, went into exile and continued his scientific work in the United States.

57 PIL 174/6 September 22, 1945, Gyula Hay writing to Rákosi.

58 PIL 274 17/6. Hay was proudly asserting that when the society's publication will appear, Hungary will be number one.

Hay made it explicit in his letter to Rákosi that Communists dominated the organization, but they made great efforts to remain in the background and to give the MSZMT a non-Communist appearance. He saw two different tasks: to attract well-known intellectuals bringing prestige to the organization and to create cells around the country involving simple people who would then be exposed to some aspects of Soviet culture. Hay was pleased to have such prominent people as Zoltán Kodály, the best-known living composer, and Imre Oltványi, the economist and FKGP politician, even though he described both of these people as "explicitly reactionary."

Obviously, under the circumstances the work was difficult. Hay wanted to organize Russian language courses, but there were no available teachers or textbooks. Contacts with the Soviet Union were never easy: the organization sent presents to the "Russian comrades" but had not received even an acknowledgment. The task was to show Russian films, stage Soviet plays, translate Russian literature, and acquaint Hungarian audiences with Russian music. In the 1945–1946 season, seven Soviet plays were appearing in Budapest theaters. MSZMT hosted prominent Soviet artists and scholars. The organization published a journal, *Jövendő* (the *Future*), that was printed in 50,000 copies.[59]

As Communist power grew, so did the size of the MSZMT. By the beginning of 1947, entire factories and schools joined the organization as units. The MSZMT organized lectures about various aspects of Soviet life. At the time of the elections in 1945, it organized lectures about the Soviet constitution, aiming to demonstrate the superiority of Soviet democracy. Gradually, more and more subsections were created, such as theater, literature, agriculture, economics, law, pedagogy, humanities, architecture, medicine, press and radio, sport, chess, film, philately, and youth. Celebrations were organized to celebrate Lenin's birthday, Red Army Day, the anniversary of the revolution of 1917, and so forth. There were more and more Soviet plays and films, more and more lectures on Soviet topics.

In November 1945, the Russians arrested the two editors of the Cultural Society's journal, *Jövendő*, accusing one of them of having a fascist past and the other of "British orientation."[60] Both men had been personally chosen to edit the journal by Zilahy. The Russians exhibited neither tact nor an appreciation of special Hungarian circumstances. Rezsö Szántó, one of the Communist leaders of the society, wrote to the Central Committee of the party in September 1946, requesting that József Révai, the man responsible for culture and ideology, should talk to the Russians and explain to them

59 PIL 274 17/6 September 22, 1945.

60 PIL 274 17/7 Hay to Rákosi.

that propaganda in favor of organizing collective farms was contrary to the publicly announced position of the party.

The organization was also a drain on the party's finances. In 1947, membership dues brought in 15,000 forints, but it cost the party an additional 50,000 to support the organization.[61] Even that was not enough, and the leaders of the organization requested that the trade unions should also make a contribution. The journal lost money, and there were few subscribers. Even according to the activists in the organization, the journal was boring, and the editors, who did not even know Russian, were incompetent. In order to attract audiences, the cultural program and lectures were free. Soviet theatrical productions often played to empty houses. The society had special difficulty in appealing to workers and especially peasants.

Although there were more and more members of the society, membership became a formality. The organization continued to exist as one of the numerous Soviet-style front organizations that attempted to give the appearance of spontaneity. The Communist leaders were well aware that the MSZMT was not achieving its purpose. They hoped that matters would improve if more Soviet artists and scientists came to Hungary and in exchange leading Hungarian intellectuals could visit the Soviet Union. In the long run, nothing helped.[62] Not only Soviet but even Russian culture remained deeply unpopular in Hungary.

61 PIL 274 17/7 September 6, 1947, Szántó to Rákosi.
62 RTsKhIDNI fond 17, opis 128, delo 315, p. 35. Report by Sándor Nográdi.

10

Foreign Relations

In the immediate postwar period, we cannot talk about a Hungarian foreign policy. The armistice severely restricted the country's sovereignty and circumscribed Hungary's relations with the rest of the world. Important matters concerning the future of the country were resolved elsewhere. Hungarian diplomats had goals and desires but no leverage. Hungarian representatives could do no more than plead, and, as we know now, their pleadings were rarely successful. Furthermore, the country had no foreign policy because different segments of the political spectrum had conflicting ideas and plans. The Communists could see no distinction between Soviet and Hungarian interests and were delighted to serve what seemed to them as the interests of world Communism. They saw increasingly clearly that they could attain power only with Soviet help and therefore feared eventual Soviet withdrawal from the country. By contrast, the non-Communist segment, represented primarily by the Smallholder Party diplomats, aimed at limiting Soviet domination and hoped for assistance from the Western powers.

From the very outset, there were two distinct channels of communication between the governing circles of Hungary and the Soviet Union: official, government-to-government contacts and exchanges between the Hungarian Communist leaders and their Soviet superiors. Members of the governments of Dálnoki Miklos and later of Ferenc Nagy were in constant contact with Voroshilov, Sviridov, and Pushkin. Sometimes the Communists and the legitimate government representatives worked for the same goals, but at other times they worked at cross purposes.

Because the country could have no official diplomatic ties for the time being, all diplomats who had been accredited to the previous regime, even from neutral countries, had to leave. Hungary was isolated and ties with other countries depended on the ACC, that is, on the Soviet occupation authorities. The foreign minister in the provisional government was János

Gyöngyösi, a moderate Smallholder politician, who in his official capacity was one of the signers of the armistice agreement. The longest serving minister in this transitional period, he had the difficult task of building up a new foreign service. Few of the diplomats from the prewar foreign ministry could be retained, because of their past collaboration with the Nazis. In Debrecen, the foreign ministry occupied three rooms, and the minister had only two assistants.[1] Even after moving the government to Budapest, the situation changed only slowly, and Hungary's diplomatic isolation in the first postwar year was not relieved.

The Soviet civilian representative, quasi-ambassador Georgii Pushkin, arrived in Hungary with the Soviet army. In March 1945, the British and the Americans also sent diplomatic representatives to Hungary, Arthur Schoenfeld from the United States and Alvary Cascoigne from Great Britain, but with the explicit understanding that their presence implied no recognition.[2] The Soviet Union, in order to bolster the legitimacy of Eastern European regimes under its control, attempted to persuade the allies to extend diplomatic recognition to these countries. The Allies resisted precisely because they wanted to express their disapproval of the antidemocratic means by which the Eastern European regimes had been established. Only in September did the United States show willingness to receive a Hungarian representative in Washington, even though at this point it did not indicate the full reestablishment of normal diplomatic relations.[3] When full diplomatic relations were finally renewed, the Americans intended to signal their approval of the Hungarian elections that had taken place in November 1945, and by contrast their disapproval of the political system that had come into being in Bulgaria and Romania. The elections in these Balkan states took place on the Soviet model; that is, the voters were presented with a single list of candidates and consequently had no choice.[4] Following British and American recognition, the foreign ministry was able to exchange diplomats with the major European countries.

The first representative in Washington was Aladár Szegedy-Maszák, who had worked in the old regime's foreign service.[5] As a liberal and anti-Nazi, he had been arrested by the Gestapo, deported to Dachau, and freed by the Americans. He took up his position in Washington in January 1946 and

1 Roman, p. 35.

2 FRUS, 1945, vol. 4, pp. 798–799. Schoenfeld had already been selected for his position in January 1945.

3 Ibid., pp. 874–875. The American note made this action conditional on holding free elections.

4 Ibid., pp. 878–879.

5 A. Szegedy-Maszák, *Az ember összel visszanéz: egy volt magyar diplomata emlékirataiból*, 2 vols, Budapest, Európa: História, 1996.

22. Hungarian delegation in Red Square, Moscow, January 1946: Ferenc Nagy, János Gyöngyösi, and Gyula Szekfű. (Source: Hungarian National Museum.)

stayed in his job until June 1947, at which time he resigned in protest of the removal of Ferenc Nagy as premier. He was a highly respected diplomat who created good will for the country he represented, though that good will had few practical consequences.[6]

The choice of first ambassador to Moscow was a curious one: Gyula Szekfű, one of the most prominent Hungarian historians, went to the Soviet Union. Szekfű, a pious Catholic, in his highly regarded scholarly works represented a deeply conservative approach to history. His prewar writings were not free of anti-Semitism, the role of the Jews in Hungary being a topic to which he devoted considerable attention. In the interwar period, he had been close to the leading political figures of the era, including István Bethlen, the prime minister in the 1920s. His coauthor of a major, multi-volume history of Hungary, Bálint Homan, was in prison at the time when Szekfű was serving the increasingly Communist-dominated state. Szekfű had been among those intellectuals who realized that Horthy's prewar political and social system was leading the country into a dead end street and had

6 Interview with Hubert Havlik, Truman Library, June 22, 1973, by Richard D. McKenzie. Havlik worked in the state department at the time when Szegedy-Maszák was ambassador. Accessed June 22, 2004 <www.trumanlibrary.org/oralhist/havlik.htm>

opposed the German orientation of foreign policy.[7] Furthermore, he also realized that in the postwar era the Soviet Union would be a decisive factor in Eastern Europe. Until the end of his career, he remained convinced that the country had no choice but to court the goodwill of the Russians and that expecting help from the West was illusory. As late as 1947, he still believed that the Soviet Union did not intend to impose Communism on his country but was primarily interested in the defense of its borders. Szekfű was almost unique among the prominent figures of the old regime in his commitment to *realpolitik*. As a Catholic intellectual, he stood at the opposite extreme from Cardinal Mindszenty. It is difficult to see how those who chose him for his position in Moscow expected him to find the proper tone to deal with the Soviet authorities. Probably, the Communists acquiesced to this appointment because they took it for granted that Hungarian Soviet relations would not be conducted primarily through the Moscow embassy. Indeed, Szekfű himself realized that the important contacts took place in Budapest between the Hungarian authorities, the ACC, and Ambassador Pushkin.[8]

After Soviet domination in Eastern Europe was complete, only relations with it really mattered. Hungarians always appeared as supplicants; they lacked the means of influencing Soviet policy. During the first year, Gyöngyösi's contacts, as the man responsible for foreign affairs, were limited to the ACC, namely Marshal Voroshilov, and to the Soviet civilian representative. There was nothing much that the foreign minister could do but send letters of protest and plead with the representatives of the Soviet authority. These appeals almost never had beneficial results. On one occasion Pushkin actually warned the foreign minister that the very submission of a request to postpone reparation deliveries "would make the worst possible impression on the Soviet authorities."[9]

In the first half of 1946, a high-level governmental delegation visited the two major world capitals, Moscow and Washington. It was inevitable that the first trip should be to the Soviet Union. The nine-day trip was something of a success. The delegation included Prime Minister Ferenc Nagy; Foreign Minister Gyöngyösi; Ernő Gerő, the only Communist in this delegation; the Socialist leader, Árpád Szakasits; and Ambassador Szekfű. The Hungarians held separate discussions with Deputy Foreign Minister Dekanozov, Molotov, and Stalin. The delegation was interested in getting help with the adjustment of Romanian and Czechoslovakian borders, the

7 Gyula Szekfű, *Forradalom után*, Ference Glatz (ed.), Budapest: Gondolat, 1983.
8 MOL XIX–J-1–j Szekfű's report to ministry on 1946, Moscow, February 23, 1947.
9 MOL XIX-J-1-j November 26, 1945.

23. Farewell meeting on occasion of the departing Allied Control Commission. From left to right: unidentified churchman; László Jékely, chief of the cabinet; Ferenc Szeder, SDP secretary; Gyula Ortutay, minister of education; and Mrs. Jékely Mátyás Rákosi. Budapest, September 25, 1947. (Source: Hungarian National Museum.)

treatment of Hungarian minorities in these countries, the repatriation of POWs, and lightening the burden of reparations. In these conversations, the Hungarians received some concessions concerning reparation: the schedule for reparation delivery was stretched from six to eight years.

Stalin received the delegation on April 11 at 9:30 pm, an hour that was not unusual for diplomatic contacts with him. On the Soviet side, Molotov, Dekanozov, and Ambassador Pushkin participated. Ferenc Nagy started his speech by saying that he wanted to report on the development of Hungarian democracy in the course of the past year. Stalin immediately interrupted him, according to the Hungarians' notes of the meeting, "stressing that the Prime Minister's words should not be called a report, but should be regarded as simply exchanging information between the heads of two friendly governments. The Soviet Union regards Hungary as a free and independent country and therefore the word 'report' is not appropriate."[10]

In the course of the conversation, Stalin said that Soviet troops would soon be withdrawn from Hungary and only a few soldiers would remain. This

10 MOL XIX-J-1-j April 11, 1946, pp. 15–24.

statement, more than any other, encouraged Nagy. When Gerő complained that the Soviets wanted payment for the repair of a Hungarian-built railroad line that was not even on Hungarian territory any longer, Stalin found the situation amusing and told Gerő that he should simply refuse to pay. The Hungarian report ends with these words:

> The great historical personality put his stamp on the entire conversation. He demonstrated a human directness that encouraged us and made us at ease. The delegation was first ill at ease to a considerable extent because in the course of the first sentences Stalin was seemingly preoccupied and listened to us morosely. But when he made his first remarks we saw that this silence did not mean coldness, but on the contrary it implied interest. And when he made his remarks Stalin's humor shined through, and then the entire delegation gained strength and confidence and the delegation of the Hungarian people's government felt that it was meeting the greatest son of a great people. It felt that it was meeting perhaps with the great figure in world history with whom it has human contacts in spite of his momentous spiritual qualities.[11]

This distastefully fawning and grammatically contorted note was not written by Communist functionaries, but by Hungarian diplomats and was approved by the participants, including the premier.[12]

The next trip took the Hungarians to Washington, London, and Paris. From the point of view of the FKGP ministers, it was important to demonstrate, at least to themselves, that Hungary retained a degree of freedom of action. However, there was a price to pay. Szekfű, in his summary evaluation of Soviet-Hungarian relations for the year 1946, remarked upon a cooling of Soviet attitudes to Hungary after the Western trip. Ambassador Pushkin and Molotov accused the Hungarians of attempting a seesaw politics between the two blocs that were coming into being.[13] Premier Nagy, who was aware of the danger of alienating Moscow by going to the United States and to Great Britain, hoped to assuage the Russians by persuading Rákosi to take part in the delegation. Ironically, Rákosi, who was predictably hostile to everything he saw in the West, was the only member of the delegation who spoke English, and therefore often was chosen as spokesman. Rákosi later gleefully reported to Stalin that aside from the promise of returning the Hungarian gold that had been taken by the Germans and returning some other Hungarian properties, such as ships, the trip brought

11 Ibid., pp. 9–10.

12 F. Nagy, pp. 272–285. Even in his exile Ference Nagy wrote with admiration about Stalin and considered the Moscow trip a success.

13 MOL XIX–J-1–j.

no political benefits.[14] Rákosi also truthfully remarked that the Americans said nothing that could be interpreted as encouraging the Hungarians to take an anti-Soviet stance. Indeed, in the course of these conversations the Western powers demonstrated that they were not in the position to provide concrete help in preventing Soviet domination. However, the Hungarian, non-Communist politicians could be forgiven for not giving up hope. Interestingly, it was the archconservative Szekfű in Moscow who from the outset realized that there was no alternative to a Soviet orientation in foreign policy and there was nothing else to do but to seek the Russians' goodwill.

Hungarians, of course, could not prevent their country from falling into the Soviet sphere of influence. The modest and realistic goals of diplomacy were only the amelioration of the crushing burden of reparations, possible border changes on the basis of ethnicity, and the defense of the Hungarian minorities that remained outside of the national borders. In all of these matters, Hungarian diplomacy failed. The fault was not in the skill of the diplomats nor in a failure to cooperate. All politicians, Communists and non-Communists alike, worked together in the defense of these national interests. However, ultimately neither the Western allies nor the Soviet Union considered it to be in their interest to help the Hungarians.

In the interwar period, Hungarian public life was utterly preoccupied with the need to remedy the historical wrongs committed at the end of the previous war, when the peace treaty, signed at Trianon in 1920, gave large chunks of territory with Hungarian majorities to the neighboring countries. With German help, the Horthy regime regained at least some of these areas. The armistice agreement, however, obliged the provisional government to withdraw from all those districts that had came under Hungarian authority after 1937. Nevertheless, in 1945 Hungarian politicians of all political parties believed that the great powers would see the justice of their cause and at least some border adjustments would be made in their favor. Ultimately, not only were the Hungarian requests not honored but also a small border change was made giving away more Hungarian land, on this occasion, to the reconstructed state of Czechoslovakia.

In 1944 and 1945, Hungarian officials were withdrawn from Carpatho-Ukraine (which now became part of Soviet Ukraine), northern Transylvania, the Bácska region of Yugoslavia, and southern Slovakia. In the closing stages of the war in all of the liberated counties, the Hungarians suffered great indignities. In northern Transylvania, in particular, the area

14 *Moszkvának jelentjük*, pp. 95–97, Rákosi's letter to Stalin dated July 5, 1946.

that was returned to Hungary in 1940 but was now reoccupied by Romanians in September and October, dreadful atrocities were committed and order returned only slowly. Hungarians were saved from Romanian nationalist brutality by Soviet troops.[15] For a few weeks under Soviet aegis, Hungarians and Romanians administered northern Transylvania together, which, from the Hungarian point of view, was an altogether unexpectedly favorable development. The behavior of the Soviet authorities in northern Transylvania made the Hungarians optimistic concerning Russian intentions for the future of the province. In Yugoslavia, Tito's Croatian partisans massacred some Hungarians and expelled others, taking over their property. Hungarian diplomats did not seriously consider presenting territorial claims against Yugoslavia, nor could there be any doubt about the future of the Carpatho-Ukraine that had belonged to Czechoslovakia between the end of World War I and the Munich agreement.

The Hungarian attitude concerning Romania and Czechoslovakia was different. Romania, after all, had been an ally of Hitler. It is true that Romania succeeded in switching sides on August 23, 1944, earlier than Hungary; however, the brutality with which the Romanians had behaved on occupied Soviet territory undermined their claim to special sympathy. As with all other issues in Eastern Europe, the Soviet Union was the decisive factor in the Hungarian-Romanian border question too. From the Soviet point of view even before the conclusion of the war, Romania, a strategically located border country, was more important than Hungary. Soviet diplomacy also favored Romania's retention of all of Transylvania as compensation for Romania's loss of Bessarabia and Bukovina to the Soviet Union. Soviet thinking probably was that Romania would be tied to the Soviet Union because it would always face a hostile Hungary and would need help from a great power.

The Soviet Union imposed Petru Groza as premier on the unwilling King Michael of Romania. Groza promised an enlightened attitude concerning the treatment of the Hungarian minority. Indeed, it was a condition of the introduction of Romanian administration into northern Transylvania that the Romanians would protect minority rights. Very soon, however, the circumstances of the Hungarian minority deteriorated, and a policy favored by

15 Mihály Fülöp and Gábor Vincze (eds.), *Revizio vagy autonomia? Iratok a magyar-román kapcsolatok történetéről, 1945–1947*, Budapest: Teleki László Alapitvány, 1998, p. 11. It is true that when Hungarians took possession of northern Transylvania they also committed atrocities. Although it is difficult to measure such matters, it appears that the Romanians in 1944 were even worse than the Hungarians in 1940. It is not that the Romanians were more likely to misbehave than the Hungarians, but the years of war cheapened the value of human lives and coarsened morality further.

24. Signing of the Soviet-Hungarian friendship agreement, April 20, 1948. (Source: Hungarian National Museum.)

Romanian nationalists was introduced. This meant that Hungarians were not allowed to return to the places of residence they had left during the war. Hungarian property was confiscated, and the original promise of maintaining a Hungarian-language university in Cluj was not kept.

The resolution of the Hungarian-Romanian border issue came to be connected with the ever more bitter struggle among the great powers. The Americans and the British did not recognize the Groza government because it was imposed by the Soviet Union against the wishes of King Michael. By supporting Hungarian attempts to regain territory, the Western allies consciously attempted to weaken the Romanian government, which they disliked, and by contrast to strengthen the Smallholders government in Hungary, which against all expectations had won a convincing victory in a free election. Ultimately, however, it was only the Soviet position that mattered.[16] At the meeting of foreign ministers in the fall of 1945, Molotov argued that in drawing the border between the two countries the Soviet Union wished only to reinforce a decision that the Allies had made already in 1920. This was a difficult point to refute, and from the point of view

16 Ibid., pp. 15–16.

of the British and American diplomats the Romanian-Hungarian border dispute was a secondary matter.

During the visit of the Hungarian governmental delegation in Moscow, the Hungarians brought up the border issue. Molotov's response was that the Hungarians should negotiate with the Romanians directly. His refusal to act as a mediator implied that the cause was hopeless. No Romanian government could give up territory without extreme outside pressure.[17] In the course of the Hungarian delegation's Western trip, the prime minister once again attempted to gain the support of the United States and Britain. But this support was not forthcoming, and therefore the adjustment of borders ceased to be a live issue. The Hungarians at this point had to limit their efforts to the defense of the minority rights of their ethnic brothers, but even in this limited goal they failed to achieve anything. Hungarians came to be a suppressed minority within the reestablished Romanian state.

Relations with Czechoslovakia were worse. The Hungarian leaders had confidence in the goodwill of Groza and did not personally blame him for the indignities the Hungarian minority had to suffer. In relation to Czechoslovakia, there was little chance of border adjustment in favor of Hungary. By the armistice agreement, Hungary undertook withdrawing from those territories that it had taken from the Czechoslovak state at the time when that country ceased to exist. Furthermore, it assumed an obligation to pay $30 million in reparations. After all, unlike Romania and Hungary, Czechoslovakia in theory was among the victor nations. The reality was more complicated. It is true that democratic Czechoslovakia had been destroyed as a result of Nazi aggression. But the puppet Slovak state, created by the Germans, where the Hungarian minority actually lived, was if anything a more willing and active ally of the Nazis than the conservative and relatively cautious Horthy regime. The clerical fascist Hlinka-Tiso regime certainly did not hesitate to send the Jews to their death. The Hungarian minority in the rump Slovak state could not be accused of being particularly enthusiastic followers of pro-Nazi policies. In fact, the nationalist policies of the Slovak fascist regime alienated the Hungarians. It was the misfortune of the Hungarians that at the end of the war, when the Czechoslovak state was recreated, the allies, who paid little attention to this matter, equated the Hungarians of Slovakia with the German minority in the Sudetenland which did in fact contribute to the destruction of the state and the Hungarian minority that had played a quite different role.

17 MOL XIX-J-1-j.

25. Hungarian police gleefully showing keys of houses abandoned by the Swabs, August 17, 1947. (Source: Hungarian National Museum.)

The end of the Second World War introduced a remarkable turn around in the nationality policies of the Czechoslovak political elite. It was a sad irony that the previously most liberal regime in Central and Eastern Europe at least for the moment was most influenced by the basest nationalist passions. In the liberal era of the interwar period, the minorities were treated reasonably well. By contrast, in the immediate postwar period the Czechoslovak state used the most brutal methods of indiscriminately expelling people. In this new era, the leadership, especially the Slovaks but also the Czechs aimed to reform their state into a purely Slavic entity in which Germans and Hungarians would have no place. The goal was to get rid of the approximately 600,000 Hungarians who had lived in Slovakia for centuries. The changes in policies and attitudes had little to do with the actual past behavior of human beings. People were punished not for actually having committed crimes. The changes instead were the consequence of a radical new thinking made possible by the great conflagration of the Second World War.

The Communists were in the forefront of the newfound nationalism. In the new Czechoslovakia, just as in Hungary under different circumstances, the Communists had to strengthen their nationalist credentials in order to counteract the criticism that they were foreign puppets. In April 1945, in

Kosice even before the conclusion of the hostilities, Klement Gottwald, the head of the Czechoslovak Communist party, expressed anti-Hungarian sentiments that foreshadowed the policies of the future state. In his speech, he said that only those Hungarians who had participated in the anti-Nazi struggle could maintain their citizenship, and the others would have a choice between staying as nonresidents or moving to Hungary.[18] Benes reaffirmed Gottwald's promises in a decree that he issued on August 3.[19] Hungarian-language schools were closed down, and the use of Hungarian language in church services was forbidden.

The deprivation of citizenship clearly had nothing to do with previous pro-German activities. That this was the case is demonstrated by the fact that the Slovak Jewry, which could not be accused of collaborating with the Nazis, suffered the same fate as the other Hungarians. (The vast majority of the Jews were Hungarian speakers.) A Slovak newspaper wrote on August 14, 1945: "Aside from a few exceptions in the previous years the Jews did not show friendship to the Slovak people and did not support the national uprising. They did not show respect to the Slovak language but spoke Hungarian or German, regarding themselves as Hungarian or German. They were the most merciless oppressors of the Slovak people. They did not respect Slovak demands, did not raise the cultural level of the people, did not support our cultural demands, but on the contrary, they sucked the blood of the people as leeches."[20] (It is not necessary to point out the absurdity of the charge that the Jews had not supported the uprising. Their countrymen had already deported them to Auschwitz.)

Hungarian diplomats as well as Communist officials complained to everyone willing to listen. They wrote to the Soviet representatives and they complained to Allied diplomats, but the matter was not considered important by anyone. The Americans at first paid attention. The state department notified Ambassador Schoenfeld in Budapest that the United States opposed the notion that people could be punished solely on the basis of their belonging to an ethnic group and mentioned that the Czechoslovak foreign minister, Jan Masaryk, had promised that only those Hungarians would be punished who had fought on the side of the Nazis.[21] Schoenfeld in a response to the state department rightly pointed out that "[t]his situation is (the indiscriminate

18 Roman, p. 54.

19 MOL XVIII-1-a-b/1945–46 Gyöngyösi's letter to Ambassadors Pushkin, Schoenfeld, and Gascoigne, November 20, 1945.

20 Ibid.

21 FRUS, 1945, vol. 4, pp. 928–951, Exchange of telegrams concerning the Hungarian minority in Slovakia.

26. Deportion of the Swabs, August 17, 1947. (Source: Hungarian National Museum.)

expulsion of Hungarians from Slovakia) particularly ironical as there had been proportionately more sincere collaborationists among Slovaks than even in Hungary."[22] Remarkably, the U.S. ambassador in Prague, Laurence Steinhardt, accepted the official Czechoslovak explanation. He approvingly quoted the Czechoslovak response, which spoke of the "audacity of Hungary and Germany, enemy states defeated only a few weeks ago in criticizing the internal affairs of one of the United Nations after what the world knows of the sufferings of the Czechs and Slovaks at the hands of the Germans and Hungarians when they were in the saddle."[23]

The Czechoslovak proposal of exchange of populations was obviously unfair. As the Hungarians pointed out repeatedly, not more than a few thousand Slovaks would opt for voluntary transfer as against the compulsory expulsion of approximately half a million poverty-stricken Hungarians. Given the dire economic situation, the arrival of so many landless peasant refugees would have disastrous consequences. At the same time, there was also an influx of dispossessed Hungarians also from Yugoslavia, Romania, and the Carpatho-Ukraine. In view of the extraordinarily cruel removal of

22 Ibid., p. 931.

23 Ibid., p. 935.

entire nations from the Caucasus just a short time before, it was naïve to expect that the Russians would be shocked at the sight of Slovak brutalities.[24]

Relations between the two "brother parties," the two Communist parties, were every bit as bad, indeed worse, than the relations between the two governments. The Hungarians constantly and indignantly complained to their superiors in Moscow. Rákosi in his report in April 1947 wrote that the Czechoslovak party did not invite Hungarian Communists to their congress. The Hungarians did invite the Czechoslovaks, but those did not even answer the invitation. When the Hungarians asked to send observers to oversee the deportations of Hungarian Communists from Slovakia, their request for visas was denied. Hungarian Communists in Slovakia felt that they were particularly harshly persecuted. Rákosi complained that the behavior of the Czechoslovak Communists would hurt the Hungarian party in the coming elections.[25] There is no evidence that the Russian comrades intervened on behalf of the Hungarians. Had they done so, we may assume that the Czechs and Slovaks at least would have become more polite. It seems that Moscow was not interested even in maintaining comity within their bloc.[26]

There is no reason to think that had the shoe been on the other foot, that is, if the Hungarians had the opportunity to impose their nationalist vision on others, they would have been more sensitive. However, in the postwar period the Hungarians were at the receiving end of persecution. Post–First World War Hungary was an ethnically more or less homogeneous country. The largest minority, not counting Jews, who were a special case, were the Swabs. This minority, which had lived in the country for centuries, played a significant role in some sections of the national life, such as the officer corps. Unlike Slovaks, Romanians, and Serbs, the Swabs, although not particularly prosperous, never considered themselves an oppressed group and had been fairly well integrated into society. Circumstances changed only in the course

24 Ultimately, only approximately 88,000 Hungarians were expelled from Czechoslovakia, and 73,000 Slovaks decided to move to Czechoslovakia. László Kővágó, *A Magyar kommunisták és a nemzetiségi kérdés, 1918–1948*, Budapest: Kossuth, 1985, p. 281. Kővágó based his information on figures from the Hungarian Statistical Office.

25 RTsKhIDNI, fond 17, opis 128, delo 315, pp. 9–11. Rákosi also wrote to Stalin making the same complaints, adding that the Yugoslav Communists attempted to intervene with the Slovaks but so far without results. *Moszkvának jelentjük,* p. 161. Rákosi also reported his complaints to Molotov at the time of his Moscow visit in April, 1947. *Moszkvának jelentjük,* pp. 200–202.

26 In September 1946, Rákosi considered organizing a conference of the Communist Parties of the Danube basin. This did not take place because of Soviet opposition. Mikhail Suslov, writing to Andrei Zhdanov, happily and incorrectly noted that the Czechoslovak Communists would not even be invited to such a meeting. Suslov went on saying that Hungarian Communists should not have a unifying role because "Hungarian successes in democratic construction are less significant than in the Slavic countries." RTsKhIDNI, fond 17, opis 128, delo 916, pp. 1–2.

of the Second World War, when Nazi Germany's racist leaders made a conscious effort to regain their long-lost racial kinsmen. It stands to reason that among the Swab minority the pro-Nazi policy of the government was more popular than among the population as a whole. At this time, some, but by no means the majority, joined the *Volksbund*, implying a newfound commitment to their German background. According to the 1941 census, out of the 477,057 people whose mother tongue was German, 300,419 considered their nationality German, and approximately 150,000 joined the *Volksbund*; a large number of the latter served in the SS. On the other hand, a significant number of Swabs formed a Hungarian patriotic organization, "Loyalty to the Fatherland," thereby indicating their desire to keep aloof from what the Nazis stood for.[27]

A vast movement of human beings, a movement both voluntary and compulsory, began during the war and continued afterward, redrawing the ethnographic map of Central and Eastern Europe. Hitler's Germany wanted to reunite Germans and resettle them on lands that were to be integral parts of the Greater Reich. At the end of the war, many ethnic Germans, fearing retaliation, followed the retreating German armies back to Germany or Austria. What happened to the Swabs in Hungary was a small part of the general movement of people that took place at the time. From Czechoslovakia and Poland, which had acquired large German provinces, approximately 8 million Germans were expelled. The involuntary moving of large populations easily fitted into the Soviet concept of human engineering. The Anglo-Saxon powers on occasion evinced doubts about the morality of collective punishment but left matters to the Czech and Polish governments and in the Hungarian case to the ACC, in effect, to the Soviet Union.

The mistreatment of Germans began even before Soviet troops entered Hungarian territory. From Romania and Yugoslavia, Soviet troops gathered ethnic Germans and deported them to the Soviet Union for labor. The same policy was immediately introduced in Hungary.[28] Even before a provisional Hungarian government was formed, in the first half of January 1945 approximately 35,000 Germans, regardless of their past politics, were deported to the Soviet Union.

The issue of the expulsion of Germans came to be connected with the problem of settling Hungarians who had to leave Slovakia, Romania, and

27 S. Balogh, 1988, p. 85.
28 Lórant Tilkovszky, *Nemzetiségi politika Magyarországon a 20: században*, Debrecen: Csokonai, 1998, pp. 124–125.

Yugoslavia. The question of what to do with the Swabs did not create great disagreement among the parties. The matter was discussed in an interparty meeting in May 1945, and all agreed that those who had compromised themselves by fighting in the German army or exhibiting pro-Nazi sympathies ought to be expelled.[29] Accordingly, the government declared the *Volksbund* to be a criminal organization. However, different political parties supported the policy of expulsion with different degrees of enthusiasm.[30]

It was the NPP that wanted to define the group of expellees as broadly as possible. A vision of Hungarian nationalism inspired the NPP leaders, a vision that excluded Jews and Germans from their definition of the nation. Furthermore, the party of poor peasants hoped to take possession of the lands of the Swabs and distribute them among the Hungarian peasantry. Ironically, perhaps, it turned out that among the Swabs it was the poorest segment that had come to be influenced by Nazi ideology. Consequently, expelling only those who had joined the *Volksbund* or who had fought on the German side, would not have satisfied the peasants' craving for the property of others. Even before the war, intellectuals who would later form the NPP expressed nationalist views that had xenophobic overtones. In 1945, unattractive anti-Swab sentiments were voiced not only by Péter Veres but also by the liberal democrat Imre Kovács. He wrote in the party's newspaper, *Szabad Szó*: "The Swabs, who came to this country with one bundle on their back, should leave the same way. They cut themselves off from the fatherland as they demonstrated with their actions that they sympathized with Hitler's Germany. Let them now share the fate of Germany."[31]

The Communists and the leaders of the FKGP did not use the same unpleasant language, but they also enthusiastically participated in formulating the policy of expulsions. The Communists, for obvious political reasons, would have liked to make an exception for the German miners. The SDP was least enthusiastic concerning expulsions. It had few adherents in the countryside and therefore was not concerned about getting lands to its followers but did not want to send away workers with German backgrounds. As a consequence, the Socialists in the long run had the least to be embarrassed about for supporting a policy of collective punishment. The protestation of

29 Tilkovszky rightly argues that all political parties found it useful to make scapegoats out of the Germans, pretending that they alone were responsible for the murder of the Jews, rather than the Hungarians themselves. Lórant Tilkovszky, *Német nemzetiség – Magyar hazafiság*, Pécs: JPTE TK, 1997, p. 167.

30 *Pártközi értekezletek*, Budapest: Napvilág, 2003, pp. 46–69.

31 Ibid., p. 81.

churches and a group of liberal intellectuals against the notion of collective punishment had little consequence.[32]

The actual process of selecting those who had to leave was bound to be haphazard. The provisional government on July 1, 1945, issued a regulation that governed the process of examining people's past behavior. In districts where the Swabs lived, committees of three were set up. These included a chairman, named by the ministry of the interior; a representative of the local national committee; and one from the "democratic German community."[33]

In November and December, the ACC discussed the issue of resettling the Swabs in Germany. The British and American representatives accepted without objection the resettlement of the expellees in their respective zones of Germany.[34] The expulsions commenced only in January 1946. In the course of that year, 135,655 Swabs were resettled in the American zone.[35] As Soviet-Western relations declined, so too did the appetite of the Anglo-Saxon powers for accepting refugees. In 1947, another approximately 50,000 Swabs were expelled, this time to the Soviet zone, the future German Democratic Republic (DDR). Ironically, the expulsion of the mostly industrious Germans in the long run harmed Hungarian interests.

32 Tilkovszky, 1998, pp. 134–141.
33 Ibid., p. 86.
34 Documents of the meetings of the ACC for Hungary, pp. 101–107.
35 S. Balogh, 1988, p. 101.

11

The Case of the "Hungarian Community"

It is obvious that the establishment of a pluralist, democratic system in Hungary failed not as a consequence of the correlation of domestic forces but because of the presence of the Soviet army. As the relations between the Soviet Union and the West became ever more hostile, the fate of the Eastern European countries liberated by the Red Army was sealed. Within limits, however, there were differences. In Romania, Bulgaria, and Poland, the chances for pluralism from the outset were close to nil. In Czechoslovakia, the decision was made only in February 1948, at which time the Communists carried out a dramatic coup. In Hungary, the growth of Communist power was gradual and incremental.[1] However, if we had to choose a time when the democratic system suffered its most significant blow, that would be the early spring of 1947.

It was a combination of considerations that made the Soviets and their Hungarian subordinates act. In the spring of 1947, it became clear to the Soviet leadership that their hopes for Italian and French Communist successes would not be realized. The Truman Doctrine and the Marshall Plan signaled that the Americans were determined not to allow the further increase of Soviet influence around the world. East-West relations quickly deteriorated, and consequently Moscow was less concerned about Western responses to its abuse of power within its own sphere. Aside from this deterioration, there was a concrete issue that encouraged the Communists to take more radical steps. In Paris, the peace treaty with Hungary was about to be signed. The treaty would, by definition, have ended the role of the ACC

1 Geir Lundestad, in his book *The American Non-policy Towards Eastern Europe, 1943–1947*, New York: Humanities Press, 1975, proposed that Soviet policy makers thought in terms of four geographical spheres of increasing importance: outer sphere, middle sphere, inner sphere, and absolute sphere. Austria, Finland, Czechoslovakia, and Hungary fell into the middle sphere, but Poland, Romania, and Bulgaria fell into the inner sphere (pp. 435–465).

in Hungary and necessitated the withdrawal of Soviet armed forces. Not only the Hungarian political parties but also the Western allies pursued a policy based on the expectation that political circumstances would profoundly change after the withdrawal of Soviet forces. The FKGP accepted defeats because its leaders believed that they just had to survive until the Russians left. Only such an expectation can explain the willingness of the moderate leaders to give concession after concession. The Communists also well understood that they had to act while there was still a Soviet military presence in Hungary.

The main reason that the decisive Communist attack on the FKGP took place in the beginning of 1947 was that the anti-Communists provided them with a golden opportunity. This opportunity was the so-called conspiracy against the republic. One hesitates whether to put the word "conspiracy" into quotation marks. On the one hand, there was a germ of truth in the accusations, in as much as a secret society (or societies) did exist, but, on the other, the gap between the truth and the accusations was so wide that the affair could fairly be characterized as the first in a series of show trials in Hungarian Communist history. The affair in itself would hardly deserve a detailed description, because the conspirators at no point presented the slightest danger to the existing political system; however, the consequences of the discovery of the conspiracy were far reaching. Some aspects of this curious story remain mysterious, but the basic outlines are clear.

The origin of the secret society went back to the 1920s. A group of gentry intellectuals, many of them coming from Transylvania, a province that Hungary had just lost to Romania, established a society, the Hungarian Community or the Hungarian Brotherly Community (Magyar Közösség or Magyar Testvéri Közösseg). The society borrowed a great deal from Freemasonry: members swore an oath, and the organization was strictly hierarchical with a "chief council," consisting of ten men, who were not elected but coopted. It had "families" and "tents," and its members had to be of "good moral standing." People who were considered to be valuable prospective members were invited to join; the society was largely made up of judges, doctors, bureaucrats, some army officers, and professors. Only people with an independent income could join, and they had to promise to serve the Hungarian cause by offering to contribute 2 percent of their income. The group was self-consciously elitist; its members thought of themselves as the cream of Hungarian society. Women and Jews were explicitly excluded. Indeed, in order to join the society, the prospective member had to demonstrate that not only his father but also his grandfather "had a Hungarian name."[2] In modern terminology, therefore, the group could be described as racist. In reality, the mental world of the people who decided to join reflected the spirit of the time: they thought of Hungarians as a special people with a particular genius. They also thought of their countrymen as oppressed and humiliated by other nations and considered it their duty to remedy these historical wrongs. Later, the Communists used these facts in their propaganda. The group's membership was never larger than about 3000. There was something theatrical, almost childish, in this organization, something profoundly different from Communist underground organizations and work. It is hard to imagine that this group at any time presented a genuine danger to any political system.

The purpose of the society was to place its members in the administration, create a genuine "Hungarian" political elite, and thereby advance a nationalist, irredentist cause. As regards the territories lost at the end of World War I, the goals of the society entirely coincided with the aim of the Horthy government, which was altogether preoccupied with this issue to the exclusion of everything else. In addition, the society aimed to bring to power "real Hungarians," as opposed to Jews and Germans in particular. One of the main concerns of the society was that "foreigners," namely Hungarian-speaking Germans, played too great a role in the leadership of the nation. In the minds of these Hungarian nationalists, the German mentality and German customs were alien to the Hungarian people whose defense and advance was the main purpose of the society. Arguably, the society was more anti-Swab than anti-Jewish: indeed, people of German background had played a major role in Hungarian political life, and they also dominated the highest ranks of the military. Members of the Hungarian Community, mostly from gentry background, did not want to compete with Jewish interests in finances and trade, but they did feel that people of German background occupied positions that should go to "genuine Hungarians," namely themselves. Of course, after the discovery of the conspiracy, it would not have served the interests of Communist propaganda to mention the anti-German aspect of the Hungarian Community.

It was Hungarian nationalism that brought the group together, but nationalists in the 1930s faced a dilemma. On the one hand, they could expect to remedy the undoubted wrongs of the Trianon treaty and regain territories only with German help, and therefore German orientation in foreign policy was unavoidable. On the other, following too closely the

2 István Csicsery-Rónay and Géza Cserenyey, *Koncepcios per a Független Kisgazda Párt szétzúzására, 1947*, Budapest: 1956–os Intézet, 1998, pp. 34–35. Also, Szent-Miklosy, pp. 13–25.

German example seemed anti-Hungarian to many. Also, the membership of the group came largely from the gentry and people from this background found Nazi politics reprehensible. Most members of the society considered the Nazis lower class and their demagogy distasteful, and only a small minority supported an explicitly pro-German orientation in foreign policy. After the German occupation of the country on March 19, 1944, the organization went into hibernation.[3] Several of the major figures of the later conspiracy, however, such as Lajos Dálnoki Veress and István Szent-Miklosy, suffered punishment in Nazi prisons for their anti-German activities. All of them supported Horthy's unsuccessful efforts to arrange an armistice with the Allies on October 15, 1944.

After the end of the war, the organization came to life once again. In 1946, it had about eight hundred members. It was not clear what kind of role it should play under the very different circumstances or what sort of organizational form it should assume. Some believed that the organization ought to reform itself into an open society, whereas others wanted to continue the old format; still others wanted to dissolve the organization altogether. In reality, the "organization" in the postwar era was nothing more than a collection of groups, only loosely connected to one another. These people were anti-Communist individuals who got together for conversations and planned for the future, a time when the Soviet troops would be safely out of the country. The groups barely knew of each other's existence. They discussed how they could form a government after the removal of Soviet troops without the participation of the Communists. They hoped to establish friendly relations with the right wing of the Socialist Party and NPP. (Indeed, one of the accused at a later trial, Aladár Weisshaus, was a Communist who had been excluded from the party "for sectarian activities.") They spent their time discussing the composition of a future government even to the extent of thinking up ambassadors to the major countries. In March 1946, some of the members established a "council of seven," and later, independently, army officers created a "council of five."[4] The most important of these circles was centered around Domokos Szent-Iványi, who had been a member of the delegation sent to Moscow in October 1944 to negotiate an armistice and now was an adviser to FKGP leaders on matters of foreign policy. As far as political ideas and strategy for the struggle were concerned, beyond a general desire to regain Hungarian sovereignty and independence, members of the group differed from one another; some were more liberal and others more conservative.

3 Csicsery-Rónay and Cserenyey use this phrase, p. 35.

4 "Council of seven" and "council of five" were titles thought up by the prosecutors at the trials rather than used by the "conspirators." Vida, 1976, p. 246.

That the members of the organization were anti-Communist and anti-Soviet can be taken for granted. At a time, however, when an imperfect, pluralist system still existed, and when anti-Communist (though not anti-Soviet) opinions could still be expressed, the Hungarian Community could hardly be described as extreme, much less as threatening the existing political order. It is true, however, that some members of the organization had ties to major figures in the Smallholder Party and urged them to take a less pusillanimous position in the political struggle.

The organization recruited a few military members and chose Lajos Dálnoki Veress as commander of an army yet to be formed. Most of the members, including the central figure of Szent-Iványi, did not know about the existence of this military cell made up of a few senior ex-army officers. Dálnoki Veress issued "order no. 1" on October 1946: this would be a major piece of evidence against the conspirators. The order spoke of an underground supreme command and of "restoring sovereignty and legal continuity," words which could be interpreted as expressing the goal of reestablishing the Horthy regime. Prosecutors at the trials argued that the conspirators had committed treason because they were conspiring against a democratically elected government. The order in fact demonstrated the political naïveté of the participants in this ill-considered action. They could not, and they did not, seriously consider expelling the Red Army from Hungary. Nor were they against the legitimately elected government that had a Smallholder majority. They, just like their Smallholder comrades, were waiting anxiously for the peace conference and the removal of Soviet troops. Instead of composing compromising orders, real conspirators would have gathered resources, compiled weapons, established contacts with friendly foreign powers, and recruited members.

In the history of this affair, it is only the role of the rather mysterious figure of László Pünkösti that remains unexplained and inexplicable.[5] Pünkösti was a war criminal, responsible for the deaths of people in workers' battalions, who in January 1945 escaped with the retreating Germans. Why he decided to return a year later and pretend that he was carrying out espionage activities on behalf of the British remains a mystery.[6] It appears that the Communist political police followed Pünkösti from the moment he crossed the border. Pünkösti's behavior gives one reason to think that he was an agent provocateur, but, if so, then it is hard to understand why he was one of only two people who were executed at the conclusion

5 On Pünkösti see Zsuzsanna Bencsik, "Egy koncepcios per elökészitése," *Budapesti Negyed* 2 (1994): 191–207.

6 Bencsik argues convincingly that Pünkösti could not have been a British agent.

of the affair. Maybe the political police captured him on his return and promised him his life in exchange for playing the role of provocateur, then reneged on their promise to cover their tracks. Of course, it is possible that the explanation is simple: perhaps Pünkösti merely suffered from megalomania and believed or pretended he was a more important person than in fact he was. In any case, Pünkösti led the authorities to the conspirators.

Given the characters of the conspirators, their actions would have been uncovered in any case. Nevertheless, this "British spy" performed a useful service to the Communist police. Pünkösti met István Szent-Miklosy, an ex-staff officer who had been involved in the military side of the organization and who was already under police observation, and János Héder, another conspirator.[7] Pünkösti asked Szent-Miklosy to introduce him to the prime minister, Ferenc Nagy, and to Dálnoky Veress. The very fact that a "British spy" asked for a meeting with the premier should have been a warning to Szent-Miklosy that he was dealing with an unreliable person. The meetings in fact did not take place. Dálnoki Veress refused to meet with him, and Szent-Miklosy did not attempt to contact the premier. Dálnoky Veress in fact now realized that the issuing of "order no. 1" was a mistake and attempted to withdraw it, but it was too late.

Szent-Miklosy was arrested on December 16 and within the next few days 260 people suffered the same fate.[8] The first legal justification for the arrests was that Hungary had not yet regained its sovereignty and without the permission of the ACC no organization could operate. Every secret organization ipso facto was against the law. The military political police (Katpol) carried out the arrests. This organization had been set up originally to examine cases and punish officers who had sided with the Nazis. There was a need for such an agency because at the end of the war the Allies were returning captured officers and soldiers. In 1947, it must have been embarrassing for the Communists in the political police to arrest these people and put them in the same cells in which they had kept Nazi collaborators, when only a few years before they had been comrades in the fight against the Nazis.[9]

7 Katpol (military-political police) rented an apartment next to Szent-Miklosy's and placed a microphone in the wall. Kornis, p. 138.

8 Szent-Miklosy, p. 136, and Palasik, 2000, p. 199.

9 When the AVH (political police) evaluated the affair in an internal memorandum twenty-three years later, matters looked different. In 1970, the fact that the "conspirators" advocated a policy of basing Hungarian policy on Anglo-American help made them most dangerous. "Jelentés a Magyar Közösség ügy értékeléséről," document, reprinted in György Gyarmati (ed.), *Államvédelem a Rákosi korszakban,* Budapest: Történeti hivatal, 2000, pp. 252–284.

Had the discovery of the conspiracy taken place a year earlier, it still would have been a great propaganda coup for the Communists. After all, the accused included a number of prominent non-Communist politicians. Kálmán Saláta, a close friend of Prime Minister Ferenc Nagy, was the only one of the accused to escape arrest by going into hiding and finally leaving the country. Endre Mistéth, an FKGP minister, and other important Smallholder politicians were also accused. But other far-right-wing individuals were members of Közösség, it turned out, such as György Donáth, a leader of the semi-fascist Party of Hungarian Life. (Donáth insisted that the Provisional Assembly had no authority to name a government, because legitimacy had been interrupted on March 19, 1944, when the Germans invaded.) The most important figure caught in this net was Dálnoki Veress, who at one point had been named by Horthy as "*homo regius,*" indicating that in the absence of Governor Horthy, he could act in his place. Consequently, it was easy to argue, albeit falsely, that the conspirators, including FKGP members of the parliament, aimed at recreating the Horthy regime. Communist propagandists could point to the danger of right-wing restoration and depict their struggle convincingly as a fight against "reactionaries."

By 1947, the Communists were no longer content to embarrass the FKGP. From the very first moments of the investigation into the Közösség, the Communist political police and Communist Party leaders had a more ambitious goal than arresting and punishing the conspirators.[10] They were now bent upon destroying the Smallholder Party by implicating not only the right-wing leadership but also the centrist leaders. It was not enough any longer to change the political composition of the FKGP by persuading its leadership to exclude the right wing.

The Communist-dominated military police tortured the accused, using methods that had been developed by their Soviet comrades. Most of the evidence presented at the trials was based on these confessions. Although the most serious accusation against the arrested was that they had planned a military counterrevolution, no storehouse of weapons was ever found. Rákosi, in his conversation with Molotov, expressed his dismay that there was no such hard evidence against the accused.[11] One of the ironies of the situation was that the head of the military-political police, György Pálffy, had

10 Rákosi wrote in his memoirs that he decided to direct the political attacks against the FKGP, rather than the Freedom Party. [The latter was a more right-wing party formed by people excluded from the FKGP and not part of the coalition.] M. Rákosi, *Visszaemlékezések, 1940–1956,* vol. 1, pp. 344–356.

11 *Moszkvának jelentjük,* p. 203. This conversation took place on April 29, 1947.

been a staff officer of Horthy's army and a secret Communist; he had been removed from the army because he had a Jewish wife. He was a colleague and acquaintance of many of the accused.[12] The goal of the torturers was to elicit compromising information concerning FGKP leaders, in particular against Béla Kovács, who, unlike Nagy and Tildy, stood for a political strategy of resisting Communist encroachments. The interrogators offered freedom to some of the accused if they were willing to testify against Kovács. They also wanted to demonstrate that the conspirators were true "reactionaries," intent on returning to the social and political order of the Horthy regime. In addition, they intended to show that the conspirators and therefore the FKGP were in contact with foreign intelligence.[13]

The available documents do not allow us to show conclusively to what degree the decision to attack the FKGP aggressively and undermine the coalition government depended on guidance from Moscow versus initiatives by Rákosi and his closest comrades. We know that the Communists were concerned about the consequences of the Paris Peace Treaty, which was signed on February 10. They well understood that in the case of Soviet withdrawal they would have no political future in Hungary, and, rightly or wrongly, they even feared for their physical safety. In Moscow Rákosi discussed with V. M. Molotov the consequences of the peace treaty. He expressed himself picturesquely, confessing his fear that after the removal of Soviet troops "our democracy will hang in the air."[14] The Soviet foreign minister assured him that for the near future the situation would not change.[15]

Clearly there was the closest possible cooperation between the Soviet occupation forces in Hungary and the Communist leadership. From Soviet behavior one must conclude that at this time Moscow's policy toward Eastern Europe, and in particular toward Hungary, changed. The decision must have been made in Moscow that the period of genuine pluralism and coalition government in Hungary had passed.

12 Pálffy rose to the rank of deputy minister of war; however, in 1949 he was executed in connection with the Rajk affair.

13 Kiszely, pp. 54–59.

14 *Moszkvának jelentjük,* p. 199.

15 Ibid., p. 196. In the same conversation the following exchange occurred. Rákosi: "We would like to know when the treaty will be ratified. This is very important for us. We must know how long the Soviet troops will remain in Hungary." Molotov: "The situation that just came into being is favorable for us. The Austrian treaty will not be signed this year, and this will happen in the best case only in the beginning of next year, therefore as long as our troops remain in Austria, they will also remain in Hungary and Romania. Even after the ratification of the Hungarian treaty a part of the Soviet troops will remain in Hungary." Of course, the Austrian treaty was signed only in 1955. After that date, Soviet troops remained in Hungary under the terms of the "Warsaw Pact."

From the very beginning, Soviet officers were involved in interrogation and torture.[16] The degree of Soviet participation in this affair surpassed previous Russian interference in Hungarian affairs. V. P. Sviridov, the head of the ACC, for example, forbade the minister of war, Albert Bartha, to meet with the accused.[17] Pálffy, who was after all at least in theory subordinate to Bartha, took his instructions from the Russians and refused to allow the minister to meet with the arrested officers. This was the first time in post-war history that the accused were completely cut off from representatives of the non-Communist parties.

On January 5, 1947, the Communist daily, *Szabad Nép,* revealed the fact that important figures had been arrested for their involvement in a conspiracy. The Communist press, supported by the Socialist newspapers, started a vicious propaganda campaign against the FKGP. It associated the party with the conspirators and insisted that the conspiracy demonstrated that the party stood for the re-creation of the old order. This publicity campaign was very effective, at least in Budapest, in putting the FKGP on the defensive.

In 1947 and 1948, six trials took place in connection with the "Hungarian Community." In the course of these, 222 accused appeared in front of the judges.[18] Up to this time, the people's courts had judged war criminals, but on this occasion many of the accused were the same people who had also suffered in Nazi prisons. Ultimately, Donáth and Pünkösti were sentenced to death. Dálnoky Veress was also sentenced to death, but his sentence was commuted to fifteen years of imprisonment. The other sentences were not particularly harsh: only thirteen people were sentenced to more than five years, and they were all freed by the revolution of 1956, at which time they left the country.

THE ARREST OF KOVÁCS AND THE RESIGNATION OF NAGY

In the first act of this drama, the Communist police, first Katpol and then AVO, arrested a number of people who had belonged to secret societies as conspirators against the existing democratic order. Although some evidence was produced under torture, the accused were tried in open court where it was possible to answer accusations and on occasion to withdraw previous

16 In his memoirs, Rákosi reports that he had requested from Stalin himself that Soviet NKVD agents be sent to Hungary, because the Hungarian Communists did not possess sufficient "technical expertise." M. Rákosi, *Visszaemlékezések, 1940–1956,* vol. 1, p. 361.

17 F. Nagy, vol. 2, p. 13.

18 Csicsery-Rónay and Cserenyey, pp. 46–47.

confessions. In the second act, the Communists turned their attention to the major figures of the FKGP, making the same accusations against them, but this time without a shred of substantial evidence. When the ministry of the interior made the first public, official announcement of a conspiracy on January 12, 1947, FKGP leaders did not realize that the Communists had decided on a frontal attack on the core of their party.[19] Prime Minister Nagy and Foreign Minister Gyöngyösi assured the American representative, Schoenfeld, that this crisis was merely a continuation of the old struggle with the Communists and there was no new threat.[20] Ferenc Nagy and President Tildy did everything within their power to distance the party from the alleged conspirators. Those implicated in the affair were asked to resign their posts and to leave the party. Immediately after the discovery of the conspiracy, the parliamentary faction of the FKGP had passed a resolution condemning all those involved in illegal activities. The FKGP supported parliamentary action to revoke the immunity of members against whom the military political police produced plausible proofs (mostly confessions of other accused achieved by torture).The deputies and the FKGP newspaper, *Kis Ujság*, called for severe punishment of the conspirators.

The Communists and the left-wing socialists extended the accusations to Béla Kovács, the chairman of the FKGP, even though there was no evidence whatsoever that he had knowledge of the plans of the conspirators. At first, they charged that as chairman of the party he had the responsibility to know of the conspirators' plans. At this point the Communists might have been satisfied with Kovács's resignation or an enforced "vacation." In truth, Kovács could not fairly be called a reactionary at all. At the time of the first arrests, in December, 1946, for example, he wrote:

> As much as we do not want a Marxist, socialist order in reconstructed Hungary, just as strictly we must distance ourselves from the reactionaries. Whoever is an opponent of the land reform or the other achievements of our democratic order, whoever would like to exchange the country of free and independent Hungarians for a country of aristocrats, big capitalists, gendarmes, is an enemy of the FKGP.[21]

The Communists, however, had long wanted to remove him from political life because of his stubborn opposition to their political tactics. By February, it was clear that the country faced its largest political crisis since the end of the war. Ference Nagy balked at revoking the parliamentary immunity of

19 F. Nagy, vol. 2, p. 11.
20 FRUS, 1947, vol. 4, p. 262.
21 Vida, 1976, p. 245.

27. Protest against the conspirators of the "Hungarian Community," January 18, 1947. (Source: Hungarian National Museum.)

Béla Kovács. Now Nagy understood that the Communists were intent upon destroying his party. On the basis of coerced and false confessions against Kovács, on February 6 the Communists demanded that his immunity be lifted, but the Smallholder majority refused. Almost two-thirds of the parliament voted for the creation of a parliamentary committee to examine all the materials relevant to the conspiracy before lifting Kovács' immunity. This solution, of course, was unacceptable to the Communists: an open examination of the materials would have revealed the flimsiness of the accusations. The affair had to remain entirely within the Communist-dominated military and political police for the charges against the FKGP to carry any weight.[22] The Communist, Socialist, and NPP delegates refused to participate in the proposed committee, and the Communists threatened to leave the coalition if the FKGP went ahead and formed it anyway.[23]

22 F. Nagy, vol. 2, pp. 78–79; M. Rákosi, *Visszaemlékezések, 1940–1956*, vol. 1, 354.

23 Rákosi's cynicism is evident from what he writes in his memoirs decades later after the affair. He mentions that almost two-thirds of the deputies in the parliament voted for creating the committee. "'It is not only a majority, it is a genuine forest' said Révai. 'We will thin it' I answered." Of course, Rákosi never pretended to be a liberal or committed to observing parliamentary niceties (p. 354).

As on previous occasions, the Communists were able to mobilize workers' demonstrations while Communist agitators in Budapest and in the rest of the country carried out a furious propaganda campaign against the conspirators and the FKGP.[24] Communist success was based primarily on their ability to get the crucial support of the occupation forces and secondarily on their ability to mobilize demonstrators and influence the parliament. Prime Minister Nagy was always concerned that in case of a political impasse the left-wing parties would withdraw from the coalition; the Communists, with Soviet help, would organize mass disorder; and the governing of the country would become impossible.[25]

In the course of the next two weeks, the political struggle concerned the fate of Kovács. The Communists and their allies insisted that his immunity had to be lifted. Finally, Kovács was willing to resign and to appear in front of the investigators without giving up his immunity. Under these terms, the political police interrogated him on February 25, and he continued to protest his innocence. However, on that very evening the Soviet authorities arrested him.[26] The Russians justified the arrest by accusing him of participation in the organization of anti-Soviet, armed, terrorist groups that aimed at carrying out spying activities against the occupying power.[27] How far-fetched these accusations were and how little the Soviet authorities cared about their plausibility is shown by the fact that neither before nor later was any other individual charged with the organization of armed, terrorist groups. Kovács remained in Soviet captivity until 1956.

The arrest of Kovács was a decisive step. He was a little stone, the removal of which started an avalanche. After all, if he was guilty then so were the other leaders of his party. The Communists demonstrated that by having Soviet power behind them, they could not be resisted. As Rákosi put it in his memoirs, "beat the iron while it is hot," meaning that the time had come for the destruction of the FKGP. The political trials that took place in the following months were intended to compromise the genuine leadership of the FKGP, first of all Ferenc Nagy and later President Tildy.

24 M. Rákosi, *Visszaemlékezések, 1940–1956*, vol. 1, p. 355.

25 FRUS, 1947, vol. 4, p. 270.

26 The circumstances of the arrest are described in detail in Mária Palasik, *Kovács Béla, 1908–1959*, Budapest: Századvég, 2002, pp. 64–67.

27 Rákosi maintained in his memoirs that the Soviet authorities arrested Kovács against his wish and advice. He feared the increase of anti-Soviet sentiments among Hungarians. Maybe he was telling the truth but probably not. M. Rákosi, vol. 1, p. 361.

The party for all practical purposes ceased to be an independent organization. On March 1, a few days after the arrest of Kovács, Rákosi lectured the Smallholders:

> The FKGP must understand the lessons of the conspiracy, both in matters of politics and also in matters of organization. From this point of view the position announced in the press today, undoubtedly includes positive features, in matters of posing issues and also in the composition of the Political Committee. But there are also worrying signs. It does not appear from the pronouncement that the FKGP wants to make a decisive and serious change in its political line. . . . For example, Béla Kovács was not excluded from the party, but his party membership was lifted. István B. Rácz was not excluded, but allowed to resign. This is the old method that wants to avoid giving the impression that these are serious matters. It does not appear that this is the sign of a new beginning. It is necessary to raise the question of the reorganization of ministries. We have to discuss the removal of the unsatisfactory FKGP ministers. We are not satisfied with Béla Varga. [Varga was the speaker of the parliament and with Tildy, Nagy, and Kovács, the most influential FKGP politician.] His last official pronouncement does not correspond to the new spirit of the FKGP.

Rákosi went on criticizing the other major figures of the party in the same hectoring tone.[28] The Socialist and NPP representatives at this interparty meeting echoed Rákosi's criticisms.

The response of the FKGP representatives at the meeting was ineffective self-justification and a pathetic request that the party's self-respect should not be harmed. The political pressure and the overwhelming force on the other side were too great for the Smallholders to resist. The FKGP carried out the demanded personnel changes by excluding thirty-two deputies from the party and once again promising "to cooperate in the struggle against any manifestation of the spirit of counterrevolution."[29]

The FKGP position was further weakened not only by the exclusion of a number of deputies who formed yet another party but also by what was going on within the two other parties in the coalition. Within the NPP, the long struggle between the moderates and the crypto-Communists ended with the resignation and flight from the country of Imre Kovács, a popular leader who had opposed bringing his party closer to the Communists. For Imre Kovács, what happened to Béla Kovács was the final proof that the Communists with Soviet help were willing to use any method to achieve ultimate power. At the same time, the Communists were strengthening their position within the SDP. In December 1946, Károly Peyer, the leader of

28 *Pártközi értekezletek*, pp. 440–441.
29 Ibid., and F. Nagy, p. 454, inter-party meeting of March 4.

the party in the Horthy era; Ágoston Valentiny, minister of justice in a previous government; and some other anti-Communist leaders presented a memorandum to the leadership in which they accused it of pro-Bolshevik policies. In February 1947 at the SDP congress, the right wing was decisively defeated, and the leadership passed to those who were willing to follow the Communist lead.[30]

It is painful to contemplate the last days of the FKGP. For public consumption, the official spokesmen of the party were compelled to use the Communists' verbiage, pretending to accept the absurd contention that their party, which had the support of the majority of the people, the office of the presidency, and premiership, had in fact been engaged in a vast conspiracy to overthrow the democratic system. In actuality, the Communists had successfully covered up their own conspiracy against the legitimate order by accusing the victims. Tildy and Nagy had to accept the imprisonment and humiliation of their colleagues and friends of decades whom they knew without a doubt to be innocent. Nagy, in particular, must have suffered as a result of repeated defeats and the persecution of his friends. At one point, he offered to resign, but Tildy persuaded him to stay. Nagy, in his memoirs, convincingly argues that he and his fellow leaders did the best they could, and by their willingness to compromise kept alive a degree of democracy and pluralism longer than any alternative political line could have achieved.[31] At the time, it was not naïve to imagine that the occupying troops would leave the country when the peace treaty was signed and that a new politics could then begin.

The democrats put their faith in Western help up to the last minute. In retrospect, it is evident that there was nothing whatsoever the Americans and the British could do to save Hungarian democracy and that sending notes to Moscow had little consequence. The Americans in their internal correspondence quite cruelly and unfairly blamed the Smallholder politicians for their lack of courage and will.[32] At the same time, it is understandable

30 On the struggle within the NPP, see Imre Kovács, *Magyarország megszállása*, already cited, and for further discussion of the SDP, see Róbert Gábor, Az igazi szociáldemokrácia . . . , also previously cited.

31 F. Nagy, vol. 2, pp. 90–92. Nagy here is defending himself against the accusation that he had behaved in a cowardly fashion. He rightly points out that the fate of the neighboring countries had been decided even earlier than that of Hungary.

32 For example, Ambassador Schoenfeld wrote to the secretary of state on January 27: "It has been clear for a long time that if non-Marxists among Hungarian leaders do not find within themselves resources of character and political will to enable them to oppose successfully encroachment of Communist monopoly it is also because they are obsessed by their identification of that minority [sic] with Soviet power which they consider irresistible." Schoenfeld apparently saw the non-Marxists as mesmerized by the specter of Soviet power. FRUS, 1947, vol. 4, p. 264.

28. Budapest youth protest against "antirepublican conspiracy," March 1, 1947. (Source: Hungarian National Museum.)

that Nagy and his comrades clung to hope until the end. The Americans urged Nagy to remain firm, but that was no help when he was facing those extraordinary pressures. The British and American representatives in the ACC did bring up the arrest of Béla Kovács at the March 4 meeting. General Sviridov rather brazenly answered: "The reasons for his arrest by the Soviet High Command have been published in the press. Are there any further remarks or comments on this subject?"[33] The entire discussion of this matter took less than a minute.

Following this exchange, on March 5 the American government sent a note to General Sviridov as de facto chairman of the ACC, demanding that the ACC together with representatives of the Hungarian government should examine all matters connected with the supposed conspiracy and the arrest of Kovács.[34] Sviridov, not surprisingly, rejected the idea and suggested that the American proposal was "a crude intervention in the internal affairs of Hungary." On Rákosi's insistence, the press waited until the Soviet response to the American note was prepared before it published the American note,

33 *Documents of the Meetings of the Allied Control Commission for Hungary*, p. 310.

34 The note and the Soviet response are printed in Csicery-Rónay and Cserenyey, pp. 369–371, and FRUS, 1947, vol. 4, pp. 273–278.

and even then while the entire Soviet note was printed, only sections of the American note appeared.[35] However, because the Voice of America and the BBC broadcasted the text, a large segment of the population knew about it.

The Western powers were unable to help the Hungarian democrats, but presumably the events in Hungary in the course of the first months of 1947 contributed to a hardening of the American position vis-à-vis the Soviet Union. On March 12, the Americans announced the so-called Truman Doctrine, namely that the United States would resist further Soviet encroachments in areas that had not already been under Soviet control. One might date the real beginning of the cold war from this moment.

There were cabinet changes in the course of which the FKGP replaced three ministers, including Bartha, the minister of war, with men more acceptable to the left-wing bloc, and once again it seemed that the crisis was surmounted. Nagy and his fellow leaders were above all concerned about Soviet intervention, but they were also very much afraid of civil war, instigated by the Communists. They were frightened by the Communists' ability to bring people to the streets. Of course, it was much easier for the Communists to mobilize workers, which they had done repeatedly, than win over peasants. The workers, under the influence of the inflammatory Communist press, once again demonstrated against the "conspirators." However, the Communists also made sustained efforts to undermine peasant support for the FKGP. Lecturing village agitators on February 4, 1947, Révai said[36]:

The time has come to deal a decisive blow to the right wing of the FKGP. This is not merely an issue for the police. We must take away their mass base in the village. We must support the left wing. The essence is that we must convince the peasants that the conspirators wanted to bring back large estates. Even the rich peasants can be our allies in this matter. The conspirators wanted to exclude the peasants from politics. The new tax system would have hurt the old and new proprietors. Let us play up to the peasants. They are the truest Hungarians. We must embrace the left wing of the FKGP. Horthyist officers were the conspirators. . . . Let us mention Béla Kovács, if they ask about whom we are talking about, but let us not mention other names, because the peasants like Ferenc Nagy and have confidence in him. We must give them questions, let the peasants mull them over. Kovács did not tell the truth to the peasants. Excluding a few leaders is not enough. We must carry on an open struggle. Let the FKGP be democratic peasant party. The FKGP has not only become a peasant party, but it has become a party of the Hungarian reactionaries.

35 *Pártközi értekezletek*, p. 478. Nagy writes in his memoirs that it was the office of Sviridov that instructed him not to have the American note published until the Soviet response was ready. Because according to the armistice agreement the ACC had the right of censorship, the demand of the chairman of the ACC could not be rejected, vol. 2, pp. 95–96.

36 PIL 274 21/21 February 4, 1947.

On the day of the formation of the new government, Révai once again lectured the agitators:

It is important for the propagandists to know what to say. You have to say that this crisis did not start now, but it has been a long process. . . . You must explain how Nagy could sink so low. He started out as a peasant politician, but he became impressed with himself and started to listen to the aristocrats. He surrounded himself with aristocratic reactionaries. We have to emphasize that we maintain the coalition. Béla Kovacs and Ferenc Nagy are not the FKGP. We must not talk about cleaning out the FKGP because then we reveal too much. . . . Among peasant women it is effective when we tell them that in Nagy's circles gentry women with red painted fingernails played significant roles. We have to stress that contrary to foreign press reports, there is no crisis. The government stays in its place. Dinnyés is going to be a good Premier. Gyöngyösi cannot stay as foreign minister. He wanted to distance us from the Soviet Union. It led to the Soviet Union's losing confidence in Hungarian democracy."[37]

Communist agitators in the villages were also encouraged to say that the Russians were retaliating for the work of the "reactionary" conspirators by not returning the prisoners of war.[38] Above all, the agitators had the task of persuading the peasants that the "reactionaries" wanted to take away their land and return it to the landlords. The party prepared resolutions condemning the conspirators, and the village meetings were asked to adopt them.

Reporting to the Soviet leadership in April 1947, Rákosi could proudly tell his comrades about the favorable consequences of the unmasking of the conspirators: the FKGP was falling apart. People did not want to be members of a party whose secretary had been arrested as a conspirator. Some ex-members of the party joined the right-wing Freedom Party (which Rákosi, grossly unfairly, described as fascist), and others joined the Communists. In his evaluation, the peasants were more willing to listen to Communist agitators than in the past. Rákosi made it clear that after the discrediting of Kovács, the next immediate task was the removal of Ferenc Nagy.[39]

The FKGP leaders hoped that with the interparty agreement signed on March 11 the most severe political crisis in postwar history had been surmounted.[40] In spite of the seeming quiet, however, the Communist struggle to remove Nagy continued. Ironically, what restrained Rákosi for the time being, as he explained to his superiors in Moscow, was that Nagy favored reducing the status of religious education in schools from compulsory to elective. Rákosi considered it essential that the Smallholders should bear

37 PIL 274 21/8 May 31, 1947.
38 PIL 274 21/7 summer 1947.
39 RTsKhIDNI fond 17, opis 128, delo 315, p. 5.
40 *Pártközi értekezletek*, pp. 485–501.

the onus for this change, which was very unpopular among the peasants and bitterly opposed by the Catholic Church.[41] He considered it difficult to demonstrate that the most popular Hungarian politician in reality was a "reactionary." However, the Russian comrades succeeded in forcing Kovács to give a compromising confession against Nagy that could be used at the appropriate moment. As far as the Communists were concerned, Nagy's fate was decided already in March.

The appropriate moment arrived in May, at a time when Nagy was vacationing in Switzerland. On May 28 in the absence of the premier, Rákosi, as deputy prime minister, called together the cabinet and notified the ministers that the Soviet authorities had delivered the text of Béla Kovács's interrogation. Kovács had confessed that Nagy also had known about the conspiracy.[42] Rákosi disingenuously remarked in his memoirs that this was the first instance of a prime minister engaged in a conspiracy against his own government.[43] The cabinet decided to ask Nagy to return and defend himself. For a short time, he hesitated whether to return and defend himself or to stay abroad. Dezső Sulyok in his memoirs blamed Nagy for not returning and accepting the role of the martyr. But István Vida, a Communist historian writing in the 1970s, more realistically argued that Nagy failed to return not because of cowardice, but because he recognized that it would serve no purpose.[44] The example of what happened to Kovács must have made it clear to him that there was no chance that he would be treated justly. For a couple of days, dramatic negotiations followed. Nagy would resign only after his five-year-old son had arrived safely from Budapest. On June 1, Nagy handed in his resignation in exchange for his son at the Swiss-Austrian border. This date can be regarded as the end of the era of imperfect pluralism in Hungary.

The next day, on June 2, Béla Varga, president of the assembly, against whom Béla Kovács had also allegedly made compromising confessions, left the country illegally. A number of FKGP politicians who feared arrest quickly made the same decision. For a short time, Tildy remained in his position, at the price of publicly denouncing Ferenc Nagy and Béla Varga. The government he appointed was in the form of a coalition. The FKGP

41 RTsKhIDNI fond 17, opis 128, delo 315, p. 8.

42 Vida, 1976, p. 292. Vida tells the story of Nagy's removal with remarkable objectivity considering that his book was published in 1976 in Hungary. Palasik's reconstruction of the event, however, is the most complete.

43 M. Rákosi, *Visszaemlékezések, 1940–1956*, vol. 1, p. 378.

44 Sulyok, p. 159. Sulyok was hostile to Nagy because Nagy was responsible for his expulsion from the FKGP in 1946.

29. Ferenc Nagy, 1903–1979.

continued to hold half of the ministries in the cabinet. In reality, however, the Communists had succeeded in removing everyone who had stood in the way of their complete dominance. The Smallholders wanted Imre Oltványi, an ex–minister of finances, to take Nagy's place, but the Russians and the Communists vetoed him. The new premier became Lajos Dinnyés, who, to be sure, had been an FKGP member of parliament since 1931 but, as Rákosi himself told Molotov, had absolutely no support within his own party.[45] He was regarded as a lightweight. In his short tenure as minister of war, he faithfully executed Communist directions, removing all army officers in whom the Communists had no confidence. He was forced on Tildy by the Soviet authorities and the Communists. Tildy accepted him because he still wanted to preserve the coalition. János Gyöngyösi, the long-serving foreign minister who had done everything within his power to maintain good relations with the Soviet authorities, also had to leave the cabinet. In the new environment, he was considered to be too independent. The wily FKGP politician and Catholic priest István Balogh was forced out of the party. He established a new party, thereby further weakening the Smallholders and dividing the anti-Communist opposition.

The personnel changes did not for a moment weaken Communist resolve to destroy the FKGP. On June 11, 1947, István Kovács lectured to a closed meeting of district party secretaries about current tasks. It is worth quoting a

45 *Moszkvának jelentjük*, pp. 199–200. Rákosi described him to Molotov as "somewhat bohemian," by which he presumably meant that Dinnyés imbibed alcohol somewhat more than he should have.

few sentences from his speech because they reveal the mentality and cynicism of the leadership in the political struggle. Among other things he said:

> We can receive information by infiltrating the opposition. . . . It was not an accident, comrades that our PB (Political Committee) knew exactly the plans of the FKGP, Hungarian reactionaries, in connection with the February 10th peace treaty. It was not an accident that we knew about the duplicitous leadership in the FKGP and what Ferenc Nagy was doing in Switzerland. . . . We must break up the FKGP. Let us call reactionaries only those for whom the people have little respect. Those who are still respected we should undermine. We recommend something – for example we should take horses away from the rich – the reactionaries will object and thereby they are uncovered.[46]

In retrospect, we may examine what the Nagy affair shows about the relationship of the Hungarian Communists with their Soviet superiors. At the time, Nagy thought that the initiative for his removal had come from the Russians. Indeed, undertaking an operation that would have international consequences could only be done with close cooperation of Soviet and Hungarian Communist authorities. The removal of the last legitimately elected premier took place at a time when the international climate had changed for the worse. Following the announcement of the Truman Doctrine, the French and Italian governments removed Communists from their coalitions. Everywhere in Eastern Europe the non-Communist parties were under siege. In Romania, Bulgaria, and in Poland in these months major non-Communist politicians were either arrested or forced into emigration. What happened in Hungary was part of the larger transformation of international relations, a step in the further intensification of the cold war. Nevertheless, it appears that Rákosi and his comrades were even more impatient than their Soviet superiors to change the postwar status quo.

Already on April 5, Rákosi wrote to the Soviet leadership: "It has become clear that Prime Minister Ferenc Nagy not only participated in the conspiracy, but in the recent past he has given advice to the conspirators."[47] At the end of April, the Hungarian Communist leader traveled to Moscow and on the 28 had extensive discussions with V. M. Molotov. At this time, he was already determined not only to get rid of Nagy but also President Tildy. He said:

> We want to unmask Ferenc Nagy. We have the confession of Béla Kovács compromising Nagy. But he is in Soviet hands. We would like to have him appear as a witness in front of the Hungarian people at least for a day, or at least two or three hours.

46 PIL 274 16/18 June 11, 1947.

47 *Moszkvának jelentjük*, p. 159.

Molotov expressed his concern that Kovács might say something embarrassing to the Soviet cause in the course of an open Hungarian trial. Then Rákosi asked if he could count on Soviet help in case of "mobilizing the people." Molotov's response was noncommittal, saying that it would depend on the circumstances.[48] Then, and later in his conversations with Soviet leaders, Rákosi always portrayed himself and his party as defenders of Soviet interests against the Americans and the British, and he formulated his attacks on the FKGP for Molotov to show it was in the interest of the Soviet Union. He stressed that the FKGP leaders were in constant contact with the representatives of the Anglo-Saxon powers.

Finally, the Soviet permission to act arrived. Rákosi described in his memoirs that in the middle of May Soviet Ambassador Pushkin asked him to go to Romania immediately for the discussion of an important matter. Rákosi met General Susaikov in Arad[49]:

> We immediately turned to the matter at hand. Susaikov handed me a hand written letter that was without signature saying that this is Stalin's personal message. The letter was hardly a page long. It said that according to Soviet information Ferenc Nagy is not resting in Switzerland, but is consulting with enemies about plans, which would make it possible to remove the communists from the government. We should use his absence and let us go on the attack, and if we miss this opportunity we would find ourselves in a difficult situation.[50]

We can safely assume that Soviet agents possessed no information concerning Nagy's contacts in Switzerland with "enemies," because there was no one to contact and no one could help. Nagy had no need to travel to Switzerland in order to consult with British and American diplomats. This was simply Stalin's way of giving the go-ahead, which was what Rákosi was waiting for. He was so excited that he refused to stay for a meal but returned to start the decisive attack as soon as possible.

From contemporary documents and from the memoir literature one may form a picture of the Soviet-Hungarian Communist relationship at this point. One wonders why it was necessary for Rákosi to travel to Arad. Would it not have been easier to deliver the short letter to him in Budapest? Stalin obviously was not thinking of the comfort of his inferiors. Also, what exactly did he mean about the Hungarian Communists finding themselves in a difficult situation if they did not act immediately? Was he ready to abandon

48 Ibid., pp.195–206.

49 General Ivan Zakharovich Susaikov had served in Hungary in 1945 as a contact person between the provisional government and the Soviet occupation forces. Later, Susaikov became deputy chairman of the Romanian ACC.

50 M. Rákosi, *Visszaemlékezések, 1940–1956*, vol. 1, p. 377.

them? Was he thinking of a major change in international relations? Why did he not even deign to sign his one-page but very important letter?

It is evident that Rákosi was more impatient to achieve complete power than Stalin was to complete making Hungary into a satellite. He could not act, however, without explicit Soviet permission. The Russians did not make his job easy. In spite of his repeated requests that Kovács be handed over to the Hungarian authorities at least temporarily, the Russians did not consent. Nor did they give any concessions at this point to help the Communists to build public support, such as supporting the Hungarian cause in the dispute with Czechoslovakia, letting prisoners of war return, or moderating Soviet demands in reparation payments.

12

Cinema

A useful perspective on the Communist struggle for power in Hungary is provided by an examination of the film industry in these years. The Communists, able propagandists as they were, wanted to use cinema in order to spread their message, and at the same time they wanted to gain sympathy for the Soviet Union. Winning over people to the Communist cause and popularizing the Soviet Union were two sides of the same coin. The exhibition of Russian films therefore was a matter of considerable political significance. In cinema life, just as in politics generally, pluralism gradually disappeared. The Communist film agency, Mafirt, acquired increasing dominance, and Western, in particular American, films were pushed out of the market. The Communist leaders, who had been educated in the Soviet Union, wanted to use methods that they had learned there. Their problem was that circumstances in Hungary were different from those existing in the mother country of Communism. In the Soviet Union, the Bolshevik Party had a complete monopoly over the means of persuasion, whereas in Hungary, the Communists still operated in a pluralist political environment, even though this pluralism was gradually diminishing and by 1948 had disappeared altogether. Pluralism meant that the Communists had to compete; they had to respond to views expressed by their opponents. The Hungarian Communist leaders recognized the obvious: the vast majority of their countrymen did not look on Soviet soldiers as liberators, and few wished to build a Communist society. Still, the Communists were convinced of the righteousness of their cause, whether the people agreed with them or not. A study of the history of the film industry also demonstrates the arrogance of the Soviet agents.

THE REVIVAL OF THE FILM INDUSTRY

No one would expect a mirror-like reflection of reality from movie screens; nevertheless, the study of a national cinema can be revealing. Autocratic and totalitarian governments almost always have regarded movies as excellent agents for spreading their ideological message, and, therefore, many devoted great attention to this industry. The methods with which governments have extended their influence over movie making and the themes which they wanted to convey or to censor can tell us much about the nature of a regime.

The Hungarian film world in the immediate post–Second World War era is particularly interesting. The organization of the industry, as compared to other Eastern European countries, was unusual inasmuch as political parties came to play important roles in making and distributing films. The Communist leaders, educated in the Soviet school of politics, took propaganda and therefore cinema far more seriously than did their opponents. Just as in the Soviet Union at that time, some of the most trivial issues concerning films were decided at the highest level of party leadership. An inexact translation of a subtitle in a Soviet film would be reported to József Révai, the person responsible for ideology within the Central Committee, and one of the four most powerful leaders of Hungary.[1]

Postwar cinema, of course, did not start with a tabula rasa. Before the Second World War, Hungary could boast a successful and, compared to the size of the country, disproportionately large film industry. Hungarian actors and actresses, such as Peter Lorrie, Béla Lugosi, Marika Rokk, and Francisca Gaal and directors, such as Alexander Korda and Michael Curtiz, acquired worldwide reputations. Béla Balázs was among the most influential theorists of the cinema during the first half century of its existence. As in other aspects of Hungarian intellectual and economic life, Jews played a decisively important role. This fact explains why many of the well-known figures, after beginning careers in their native country, made their most significant contributions abroad. After 1938, laws were introduced limiting the role of the Jews in the economic and cultural life of the nation, and these laws did exceptionally great damage to the film industry.

Conservative interwar governments took a great interest in the film industry. The success of Hungarian film was a matter of prestige for the bureaucrats, and at the same time they were convinced that it was their duty to prevent this popular art form from conveying subversive messages. Government censorship was often foolish. On one occasion, for example,

1 PIL 274 23/24 p. 23.

a scene had to be cut that showed horses kicking up dust on a road, because according to the censor that might have given the impression that Hungarian roads were dusty. Another scene, which showed a government minister running upstairs, was found unacceptable because it depicted a public official in an undignified manner. Although the vast majority of the films were made for simple entertainment, after the outbreak of the war studios also aimed at advancing patriotism.[2]

Given the small size of a prospective audience and the small number of screens (approximately five hundred), making Hungarian films was unlikely ever to become a money-making proposition.[3] Without government subsidies, the film industry would not have succeeded. However, as it was, in terms of output in the interwar years Hungary was ahead of the economically more advanced Czechoslovakia and Austria. Approximately eight to ten films premiered annually. The studios were well equipped, which allowed some less developed countries to take advantage of them. For example, the first two Bulgarian sound films were made in Hungary. These studios were good enough to be used by Western, including American, filmmakers.[4] American films were copied in Budapest for distribution in the countries of southeastern Europe, which the American industry paid for by providing raw material for Hungarian films.[5]

It is a testament of the desire of human beings to create at least the appearance of normality that for all practical purposes filmmaking never stopped, even during the last year of the war. As late as October 1944, a new Hungarian film premiered in the theaters. (In this respect, Hungary was no different from Nazi Germany, where filmmaking also continued right up to capitulation.) Some of the films for which the shooting had begun before the Soviet occupation were finished only afterward. In November 1944, at a time when the city was surrounded by the Soviet army, newsreels were still made in the Hunnia studios. Members of the Arrow Cross planned to move the entire factory to Germany, but they did not succeed: Soviet troops reached the studio on December 25.[6]

A little over a month later, the newly appointed Smallholders Party mayor of Budapest, János Csorba – even while the fighting was still going on for

2 On pre–Second World War cinema, see István Nemeskürty, *A képpé varászolt idő*, Budapest: Magvető, 1983.
3 Gábor Szilágyi, *Tüzkeresztség: A magyar játékfilm története 1945–1953*, Budapest, Magyar Filmintezet, 1992, p. 14.
4 Nemeskürty, p. 638.
5 PIL 274 23/24 p. 12, Mafirt report to the Central Committee of the Communist Party.
6 Tibor Sándor, *Örségváltás*, Budapest: Magyar Filmintezet, 1997, p. 224.

the city – concerned himself with the problems of the film industry. On January 30, he directed the union of artists to organize themselves in order to prepare to begin to work again.[7] Given the fact that even before 1945 the industry had come under the ministry of religion and public education and that the government had named the directors of studios, no one considered it unusual that the authorities took an interest in the revival of the industry. Csorba's directive, however, was only a first step. In the course of 1945, several attempts were made to create a body that would have the authority to make necessary decisions concerning allocation of resources, choice of scripts, and so forth. Finally, in October 1945, the government established a committee largely made up of representatives from political parties, ministries, and social organizations, such as trade unions. Of the twenty-four members, only four came from the filmmaking community. This organization, in effect, came to be a censorship body, for it had the obligation first of approving scripts and finally of approving the finished product before it could be exhibited.[8] At this time, at least, all filmmakers, including Communists, deplored the idea of preliminary censorship. Nonparty artists complained that preliminary censorship made it almost impossible to acquire the capital that was necessary for making movies.

In 1945, neither Hungarian nor Soviet politicians had a clear vision of the future of the nation in general and the organization of the film industry in particular. In Hungary, unlike other Soviet-occupied countries, such as Poland, Romania, and Bulgaria, the film industry was not immediately nationalized.[9] Instead, after liberation, the four major political parties in the governing coalition, the Smallholders' Party, the Communist Party, the SDP, and the NPP, agreed to take control of and distribute among themselves the majority of the movie theaters. Eventually, the parties established film companies. (The Communist film organization was Mafirt, the Socialist organization was Orient, the Peasant Party organization was called Sarlo [sickle], and the Smallholders' Party organization was called Haladás [Progress]).

These companies all made short films and newsreels, had rental agencies, and owned movie theaters. The cinema world was politicized: Communist-owned movie theaters, for example, would refuse to carry advertisements for Smallholder newspapers, and the major Communist paper, *Szabad Nép*, was admonished not to write negative reviews of Communist-financed short

7 Szilágyi, p. 15.

8 Ibid., p. 17.

9 On post–Second World War Eastern European cinema, see Mira Liehm and Antonín J. Liehm, *The Most Important Art: Eastern European Film after 1945*, Berkeley: University of California Press, 1980.

films.[10] Gradually and not surprisingly, as the Communist Party came to play an ever more dominant role in political life, it was the Communist film organization, Mafirt, which came to be the most powerful. It soon acquired a studio and a laboratory where 16-mm films and newsreels could be made and feature films could be copied.

However, the major studio, Hunnia, was a national property that came under the ministry of industry, which at this time was headed by a Socialist minister. Consequently, in Hunnia Socialist artists and politicians had a decisive role to play. The director, a Social Democrat, István Szegő, constantly annoyed the Communists by refusing to collaborate with them and instead worked with representatives of right-wing parties. In fact, in film affairs the major conflict in 1947 was between the Socialist and Communist Parties. The Socialists controlled the ministry of industry, but the Communists had the ministry of the interior, which had control over the movie theaters. Mafirt repeatedly complained to the Central Committee of the Communist Party concerning what seemed to them as undue Socialist dominance in the film industry.

The expectation was that parties or private companies, of which there had been many before 1945, could rent studio space from Hunnia. Thus political parties became competitors of private enterprise in the film industry. This confusing situation used scarce resources inefficiently and occasioned fierce debates, but at least for awhile it delayed the imposition of a Stalinist straightjacket. Ideological conformity came to be the rule only in "the year of the turning point," 1948, with the nominal unification of the Socialist and Communist Parties (in fact the absorption of the SDP by the Communists) and the destruction of all non-Communist political forces.

The difficulties in actually making films were considerable. Studios were damaged, and many of the theaters all over the country were in ruins. Some of the actors and directors who had compromised themselves by cooperating with the Nazis could not appear in the newly made films, and, indeed, even those films, which were from a political point of view acceptable but included actors on the blacklist, could not be shown any longer. Film stock was limited and could be obtained only with convertible currency, which was scarce at this time because of extreme demands on the national purse. The greatest problem, however, was the lack of capital. The government would have liked to attract private capital, but given the uncertainties and

10 PIL 274 23/22 p. 117, Mafirt to Central Committee, November 6, 1946.

the likelihood that censorship would prevent the distribution of a completed work, this was not very successful. Finally, the money came almost exclusively from the government.

Curiously, in 1945 three films were made, but none in 1946. The first film actually exhibited was *Tanítónő* [*The Woman Teacher*], which premiered in September 1945. It was based on a turn of the century play, making it relatively safe from a political point of view. The Socialist Márton Keleti directed the film, but Gyula Hay, a Communist, wrote the script. That the male lead was played by the popular actor, Pál Jávor, who because of his courageous anti-fascist stand had not been able to appear in films in the recent past, contributed a great deal to the success of the film. The film certainly did not express the correct class point of view, as Communist reviewers were quick to point out: at the center of the story was a love affair between a poor teacher and the son of a landlord.[11] In spite of the technical problems in the war-damaged studio (it took three times as long to complete as pre-1945 films), it was a reasonably well-made and successful product. The Socialist newspaper, *Népszava*, wrote that this was the first film that showed life as it really was; however, the technical means for making a first-rate picture did not yet exist.[12] The other two films appeared only in 1946 and were less successful according to contemporary reviews; they disappeared quickly after a short run.

In these years, the Hungarian film industry was full of unrealized projects. Dozens of scripts were submitted and discussed, usually without result. Even when a film was completed under extraordinarily difficult circumstances, it often could not be shown. In 1947, five films were made in Hungary, but of these only two could be exhibited. It is worth discussing all five in some detail because such a discussion shows the constraints and problems of filmmakers.

One of the films not shown was evidently among the finest, *Ének a Buzamezőkről* (*Song of the Wheat Fields*). István Szöts, a man of great prewar reputation, made it on the basis of a 1927 novel by the populist writer, Ferenc Móra. Szöts planned to make this film in 1942, but the authorities, considering the theme pacifist, did not allow him to proceed. In 1947, Szöts chose as artistic adviser for this film a renowned librettist, film theorist, and life-long Communist, Béla Balázs. *Ének a Búzamezőkről* was a ballad-like melodrama, taking place in a gloomy village. Set in World War I, it portrayed a Russian POW who, in escaping from a POW camp, fails to

11 *Szabad Nép*, December 24, 1945.

12 *Népszava*, December 28, 1945.

share his food with a fellow escapee, who dies. Consumed by guilt, he is then rescued and has an affair with a Hungarian woman. The religious overtones of the film were enough to alienate Communist censors, and the minister of the interior also objected to the affair between the Russian soldier and the Hungarian woman. Szöts desperately wanted to make this film and was willing to make artistic compromises but nothing helped.[13] When the completed film was shown in the Communist Party headquarters, Mátyás Rákosi got up and left after the first scenes.[14] In Hungary, just as in the Soviet Union at the time, decisions about the fate of a film were made this way. Rákosi's hostile response was enough to seal the fate of the film.

The decision not to distribute the film was made easier by the fact that it was made in the Communist film studios. But perhaps the main reason that the film was never shown was that the topic of POWs was too sensitive at a time when there were still tens of thousands of POWs in Soviet captivity. That issue was one of the most troubling ones for Hungarians at the time and calling attention to it in a movie seemed to be unwise. Szöts left Hungary and never again attempted to make a film in his native country.[15]

One of the two other films not exhibited was an insignificant comedy, *Könnyű Múzsa* (*Light Muse*). This film did not appear in the theaters because it was considered to be artistically weak. The other, a more substantial work, *Mezei Próféta* (*Village Prophet*) failed to win approval because of its religious content. Characters looked for solace to their problems in their faith.[16] Evidently, the directors did not understand any better than others how the political climate was changing at the end of 1947.

Beszterce Ostroma (*The Siege of Beszterce*) was allowed to be exhibited. This was a costume drama, made on the basis of an 1895 novel by the great Hungarian writer Kálmán Mikszáth. The director and the screenwriter quite shamelessly changed the story and characters to suit contemporary political demands. From an artistic point of view, the film was a failure.

At the other end of the aesthetic spectrum was the film *Valahol Europában* (*Somewhere in Europe*). Géza Radványi, another highly regarded Hungarian director, made the film. Balázs and Radványi themselves wrote the script, and it was produced by the Communist film organization Mafirt. This film has come to be considered not only the best of this period but also

13 PIL 274 23/23 pp. 112–113, Szöts to Mafirt, June 24, 1947.
14 Szilagyi, p. 52.
15 I base my evaluation of the film on Szilagyi, pp. 48–49.
16 Ibid.

among the dozen finest Hungarian films of all time.[17] Indeed, it is fair to say that immediately after the war there were few films made anywhere in the world that depicted the postwar world with comparable realism, passion, and emotional truth. The style of the film is somewhat in the vein of Italian neorealism. It is not so much that Hungarian artists copied the style of Italian neorealism, though they were acquainted with the work of the Italian directors. It is more likely that similar background and circumstances created similar results.

Although other directors chose safe topics, usually based on prewar novels or dramas, this film was altogether contemporary. The story took place immediately after the war, and it showed the most pitiful victims of the destruction: abandoned children. The audience saw a destroyed, desolate landscape, which indeed could have been anywhere in Europe. But the subject of the film is not material but psychological destruction. The orphaned children (on one occasion we see a mother throwing a child out of a moving train, one traveling, presumably, toward Auschwitz) left on their own to find each other and revert to the law of the jungle. They behave like delinquents. They have no choice, and they do not know any better. They take possession of an abandoned castle, where they find an elderly man, a musician, whom they at first want to harm, but ultimately the old man finds a way to communicate with them, gains their allegiance, and reawakens their humanity. The film bears some similarity to Nikolai Ekk's film, *Road to Life* (1931), which is perhaps not an accident because Balázs spent the interwar years in Moscow and had reviewed this film for a Soviet journal. *Road to Life* also deals with abandoned children who find their way back to society.

In the politically complex and confused situation, it was difficult to find acceptable scripts, but an even more fundamental problem was the lack of capital. Negotiations with foreign, specifically American, companies about coproductions that would have generated capital for the making of Hungarian films did not lead to anything as the cold war developed, and the

17 This is the only Hungarian film of the immediate postwar era available today on video. There is even a version with English subtitles. At the time and ever since this film has received high praise. Miklos Molnár, later a comrade of Imre Nagy, wrote in the Communist newspaper *Szabad Nép* (December 24, 1947) that the new Hungarian art of cinema begins with this film. The Socialist newspaper, *Népszava*, commented that the film was made with the purest artistic means. The film was also shown with great success in Germany and France. Graham Petrie in his book on Hungarian cinema wrote: "In 1947 also appeared one of the most remarkable of all Hungarian films, *Somewhere in Europe* – a film that deserves to be much better known than it is and at least to rank alongside such Italian neorealist works as *Open City* and *Bicycle Thieves*." Petrie, *History Must Answer to Man*, Budapest: Corvina, 1978, p. 7.

film people had to operate under ever more restrictive conditions. In the summer of 1946, Mafirt, the Communist film agency, negotiated with the representatives of American studios concerning the import of sixty to eighty American films. Mafirt hoped that the prewar arrangement would be resumed, according to which copies of American films for the Eastern European markets would be made in the Budapest studios. The possibility even emerged that the American studios would make small-budget English-language films in Hungary where labor was cheap. In July 1946 Mafirt's report to the Central Committee of the party was full of optimism concerning cooperation with the Americans and the possibility of making money. The Mafirt representative wrote: "It is my conviction that this kind of factory, laboratory and import-friendly cooperation opens up the nicest perspectives for us."[18]

How much the political situation changed in the course of one year can be seen in a letter written in March 1947 from the same Mafirt organization to Mihály Farkas, one of the top leaders of the party. The writer expressed concern about the dumping of American films in Hungary and the removal of the accumulated profit. He was obviously concerned about the "ideological poison" that was inherent in Hollywood products. Further, he complained that the Hunnia factory was preparing a French-Hungarian coproduction that was in a "reactionary sprit."[19]

Anxious to see films, the moviegoing public had to be satisfied under the circumstances with seeing pre-1945 Hungarian and foreign, at first only Russian, films. Many of the pre-1945 films were considered unsuitable for screening, most often not because of the political content of the film but because of the unsavory past of some of the major actors. In order to alleviate the film hunger, József Révai suggested that scenes in which discredited actors appeared could be cut and reshot.[20]

Before 1945, of course, private persons owned movie theaters. The new regime, however, experimented with a new and unusual method of ownership. Already in July 1945, the representatives of the major political parties came to an agreement according to which the theaters would be distributed among themselves: 80 percent of the largest theaters (250-person capacity or more) were distributed among the political parties (the remaining 20 percent were given to various social organizations and unions). Of the smaller

18 PIL 274 23/27 p. 6, Mafirt to HCP (Hungarian Communist Party) Central Committee, Economics Department, July 30, 1946.
19 PIL 274 23/27 p. 128, Mafirt to Farkas, March 29, 1947.
20 PIL 274 23/27 p. 259, principles of the new Hungarian film industry, May 5, 1948.

theaters, the parties distributed among themselves only 20 percent, and the rest were given to the ministry of the interior for distribution.[21] These could be given to private individuals after checking their political reliability. Not surprisingly, the Communist Party was the most successful in the struggle for theaters. With Soviet help, the Communist Party took control of the largest and most desirable theaters in Budapest. In the countryside, for example, Communist Party–owned theaters could accommodate 15,817 people, whereas the Smallholders' Party had theaters with the capacity of only 13,407, in spite of the fact that the FKGP had attracted more than three times as many votes as the Communists in the 1945 national election.[22] As time went on, Mafirt owned more and more theaters, and by the middle of 1947 according to some sources it had 40 percent and according to others 70 percent of the theaters. Licenses were given out by the Communist-dominated ministry of the interior, which paid no attention to the Smallholders' repeated protests.[23]

There remained 250 small movie theaters for which there was considerable competition. Evidently, people believed that there was money to be made. The ministry of the interior was determined that the licenses should not go to the well-to-do or to those who might have contacts with foreign studios but instead should go to reliable people who could be trusted in the choice of films they would exhibit. The desire to own or rent movie theaters showed a considerable degree of optimism. Such optimism was shown not only by private investors but also by the political parties. Politicians believed that the profit made from movie theaters would go to the coffers of the party, and at the same time would enable their own film studios to make ideologically desirable films. Fairly soon, it became clear that the optimism was unwarranted. The cinemas operated at a loss. Most of the theaters were in bad shape, many had suffered heavy damage during the long siege of Budapest, and capital was not available for their renovation. But most important, the government also wanted its share of the profit and therefore taxed movie tickets much too heavily. In 1946, movie tickets were taxed 52 percent (20 percent entertainment tax, 20 percent sales tax, 12 percent special tax for the ministry of the interior), and at the same time film rentals were expensive because of the shortage of films. Mafirt suggested an interparty conference in order to demand from the government the lowering of taxes on movie tickets.[24]

21 PIL 274 23/27 p. 6, Mafirt to HCP Central Committee Economics Department, July 30, 1945.
22 PIL 274 23/27 p. 100, Kovacs to Central Committee Economics Department, November 5, 1946.
23 PIL 274 23/27 pp. 145–148, report May 20, 1947.
24 PIL 274 23/27 pp. 64–68, Mafirt report to Central Committee KP, October 10, 1946.

A particularly interesting situation arose in the making and distribution of newsreels. All parties, of course, understood the political significance of newsreels. Each party enterprise made its own, expressing its own agenda and slant on events, and showed them in its own movie theaters. Not surprisingly, the Communists, the most active propagandists, were the most active newsreel makers. At first, they produced one newsreel every two weeks, and then they succeeded in making them weekly. In the summer of 1946, on Communist initiative, the parties made an attempt to reconcile their differences and agree on a common newsreel, but the attempt failed. The Communists proposed that the ministry of the interior would make the showing of their newsreels compulsory. As a concession, they offered the creation of an interparty committee that could edit the newsreels. The letter from Mafirt to the Central Committee of the party assured the leaders that there was nothing to fear, for the technical means of making these newsreels would be safely in Communist hands.[25] Communist-made newsreels, however, were sometimes, but not always, shown in Socialist and Peasant Party movie houses. The Peasant Party, however, which the Communists regarded as their Trojan Horse among the peasantry, on occasion balked at showing Communist newsreels, which seemed to be pure propaganda. Indeed, in some localities, the local Peasant Party movie theaters had the temerity to show Smallholder Party (FKGP) newsreels. On such occasions, Mafirt found it necessary to request the highest authorities of the party to intervene with the leaders of the Peasant Party so that such things would not happen again.[26] In addition, Communist-controlled theaters also played Russian-made newsreels and for a while received material from the French Communist Party also.

The Communist Party was far more active in making 16-mm films than the other parties and soon had a monopoly. For the Communists, making these films was a political rather than an economic matter. They alone realized the propaganda significance of showing these films and alone were willing to make the material sacrifices. The portability of this format made 16-mm film most useful for propaganda purposes.

Unlike in the elections of 1945, newsreels and 16-mm films played a considerable role in the 1947 elections. Hungary was the only country in southeast Europe that had the laboratories to make 16-mm films. The agitators attributed great significance to the showing of these films in the course of propaganda campaigns. During the 1947 campaigns, these 16-mm films

25 PIL 274 23/22, Mafirt to Central Committee, August 6, 1946.
26 PIL 274 23/22, Mafirt to Central Committee, October 16, 1946.

were shown in Communist movie houses; in villages where there were no available theaters, agitators brought projectors on trucks provided by the Soviet army and exhibited the films in schoolrooms or wherever a large room was available.[27] The short films and newsreels showed "Communist achievements" in reconstruction and also the achievements of other, neighboring Communist regimes. These were some representative titles: *We Build the Country of Toilers, Liberated Hungary*, and *How to Vote*. In Communist theaters, the showing of propaganda films was combined with oral agitation. Mafirt reported to the Central Committee that almost half a million people saw these short films.[28]

Although in 1946 Mafirt was looking forward to successful cooperation with Mopex, the representatives of American studios in Budapest, in the following year Mafirt saw the situation altogether differently. By this time, the Communists at the film agency would have liked to limit the influx of American films because of ideological concerns. The problem was that the Hungarian industry could produce only a few films, and Hungarian audiences rejected Soviet films. There simply were not enough films that were "progressive" enough in the opinion of the Communists. Mafirt considered basing itself on the French industry more than on Hollywood, but that also was not successful, inasmuch as the French also did not produce satisfactory films in large enough numbers. According to their self-evaluation, Mafirt in its own cinemas could play only 25–30 percent "progressive" films, and for the rest it attempted to find apolitical, amusing films. At the same time, the Communists believed that even such apparently apolitical films carried a hostile and dangerous message. Mafirt attempted to reassure the party's Central Committee that apolitical films would be accompanied in the theaters by newsreels and shorts carrying satisfactory political messages.[29]

SOVIET FILMS

In August 1946, Béla Balázs, who had excellent contacts in the Soviet film world, traveled to Moscow in order to discuss the showing of Soviet films in Hungary and to ask for help in overcoming the difficulties of making "progressive" films. On his return, he wrote a letter to the Communist Party Central Committee in which he expressed his concerns about the

27 PIL 274 23/23 pp. 126–130, Mafirt to Central Committee, June 1947.
28 PIL 274 23/23 pp. 163–164, Mafirt report to Central Committee, August 1947.
29 PIL 274 23/23 pp. 125–130, Report on Mafirt's work to Central Committee for May–July 1947.

difficulties of the film industry. He complained that up to this time the industry had managed to make only three rather weak films. He believed that it was important to begin making better and from an ideological point of view more useful films in order to increase the influence of the party. Otherwise, he argued, reactionaries with American financial support would be the first to use the available technical and human resources. Because the lack of raw film stock was one of the chief problems, Balázs suggested that the Communist leaders ask for this material from the Soviet Union. The Soviet Union had already provided such help to the East German film industry, and Balázs understood from his discussions in Moscow that a Hungarian request would also be favorably considered.[30]

In fact, contrary to Balázs' optimistic predictions, cooperation with the Soviets turned out to be extremely difficult from the very beginning. It is true that the Communist Party and its related organizations, including Mafirt, received help and support from the Soviet Union in competition against the other parties. On the other hand, the collaboration with the Russians was very difficult. From the documents, it is evident that the Russians were unprofessional and, above all, arrogant. Mafirt was put in an impossible situation: on the one hand, the party leaders constantly urged it to make a profit and help the party's finances, but, on the other, Mafirt was compelled to show Soviet films. Showing these to a Hungarian audience was bound to be a money-losing proposition, and, therefore, Mafirt was a constant drain on Communist finances.

The Communists regarded the popularization of Soviet culture as one of their major political tasks. The showing and advertising of Soviet films was simply part of the larger effort to make Hungarians like and admire the Soviet Union. It was a difficult job: Hungarians had been traditionally hostile to the Russians, and the behavior of the Red Army had made everything a great deal worse. The Communist leaders were well aware of these problems and discussed the matter among themselves repeatedly. In their internal correspondence, they openly admitted the anti-Sovietism and anti-Communism of the Hungarian people, and they blamed twenty-five years of successful reactionary propaganda for what they considered an anti-Soviet prejudice.[31]

In the summer of 1945 on Communist inspiration, a pseudo-voluntary Hungarian-Soviet Friendship Society was formed in order to propagate

30 PIL 274 23/22 pp. 106–108, Balázs to Central Committee, November 25, 1946.
31 See for example, PIL 274 11/11, the report of Tömpe to Central Committee from the town of Mako, March 6, 1946.

Soviet culture. In the following three years, individual cells were created in towns and factories. A film subsection was also a part of the society. In 1946, the party directed Communist-dominated mass organizations, such as the organization for youth, MADISZ, and organization for women, MNDSZ, to show and popularize Soviet films. The party also set up special film propaganda sections within the district organizations. The sections organized lectures, screenings of Soviet 16-mm scientific and travel films, and Sunday morning film matinees. (Surely, it was not an accident that films were shown at the time of religious services.) These sections also organized mass viewings of Soviet films in factories and schools and rewarded selected workers with free tickets to cinemas showing Soviet films. A report from the propaganda section of Mafirt to the Central Committee complained about the viewing public's lack of interest and admitted that the propaganda of Soviet films was exclusively a Communist affair.[32] At the end of this report, Zsigmondi, the head of the propaganda section in Mafirt, expressed pessimism:

> I regard it as a failure of my work that in spite of my determined and many faceted work, I have not succeeded in making a significant change in the Hungarian public's interest in Soviet films. This was the chief goal of my work and everything else was subordinated to it. . . . I do not want to talk about the objective difficulties. There is a broad, but indifferent audience, which includes even a majority of the Party members, who find the mentality of the Soviet films alien.

The main problem was the nature and quality of Soviet films, but the Soviet representatives made the task of the Hungarians much more difficult. Major Piskarev, a representative of Sovexportfilm (the export-import organization for Soviet films), arrived in Budapest as early as May 1, 1945, less than a month after the complete liberation of the country.[33] There is an agreement among everyone who met him that Piskarev was an extremely unsuitable person for the job. He not only knew nothing about the particular Hungarian circumstances but also knew little about cinema. He behaved tactlessly and made the situation of the Hungarian Communists, who had the most fervent desire to serve Soviet interests, more difficult. He was a typical representative of an occupying power, not interested in soothing Hungarian sensibilities. On one occasion, for example, Soviet soldiers took possession of Soviet films that had been shown in provincial theaters, saying that because these were Soviet films, they were the legitimate owners. In vain

32 PIL 274 23/24 pp. 31–34, Mafirt report to Central Committee on organization of propaganda for the first half of 1946, July 9, 1946.

33 PIL 274 23/24 pp. 5–6, Mafirt director, Kovács to Central Committee July 26, 1945. Both Rákosi and Révai expressed interest in the content of the letter. Their initials are on the letter.

did Hungarian authorities appeal to Piskarev for help. The Soviet Union also took possession of one of the finest theaters in Budapest, the Uránia, arguing that it had been German property, and therefore under the agreement concerning German war reparations now it became Soviet property.[34]

In 1945, there was practically no competition for Soviet films; the Soviets had the market to themselves. Under the circumstances, Mafirt, which signed an agreement with Soviet representatives and became the sole distributor, was in an excellent position to take advantage of Soviet contacts and popularize Soviet films, which in Hungary for all practical purposes were unknown. It is unlikely that even in the best of circumstances the Communists would have succeeded in making these films very popular among the hostile Hungarian people. The Soviet films that had been made before or during the war were not such as would appeal to Hungarian viewers. Hungarian audiences were reared on prewar films that were meant to entertain: The viewer saw well-appointed apartments and well-dressed, pretty women and took vicarious satisfaction in the lives of the rich. The films had also been formulaic: rich men fell in love with poor women, or much more rarely, rich women fell in love with poor men. And, of course, they overcame all obstacles. The style and content of Russian films could hardly have been more different.

The post–Second World War period was the worst in the history of Soviet cinema.[35] First of all, very few films were made in these years, and therefore most of the films that Sovexportfilm sent to Hungary had been made ten to fifteen years earlier. The films that were made in this period were dull, without conflict, and burdened with excessive Russian nationalism, and they were so formulaic that even contemporary Soviet critics pointed out that scenes and dialogs could easily be moved from one film to another and the viewers would not notice. The representatives of Mafirt resisted, for example, the showing of *Lermontov*, pointing out that the film was exactly the same as *Pushkin*, which had just appeared in Hungarian theaters.[36]

In March 1946, Mafirt and Sovexportfilm signed a contract in Moscow. It is characteristic of the casual and unprofessional behavior of the participants of this meeting that the Russian text included a decisively important point that was not in the Hungarian version. According to point five in the Russian version, Communist film theaters limited themselves exclusively to

34 PIL 274 23/24 May 16, 1946, Mafirt to Farkas. Russians took Uránia as previous German property.
35 On Soviet films of this era see Peter Kenez, *Cinema and Soviet Society, 1917–1953*, Cambridge; New York: Cambridge University Press, 1992, pp. 209–246.
36 PIL 274 23/28 p. 182, Mafirt report, and PIL 274 23/23 p. 251, memorandum o polozhenii sovetskikh kinofil'mov v Vengrii.

exhibiting Russian and new Hungarian films. Because there were practically no new Hungarian films, this arrangement meant that the theaters showed nothing but Soviet films. Such an obligation imposed an enormous financial burden on the Hungarians. The Hungarian understanding was that they obligated themselves only to be the Hungarian agents of Sovexportfilm.[37]

Pointing to the contract signed with Mafirt, Piskarev repeatedly insisted that Mafirt theaters show dozens of Soviet films, without any possibility of choosing films that would be appropriate for Hungarian audiences. The Hungarians had not been told what might arrive from Moscow and had no say in what kind of films the Russians would send. Under the circumstances, they could not advertise the films ahead of time. They were obliged to show whatever was available. Sometimes they received only one copy of a film, sometimes several. Sometimes negatives, which would have enabled the Hungarians to prepare copies, had not been sent. On several occasions, films were missing reels. Piskarev did not hesitate to intervene in the smallest matters. In the summer of 1945, Budapest theaters were playing the Aleksandrov comedy, *Shining Path*. The Hungarians wanted to cut the film in order to have time to show a newsreel that included a speech by Rákosi. Piskarev insisted that instead of cutting the film, Rákosi's speech had to be cut.

One of the lesser problems in popularizing Soviet films was the lack of personnel to translate. The subtitles were prepared in the most haphazard fashion, often by people with only a rudimentary knowledge of Russian. This sometimes led to hilarious errors in the Hungarian subtitles. In June 1946, Piskarev complained to Mafirt about such errors. He mentioned examples in the film made by Mark Donskoi from Gorkii's autobiographical trilogy. In one famous scene, the impoverished grandfather is finally reduced to begging. In the Russian version, he says: "For the love of Christ, give me alms!" The Hungarian translation was "Give me a little liver pate." At other places, the translation was exactly the opposite of the original. When the little handicapped boy asks his friend, the young Gorkii, whether a little mouse can grow up to be as large as a horse, Gorkii answers, "yes." In the Hungarian version, he says, "no."[38]

The original idea of entrusting the political parties with film theaters was that they could make money and help finance their political activities.

37 PIL 274 23/28 pp. 61–85, protocols of the meeting between representatives of Mafirt and Sovexportfilm, November 14, 1946.

38 PIL 274 23/24 p. 23, Piskarev to Mafirt, June 6, 1946. The letter was forwarded to Révai, who demanded an explanation.

In the case of Mafirt, however, this did not happen, largely because Mafirt had close connections and contracts with the Soviet film export agency. In 1947 alone, Mafirt lost 200,000 forints exclusively as a result of showing Soviet films. (After the stabilization of the forint on August 1, 1946, the loss of 200,000 was a major burden for Communist finances.) Mafirt's report to the Central Committee on October 6, 1946, blamed the problems on the behavior of the Soviet representatives, who insisted that the theaters show almost exclusively Russian films, without any possibility of selection. Such films created a negative attitude among Hungarians against all Soviet films, and so this kind of programming was counterproductive. But the report also admitted a general hostility against all Russian films: "There is a social boycott against Russian films. A manifestation of this hostility is that the Smallholder Party warned its members against seeing Russian films."[39] Most likely, the accusation against the Smallholders was a figment of the report writer's imagination; nevertheless, the lack of interest and, indeed, hostility toward all things Soviet, in particular films, was obviously true.

In the spring of 1947, Mafirt with the help of the Central Committee of the Communist Party succeeded in renegotiating the terms of the previous contract with the Soviet film export agency. The Russians accepted the Hungarian version of the original contract; the two sides agreed to divide income 50–50. This was a much less favorable arrangement than the Hungarian distributors of American films had. The new contract allowed the Hungarians greater freedom in selecting films and allowed them to show Soviet films alternating with Western, largely American, films. The possibility of selection, however, was to some extent theoretical. When in 1947 a Hungarian delegation traveled to Moscow in order to sign a contract for the import of sixty to eighty films, in their several stay of weeks they were able to see only five films, two of which were German. Time and again, Sovexportfilm did not live up to the contract: it did not deliver the promised films. The Russians insisted that no Soviet film could be cut without their express permission, even though the films included scenes that could not possibly make sense to a Hungarian audience. They insisted that only their posters should be used in advertising the films. It was not easy to deal with Soviet bureaucracy. Cooperation did not become easier because the fundamental problem was not solved and, indeed, could not be solved: when they had a chance, Hungarian audiences preferred films other than Soviet. The financial loss that Mafirt suffered was a major drain on Communist Party

39 PIL 274 23/27 pp. 64–68, Mafirt report, October 6, 1946.

finances. The economics department of the Central Committee constantly and unrealistically urged Mafirt to make a profit.

The Russians and the Hungarians continued to blame one another for the failure. It is worthwhile to discuss in detail the protocols of a meeting between Hungarian and Soviet representatives on October 22, 1947, for the protocols show not only the problems Soviet films faced in Hungary but also the style with which the Russians treated their Hungarian comrades. They treated them like servants. They attacked Mafirt for showing "reactionary" American and French films, such as *The White Cliffs of Dover*, *Lost Weekend*, and *Symphony Pastorale*. The representative of Sovexportfilm, Quin, blamed Mafirt for insufficient efforts to win over the population for Soviet films.[40] He argued that Mafirt's interest was purely commercial, by pointing out that those Soviet films were the most successful in Hungary that had the least to do with propaganda, as if that was Mafirt's fault. The most successful film, indeed, was *Stone Flower*, a beautiful film for children. (The film actually was made in Prague Barrandow studios and was the only Soviet film made in the immediate postwar years that one can watch today with pleasure.) This was the only Soviet film that was shown in all theaters owned by Mafirt and attracted the largest audiences. Angyal, representing Mafirt, responded that since August 1, 1946, Mafirt had lost 600,000 forints showing Soviet films. When Soviet films were shown, 80 to 90 percent of the seats remained empty. He argued that the loss was even greater if one considered that Mafirt could have made a profit in the same theaters by showing films other than Soviet. The major problem was

> Hungarians are not only hostile to progressive films, but those who have money actually like reactionary films. We have started the struggle against American films . . . [but] if we did not play American films in our theaters, all that we would have achieved is that other movies would have played them and the audiences would have gone to see them all the more.[41]

In the course of these heated discussions, another problem was mentioned. The ideas inherent in Soviet films did not always correspond to the propaganda themes of the Hungarian Communists. For example, the Hungarian Communists in the immediate postwar years were well aware of the great hostility of the peasantry to the *kolkhoz* system. Indeed, anti-Communists repeatedly warned the peasants that in the case of Communist victory they would be compelled to give up their lands. Communist agitators

40 PIL 274 23/23 pp. 175–180, protocols of meeting between representatives of Mafirt and Sovexportfilm, October 22, 1947.

41 PIL 274 23/28 protocol, November 14, 1947.

in the villages felt it necessary to counteract enemy propaganda and described the talk about collective farms as "*kolkhoz* fairy tales," entirely thought up by the enemy, implying that the party had no intention at all of copying the Soviet model. Showing Soviet *kolkhoz* films obviously undermined the propaganda efforts of the village agitators.[42]

There was another problem. In the given circumstances when the Communists were compelled to compete for votes, it was essential to make the people believe that their policies were moderate. Sebes, another Mafirt representative, pointed out: "The Party established that it was an error to exhibit *Vyborg Side* in a public movie house in front of a large audience, because what the public saw was that the masses dispersed the Constituent Assembly and therefore the people became distrustful concerning our Party, because they believe we want to do also." He added that it would have been all right to show the film to worker audiences. The Soviet representative could respond only: "According to you any film which has a kolkhoz is bad. Any film which has revolution is bad." Then he added this non sequitur: "The worst Russian film is better than an American one."[43]

The Soviet representative ended the meeting with an extraordinary threat: "We will continue to watch the work of Mafirt with great attention. I declare that if there will be no improvement in the work of Mafirt in the propagation of Soviet films then we will raise the issue differently with the inclusion of different organs." One wonders what he had in mind. Perhaps Quin was threatening his Communist colleagues with the Soviet political police.

This was not an idle threat. On December 20, 1947, a certain Major Gurkin, a Soviet political representative in Budapest, sent his report to the foreign department of the Central Committee of the Soviet Communist Party. In it, he accused the leadership of Mafirt and, in particular, the director, Angyal, of conscious sabotage of Soviet films. He blamed the Central Committee of the Hungarian Party for not paying enough attention to this serious matter and even attempting to defend Mafirt's leadership. He made two recommendations: 1. as of January 1, 1948, forbid the showing of American films altogether in Hungary, as had already been done in Romania, and 2. repudiate the existing contract with Mafirt. Instead of working through Mafirt, Sovexportfilm should establish its own distribution company in Hungary.[44]

In retrospect, the Communists called 1948 the year of the turning point. Indeed, in this year the ever-narrowing pluralism of the immediate postwar

42 Ibid.

43 Ibid., October 22, 1947

44 RTsKhIDNI fond 17, opis 128, delo 524.

years ended. From this point on, Mafirt did not have to compete with other film enterprises. Film studios and theaters were nationalized. The films that were made in Hungary in and after 1948 fully reflected the Communist point of view; American and French films presented less and less competition for Soviet films. The choice that remained for the audiences was either to see "progressive" films or to stay at home.

13

The End of the Pluralist Political Order

THE AUGUST 1947 ELECTIONS

When Ferenc Nagy was forced out of office as prime minister, it should have been clear to everyone that this act was the last and final blow to a genuinely democratic political system. The forms of pluralism, however, remained in existence for a short time: there still was a multiparty system, issues were still debated in the parliament, and newspapers still represented different points of view. However, the substance of pluralism was already gone. The last major anti-Communist political force, the FKGP, had been emasculated and was now led by people willing to follow Communist instructions. The second half of 1947 and the first half of 1948 saw the destruction of even the appearance of pluralism. The elections of August 1947 ended the parliamentary majority of the FKGP. The "unification" of the SDP and the MKP in June 1948 into the Party of Hungarian Workers (Magyar Dolgozok Pártja, MDP) was the last step in the creation of a Soviet-style one-party state. The nationalization of industry was part of the process of creating an economic system like that introduced in the Soviet Union decades earlier. The nationalization of church schools demonstrated that even the Catholic Church, which had been the most determined opponent of the Communists, could no longer resist.

The Communist leadership in the late spring of 1947 decided that it was in its interest to hold new elections before the end of the tenure of the current parliament, which was scheduled to take place only in 1949. The Communists argued truthfully that much had changed since the last elections. The decision to hold elections ahead of time was not based on an optimistic assumption that the party had gained many more followers since November 1945. The experience of the previous elections taught the leadership the dangers of excessive optimism, and Rákosi and his comrades continued to grumble about the reactionary nature of the Hungarians.[1] Reports from the countryside indicated clearly that the great majority of the people remained hostile to what the Communists stood for. However, the Communist leaders well understood that their most powerful political opponent, the FKGP, was falling apart. Because of Soviet intervention the leaders of the Smallholders could not defend themselves against the spurious charge that they had conspired against the republic. As a consequence, the most popular leaders of the party were already in exile or in prison. Under the circumstances, the Communists could take it for granted that their most powerful political opponents would not be able to repeat the performance of 1945.

To improve their chances, the Communists chose August as the date for the elections. They assumed that following the harvest the economic situation of the country would be the most favorable, and they planned to take credit for the improvements. Further, the Communists insisted on reducing the electoral rolls and narrowing the suffrage. By the middle of 1947, both the NPP and the SDP had gotten rid of their right-wing leaders, meaning that the Communists had the full support of both parties in interparty conferences determining who could vote and who could run for parliament.[2] The new electoral law, submitted by the Communists and accepted by the parties of the coalition, took away suffrage from members of approximately thirty prewar political organizations and societies, from those who had returned from the West only after October 1, 1945, and from those who had lost their jobs after 1945 for political reasons.[3] Forbidding the political participation of people who had played active roles during the Horthy regime was aimed against politicians who had managed to irritate the Communists the most. Right-wing FKGP deputies, who had been excluded from the party in 1946, established an explicitly anti-Communist Hungarian Freedom Party. The central figure, Dezső Sulyok, intended to unite the anti-Communist opposition. Because the right to run for reelection was taken away from the better-known leaders of this party, including Sulyok, the party was forced to dissolve itself in July 1947.

The interparty agreement reduced the number of people entitled to vote by something between 100,000–200,000, out of an electorate of

1 PIL 274 2/42 September 11, 1947. Rákosi speaking to party activists described Hungary as a "reactionary country."

2 *Pártközi értekezletek* July 10–12, 1947, pp. 534–633.

3 László Hubai, "A Magyar társadalom politikai tagoltsága és a 1947-es választások," in István Feitl, Lajos Izsák, and Gábor Székely (eds.), *Fordulat a világban és Magyarországon, 1947–1949*, Budapest: Napvilág, 2000, p. 99.

approximately 5 million.[4] However, the number of people who could not vote was much larger than those who had been explicitly excluded. Communist functionaries prevented many who were expected to support the opposition from voting. They simply removed those voters' names from the electoral rolls, maintaining that these individuals had made errors in filling out forms.[5] Rákosi himself after the elections spoke of taking the right to vote away from about half a million people.[6]

It was part of the Communist strategy to have the elections over as quickly as possible. The decision to hold elections was not made public until the middle of July, and the elections were to be held on August 31. The Communists encouraged the formation of "bourgeois" parties, in the correct expectation that the centrist and right-wing votes would be dispersed. These newly formed parties were allowed to participate in the election, but because they did not possess newspapers and had no time to organize mass meetings, let alone an election campaign, they were at an obvious disadvantage. Aside from the four parties of the coalition, six other parties participated in the elections. The new parties were similar to one another in their ideology, differing chiefly in the personalities of their leaders. Most of these politicians had previously been members of the FKGP. The parties even had similar names. One, called the Independent Hungarian Democratic Party, was led by István Balogh; the Democratic People's Party, led by István Barankovics, was closest to the ideology of European Christian socialism. Zoltán Pfeiffer, another ex-FKGP politician, established the Hungarian Independence Party, which was a revival of the recently dissolved Freedom Party of Dezső Sulyok. The Citizens' Democratic Party was a revival of an organization that had been established in 1945 by Géza Teleki. The Hungarian Radical Party's leading figure was Károly Peyer, a right-wing Socialist who had led his party in the interwar period but under Communist pressure had been excluded from the SDP. Aside from these parties, there was also an unusual addition, the Christian Women's Camp, created by Margit Slachta.

The Communists prepared for the elections with their customary care and talent. They organized mass meetings and drew up elaborate plans for agitators to carry out "neighborly visits." They printed hundreds of thousands of posters. Their front organization for women, MNDSZ, for example, had set up separate agitation groups for industrial workers, for the intelligentsia, and also for domestic workers. MNDSZ members were asked to write letters to peasants whether they knew people in the villages or

4 S. Balogh, 1975, p. 483.

5 Palasik, 2000, p. 259.

6 PIL 274 2/42 September 11, 1947, Rákosi, election results, Központi Vezetőség meeting.

not. Indeed, according to Communist figures, 18,000 women participated in this letter-writing campaign. MADISZ, the youth organization, was instructed to attempt to influence parents of the young people to vote "correctly." (The minimum voting age was twenty years.) Even young children were mobilized. Pioneer groups decorated playgrounds that had been renovated by MKP volunteers. In the course of ceremonies opening these playgrounds, in the presence of their parents, children thanked the MKP for help. The participating children received Rákosi pictures, small flags, and balls with party emblems painted on them.[7]

In the historical literature, these elections came to be known as "blue tag elections." The Communists distributed blue pieces of paper among their activists on the pretext that activists' official duties on election day would put them in districts other than their places of residence. These blue tags allowed them to vote wherever they happened to be. The communists distributed 200,000 such tags among their members. Because this crude method of cheating was almost immediately recognized, ultimately only 62,000 such tags were used. (The amount of cheating was smaller because that number included some legitimate votes.)[8] Unfairly excluding half a million people from the right to vote helped the Communists more than these blue tags, but the impudence of this scheme made a most unfavorable impression. On the day of the election and afterward complaints poured in and not only from right-wing parties. Socialist and NPP leaders also reported that their supporters had been excluded from the election rolls and that Communist activists had intimidated their followers.[9]

In spite of the high-handed and arbitrary Communist behavior, in spite of intimidation, in spite of cheating, in spite of denying hundreds of thousands of people the opportunity to vote, the results of the elections did not show great success for the Communists in winning over the people since the previous elections or a general move to the left by the population. Votes for the Socialist Parties (MKP, SDP, NPP) grew only 4 percent (from 41 percent to 45 percent). The Communists did manage to increase their vote by approximately 300,000, from 17 percent to 22 percent, and emerge as the largest party in the parliament. As was expected, the MKP did well in Budapest and in other industrial centers, and it did succeed in attracting a substantial segment of working-class support. Just as in 1945, men were much more likely to vote for the Communists than women.

7 PIL 274 17/2 July 1947.

8 Hubai, in Feitl, Izsák and Székely, 2000, p. 100.

9 PIL 284 8/2 September 8, 1947, report from Csoma. The NPP local secretary was so dismayed by Communist behavior that he announced his retirement from politics.

30. Meeting before 1947 elections. (Source: Hungarian National Museum.)

In spite of their mediocre performance, the Communists achieved their immediate goal. Their party became by far the largest within the leftist bloc, because the SDP performed poorly, by getting somewhat less than 15 percent of the votes. More important, the FKGP, which had dominated parliamentary life from the November 1945 elections to the first half of 1947, fell apart losing almost 2 million votes. A majority of these votes went to one or another of the new political groups, most significant among them being the Democratic People's Party, which with 16.5 percent of the vote became the second-largest party in the country. The Hungarian Independence Party also got 13.5 percent of the vote.[10]

After the elections, Rákosi expressed surprise that in spite of their difficulties the "reactionary" parties performed as well as they actually did. He went on saying with remarkable honesty and cynicism:

> I heard: we must have three things in mind: let the elections be clean, let them take place in good order and let them bring communist victory. And I say: the order is incorrect. A clean election is one in which the communists perform well, because that helps democracy.[11]

10 S. Balogh, 1975, pp. 525–532.

11 PIL 274 2/42 September 11, 1947, Rákosi.

Indeed, compared to the free elections of 1945, these elections were a great step backward. On the other hand, this was the last occasion when a variety of political positions could be articulated, and people were able to express their political preferences. The elections that were held two years later were in the Soviet style: the voters had no choices.

Extralegal steps against the newly formed opposition parties followed the elections almost immediately. The brutality and open violation of legality, which marked these new developments in Hungary, were characteristic of the major changes occurring throughout the Communist Bloc in the fall of 1947. On September 21 in Szklarska Poreba in Poland, the Communist Parties of Eastern Europe (and the French and Italian Communist Parties) established the Communist Information Bureau (Cominform).[12] Andrei Zhdanov and Georgii Malenkov, representing the newly formulated Stalinist policy, made it clear to the assembled leaders that in the changed circumstances the Soviet Union no longer supported the policy of "popular fronts."[13] Europe was now divided into two hostile camps, and within the "Socialist camp" a dreadful uniformity was imposed. The two Hungarian delegates at the meeting, Révai and Farkas, returned from the gathering with the clear understanding that they no longer had to be concerned about the Western response. The Communists now could proceed in building a Soviet-style, one-party system: the days of coalition politics had ended.

Because Communist ascendancy had been gradual, few people in the country appreciated that the establishment of the Cominform implied a major change in Soviet policy. Even before the elections, Hungary had not been a democracy where matters were decided by the correlation of parliamentary forces. Communist and Soviet collusion in the destruction of the FKGP in the spring of 1947 was so obvious that the extralegal steps against the anti-Communist forces after the elections were hardly surprising. None of the newly formed parties participated in political life for long. The first victim of the Communists' merciless attacks was the Hungarian Independence Party. In his speech to the Central Committee of the party on September 11, Rákosi promised that the fight against that party would not be limited to a parliamentary struggle but would aim at the removal of the party from political life altogether.[14] The Communists trumped up charges against the party, claiming that the necessary signatures for its participation in

12 The meeting was secret, and its decisions were revealed after it was finished. Even then the pretence was made that the gathering took place near Warsaw, when in fact it had taken place in Silesia. Adam Ulam, *Stalin: The Man and His Era*, Boston: Beacon Press, 1989, p. 660.

13 On the establishment of the Cominform, see Charles Gati, pp. 108–123.

14 M. Rákosi, *Visszaemlékezések, 1940–1956*, vol. 1, p. 433.

the elections had been forged. The president of the court charged with overseeing the elections was the Communist Ákos Major. Rákosi instructed him to make sure that the party would be disqualified as a result of the charges. Pfeiffer attempted in vain to defend his party. When he was threatened with the lifting of his parliamentary immunity and therefore arrest, he fled the country, and the Communist minister of the interior, László Rajk, dissolved the party on November 20, 1947.

The other parties did not fare much better. They continued a shadowy existence for a while, but because they did not possess a network of national organizations, their political role was limited to parliamentary speeches.[15] For a very short time, critical speeches could still be heard in the parliament. The coalition of the four parties remained in existence, but after the formation of the new government, the coalition was a mere pretense. In the newly formed government, the Communists, in recognition of their increased popular support, received five portfolios, but Lajos Dinnyés, a Smallholder party politician, remained premier. At this point, the actual composition of the government did not matter much. All the important ministries were in the hands of the Communist Party members or crypto-Communists.

NATIONALIZATIONS AND THE THREE-YEAR PLAN

In early 1945, the political struggle among the various political groupings was already bitter, but the conflicting economic programs of the parties did not cause this bitterness. As long as the task was economic reconstruction, there was considerable unity among the parties. Immediately at the end of the war, following Stalin's instructions, the Communist plans were hardly radical. It was obvious that the immediate task had to be reconstruction. In May 1945, József Révai said at a party conference: "It is very important to understand that we must work together not only with the working classes, the peasantry and intelligentsia, but also with the entrepreneurs and with a segment of the bourgeoisie."[16] Of course, the Communists wanted to build a Soviet-type Socialist economy and society in the long run, but as a matter of practical politics they envisaged an indefinite period of transition. Would it last for a couple of years or for decades? It needs to be repeated that the Soviet leadership, and therefore the Hungarian Communists, clearly expected a longer transition period than actually came to be.

15 Lajos Izsák, *Polgári pártok és programjaik Magyarországon, 1944–1956*, Pécs: Baranya Megyei Könyvtár, 1994, p. 125.
16 Iván Pető and Sándor Szakács, p. 68.

It was not conflicting economic doctrines that were the source of disagreements but concrete issues as they emerged. The first of these was the character of land reform. The second was the nature of long-term economic relations with the Soviet Union. The third was the role and power of the Economic Council in which the Communists came to play the dominant role. The fourth issue was the nature and speed of nationalization.

Even in pre-1945 Hungary, the state possessed a significant proportion of the national wealth. The railroads, postal service, and utilities had all been state enterprises. Military contracts during wartime, naturally, further increased the role of the state in the economy. In the course of land reform, the state took possession of previously privately held forests, lakes, and experimental agricultural stations. The coal mines were nationalized in the winter of 1945–1946 as a consequence of a national emergency. Although the Communists were usually the first to suggest nationalization, the other parties of the coalition did not protest. Just as in the case of land reform, the previous owners were promised compensation; in reality, however, as a result of the inflation and the changing political situation, they ultimately received nothing.

Because the largest industrial enterprises mostly worked to satisfy reparation demands, the government itself was the primary customer. This necessarily large state involvement meant that at the end of 1946, when large-scale nationalization began, the changes were at first not perceived as radical. Even before nationalization, the power of management had already been circumscribed by state intervention and by the institution of Communist-dominated factory committees. The largest nationalized enterprises came under the authority of the Chief Economic Council, which was directed by Zoltán Vas. The Communists on the basis of their Marxist convictions assumed that under government ownership the large factories and mines would function more efficiently then before. Their faith in the economic rationality of central planning turned out to be misplaced.

At first, nationalization was driven by the dire economic situation, but later political consideration came to play a major role. The Communists believed that confiscating the wealth of the bourgeoisie would undermine the strength of their enemies and at the same time would increase working-class support for their cause. From about the second half of 1946, the Communists demanded the nationalization of a larger and larger share of the economic life of the nation. The nationalization of large mills was first suggested by the NPP in the name of the left-wing bloc in November 1946.[17]

17 *Partközi értekezletek*, November 12, 1946, p. 373.

The NPP leaders reasoned that because private entrepreneurs charged too much for milling, nationalization would serve the interests of the poor peasants, their constituency. The FKGP politicians did not oppose nationalization on principle, but their representatives pointed out that the reconstruction of the mills required a great deal of capital, and the government did not have the resources. They argued that increased nationalization would make it impossible to attract foreign capital even in that segment of the economy that remained in private hands.

As long as the coalition government existed, the directorships of the large, newly nationalized factories were distributed among the parties. If the director were nominated by the FKGP, for example, his deputy would come from the MKP, and vice versa. This was hardly an efficient system, because economic issues often came to be subordinated to political ones. It is fair to say that by and large the Communist Party, more disciplined than the others, had much to gain from accumulating these positions. In any case, they were utterly shameless in taking advantage of the opportunities offered for patronage.

By the end of 1946, the issue of nationalization had become highly politicized. The Communists wanted to step up nationalization, and the FKGP was increasingly reluctant to go along. A particularly contentious issue was the nationalization of the banks. In reality, that too was a gradual process because from the outset, and certainly after the stabilization of the currency in August 1946, the banks had been under governmental scrutiny, and the rights of ownership were already very much limited. The struggle among the parties became more ideological. Rákosi in another interparty meeting spoke of the "alliance of the banks against democracy."[18]

In May 1947, the Communists wanted to move from the supervision of the largest banks to nationalization. Here they met with strong opposition. Prime Minister Nagy objected, saying that the nationalization of the largest banks implied that the most important factories should also come under governmental supervision because they all operated on the basis of credits. He rightly saw this move as a major restriction on the role of private enterprise, and he believed the nationalized enterprises would gradually come under Soviet supervision, which would mean a further restriction on Hungarian sovereignty.[19] Before embarking on his ill-fated Swiss vacation in May 1947, he made his fellow FKGP leaders promise that in his absence they would not give concessions to the Communists on this issue.[20] The nationalization of the banks came to be the most contentious issue in the entire

18 Ibid., November 15, 1946, p. 396.
19 F. Nagy, pp. 128–129.
20 Ibid., p. 131.

process through which the free enterprise system was ultimately destroyed. The Communists raised the issue in May 1947, at a time when the political crisis was the sharpest. In this matter, even the SDP did not support the Communist position, and the FKGP opposed it with determination.

The nationalization of the banks came about in a gradual process of ever more intrusive supervision. The Communists argued that increased supervision was necessary because the bankers would have liked to remove their capital from the country, and capital flight had to be prevented. The appointed supervisors increasingly came to control the work of the credit institutions. The Communists succeeded in placing their people in positions of control in the most important banks. In the National Bank, for example, the director of the department of convertible currencies was László Hay, a Moscow-trained Communist functionary.[21]

The banks were formally nationalized only at the end of 1947, when the FKGP had already been emasculated. This was not an unpopular move. A contemporary public opinion survey showed that 53 percent of respondents approved the idea of nationalizing the largest banks and only 36 percent opposed.[22]

The nationalization of the largest factories created mixed reactions. A majority of workers at first enthusiastically approved because they naïvely expected an immediate rise in their income. When this did not happen, and when they learned that strikes for higher wages had, in fact, been outlawed, the workers were understandably disappointed. The technical intelligentsia, the engineers, bookkeepers, and so forth, were generally hostile to the idea of nationalization from the outset.[23]

The nationalization of factories in which foreigners had a stake presented a special problem. American and British diplomatic representatives repeatedly protested when the economic interests of their nationals were harmed. At first the government proceeded cautiously. In each instance, it had to have the backing of the Soviet representatives in order to disregard the protests. The complete nationalization of British and American property occurred in 1948 and 1949. At this time, foreign executives in these companies were accused of espionage. The most famous cases were the arrests of the executives of Standard Electric, of Lever and Hutter, and of the Hungarian-American Oil Company (MAORT).[24] Perhaps it is needless to add that the charges were completely without foundation. By the end

21 RTsKhIDNI fond 17, opis 128, delo 315, p. 24.

22 PIL 283 32/31 July 10, 1947. The same survey also showed that 80 percent of the respondents approved of taking away wealth greater than 75,000 forints. Respect for private property in Hungary was not widespread.

23 PIL 274 21/7 and 21/53.

24 L. Borhi, 2000, pp. 49–63.

of 1949, foreign capital was completely excluded from the economic life of the nation. (Not counting, of course, factories that the Soviet Union had taken over in 1945.)

The nationalization of the banks was connected with the chief Communist economic political program, the institution of the three-year plan. Capital for investment in reconstruction could not be assured without complete control over banking. Economic planning by the government was not new. In 1945, the reconstruction ministry under Ferenc Nagy, the future premier, had to operate on the basis of a plan. The great involvement of the government in the economy from the beginning implied a degree of planning. The Communists, on the basis of their Marxist convictions, were the most devoted proponents of economic planning. Indeed, the idea was first introduced in 1945 in the context of the party's economic program. It was the first time that a year-to-year plan was mentioned. At this point, it was only a vague idea concerning how reconstruction could best be accomplished. A year later, however, at the Third Congress of the party in September 1946, the development and then realization of a three-year plan was at the center of the economic program of the party. Rákosi mentioned wistfully that the neighboring countries were already functioning on the basis of planned economies. Hungary could not be left behind in this competition.[25]

In the following months, Socialist and Communist economists together worked out the main outlines of a three-year plan and began negotiations with the FKGP in April. An interparty conference on May 30, 1947, came to an agreement concerning the investment program for the three-year plan.[26] In the development of the project, the Communist participants self-consciously followed the Soviet example. However, at least at this time, Soviet-style economic planning was still considered to be premature. In the middle of 1947, only a segment of the economy was nationalized. Just as with the issue of nationalization, FKGP politicians did not object to economic planning in principle. They, believed, however, that the plan could be realized only if the country received substantial foreign (i.e., Western) loans. To accept or not to accept Western help came to be a contentious issue. The Communists, and behind them the Soviet representatives, vociferously objected. The Smallholder economists did not believe that the country would be capable of producing the 6.5 billion forints of investment capital that was a fundamental condition for the success of the three-year plan.

25 M. Rákosi, *Visszaemlékezések, 1940–1956*, vol. 1, p. 320.
26 *Pártközi értekezletek*, pp. 507–516.

The plan came into effect on August 1, 1947. At this point, it was not much more than a set of decisions concerning investment priorities in various segments of the economy. However, the introduction of the plan necessitated the creation of a new bureaucratic institution, the National Planning Office, naturally under Communist leadership. The planners still thought in terms of reconstruction rather than a thorough "Socialist" reorganization of the economy, and therefore plans were relatively modest. It was not yet a Soviet-type of plan setting output goals for each segment of the economy, breaking down goals to economic sectors, and ultimately to the individual factory level. Nor did the plan foresee the destruction of the institution of private property. The goal was only to achieve the prewar level of production in industry and agriculture by the middle of 1950. Although the economists envisaged a slight increase in the standard of living of the working class as compared to 1938, they still placed stress on heavy industry as opposed to the production of consumer goods. The plan called for 11 percent investment of the national income, which at the time seemed ambitious.[27] (By contrast, in the 1950s, investment reached 22 percent, which, of course, was possible only with a significant depression of the standard of living.) Capital for the investment was to be created by heavy taxation of the well-to-do.

By the spring of 1947 Hungary was in the midst of extremely rapid domestic and international political change. Soviet leaders no longer advised moderation, and the domestic non-Communist political forces had, already for all practical purposes, been destroyed. When the Communist economists were developing their plan, there was no mention yet of the destruction of the economy based on private property. However, in the following months, it increasingly came to resemble a Soviet-style economic plan.

The creation of a Soviet-style economy, that is, the nationalization of industry and commerce, took place only when the Communist Party had succeeded in destroying all political opposition. The first step was to take over factories that had employed more than a hundred workers, and then, a little later, the entire industry. In the fundamentally transformed political situation, the road was open for the Communist leadership to move "to the building of Socialism," much ahead of the previously envisaged schedule. These leaders did everything within their power to "catch up" with Bulgaria, Romania, Poland, and Yugoslavia in the establishment of the Soviet type of state. In the economic sphere that meant large-scale nationalizations and rethinking the nature of the three-year plan, only recently introduced. As a consequence, following the nationalization of banks at the end of 1947,

27 Vas, vol. 2, pp. 231–232.

58 percent of the workers in industry suddenly worked in state-owned enterprises.[28]

From the beginning of 1948, the control of economic and political life was entirely in Communist hands. The Communists no longer had to take into consideration the inconvenient objections of their political opponents. As Gerő, the man primarily responsible for the economic policies of his party, put it in March 1948: "It would be an error to stick to our original plans and not to take advantage of the favorable opportunities."[29] The first step that took place entirely as a result of Communist planning was the nationalization of all enterprises that employed more than a hundred workers. Although previous nationalizations had been preceded by long discussions, now the moves came as a surprise. There was no longer any need for mass mobilization and demonstrations in favor of Communist plans. In the course of 1948 following in the wake of mines, banks, and the largest chemical and heavy industrial enterprises, most light industry also became state property. In the new economic context, even smaller enterprises found it difficult to function, and many of them were forced to close down. In 1949, nationalization was extended to all factories that employed more than ten workers. Within a short time, private enterprise of any kind, including retail stores and even handicraft businesses, found it impossible to function and closed their doors.

THE FOUNDING OF THE HUNGARIAN WORKERS' PARTY

The last act in the destruction of political organizations possessing a modicum of autonomy was the "unification" of the two Marxist parties, that is, the incorporation of the left wing of the Socialist Party into the MKP. With the disappearance of the SDP, the *Gleichschaltung** of Hungarian political life was fully accomplished.

The Communists' worldview impelled them to recognize no middle way, because they "knew" that they and they alone were in possession of the truth. One could not be half right. As they saw it, the world was divided between "us" and "them," and therefore they could not have genuine friends. "Whoever is not with us is against us" was their implicit understanding. It is inherent in this ideology to aim for complete control. Rákosi and his fellow

* *Gleichschaltung* is a German word, sometimes translated as synchronization, meaning putting things in the same gear. The Nazis used this term to express their commitment to bringing all aspects of German life under the party's authority.

28 Pető and Szakács, p. 95.

29 Ibid., p. 97.

leaders had particular venom against the Social Democrats. From their point of view failing to follow the correct Marxist revolutionary strategy was worse than repudiating Socialism altogether. The experience of 1919, when a Communist-Socialist coalition government under Béla Kun existed for 133 days, contributed to a mutual hostility: the two participating parties blamed each other for the failure. The "lesson" learned by the Hungarian Communists, and all the other Leninist parties as well, was that cooperation with "traitors" was bound to lead to defeat.[30] Also, Communists and Socialists competed for the same constituency, the working classes. In addition, the Communists aimed to gain support at the expense of the Socialists within the trade unions.

Although one can speak of a uniformly hostile Communist attitude, it is not possible to speak of a united Socialist response, because the Socialist movement had never been homogeneous. There were Socialists who distrusted the Communists from the outset, but there were others for whom the Communists were brothers in the common struggle. The memory of 1919 contributed greatly to internal struggle within the SDP. The fact that Károly Peyer had opposed the establishment of the Soviet republic in 1919 was held against him even by those who in the postwar situation might have been his allies, such as Vilmos Böhm, a moderate leader, but one who had played a major role in the short-lived Soviet republic.[31]

In 1935, under the threat of a resurgent Germany, the international Communist movement had changed tactics and called for a policy of antifascist "popular fronts," which, of course, included the Socialists. It was the policy of these fronts that was revived in the Soviet-occupied Eastern European countries in 1945. For the Communists, of course, the "national front" policy was always tactical and not for a moment implied genuine trust and recognition of the legitimacy of the programs and goals of the other Marxist party. The picture that emerges from internal, Hungarian, Communist correspondence is bitter hostility and on occasion contempt for their Socialist allies. The Communists drew little or no distinction between Károly Peyer, a right-wing anti-Communist statesman of long standing, on the one hand, and Árpád Szakasits, a left-wing SDP leader in the postwar era who very much wanted to cooperate with the Communists.[32]

30 On the "lessons" of 1919, see Peter Kenez, "Coalition Politics in the Hungarian Soviet Republic," in Andrew C. Janos and William B. Slottman (eds.), *Revolution in Perspective: Essays on the Hungarian Soviet Republic*, Berkeley: University of California Press, 1971, pp. 61–84.

31 *Vilmos Böhm Válogatott politikai levelei: 1914–1949*, Éva Szabó and László Szücs (eds.), Budapest: Napvilág, 1997. In his letters Böhm writes about Peyer with extraordinary bitterness.

32 *Moszkvának jelentjük*, p. 260. When Márton Horváth, the editor of the Communist daily, held discussions in Moscow in April 1948, he characterized the left-wing Socialist leaders. He described Szakasits as corrupt, vain, inconsistent, and weak. Marosán, whom he described most favorably,

It is not surprising that in the postwar years there was a movement away from the SDP toward the MKP. Those who wanted to switch allegiance did not necessarily do so for opportunistic reasons. Radicals who in the interwar period could not or did not want to join an illegal party now naturally gravitated to the Communists. Often the Communist leaders discouraged these people, explaining to them that they could provide more help by staying in their party and moving it in the right direction.[33] Sándor Rónai, for example, a leader of the SDP, expressed his desire to join the MKP in January 1945. The Communists persuaded him to stay with the socialists. In his capacity as a Socialist leader, he performed valuable services for the Communists. In the name of the SDP, he signed an agreement that created a committee for the purpose of reconciling Communist and Socialist policies. It was agreed that in cases of unresolved issues, the decision of the leadership of the MKP would be decisive. That such an agreement was possible in spite of the fact that the MKP was miniscule compared to the SDP at the time demonstrates the overwhelming power of the Communists even at this early date.

As time went on, Communist policy became bolder and more aggressive, and their denunciations of the Socialists became ever stronger. Communists in the countryside regarded the Socialists with hostility. They often reported that the SDP was in the hands of the reactionaries, and at times they described their relations with the Smallholders as better than with the Socialists.[34]

Although the Socialists gradually forced right-wing and centrist figures out of their party's leadership, nevertheless Communist attacks on them did not abate but became ever stronger. Rákosi repeatedly complained to his Soviet superiors about the Socialists; in fact, he spent more time denouncing them than the "reactionaries." In his reports to Moscow, Rákosi maintained that even left-wing leaders of the SDP were supported by the British. Although it was true that some of the SDP leaders looked to the Labour Party for support, there was no evidence whatever that in fact such support was forthcoming. Rákosi ridiculed Szakasits, the man who did more than anyone to move the SDP to the left. There seemed to be something deeply personal in Rákosi's hatred of the Socialists and in his desire to destroy the SDP.[35]

he considered ideologically weak. Rónai, who was a crypto-Communist, he described as corrupt. He described Ries as a possible traitor "who often travels abroad" and also corrupt. He considered Zoltán Horváth, the editor of *Népszava,* insincere. These were the leaders who supported fusion of the two parties.

33 *Moszkvának jelentjük,* Farkas to Rákosi, January 7, 1945, pp. 39–41.

34 PIL 274 21/21, Zalántai from Kalocsa reporting on a meeting of agitators December 12, 1947. Also 274 21/26, Farkas from Kétegyháza, November 1947.

35 In his memoirs, *Visszaemlékezések,* written some twenty years later, Rákosi's hostility to the SDP remained unabated.

In a report that he wrote in 1947 he complained, once again completely without foundation, that when the FKGP was falling apart, many of the "bourgeois" elements found a political home in the SDP.[36] In reality, as the results of the 1947 elections demonstrated, those who had left the FKGP were most likely to join the newly formed centrist or right-wing parties. The Socialists, in fact, were losing support, and many of their party members decided it was time to join the Communists.

There was nothing the Socialists could do. They excluded the old moderate leaders, such as Károly Peyer and Ágoston Valentiny, and on each and every major issue the Socialist representatives supported the Communist position in interparty conferences, but it still was not enough. By the beginning of 1948, it was clear that the Communists would not tolerate any genuinely autonomous organization. The post-1945 SDP was in a constant political crisis. The Socialist leaders were an extremely varied group. Peyer was an anti-Communist who never expected anything good from the MKP. Valentiny also had the gravest reservations concerning collaboration with the Communists after his experience as minister of justice in the first provisional government. Böhm, an outstanding figure with an international reputation, had spent the war years in Swedish exile and wanted to make a common cause with the Communists and to cooperate with them while preserving the independence and autonomy of the SDP. On the other extreme, there were people like Rónai and György Marosán who were Communists in everything but name.

The gap between the left and right wings became increasingly wide. The best-known figures of the prewar party, Károly Peyer, Vilmos Böhm, and Anna Kéthly, were marginalized. Centrists who desired to cooperate with the Communists and who recognized the decisively important role of the Soviet Union in the future of Hungary, nevertheless also wanted to maintain the independence of their party from the Communists. The position of these centrists became increasingly difficult and their task increasingly hopeless. It was a tragic situation: people who had devoted their lives to the struggle for Socialism, people who had been forced into exile by the reactionary Horthy regime, now found themselves under bitter attack within their own party, very soon to be forced into exile once again. (One might add, however, that their opponents within the party had an even more tragic fate. They achieved their goal, the unification of the two Marxist parties, but within a short time almost all found themselves in prison. In this instance, it turned out, it was better to be on the losing side.)

36 RTsKhIDNI fond 17, opis 128, delo 315, May 30, 1947, pp. 6–11. For Rajk's report, see pp. 18–19.

What was considered to be left, center, and right in the party constantly changed. As the right wing was pushed out of party positions, leaders who had originally considered themselves to be centrists became representatives of the right wing, and some left-wing leaders now were considered to be centrists.[37] Antal Bán, just to mention one example, was a leader of the left in 1945, was considered a centrist in 1946, and in February 1948 was excluded from the party as a right-wing leader. The right wing in December 1946 attempted to make a comeback and sent a memorandum to the leadership in which it criticized its pro-Communist policies. This attempt failed because at the Thirty-Fifth Congress of the party, which was held in January 1947, the left wing was in full control. Nevertheless, for a brief time an open break was avoided. The events of the spring of 1947, that is, the case of the "Hungarian Community" and the removal of Ferenc Nagy, persuaded the right wing of the SDP to leave the SDP altogether. Peyer established a new party that participated in the elections of August 1947.

The Communists contributed to the crisis within the SDP by supporting the left wing and attacking the right and center. They constantly agitated among the working classes against the Socialists and attempted to persuade workers to switch parties. In this effort, they were increasingly successful. The Socialist leadership protested in vain. The Communists repeatedly promised to stop their anti-Socialist agitation, but they never kept their promise. They were, however, not primarily responsible for the lack of unity among the Socialists. Just as in the FKGP and in the NPP, there were genuine disagreements in the SDP concerning what policy to follow in the new circumstances. The relatively poor performance of the party in the August 1947 elections contributed to a sense of crisis within the party. Both the left and the right wing of the party recognized that tens of thousands of voters did not choose the SDP because the Communists had already indicated their desire to fuse with the SDP, and under the circumstances non-Communist sympathizers chose "bourgeois" opposition parties rather than the SDP.[38] However, the decisive reason for the disappearance of the SDP was not internal problems but Soviet and Communist pressure. Once the Soviet decision was made and communicated to the Eastern European Communist leaders at the founding meeting of the Cominform that no "third road" would be tolerated within the zone of Soviet domination, the fate of the SDP was sealed. At this time, the Romanian Socialist Party had

37 The most detailed description of the struggle within the SDP is to be found in Róbert Gábor, *Az Igazi Szociáldemokrácia*, op. cit.

38 The crisis within the SDP is discussed in a letter of Vilmos Böhm to the party leadership, September 26, 1947, *Vilmos Böhm*, pp. 381–389.

already been destroyed, but the Czech and Polish parties still managed to hold onto an independent existence. At the end of 1947, the real choice for the SDP leaders was to dissolve the party or to accept incorporation into the MKP. Under the existing political circumstances, a genuine Socialist Party could not possibly function.

From the Communist point of view, a self-dissolution would have been something of an embarrassment, although by no means a major political setback. A Communist tactic was to attempt to persuade the Socialists that once they had removed their "right-wing" leaders – and the definition of "right wing" always changed – they could preserve their independent existence in close cooperation with the MKP. The Communists were already discussing the process of unification at a time when the Socialist leadership, including the left-wing party secretary, Szakasits, was still hoping to avoid it.[39]

The Communists took an active role in the destruction of the SDP by supporting left-wing Socialists and organizing Communist sympathizers within the trade unions.[40] Their propaganda attacked Western Socialist Parties, in particular the Labour Party government in England, in order to connect the right wing of the Hungarian SDP with the Western "imperialists." After the division of Europe into two hostile camps, symbolized by the establishment of the Cominform, association with the "imperialists" was ominous for Hungarian politicians. Within the SDP leadership, an eight-member committee came into being that took on itself the organization of the left wing and preparation for the unification with the MKP. The leader of the committee was György Marosán, who persuaded the right-wing and centrist leaders of the SDP to resign in February 1948 while Szakasits was in Moscow. The penultimate, Thirty-Sixth Congress of the party opened on March 5, 1948.[41] The congress unanimously accepted the proposition that the leadership without delay should begin negotiations with the MKP for the purpose of unifying the two parties.[42]

Probably the initiative for the "unification," that is, destruction of the SDP, came from the Hungarian Communists, in particular from Rákosi, rather than from Moscow. In any case, during a visit to Moscow in February 1948, Szakasits got the impression from Stalin that he considered the coexistence of the two workers' parties desirable for the time being.[43]

39 Gábor, pp. 264–265.
40 Erzsébet Strassenreiter, "Egyesülés? Beolvadás? Likvidálás?" in Feitl, Izsák and Székely (eds.), p. 253.
41 György Marosán, *Az uton végig kell menni*, Budapest: Magvető, 1980, pp. 251–255.
42 Gábor, pp. 275–276.
43 Márton Horváth's discussions in Moscow, April 19, 1948, *Moszkvának jelentjük*, p. 259.

31. Unifying congress of the two workers' parties. In front, Mátyás Rákosi and Mihály Farkas, Budapest, June 12, 1948. (Source: Hungarian National Museum.)

The new party's name was decided in Moscow. Rákosi on March 22 requested advice from the Central Committee of the Soviet Party and suggested "Hungarian Worker-Peasant Party." Gerő suggested "Socialist Party," arguing that this was the name of the unified parties in 1919. The Soviets rejected Gerő's idea and also objected to including "Peasant" in the name of the party, for such a choice in their opinion would not demonstrate the hegemony of the proletariat. They proposed instead "Hungarian Workers' Party." At a meeting of the unifying committee on April 22, MDP (Hungarian Workers' Party) was accepted. Révai added: "Maybe later, in brackets we can add 'Communist.'"[44]

The next task was to set up committees to prepare the unification. A committee had existed from the time of the end of the war that had the task of reconciling programs and discussing problems that might arise between the two parties. Now committees were set up that had the responsibility of removing those SDP members who were not considered suitable for membership in the new Communist Party. These selections took place not only in the localities but also among the members of the

44 *Moszkvának jelentjük*, pp. 255–256.

Socialist youth and women's organizations. Reliable cadres went out of Budapest to the towns and villages to supervise the work of local committees. In the course of this work, thousands of Socialists were excluded. The SDP had about three-quarters of a million members in the middle of 1947. About 100,000 to 150,000 left the SDP for the MKP by the end of that year. The exodus continued during the first half of 1948, when another 240,000 ex-Socialists became Communists. At this time the Socialists were forbidden to admit new members without explicit permission from the unification, committees.[45] Between March and May 1948 22,000–24,000 Socialists were excluded from the SDP by the committees, which were instructed to be firm because "any compromise with the right wing would be a serious political error."[46] Even before the unification, the SDP had lost more than half of its previous members. When unification was completed, out of the 1.25 million members of the MDP about 350,000 were ex-Socialists.

Naturally, the press and the property of the SDP now became the property of the united party.[47] Not only human beings were removed from the lists of Socialists, but also books from the bookshelves written by prominent Socialists. The local committees drew up the list of proscribed books. The authors included the prominent Austrian Socialists Victor Adler and Otto Bauer, and the great names of the Hungarian party, including Böhm, Bán, Kunfi, and Kéthly.[48] One of these committees also found it advisable to refuse republication of a book by Szakasits himself.[49]

On June 12, 1947, the SDP held its thirty-seventh and last congress. At the same time, the MKP held its fourth congress. These were followed the next day by the unification congress, the first congress of the MDP. Szakasits assumed the largely ceremonial role of chairman of the party and Rákosi its secretary.

THE COMMUNISTS AGAINST THE CHURCH

As the political struggle became sharper in 1946, the Communists carried out ever more aggressive attacks against the Catholic Church. Most of these, though not all, had something to do with the desire of the Communists to

45 PIL 274 16/33 March–May 1948

46 PIL 274 16/33 April 7, 1948. A report from Abauj County stated that excluded Socialist leaders went around in the neighborhood showing their letters of exclusion and telling people that when the Americans came they would be able to demonstrate they were against the Communists. The party secretary concluded that excluded members of the Socialist Party should not be notified with a letter.

47 Gábor, p. 278

48 PIL 283 34/6 April 8, 1948.

49 Gábor, p. 281.

deprive the Church of its influence on the youth. A first and very significant step was the dissolution of KALOT and other Catholic youth organizations, such as KALÁSZ, (Katolikus Leanykörök Országos Szövetsége) National Union of Catholic Girl Circles, which was an organization of Catholic village girls. At the same time, the Communist minister of the interior, László Rajk, also dissolved the Boy Scout movement. The Communists from the very beginning had been hostile to the Scouts. Rákosi, in a speech to young Communist activists in June 1945, complained that the Scout movement was under the influence of the Catholic Church and described the founder of the Boy Scouts, Lord Baden Powell, as a "British spy."[50] On the one hand, as mentioned before, the charge that KALOT, the organization of village youth, had cooperated in the past with right-wing radicals was not without foundation. But on the other hand, no Catholic group did as much as this one to bring about some sort of modus vivendi between the Church and the new regime.* The leaders of KALOT, Kerkai and Töhötöm Nagy, deeply disapproved of Mindszenty's uncompromising policy, and feared that the cardinal would attempt to destroy the organization. Nagy, who had good contacts in Rome, once again traveled to Italy and received the support of the Vatican as a defense against Mindszenty.[51] But the compromise for which Nagy was working became ever more remote: Mindszenty had never intended to work with the new authorities, whom he regarded as illegitimate, and the Communists by this time were strong enough to carry out a frontal attack on the Church, which they had always disliked and feared.

The immediate pretext for closing down Catholic youth organizations was the assassination of two Soviet soldiers by a young man, Pénzes István, on July 17,1946.† The Soviet chairman of the ACC, General Sviridov, used the opportunity to move against Catholic youth organizations, but in all probability the initiative came from the Hungarian Communist Party. As it happens, Töhötöm Nagy of KALOT had excellent relations with the Soviet High Command, and therefore it is unlikely that the Russians on their own would have turned against this organization. Töhötöm Nagy had also been working in order to find a compromise between the Church in Rome and the Soviet Union. Nonetheless, the Communists found the Soviet backing needed to persuade their coalition partners to move against church organizations. The government of Ferenc Nagy of the Smallholders' Party simply could not defy the ACC. Although moderate

* See Chapter Eight.

† The Pénzes affair was discussed in chapter 6.

50 PIL 274 18/2 June, 16, 1945.

51 The relations between Mindszenty and KALOT are described by Töhötöm Nagy, pp. 232–247.

politicians pointed out that the destruction of KALOT was likely to backfire because it would demonstrate to Catholic public opinion that Mindszenty had been right all along and compromise with the Communists was impossible, still the Communists were not put off.

The cardinal used the incident to send a most strongly worded letter to the minister of foreign affairs, a Smallholder politician, János Gyöngyösi, protesting the dissolution as an attack on the freedom of religion.[52] He wrote to the foreign minister, because it was he who had the responsibility to maintain ties with the ACC. Mindszenty threatened to turn to world public opinion and enumerate all the indignities that the Church had suffered in the previous year and a half. He also threatened to excommunicate those who had ordered the dissolution of the Catholic organizations as well as those who had carried out the order.[53] Gyöngyösi, in his response, pointed out that Soviet hostility to the Catholic Church started not with the recent assassination but as a consequence of Mindszenty's letter attempting to influence the elections in the previous year and his various political pronouncements more recently. The public, he wrote, perceived these pronouncements as anti-Soviet and antidemocratic.[54] Mindszenty did not let the matter rest but wrote to the premier, Ferenc Nagy, repeating many of his earlier arguments. Remarkably, even at this time he described himself not only as the leader of 5.5 million Catholics but also as the "highest officer of the land" (*Magyarország elsö közjogi méltosága*), implying his lack of recognition of the republic.[55]

Shortly after, the government allowed the re-creation of some Catholic youth organizations. The minister of the interior, Rajk, authorized the formation of KAPSZ (*Katolikus Parasztifjusági Szövetség*, Catholic Peasant Youth Organization), which was to take the place of KALOT but unlike KALOT lacked autonomy. Kerkai and Nagy could not participate in the leadership (though for a while from behind the scenes they continued to play a role), but the leadership was chosen in agreement between László Banass, the bishop most willing to compromise, and the Communist minister of the interior. Mindszenty would have nothing to do with KAPSZ. In order to remove Nagy and Kerkai, he arranged for the Vatican to send Nagy to Latin America, and he sent Kerkai to a distant village. It is fair to say that

52 Mindszenty in his memoirs gave a fanciful description of this incident. He maintained that it was one Russian that shot the other, and the Communists beat to death Pénzes, who had nothing to do with the murder. Mindszenty, pp. 134–135.

53 PIL 274 7/247 Mindszenty to Gyöngyösi, July 22, 1946, pp. 73–77.

54 Ibid., pp. 69–72.

55 Ibid., Mindszenty to Nagy, July 31, 1947, pp. 77–82.

the Communist Party and Mindszenty collaborated in the destruction of KALOT.

Although Mindszenty's pastoral letter in 1945 probably managed to increase the popular vote for the Smallholders, none of his other interventions in the political life of the nation achieved much success. He certainly did not find support in his opposition to the land reform law or in his protest against the nominal abolition of the monarchy.[56] (Nominal, because in fact the monarchy had ceased to exist in 1918.) Even the destruction of the Catholic youth organizations in the summer of 1946 failed to create much popular indignation. It was altogether different in the case of compulsory religious instruction in schools, and later in the matter of the nationalization of church schools. On these issues, the Communists encountered powerful resistance, especially in the villages.

Before the government embarked on the nationalization of church schools, it attempted to limit clerical influence on the youth by first introducing monopoly over the publication of textbooks. Mindszenty, of course, protested.[57] The premier in his response attempted to allay the cardinal's fears by pointing out, mistakenly, that the only textbooks in question concerned natural sciences and therefore could not be considered relevant to religion.

The next source of conflict was the government's attempt to make religious instruction in state schools voluntary. This struggle was a preview of what was to come over the more important issue of nationalizing church schools altogether. Remarkably, at least temporarily, the Church prevailed. The matter was raised not by the Communist Party, but by politicians on the left wing of the Smallholders, in particular, Gyula Ortutay, the new minister of education and culture. A meeting of the representatives of the parties of the coalition in March 1947 agreed on the introduction of the voluntary study of religion and a state monopoly on textbook publishing.[58] There were senior churchmen, such as Banass, bishop of Veszprém, who were inclined to go along and accept the new situation in which the church found itself. However, Mindszenty and the bishops who supported him managed to mobilize Christian public opinion to a surprisingly large extent.

56 Seventy-six percent of the population supported the abolition of the monarchy. *Közvélemény* (Public Opinion), 1947, p. 6.

57 PIL 274 7/247 Mindszenty to Nagy, October 22, 1946.

58 *Moszkvának jelentjük*, p. 204, protocol of Rákosi's conversation with Molotov in Moscow, April 29, 1947. Rákosi said that the Communist Party supported the reform at least partially because it assumed that it would undermine the relationship between the Church and the Smallholder Party.

Mindszenty, once again in the name of the bishops, issued a pastoral letter. In the most uncompromising manner, he denounced the authorities as enemies of religion and good morals. He found it necessary to respond to the argument that in most democratic states the study of religion was voluntary. He wrote:

> Those who oppose compulsory religious education bring up the example of the outside world. We do not regard foreign countries always as an example to follow. We do not regard every intellectual current and point of view as worthy of import. We had and we have opportunities to compare the results of our moral education with that of foreigners, and it is not to our disadvantage.[59]

In the conflict between the democratic West and the Communist Soviet Bloc, the cardinal, of course, passionately sided with the West. But had there been no such conflict, he would have opposed the liberal democracies with just as much determination.

The reformed churches also participated in the struggle to maintain compulsory religious instruction in schools. The churches organized demonstrations and letter-writing campaigns, which were successful even among the industrial workers. The largest demonstration took place in the town of Szeged, where the students, surprisingly, demanded compulsory teaching of religion. Police had to be used to disperse the demonstrators. The Communists were glad it was not they who had raised the issue, but, of course, from the outset they were the most enthusiastic supporters of the reform. Christian opinion blamed them, although they tried to remain in the background and they decided to back down. Sándor Zöld, the party secretary of Szeged and a major figure in the party's leadership, warned his colleagues:

> The demonstration planned by the Church was transformed from a silent to a noisy one. On this issue the shopkeepers and tradesmen sympathize with the Church. Let us not be in the front line in the question of teaching religion in schools.[60]

Although Ortutay, himself a Catholic scholar, had prepared a draft law concerning religious education in schools, the government dropped the issue from further consideration.[61]

By the time the greatest struggle between the ever more dominant Communist Party and the Church took place, the political situation in Hungary had fundamentally changed. The only organized opposition that remained was the Catholic Church, and the courageous, open opposition

59 Mindszenty, p. 174.
60 PIL 274 1/16 April 12–13, 1947, meeting of county and district secretaries.
61 Gergely, 1985, p. 55.

of the cardinal could not be tolerated. Although the Vatican had been anti-Communist and anti-Soviet even before 1945, nevertheless by the conclusion of the war some sort of coexistence with the newly established Eastern European regimes could be envisaged. After all, it was not clear what kind of regimes were to be established there. By 1948, however, Rome was also uninterested in compromise and openly took sides in the ever more bitter cold war. Diplomatic relations between the Hungarian government and the Vatican, broken in 1945, were not reestablished. The struggle between Catholics and Communists was an international one, and the fundamental decisions were made in Rome and Moscow. In the Hungarian case, this struggle was especially bitter because of the character of Cardinal Mindszenty. Power was on the side of the Communists, and therefore at least in the short run it was inevitable that the Church would lose.

In June 1947, Mindszenty traveled to Canada to participate in a world congress honoring the Virgin Mary. On his return he conceived the idea of a "Year of the Virgin" in Hungary with the slogan "Hungary is Virgin Mary's country." There is no reason to doubt Mindszenty's genuine religious inspiration. However, it must have also occurred to him that by organizing mass meetings, prayers, and pilgrimages, the Church would be able to show that it was capable of mobilizing a sizeable part of the population. Indeed in the second half of 1947 and the first half of 1948 in various parts of the country, including the capital, hundreds of thousands of people gathered to pray and to listen to sermons. The cardinal, in his numerous speeches to the faithful, often found it necessary to remind them that Satan was ever present. The political implications of his sermons were clear to all.[62] The Communist authorities certainly perceived these activities as a challenge.

In a speech to party functionaries on January 10, 1948, Rákosi announced that "clerical reaction" must be defeated. He said:

> It is the task of our democracy in the coming year to resolve the issue of the relationship between the Church and the People's Republic. We must not allow this impossible situation to continue in which the majority of the enemies of the people hide behind the cassocks of priests, in particular of the Catholic Church.[63]

The Communists found it increasingly intolerable that the Church was still in a position to spread its message among the youth, a message that was inevitably hostile to their ideology.

62 Mindszenty, pp. 194–201. According to Mindszenty, almost 5 million people, more than half of the population of the country, participated in one form or another in the celebrations.
63 PIL 274 1/22 MKP third national meeting of functionaries, January 10–11, 1948.

In February 1948 the minister of culture, Gyula Ortutay, traveled to Esztergom to negotiate with the cardinal; the discussions proved fruitless, even though the nationalization of Catholic schools was not mentioned. Mindszenty insisted that before the outstanding issues between Church and state could be resolved, the various indignities suffered by the Church in the past had to be remedied. For their part, the Communists, in whose name Ortutay negotiated, required the cardinal to recognize the republic and the existing social-political order before they would be willing to listen to his various complaints.[64] (A minority of the senior leaders of the Church, such as Gyula Czapik, the archbishop of Eger, and László Banass, the bishop of Veszprém, did not approve of Mindszenty's rigid position. To the great irritation of the cardinal, they made their position public.[65])

It is remarkable that the nationalization of schools aroused far stronger popular opposition than land reform, the nationalization of factories and businesses, or even the collectivization of land that would soon take place. The Communists first announced their intention to nationalize schools at the end of April 1948 and presented their reform law on May 15.[66] Because the Catholic Church had demonstrated that it still had the power to mobilize people, the government realized that it had to proceed cautiously. It attempted to lessen resistance by promising the retention of compulsory religious instruction in the nationalized schools, by offering the churches the possibility of retaining some schools and leaving entirely in their hands the training of priests and ministers. (Not surprisingly, the government did not keep its promise: a year later compulsory religious instruction in the schools was abandoned.) The government achieved a great success when it managed to divide the churches. The Protestants were willing to accept the compromise, which they regarded as something inevitable, but the Church led by Mindszenty remained unbending.

Up to this time, the churches had played a decisively important role in public education. As late as 1948, more than half of the students in primary schools attended schools administered by the churches, among which the Catholic Church was by far the most important. (Out of 1.2 million students, 632,000 attended religious schools; out of these, 445,000 attended Catholic schools.[67]) The churches also maintained some of the best mid-level schools, the so-called gymnasia. These were in the hands of religious orders. Given

64 Jenö Gergely, "1948 és az egyházak Magyarországon," in Feitl, Izsák, and Székely (eds.), pp. 143–144.
65 Gergely, 1985, pp. 60–61.
66 Gergely, in Feitl, Izsák, and Székely (eds.), p. 144.
67 Gergely, 1985, p. 63.

the great role of the churches in education, where a sizeable portion of the teaching staff were priests and nuns, the coming reform was a major and difficult undertaking.

Mindszenty again issued a pastoral letter that was read in churches all over the country. He bitterly denounced the government's plan and incited opposition.[68] He promised excommunication to those who would vote for nationalization in the parliament and forbade priests and nuns to continue their teaching work in nationalized schools. Catholic churches became the focal points of protest. The organization of the Alliance of Catholic Parents joined the struggle. There were protest meetings in towns and villages, and the government received thousands of letters opposing the reform plan.

In May 1948, the Central Committee of the Communist Party summarized reports from village agitators in these words:

> In Catholic schools the priests oppose lay teachers. Mindszenty's letter made a great impression. In some places nationalization is regarded as a Hitler-like act. One priest said: "the priesthood will oppose nationalization with full force. Nationalization is done by a party that is in a minority and wants to rule against the wishes of the majority." There are reports that at places people express pleasure that finally someone is opposing the communists. Nationalization of schools is a far more important issue for the people than the unification of the two parties.[69]

Communist agitators from the countryside reported on the mood of the people. Reports of mass demonstrations, which occasionally had to be dissolved by the police using water cannon and firing into the air, came in from everywhere. The opposition in the countryside, where the Church was much more influential than in the cities, was stronger. Usually women were in the forefront of the protest. The agitators wrote that the people were praising Mindszenty, and all sort of rumors were spreading. It was said that Jewish teachers would replace Catholics in schools and that the nationalization of schools would be followed by nationalization of the land. People objected to mixing students of different religions in one school because in their view that would make it impossible to teach religion and morality.[70]

The Communist tactic under these difficult circumstances was to hide behind the politicians of the Smallholders' Party. Ortutay, the minister of culture, who was responsible for the school reform, at least nominally was a member of the Smallholders' Party, even though he had been carrying out policies desired by the Communists. At least for a while, he became the most unpopular politician in the country. Communist agitators were

68 PIL 274 7/268.

69 PIL 274 21/7.

70 PIL 274 16/23, 21/15.

instructed to emphasize that they were not against religion, that the schools would become cheaper and better, and that this was a reform that was long overdue. They were told to emphasize that religion would continue to be taught and were encouraged to call attention to the fact that the Protestant churches, unlike the Catholic ones, were willing to accept the reform.

On June 3, 1948, two weeks before the parliament was to vote on the nationalization of schools, an incident occurred in the village of Pócspetri that would serve the interests of the Communists. A crowd of approximately five hundred people gathered in front of village administrative offices, protesting the nationalization of schools. The police attempted to disperse the demonstrators, and in the ensuing melee a policeman was shot. The exact sequence of events remains controversial to this day. At the time, the authorities arrested twenty-three people. One of them, Miklós Királyfalvy, confessed to the murder. The local priest, János Asztalos, was also arrested and charged with incitement to murder. Asztalos and Királyfalvy were both sentenced to death, but Asztalos's sentence was reduced to life imprisonment.[71] Mindszenty in his memoirs maintained that the policeman accidentally shot himself.[72]

The affair turned into a cause célèbre. József Révai wrote the lead article in the party's newspaper. Communist agitators everywhere used the Pócspetri affair as an example of the danger of "clerical reaction" and used the opportunity to take coercive measures against priests or against anyone who resisted. It is unlikely, but possible, that the Pócspetri affair was a preplanned provocation, but the Communists took full advantage of the opportunity, just as they had two years before, at the time of the murder of the two Soviet officers. The nationalization of schools was soon completed. The state could manage fairly well in replacing teachers in primary schools, but it was more difficult in the case of the gymnasia. In the 1948–1949 school year, there were 250 open positions for teachers.[73]

By the time the next academic year started, in early fall of 1948, in Hungary, as everywhere in Eastern Europe, a Soviet-style system was firmly established. The last vestiges of pluralism had disappeared. By the time the cardinal was arrested in December of that year and subjected to one of the first show trials in Eastern Europe on the basis of entirely trumped up charges, the Hungarians lived in a totalitarian society.

Mindszenty stayed in prison until the revolution of 1956 liberated him. After the failure of that revolution he took refuge at the American embassy.

71 *Szabad Nép.*, June 6, 1948, p. 1.
72 Mindszenty, pp. 205–206.
73 Gergely, p. 71.

His name became a symbol of resistance to Communist tyranny in Hungary and beyond. His legacy, however, remains ambiguous. On the one hand, he demonstrated courage and determination. But on the other, it is obvious that he was opposing the Communists not in the name of a modern, democratic, and liberal society, but in defense of an anachronistic, semifeudal system. At a time when the partisans of the old order had been discredited and marginalized in politics, it was Mindszenty alone who could speak up in the name of a powerful organization, the Catholic Church, for the old order and for legitimacy. For the future of a democratic Hungary, it would have been beneficial if the opposition to Communist rule had come from a united, democratic front. Mindszenty was not part of a united opposition. He was a divisive figure, and his memory remains a divisive force even in our days.

What conclusions could one draw from this examination of the relationship between the Catholic Church and the Hungarian Communist Party in the immediate postwar period? First of all, it is evident that among the many opponents of the Sovietization of the country, the Catholic Church was the strongest. The Church possessed a network of village priests that was able to mobilize the believers at a moment's notice. Unlike the anti-Communist politicians, the leaders of the Church, above all the cardinal, never hesitated to engage in ideological combat with the hated Communists.

Second, the Communists were well aware of the power of the Church and at least in the early period made every attempt to ameliorate conflict. They tried to convince Hungarians that they had nothing against religion and only wanted to combat reactionary church leaders. This task was made easier by the behavior of Mindszenty, who did not hesitate to undertake political tasks even at the earliest period. He could easily be depicted as a reactionary, as a legitimist, as a partisan of feudal, prewar Hungary.

Third, this story demonstrates the gradual process by which the Communists took complete power. The year 1945 was very different from 1946, and 1947 very different from 1948. Church-party relations, of course, cannot be taken out of the larger domestic and international context. In 1945, both the papacy and the Moscow leadership exhibited some desire to find a modus vivendi, but this possibility gradually disappeared.

Fourth, there is no evidence that Soviet leaders interfered in the development of the Hungarian Communist Party's policy toward the Church. If anything, the Soviet authorities in Hungary were more willing to compromise. Töhötöm Nagy, the Jesuit priest who sought collaboration with the new authorities, had better relations with the Soviet command in Hungary than he had with the Communist leaders. On the other hand, when the

Communists decided to attack the Church, they quite unfairly used the murder of a Soviet officer as an excuse, and the Soviet authorities did not interfere. Only in retrospect, after full Sovietization, did Moscow criticize the Hungarian Communists for having taken too soft a line in its anticlerical struggle.

Fifth, it is evident that although the Hungarian Communists had considerable autonomy in their policies, they willingly operated within a framework that had been established in Moscow. Mutatis mutandis, the outcome of the Church and Communist Party struggle was the same in every Soviet-controlled Eastern European country. Had the papacy and Stalin succeeded in 1945 in reaching some sort of compromise, the history of Hungarian Church and state relations would also have been different.

14

Conclusions

The history of the years between 1920 and 1947 is a divisive subject in current Hungarian political life. Nationalist and conservative politicians regard themselves as the legitimate heirs of the nation's pre–Second World War history and aim to present the Communist era as an exception, an aberration. Mutatis mutandis, they accept much from the ideology of the Horthy regime and are partial to a certain exclusivist, almost racialist nationalism. They find much to admire in the nation's pre-1945 history and, consequently, cannot be expected to be enthusiastic about the destruction of the social and political order in 1945. They date the beginning of Soviet oppression immediately at the end of the war, and for them the postwar period is chiefly characterized by the underhanded methods used by Communists in their struggle for power. Liberal and Socialist historians, by contrast, look favorably on the achievements of the social revolution that took place at the end of the Second World War and find inspiration in the avowed aims of democratic and progressive politicians of that time.

A person's view of the past determines his current politics, or, perhaps, vice versa. Political struggles, which are bitter, are often played out in the guise of historical debates. Any discussion of post–Second World War history willingly or unwillingly will bring the historian into a political arena that is hotly contested.

The list of recent genuine and pseudo-historical disputes is endless. For example, a few years ago the most passionately debated issue was whether the crown, "the symbol of Hungarian statehood," should be kept in the National Museum, where it belongs, or in the Parliament. In this instance, the view of the right wing prevailed. The decision to regard the crown as a political symbol rather than a historical relic signalled a return to the rhetoric of the interwar Horthy regime, and warned neighboring countries that this government in some form continued to claim a legitimate interest in those lands that once had come under the crown of St. Stephen.

In 2004, right- and left-wing politicians and intellectuals passionately debated whether it was morally correct to erect a statue honoring Paul Teleki, Hungarian premier between 1939 and 1941. Teleki committed suicide rather than acquiesce to using Hungarian territory and troops in attacking Yugoslavia. On the other hand, the very same, obviously courageous, and, according to his own opinion, moral man, helped to pass anti-Jewish legislation in the Parliament that in some ways was more punitive than contemporary Nazi laws. Further to the right, the extreme right-wing and pathologically anti-Semitic Party of Hungarian Truth and Life (Magyar Igazság és Élet Pártja) a few years ago asked for the rehabilitation of Premier László Bárdossy, the man who took Hungary into the Second World War in 1941.

In 2002, a "Museum of Terror" opened in Budapest. The ostensible purpose of the museum was to commemorate the victims of the Nazi, Soviet, and Hungarian Communist murderers. The museum was the brainchild of the center right-wing (Fidesz) government that was then waging a desperate electoral battle against a resurgent SDP. The opening of the museum occasioned considerable debate, for the immediate political purpose behind its construction was transparent. As critics pointed out, the exhibition was based on the assumption that terror began in Hungary on October 15, 1944, that is, when Szálasi, a German puppet, took control. By implication, the interwar Horthy regime was blameless. In any case, the vast majority of the exhibition is devoted not to Nazi but to Communist terror. As visitors enter the first hall, they are confronted with a map showing the "tragedy of Trianon," the great loss of territory and population that Hungary suffered at the conclusion of the First World War. The implication is that Hungarian history began in 1920, and Hungarians have always been victims, which again recalls the ideology of the Horthy regime. This is a point of view that is congenial to right-wing politicians and thinkers. By creating the museum, the government in power attempted to score points against the opposition. The exhibition calls attention to Communist wrongdoings, and in the view of right-wing politicians, the Socialists are the successors of the Communists and therefore somehow responsible for the previous crimes.

As we saw, the period between the end of the war and the full establishment of a Communist regime was eventful. In a short time, great changes took place. The population became even more homogeneous with the expulsion of the Germans, the voluntary departure of Slovaks, and the return to Hungary of ethnic Hungarians from Slovakia, Romania, Yugoslavia, and the Soviet Union. The government carried out a land reform, which destroyed the antiquated, semifeudal social order forever. The people's courts tried war criminals. The Horthyist administrative structure was dismantled, and new people took jobs in the bureaucracy. The economy revived after great devastation, and then most of it was nationalized. The Communists removed the churches from the business of education. The future seemed open; politicians of different persuasions articulated a variety of political programs. Indeed, a primary characteristic of the time was that different parties stood for different principles, and political parties – other than the Communist Party, which was homogeneous and disciplined – were themselves heterogeneous and constantly evolved as times changed.

Reading about the postwar period, one is impressed by the strength of indigenous democratic forces. It is true that the right wing of the political spectrum was discredited by collaboration with the Nazis and therefore disenfranchised. The majority of the Hungarian people who voted for the most popular party, the Smallholders Party, approved its progressive stance. Zoltán Tildy, Ferenc Nagy, and Béla Kovács, the leaders of the party, were genuine democrats who had no desire to return to the past. Even though they shared with the Hungarian people an almost visceral dislike of Russians and were understandably skeptical of Soviet intentions, they nevertheless recognized the necessity of cooperating with the occupying power for the foreseeable future.

Election results clearly demonstrated the extent of Communist support. In the perfectly honest 1945 elections, the Communist Party received 17 percent of the vote, and in the already compromised, but not meaningless, 1947 elections, the party received 22 percent. It is fair to say that the Communist program never had more support than that of a fifth of the population. The Communists competed, but competed on a playing field that was anything but level. From the outset, they controlled and used the political police to their political advantage. They copied Soviet methods of propaganda and agitation, but they had to act in an environment where the falsity of Communist claims could still be demonstrated. Politicians could openly protest, and newspapers could point out Communist lies and wrongdoings. As time went on, however, the opposition found it increasingly difficult to contradict Communist assertions.

The picture of the top Communist leaders that emerges from this study is not attractive. They were utterly subservient to a foreign power to the extent of being unable even to imagine that the interests of Hungary and that of international Communism might not coincide. They were ruthless and petty, and, when they came to realize that the Hungarian people could not be persuaded to support their cause, they were willing to use increasingly crude and brutal methods to achieve power. A contributing factor in explaining their brutality, though this is by no means a full explanation, was that in their view of politics the victor always destroyed the defeated. In case of a possible Soviet withdrawal, they feared for their own lives.

A decisively important fact was that in Hungary, unlike anywhere else in Eastern Europe, the top leadership was entirely Jewish. The four people who made up the top of the hierarchy were all Jews; all of them had spent the war years in Moscow, and very likely their stay in the Soviet capital had deformed them as human beings. From the point of view of the Hungarians, this fact made the top leadership doubly alien: they were the agents of Moscow, and, as far as the majority of Hungarians were concerned, they were not Hungarian at all. Of course, the Communists did not consider themselves Jewish, but there was nothing that they could do to prevent others from considering them to be Jewish. The Communists, well aware of the problems of being identified as Jews leading a Jewish party, attempted to play the nationalist card. In this, they were rarely successful. They did everything within their power to cover up their background. The party made great efforts to recruit ex-Nazi party members who had played only minor roles in politics in the past. Consequently, in the localities some of the party secretaries were explicitly anti-Semitic.

It was obvious to everyone, including to the leading Communists, that the success of Communism in Hungary depended on the presence of the Red Army. It was therefore a major and very difficult political task to increase the popularity of the Soviet Union and of Soviet culture in particular. According to all available evidence, such efforts were a resounding failure. Hungarians continued to fear and at the same time look down on Russians. Moviegoers in Hungary, as elsewhere in the world, when they had a choice, preferred American to Russian films. The behavior of the Red Army and of Soviet agents in Hungary did not help the Communists.

Examinination of the relationship between the Hungarian Communist leaders and their superiors in Moscow reveals an interesting and ambiguous story. That the major lines of policy and the most important personnel decisions were made in Moscow is not open to doubt. But it is also evident that the Russians neither could nor wanted to decide everything. We find not so much that the Russians were telling the Hungarians what to do in each instance, but on the contrary, the Communist leaders were begging their Russian comrades for guidance. Whether the Hungarian Communist policy was more aggressive than policy made in Moscow depended on circumstances, which varied. It is fair to say that the Hungarian Communist leadership simply could not envisage circumstances in which Soviet and Hungarian interests would not coincide. In this sense. they were always happy and willing to serve. From the documentary evidence, it appears that the Communist leaders frequently gave reports to their superiors and hoped that the policy implicit in the reports won the approval of the higher authorities. There is little evidence in the archives that the Russians simply gave instructions. The local Communists usually had to divine Soviet intentions. This did not mean there were no disagreements between Soviet agents in Hungary and the Hungarians. Rákosi and his comrades on occasion tried to find help in Moscow against the Czechoslovak and Romanian Communists and hoped that some border adjustments would be possible. They also asked for help in alleviating the cruel fate of the Hungarian minorities in Romania and Czechoslovakia. But such help was not forthcoming. The Hungarian Communists sometimes rightly felt that they understood circumstances better and that Soviet "advice" was harmful for their common cause. Nevertheless, the Soviet recommendations usually prevailed.

The Soviet Union sent writers, scientists, and musicians to win friends for Soviet culture. In this effort, the propagandists obviously failed. Moscow also sent representatives to almost all institutions. Most important of these were the "advisers" to help the work of the political police. On the basis of the available documents, it is difficult to establish the exact role of Soviet advisers during the first years of the political police, but we may assume it was substantial. After all, the Soviet representatives possessed considerable experience in these matters. The success of the cooperation very much depended on the sensitivity and intelligence of the Soviet representative. Some were brutally demanding, even obliquely threatening.

One can easily chart the evolution of Soviet foreign policy in the postwar years. In 1944, Stalin instructed the Hungarian Communists to be moderate and patient and pose as defenders of private property. At the outset, Soviet authorities helped in the establishment of non-Communist parties and were active agents in creating a meaningful coalition of genuine political forces in Hungary. Their main interest at this point seemed to be the exploitation of Hungarian resources. They simply wanted to take as much as possible as quickly as possible. Gradually, Soviet intervention in Hungarian political life became more blatant. By 1947 with the utterly lawless arrest of Béla Kovács on trumped up charges, they demonstrated that they were the real masters in the occupied country. The final decision to create a group of satellites including Hungary came in September 1947 when at Szklarska Poreba Stalin's representatives, Andrei Zhdanov and Georgii Malenkov, informed the assembled Eastern European Communist leaders that there could be no middle way between the two hostile blocs. This declaration instructed the Hungarian Communists that the time had come to take power.

The years that followed the establishment of full Communist control in 1948 until Stalin's death in March 1953 were the gloomiest in the second half of the century. This was a time of poverty, privation, and terror. The Communist leadership followed the Soviet example: fast-paced industrialization called for high investment, which came at the expense of consumption and a depressed standard of living. The investment decisions made little economic sense. For example, Hungary was to be a country of steel and iron and even a new town, Stalinváros, was built, devoted to heavy industry; however, Hungary lacked the raw material: the country had no iron ore. Beginning in 1949, everything down to the corner barbershop and shoe repair shop was nationalized. The overcentralized economy turned out to be woefully inefficient. The population paid a high price for the irrational, ideology-driven economic policies of the regime. After 1949, the real wages of the workers actually fell from an already abysmally low level.

The situation in the countryside was particularly depressing. Just as in the Soviet Union in the early 1930s, the process of collectivization was accompanied by a brutal attack on the *kulaks*, that is, the most efficient peasants. Quoting Stalin, the propagandists of the regime spoke of sharpening class struggle in the villages, which in concrete terms meant persecuting well-to-do peasants. A combination of poor leadership on the newly established collective farms, extremely high requisition requirements, and the artificially low prices for agricultural products set by the regime's central planners destroyed initiative. The income of peasant families, low even after the land reform, fell further. Land reform may have erased a landed upper class, but it did not improve the lot of the majority of the peasants.

These were also years of mindless terror. Hungary had the unhappy distinction of having a larger percentage of victims than any of the other satellites. Cardinal Mindszenty, arrested in December 1948, was only the first of the prominent victims. It was not surprising that the regime chose him for this role: he had been a thorn in the side of the Communists from 1945. But those who had smoothed the road to power of Rákosi and his comrades were not treated any better. Zoltán Tildy, the Smallholder president of the republic, who did everything within his power to find a modus vivendi with the Communists, was among the arrested. Almost the entire leadership of the SDP suffered. Those who did not go into exile, such as Anna Kéthly, were arrested and spent years in prison, including Árpád Szakasits, previously president of Hungary, and such staunch pro-Communists as György Marosán. Finally, it was the turn of the Communists. The most prominent victim was László Rajk, the ex–minister of the interior, a person just as responsible for repression as the other leaders. His show trial was the most spectacular case: dozens were arrested, and at least fifteen people were executed. Rajk and his fellow victims were accused among other things of being agents of Tito. Who became victims seemed to be almost random, although those Communists who had spent the war years in Hungary, and who therefore had engaged in active resistance to Nazism, were more likely to suffer; by contrast, having spent the war years in Moscow seemed to provide a degree of protection. János Kádár, the future head of the regime, also spent years in prison.

It was not only prominent people who were affected by terror. Between 1948 and 1953, incredibly, in a country of fewer than 10 million people, approximately 1.3 million came before tribunals, and almost 700,000 were sentenced, ranging from capital punishment to firing from jobs.[1] In addition, thousands of "class alien" people were deported, primarily from Budapest, but also from some other major cities into the countryside, where they were forced to live in extremely difficult material circumstances. Some of these deported had recently returned from Nazi concentration camps. Their apartments and belongings were taken over by a new party elite.

Most of the Hungarians who in 1945 looked to the future with optimism found their hopes gradually destroyed and had to endure years of privation under merciless oppression.

1 Miklós Molnár, *A Concise History of Hungary*, Cambridge: Cambridge UP, 1996, p. 303.

Bibliography

Archives

The most important primary sources come from the archives of the Political History Institute in Budapest: *Politikatörténeti Intézet Levéltára* (PIL). The extensive records of the Communist Party are to be found in fond 274. The documents of the Socialist Party are in fond 283, and the papers of the NPP are in fond 284. In addition, fond 286, which contains records of mass movements, also proved useful. In Budapest, the Hungarian National Archives, *Magyar Országos Levéltár* (MOL), contain documents concerning foreign relations, reparation questions, and the work of the people's courts in the postwar years. Useful Russian documents are to be found in Moscow at the Russian Center for the Preservation and Study of Documents of Modern History (RTsKhIDNI). I also read contemporary newspapers, *Népszava* and *Szabad Nép,* in the parliament's library in Budapest. With the exception of portraits, illustrative photographs come from the Historical Photo Archives of the Hungarian National Museum in Budapest.

Documents in Print

Balogh, Sándor, and Margit Földesi, eds. *A magyar jóvátétel és ami mögötte van: Válogatott dokumentumok, 1945–1949* [*Hungarian reparations and what is behind them: Selected documents*]. Budapest: Napvilág, 1998.

Cseh, Bendeguz Gergő, ed. *Documents of the Meetings of the Allied Control Commission for Hungary, 1945–1947*. Budapest: MTA Jelenkor-kutató Bizottság, 2000.

Csicsery-Rónay, István, and Géza Cserenyey. *Koncepciós per a Független Kisgazdapárt szétzúzására 1947: Tanulmány és válogatott dokumentumok* [*Show trial for the destruction of the Smallholders Party 1947: An essay and selected documents*]. Budapest: 1956–os Intézet, 1998.

Földesi, Margit, ed. "A csehszlovák-magyar jóvátételi egyezmény 1946-ban" ["The Czechoslovak-Hungarian reparation agreement in 1946"]. *Múltunk* 1 (1998): 194–217.

Foreign Relations of the United States (*FRUS*). Washington, DC: U.S. Government, 1945–1948.

Fülöp, Mihály, and Gábor Vincze, eds. *Revízió vagy autonómia? Iratok a magyar-román kapcsolatok történetéről, 1945–1947* [*Revision or autonomy? Documents concerning the history of Hungarian-Romanian relations, 1945–1947*]. Budapest: Teleki László Alapítvány, 1998.

Izsák, Lajos, ed. "A Demokrata Néppárt alapvető dokumentumai, 1946–1947" ["The fundamental documents of the Democratic People's Party, 1946–1947"]. *Múltunk* 1 (1991): 137–166.

Moszkvának jelentjük–: Titkos dokumentumok, 1944–1948 [*We report to Moscow: Secret documents, 1944–1948*]. Budapest: Századvég Kiadó, 1994.

Pártközi értekezletek: 1944–1948 [*Interparty negotiations: 1944–1948*]. Budapest: Napvilág, 2003.

Poth, Piroska, ed. "Rákosi Mátyás előadása Moszkvában 1945 juniusában" ["The lecture of Matyas Rakosi in Moscow in June of 1945"]. *Múltunk* 4 (1999): 199–223.

Rákosi, Sándor, Lajosné Ikladi, and Lajos Gál, eds. *A Madisz, 1944–1948: Dokumentumok az ifjusági mozgalom felszabadulás utáni történetéböl* [*Madisz 1944–1948: Documents from the history of the youth movement after liberation*]. Budapest: Kossuth, 1984.

Standeisky, Éva, ed. "Losonczy Géza levele Révai Jozsefnek 1949, július 14-én" ["Losonczy Géza's letter to Révai Jozsef July 14, 1949"]. *Budapesti Negyed* 2 (1995). Accessed July 22, 2005 <http://www.bparchiv.hu/magyar/kiadvany/bpn/08/losonczy.html>

Svéd, László, ed. *Megforgatott világmegforgatók: A magyar népi kollégimi mozgalom dokumentumai* [*Those who turned the world upside down: Documents of the Hungarian people's college movement*]. Budapest: Politikatörténeti Alapitvány, 1994.

Szabó, Éva, and László Szücs, eds. *Böhm Vilmos válogatott politikai levelei, 1914–1949* [*Selected political letters of Vilmos Böhm, 1914–1949*]. 1. kiad. ed. Budapest: Napvilág, 1997.

Vass, Henrik, ed. "Dokumentumok Rákositól-Rákosiról" ["Documents from Rakosi about Rakosi"]. *Múltunk* 2–3 (1991): 245–288.

Volokitina, T. V., ed. *Sovetskii faktor v Vostochnoi Evrope 1944–1953: Dokumenty* [*The Soviet factor in Eastern Europe, 1944–1953*], 2 vols. Moskva: ROSSPEN, 1999.

Primary and Secondary Sources

Balogh, Margit. *A KALOT és a Katolikus társadalompolitika, 1935–1946* [*KALOT and Catholic social policy, 1935–1946*]. Budapest: MTA Történettudományi Intézete, 1998.

Balogh, Sándor. *Parlamenti és pártharcok Magyarországon, 1945–1947* [*Parliamentary and party struggles in Hungary, 1945–1947*]. Budapest: Kossuth Könyvkiadó, 1975.

Balogh, Sándor. *Magyarország külpolitikája 1945–1950* [*Hungary's foreign policy 1945–1950*]. Budapest: Kossuth Könyvkiadó, 1988.

Balogh, Sándor. *Választások Magyarországon, 1945: A törvényhatósági, fővárosi és nemzetgyülési választások* [*Elections in Hungary 1945: Budapest and National elections*]. Budapest: Kossuth Könyvkiadó, 1984.

Balogh, Sándor. *Magyarország és szomszédai, 1945–1947* [*Hungary and its neighbors 1945–1947*]. Budapest: MTA Történettudományi Intézete, 1995.

Bautz, Friedrich Wilhelm, ed. *Biographisch-Bibliographisches Kirchenlexikon*, vol. 5. Hamm (Westf.): Traugott Bautz, 1993.

Bay, Zoltán. *Az élet erösebb* [*Life is stronger*]. Budapest: Püski, 1990.

Berend, T. Iván. *Ujjáépités és a nagytöke elleni harc Magyarországon, 1945–1948* [*Reconstruction and the struggle against big capital in Hungary, 1945–1948*]. Budapest: Közgazdasági és Jogi Könyvkiadó, 1962.

Berend, T. Iván, and György Ránki. *The Hungarian Economy in the Twentieth Century*. London: Croom Helm, 1985.

Berend, T. Iván, and György Ránki. *Hungary: A Century of Economic Development*. New York: Barnes & Noble, 1974.

Bibó, István. *Demokratikus Magyarország: Válogatás Bibó István tanulmányaiból* [*Democratic Hungary: Selected essays of Istvan Bibó*]. Budapest: Magvető, 1994.

Bibó, István. *Zsidókérdés Magyarországon 1944 után: Néhány kiegészitő megjegyzés a Zsidókérdésröl* [*The Jewish question in Hungary after 1944: Some additional comment on the Jewish question*]. Budapest: Katalizátor Iroda, 1994.

Bischof, Günter, and Stephen E. Ambrose, eds. *Eisenhower and the German POWs: Facts against Falsehood*. Baton Rouge: Louisiana State University Press, 1992.

Borhi, László. *Hungary in the Cold War, 1945–1956*. Budapest, New York: CEU Press, 2004.

Borhi, László. *A vasfüggöny mögött: Magyarország nagyhatalmi erötérében, 1945–1968* [*Behind the iron curtain: Hungary in the foreground of the struggles of the great powers, 1945–1968*]. Budapest: Ister, 2000.

Chuev, Feliks Ivanovich, and Vyacheslav Mikhaylovich Molotov. *Sto sorok besed s Molotovym: Iz dnevnika F. Chueva* [*One hundred and forty conversations with Molotov: From the diaries of F. Chuev*]. Moscow: Terra, 1991.

Connor, Walter D., and Zvi Y. Gitelman. *Public Opinion in European Socialist Systems*. New York: Praeger, 1977.

Cserhalmi, Imre, and Viktória Vagyóczkyné, eds. *Az Ideiglenes Nemzetgyűlés és az Ideiglenes Kormány megalakulása: 1944: December 21–22* [*The Provisional National Assembly and the establishment of the provisonal government, 1944, December 21–22*]. Budapest: Kossuth, 1984.

Demény, Pál. *A Párt foglya voltam: Demény Pál élete* [*I was a prisoner of the party: The life of Pal Demeny*]. Budapest: Medvetánc, 1988.

Dessewffy, Tibor. *Iskola a hegyoldalban* [*School on the mountainside*]. Budapest: Uj Mandátum, 1999.

Dreisziger, N. F., ed. *Hungary in the Age of Total War*. New York: Columbia University Press, 1998.

Farkas, Vladimir. *Nincs mentség* [*There is no excuse*]. Budapest: Interart Studio, (1990).

Feitl, István, ed. *Az ideiglenes nemzetgyülés és az ideiglenes nemzeti kormány, 1944–1945* [*The provisional parliament and the provisional government 1944–1945*]. Budapest: Politikatörténeti Alapitvány, 1995.

Feitl, István, Lajos Izsák, and Gábor Székely, eds. *Fordulat a világban és Magyarországon, 1947–1949* [*Turning Point in the World and in Hungary, 1947–1949*]. Budapest: Napvilág, 2000.

Föglein, Gizella. *Államforma és allamfői jogkör Magyarországon, 1944–1949* [*The constitution and the authority of the head of state in Hungary, 1944–1949*]. Budapest: Osiris, 2001.

Földesi, Margit. *A Szövetséges Ellenőrző Bizottság Magyarországon: Visszaemlékezések, diplomáciai jelentések tükrében, 1945–1947* [*The Allied Control Commission in Hungary in the mirror of memoirs and diplomatic reports, 1945–1947*]. Budapest: Ikva, 1995.

Földesi, Margit. *A megszállók szabadsága* [*The freedom of the occupiers*]. Budapest: Kairosz, 2002.

Gábor, Róbert. *Az igazi szociáldemokrácia: Küzdelem a fasizmus és a kommunizmus ellen, 1944–1948* [*Genuine social democracy: Struggle against fascism and communism, 1944–1948*]. Budapest: Századvég, 1998.

Gati, Charles. *Hungary and the Soviet Bloc.* Durham, NC: Duke University Press, 1986.

Gazdag, Ferenc. *Franciaország története, 1945–1988* [*The history of France, 1945–1988*]. Budapest: Kossuth, 1989.

Gergely, Jenő. *A politikai Katolicizmus Magyarországon: 1890–1950* [*Political Catholicism in Hungary: 1890–1950*]. Budapest: Kossuth, 1977.

Gergely, Jenő. *A Katolikus Egyház Magyarországon, 1944–1971* [*The Catholic Church in Hungary, 1944–1971*] Budapest: Kossuth, 1985.

Gunst, Péter, ed. *A magyar agrártársadalom a jobbágy felszabadulástól napjainkig* [*Hungarian agrarian society from the serf liberation to our days*]. Budapest: Napvilág, 1998.

Gyarmati, György. *Államvédelem a Rákosi korszakban: Tanulmányok és dokumentumok a politikai rendőrség második világháboru utáni tevékenységéröl* [*Defense of the state in the Rákosi era: Essays and documents concerning the work of the political police after the Second World War*]. Budapest: Történeti Hivatal, 2000.

Györi Szabó, Róbert, and György Borsányi. *A Kommunista Párt és a Zsidóság Magyarországon: 1945–1956* [*The Communist Party and the Jewry in Hungary, 1945–1956*]. Budapest: Windsor, 1997.

Gyurgyák, János. *A Zsidókérdés Magyarországon: Politikai eszmetörténet* [*The Jewish question in Hungary: The history of a political ideology*]. Budapest: Osiris, 2001.

Haas, György. *Diktaturák árnyékában: Tildy Zoltán élete* [*In the shadow of dictatorship: The life of Zoltan Tildy*]. Budapest: Magyar Napló, 2000.

Hegedüs, András. *Élet egy eszme árnyékában: Életrajzi interjú* [*A life in the shadow of ideology: An autobiographical interview*]. Vienna: Zsiller Zoltán, 1985.

Hegedüs, András. *A Történelem ás a hatalom igézetében: Életrajzi elemzések* [*Under the spell of history and power: An autobiographical analysis*]. Budapest: Kossuth, 1988.

Hubai, László, and László Tombor, eds. *A magyar parlament 1944–1949: Tanulmányok* [*The Hungarian parliament 1944–1949: Essays*]. Budapest: Gulliver, 1991.

Huszár, Tibor, ed. *István Bibó: Beszélgetések, politikai-életrajzi dokumentumok* [*István Bibó: Conversations, political-biographical documents*]. Budapest: Kolonel Lap és Könyvkiadó, 1989.

Huszár, Tibor. *Kádár János politikai életrajza, 1912–1956* [*The political biography of János Kádár*]. Budapest: Szabad Tér: Kossuth, 2001.

Izsák, Lajos. *Az 1944–1946-os évek alternativái Magyarországon* [*The alternatives of the years 1944–1946 in Hungary*]. Budapest: Korona, 1995.

Izsák, Lajos. *A Keresztény Demokrata Néppárt és a Demokrata Néppárt, 1944–1949* [*The Christian Democratic People's Party and the Democratic People's Party, 1944–1949*]. Budapest: Kossuth, 1985.

Izsák, Lajos. *A koalició évei Magyarországon 1944–1948* [*The years of coalition in Hungary, 1944–1948*]. Budapest: Kozmosz Könyvek, 1986.

Izsák, Lajos. *Polgári pártok és programjaik Magyarországon, 1944–1956* [*Political parties and their programs in Hungary, 1944–1956*]. Pécs: Baranya Megyei Könyvtár, 1994.

Izsák, Lajos, ed. *Vissza a történelemhez* [*Return to history*]. Budapest: Napvilág, 1996.

Janos, Andrew C. *East Central Europe in the Modern World: The Politics of the Borderlands from Pre- to Postcommunism*. Stanford, CA: Stanford University Press, 2000.

Janos, Andrew C. *The Politics of Backwardness in Hungary, 1825–1945*. Princeton, NJ: Princeton University Press, 1982.

Janos, Andrew C., and William B. Slottman, eds. *Revolution in Perspective: Essays on the Hungarian Soviet Republic of 1919*. Berkeley: University of California Press, 1971.

Kádár, Gyula. *A Ludovikától Sopronkőhidáig: Visszaemlékezések* [*From Ludovika to Sopronkohida: Memories*]. Budapest: Magvető, 1978.

Kállai, Gyula. *Két világ határán* [*At the edge of two worlds*]. Budapest: Kossuth, 1984.

Karády, Viktor. *Zsidóság az 1945 utáni Magyarországon* [*Jewry in post-1945 Hungary*]. Párizs: Magyar Füzetek, 1984.

Karády, Viktor. *Zsidóság, polgárosodás, asszimiláció: Tanulmányok* [*Jewry, becoming middle class, assimilation: Essays*]. Hungary: Cserépfalvi Kiadása, 1997.

Karsai, Elek, ed. *"Szálasi Naplója": A Nyilasmozgalom a II. Világháború idején.* [*"Szalasi's diary": The Arrow Cross movement at the time of the Second World War*]. Budapest: Kossuth Könyvkiadó, 1978.

Kenez, Peter. *The Birth of the Propaganda State: Soviet Methods of Mass Mobilization, 1917–1929*. New York: Cambridge University Press, 1985.

Kenez, Peter. *Cinema and Soviet Society, 1917–1953*. New York: Cambridge University Press, 1992.

Kenez, Peter. *Varieties of Fear: Growing Up Jewish under Nazism and Communism*. Washington, DC: American University Press, 1995.

Kertesz, Stephen Denis. *Diplomacy in a Whirlpool: Hungary between Nazi Germany and Soviet Russia*. Notre Dame, IN: University of Notre Dame Press, 1953.

Király, Béla K. *Honvédségből néphadsereg: Személyes visszaemlékezések, 1944–1956* [*Out of the army a people's army: Personal memories 1944–1956*]. Párizs, New Brunswick, New York: Magyar Füzetek, 1986.

Kiszely, Gábor. *ÁVH: Egy terrorszervezet története* [*AVH: The history of a terror institution*]. Budapest: Korona, 2000.

Kornis, Pál. *Tanuként jelentkezem* [*I appear as a witness*]. Budapest: Zrinyi Katonai Kiadó, 1988.

Kovács, Imre. *Magyarország megszállása* [*The occupation of Hungary*]. Toronto, Canada: Vörösváry, 1979.

Kővágó, László. *A Magyar kommunisták és a nemzetiségi kérdés, 1918–1948* [*The Hungarian Communists and the nationality question, 1918–1948*]. Budapest: Kossuth, 1985.

Kövér, György. *Losonczy Géza, 1917–1957* [*Geza Losonczy, 1917–1957*]. Budapest: 1956–os Intézet, 1998.

Leonhard, Wolfgang. *Child of the Revolution*. Chicago: Henry Regnery, 1967.

Levy, Robert. *Ana Pauker: The Rise and Fall of a Jewish Communist*. Berkeley: University of California Press, 2001.

Liehm, Mira, and Antonín J. Liehm. *The Most Important Art: Soviet and Eastern European Film after 1945*. Berkeley: University of California Press, 1980.

Lundestad, Geir. *The American Non-policy towards Eastern Europe, 1943–1947: Universalism in an Area Not of Essential Interest to the United States*. New York: Humanities Press, 1975.

Macartney, C. A. *October Fifteenth: A History of Modern Hungary, 1929–1945*, 2 vols. Edinburgh, Scotland: University Press, 1956.

Major, Ákos. *Népbiráskodás, forradalmi törvényesség: Egy népbiró visszaemlékezései* [*Being a judge in the people's court, revolutionary justice: Memoirs of a people's judge*]. Ed. Tibor Zinner. Budapest: Minerva, 1988.

Márai, Sándor. *Napló, 1945–1957* [*Diary, 1945–1957*]. Washington: Occidental Press, 1958.

Márai, Sándor. *Föld, Föld! Emlékezések* [*Land, land! Memories*]. Toronto, Canada: Vörösváry, 1972.

Marosán, György. *Tüzes kemence* [*Fiery furnace*]. Budapest: Magvető, 1968.

Marosán, György. *Az uton végig kell menni* [*We must go to the end of the road*]. Budapest: Magvető, 1972.

Mastny, Vojtech. *Russia's Road to the Cold War: Diplomacy, Warfare, and the Politics of Communism, 1941–1945*. New York: Columbia University Press, 1979.

McCagg, William O. *Stalin Embattled, 1943–1948*. Detroit, MI: Wayne State University Press, 1978.

Mendelsohn, Ezra. *The Jews of East Central Europe between the World Wars*. Bloomington: Indiana University Press, 1983.

Mészáros, Tibor. *Akit az övéi be nem fogadtak: Mindszenty Biboros titkárának visszaemlékezései* [*The man who was not received by his own people: The memories of the secretary of Cardinal Mindszenty*]. Pécs: Pro Domo, 1997.

Mészáros, Tibor. *A számüzött Biboros szolgálatában: Mindszenty József titkárának napi jegyzetei, 1972–1975* [*Serving the exiled cardinal: The daily notes of the secretary of Jozsef Mindszenty*]. Abaliget: Lámpás, 2000.

Mindszenty, József. *Emlékirataim* [*My memoirs*]. Toronto: Vörösváry, 1974.

Molnar, Miklos. *A Concise History of Hungary*. Cambridge, UK: Cambridge University Press, 1996.

Nagy, Ferenc. *Küzdelem a vasfüggöny mögött* [*Struggle behind the iron curtain*], 2 vols. Budapest: Európa, 1990.

Nagy, Kázmér. *Elveszett alkotmány: A magyar politikai emigráció, 1945–19*75 [*The lost constitution: The Hungarian political emigration, 1945–1975*]. Budapest: Gondolat, 1984.

Nagy, Töhötöm. *Jezsuiták és Szabadkőművesek* [*Jesuits and Freemasons*]. Szeged: Universum Kiadó, 1990.

Naimark, Norman M. *The Russians in Germany: A History of the Soviet Zone of Occupation, 1945–1949*. Cambridge, MA: Belknap Press of Harvard, 1995.

Naimark, Norman M. *Ethnic Cleansing in Twentieth Century Europe*. Seattle, WA: Henry M. Jackson School of International Studies, University of Washington, 1998.

Naimark, Norman M., and L. I. A. Gibianskii, eds. *The Establishment of Communist Regimes in Eastern Europe, 1944–1949*. Boulder, CO: Westview Press, 1997.

Nemeskürty, István. *A képpé varázsolt idő: A magyar film története és helye az egyetemes kulturában, párhuzamos kitekintéssel a világfilmmüvészetére [Time transformed magically into picture: The history of Hungarian film and its place in universal culture, comparing it to world film history]*. Budapest: Magvető, 1983.

Okváth, Imre, ed. *Katonai perek 1945–1958 [Military trials 1945–1958]*. Budapest: Történelmi Hivatal, 2001.

Orbán, Sándor. *Két agrárforradalom Magyarországon: Demokratikus és szocialista agrárátalakulás, 1945–1961 [Two agrarian revolutions in Hungary: Democratic and Socialist agrarian transformation, 1945–1961]*. Budapest: Akadémiai Kiadó, 1972.

Orbán, Sándor. *Social Transformation of the Hungarian Peasantry after the Liberation: On the Historical Postponement of the Disintegration of the Peasantry in East Europe*. Budapest: Akadémiai Kiadó, 1980.

Palasik, Mária. *A jogállamiság megteremtésének kisérlete és kudarca Magyarországon, 1944–1949 [The attempt to establish a law-based state in Hungary and the failure of that attempt]*. Budapest: Napvilág, 2000.

Palasik, Mária. *Kovács Béla: 1908–1959 [Béla Kóvács: 1908–1959]*. Budapest: Századvég, 2002.

Pelle, János. *Az utolsó vérvádak: Az etnikai gyűlölet és a politikai manipuláció Kelet-Európai történetéből [The last blood libels: Ethnic hatred and political manipulation from the history Eastern Europe]*. Budapest: Pelikan, 1996.

Pelle, János, and György Haraszti. *A gyűlölet vetése: A Zsidótörvények és a magyar közvélemény 1938–1944 [The sowing of hatred: Jewish laws and Hungarian public opinion, 1938–1944]*. Budapest: Európa, 2001.

Pető, Andrea. *Women in Hungarian Politics, 1945–1951*. Boulder, CO; New York: East European Monographs, distributed by Columbia University Press, 2003.

Pető, Iván, and Sándor Szakács. *A hazai gazdaság négy évtizedének története, 1945–1985 [The history of four decades of the national economy, 1945–1985]*. Budapest: Közgazdasági és Jogi Könyvkiadó, 1985.

Petrák, Katalin. *Magyarok a Szovjetunióban, 1922–1945 [Hungarians in the Soviet Union, 1922–1945]*. 1. kiad. ed. Budapest: Napvilág, 2000.

Petrie, Graham. *History Must Answer to Man*. Budapest: Corvina, 1978.

Polonsky, Antony, ed. *Studies in Polish Jewish Jewry*. London: Littman, 2000.

Pokorny, Herman. *Emlékeim: A láthatatlan hirszerző [My memoirs: The invisible informant]*. Budapest: Petit Real, 2000.

Pótó, János. *Emlékmüvek, politika, közgondolkodás: Budapest köztéri emlékmüvei, 1945–1949 [Monuments, politics and public opinion: Budapest monuments, 1945–1949]*. Budapest: MTA Történettudományi Intézet, 1989.

Pünkösti, Árpád. *Rákosi a hatalomért: 1945–1948 [Rakosi's struggle for power: 1945–1948]*. Budapest: Európa, 1992.

Rainer, M. János. *Nagy Imre: Politikai életrajz, 1896–1953* [*Imre Nagy: A political biography, 1896–1953*], vol. 1. Budapest: 1956–os Intézet, 1996.

Rákosi, Mátyás. *Visszaemlékezések, 1940–1956* [*Memories, 1940–1956*], 2 vols. Budapest: Napvilág, 1997.

Rákosi, Mátyás. *Visszaemlékezések, 1892–1925* [*Memories, 1892–1925*], 2 vols. Budapest: Napvilág, 2002.

Ramet, Sabrina, ed. *Eastern Europe since 1939*. Bloomington: Indiana University Press, 1998.

Roman, Eric. *Hungary and the Victor Powers, 1945–1950*. New York: St. Martin's Press, 1996.

Romsics, Ignác. *Magyarország története a XX. században* [*The history of Hungary in the twentieth century*]. Budapest: Osiris, 1999.

Romsics, Ignác. *Mitoszok, legendák, tévhitek a 20. századi magyar történelemröl* [*Myths, legends, and false beliefs from twentieth century Hungarian history*]. Budapest: Osiris, 2002.

Sándor, Tibor. *Örségváltás: A magyar film és a szélsőjobboldal a harmincas-negyvenes években: Tanulmányok, dokumentumok* [*The changing of the guard: Hungarian film and the extreme right wing in the thirties and forties: Essays, documents*]. Budapest: Magyar Filmintézet, 1997.

Schifferné Szakasits, Klára. *Fent és lent, 1945–1950* [*Up and down, 1945–1950*]. Budapest: Magvető, 1985.

Sulyok, Dezső. *A magyar tragédia* [*The Hungarian tragedy*]. New Brunswick, NJ: Sulyok, 1954.

Szabó, Ferenc. *Egy millióval kevesebben* [*One million fewer*]. Pécs: Pannonia, 1998.

Szakács, Sándor. *Földosztás és agrárfejlődés a magyar népi demokráciában, 1945–1948* [*Land reform and agricultural development in the Hungarian people's democracy, 1945–1948*]. Budapest: Közgazdasági és Jogi Könyvkiadó, 1964.

Szakály, Sándor. *A magyar katonai elit, 1938–1945* [*The Hungarian military elite, 1938–1945*]. Budapest: Magvető, 1987.

Szakály, Sándor. *A magyar tábori csendőrség története, 1938–1945* [*The history of the Hungarian gendarmerie, 1938–1945*]. Budapest: Ister, 2000.

Szász, Béla. *Minden kényszer nélkül: Egy műper története,* [*Without coercion: The history of a show trial*]. Budapest: Europa, 1989.

Szegedy-Maszák, Aladár. *Az ember ősszel visszanéz: Egy volt magyar diplomata emlékirataiból* [*A man looks back in autumn: From the memoirs of an ex-Hungarian diplomat*], 2 vols. Budapest: Európa, 1996.

Szekfű, Gyula. *Forradalom Után* [*After the revolution*]. Ed. Ference Glatz. Budapest: Gondolat. 1983.

Szent-Miklosy, István. *With the Hungarian Independence Movement, 1943–1947: An Eyewitness Account*. New York: Praeger, 1988.

Szilágyi, Gábor. *Tűzkeresztség: A magyar játékfilm története, 1945–1953* [*Baptism by fire: A history of the Hungarian feature film, 1945–1953*]. Budapest: Magyar Filmintézet, 1992.

Teleki, Éva. *Nyilas uralom Magyarországon: 1944 október 16/1945 április 4* [*The rule of the Arrow Cross in Hungary: October 16, 1944–April, 4 1945*]. Budapest: Kossuth, 1974.

Tilkovszky, Lórant. *Német nemzetiség, Magyar hazafiság* [*German nationality, Hungarian patriotism*]. Pécs: JPKE TK, 1997.

Tilkovszky, Lórant. Nemzetiségi politika Magyarországon a 20. században [*Nationality policy in Hungary in the twentieth century*]. Debrecen: Csokonai, 1998.
Ulam, Adam Bruno. *Stalin: The Man and His Era*, expanded edition. Boston: Beacon Press, 1989.
Ungváry, Krisztián. *Budapest ostroma* [*The siege of Budapest*]. Budapest: Corvina, 1998.
Ungvári, Tamás. *Ahasvérus és Shylock: A "Zsidókérdés" Magyarországon* [*Ahasverus and Shylock: The "Jewish question" in Hungary*]. Budapest: Akadémiai Kiadó, 1999.
Valuch, Tibor. *Magyarország társadalomtörténete a XX. század második Felében* [*Hungary's social history in the second half of the twentieth century*]. Budapest: Osiris, 2002.
Varsori, Antonio, and Elena Calandri. *The Failure of Peace in Europe, 1943–48*. New York: Palgrave, 2002.
Vas, Zoltán. *Akkori önmagunkról* [*About our past selves*], vol. 2. Budapest: Magvető, 1982.
Vida, István. *A Független Kisgazdapárt politikája 1944–1947* [*The politics of the Independent Smallholders' Party, 1944–1947*]. Budapest: Akadémiai Kiadó, 1976.
Vida, István, ed. *Koalició és pártharcok, 1944–1948* [*The coalition and party struggles, 1944–1948*]. Budapest: Magvető, 1986.
Vida, István, József Kiss, and Magda Somlyai, eds. *Az 1944. évi december hó 21-re Debrecenbe összegyűlt majd később Budapestre összehivot Ideiglenes Nemzetgyűlés Almanachja, November 21–29, 1945* [*The almanac of the Provisional National Assembly convened in Debrecen on December 21, 1944, and later moved to Budapest, November 21–29, 1945*]. Budapest: Magyar Országgyűlés, 1994.
Vigh, Károly. *Tildy Zoltán Életútja* [*The life of Zoltán Tildy*]. Békéscsaba: Tevan, 1991.
Vincellér, Béla. *Szálasi hat hónapja: 1944 október–1945 május* [*Szálasi's six months: 1944 October–1945 May*]. Budapest: Volos, 1996.
Zinner, Tibor, and Péter Róna. *Szálasiék Bilincsben* [*Szálasi and his comrades in shackles*], 2 vols. Budapest: Lapkiadó Vállalat, 1986.

Journal Articles

Bándy, Sándor, "Lakatos Imre arcai" ["The faces of Imre Lakatos"]. *Beszélő* 12 (2003): 92–98.
Baráth, Magdolna. "Valaki figyel" ["Someone is listening"]. *Beszélő* 11 (1999). Accessed July 22, 2005 <http://beszelo.c3.hu/99/11/08barat.htm>
Bencsik, Zsuzsa. "Egy koncepciós per előkészítése" ["The preparation of a show trial"]. *Budapesti Negyed* 2 (1994): 191–207.
Borhi, László G. "The Merchants of the Kremlin: The Economic Roots of Soviet Expansion in Hungary." Working papers, Woodrow Wilson Center for Scholars, 2000.
Farkas, Vladimir. In *Élet és Irodalom*, July 14, 2000.
Gyarmati, György. "A Politika Rendőrsége" ["The police of politics"]. *Beszélő* 9–10 (2000):
Hubai, László. "A Magyar Kommunista Párt gazdálkodása, 1944–1948" ["The economic policy of the Hungarian Communist Party, 1944–1948"]. *Múltunk* 2 (1998): 77–119.

Hubai, László. "A politikai irányzatok választási eredményeinek kontinuitása, 1920–1947" ["The continuity of political trends and election results"]. *Múltunk* 1 (1999): 44–69.

Korom, Mihály. "A Magyar kommunista emigráció vezetöinek tevékenysége a Szovjetunióban a Második Világháború idején" ["The activities of the leadership of the Hungarian Communist emigration in the Soviet Union at the time of the Second World War"]. *Múltunk* 2 (1997): 3–51.

Murashko, A. F. "Néhány ecsetvonás Rákosi Mátyás politikai portrétjához" ["A few sketches for the political portrait of Matyas Rakosi"]. *Múltunk* 2 (1999): 160–169.

Murashko, A. F., and G. P. Noszkova, eds. "A Szovjet tényező Kelet Európa országainak háború utáni fejlődésében, 1945–1948" ["The Soviet factor in the development of the countries of Eastern Europe after the war, 1945–1948"]. *Múltunk* 2 (1996): 58–59.

Pető, Andrea. "Átvonuló hadsereg, maradandó trauma" ["Passing army, lasting trauma"]. *Történelmi Szemle* 1–2 (1999). Accessed July 22, 2005 <http:www.itt.hu/tsz99 1 2 peto andrea.htm>

Pető, Andrea. "Budapest ostroma 1944–1945-ben nöi szemmel" ["The siege of Budapest in 1944–1945 through feminine eyes"]. *Budapesti Negyed* 3–4 (2000). Accessed July 22, 2005 <http:www.bparchiv.hu/Magyar/kiadvany/bpn/29/30/peto.htm>

Rieber, Alfred. "The Crack in the Plaster: Crisis in Romania and the Origins of the Cold War." *Journal of Modern History* 76.1 (2004): 62–106.

Simon, István. "A szociáldemokrácia 'Uj Arca' 1945-ben" ["The new face of social democracy in 1945"]. *Múltunk* 1 (2001): 208–232.

Tóth, István. "A Nemzeti Parasztpárt tevékenységének finanszirozása 1945–1948" ["Financing the activities of the National Peasant Party, 1945–1948"]. *Múltunk* 1 (1999): 116–137.

Ungváry, Kristián. "Második Sztálingrád" ["The Second Stalingrad"]. *Budapesti Negyed* 3–4 (2000): 29–30.

Varga, László. "Forradalmi törvényesség" ["Revolutioanary legality"]. *Beszélő* 11 (1999). Accessed July 22, 2005 <http:www//beszelo.c3.hu/99/11/09varga.htm>

Varga, László. "Várostörténet: 1945–1956" ["History of the town, 1945–1956"]. *Budapesti Negyed* 2–3 (1998). Accessed July 22, 2005 <http://www.bparchiv.hu/magyar/kiadvany/bpn/20_21/varga.htm>

Vass, Henrik, and László Zalai. "Tájékoztatás és hatalmi harc, 1944–1948" ["Information and the struggle for power, 1944–1948"]. *Múltunk* 2–3 (1993): 202–218.

Index

For EU product safety concerns, contact us at Calle de José Abascal, 56–1°,
28003 Madrid, Spain or eugpsr@cambridge.org.

www.ingramcontent.com/pod-product-compliance
Ingram Content Group UK Ltd.
Pitfield, Milton Keynes, MK11 3LW, UK
UKHW042150130625
459647UK00011B/1276
* 9 7 8 0 5 2 1 7 4 7 2 4 0 *